THE ROYAL INSTITUTE OF INTERNATIONAL AFFAIRS is an unofficial body which promotes the scientific study of international questions and does not express opinions of its own. The opinions expressed in this publication are the responsibility of the authors.

The Institute and its Research Committee gratefully acknowledge the comments and suggestions of the following who read the manuscript: Professor W. J. M. Mackenzie, Andrew Shonfield, and Professor David Vital.

THE FOREIGN POLICY PROCESS IN BRITAIN

William Wallace

THE ROYAL INSTITUTE
OF INTERNATIONAL AFFAIRS
LONDON

Chatham House, 10 St James's Square, London W.1

ISBN 0 905031 01 6

Printed in Great Britain
by W & J Mackay Limited, Chatham

Contents

Preface

THE STUDY OF THE PROCESS of making British foreign policy has until
recently been neglected, disowned by most students of domestic politics,
distantly acknowledged by scholars of international relations. In the
United States, by contrast, foreign policy-making has for long been
examined and criticized in the utmost detail. There have been some
eighty official reports within the last thirty years on aspects of the
organization and conduct of US foreign policy; as I write another full-
scale investigation is under way. Library shelves are covered with critical
studies of the State Department, of US management of foreign aid or
information policy. In Britain, until the publication of David Vital's
short and pioneering study (*The Making of British Foreign Policy*) in
1968, the interested observer was forced to rely upon diplomatic
memoirs and parliamentary debates for enlightenment, supplemented
by what he could glean from the press. Many participants – and even
some academics – denied the existence of an identifiable process of
policy-making in foreign affairs in any sense comparable to the process
observed in domestic policy. Too many students of domestic politics
excluded the international dimension of policy from their concerns,
assuming that the traditional boundaries which divided foreign policy
from domestic politics still held firm.

This book has two primary objectives. The first is to uncover and
describe the process through which foreign policy is made. It will be
argued that foreign policy-making is as deeply affected by the domestic
political environment as by international constraints, and that an understanding of this political environment is necessary to any full understanding of the evolution of British foreign policy. The second is to explore the
extent to which the traditional boundaries between foreign and domestic
policy have been undermined by the increasing interdependence of the
developed industrial countries of the North Atlantic area – to ask whether
it is still possible to distinguish any separate and discrete field of policy
which we can label 'foreign', or whether it would now be more accurate
to talk about an international dimension which touches most important
areas of domestic policy. This cannot, of course, be an exhaustive study.
It has little to say on international agricultural policy, for instance, or on
the highly sensitive problem of political and economic relations with the
countries of Eastern Europe. In retrospect I would have wished to pay
more attention to the management of relations with the Arab states, and
to the international aspects of British energy policy – but when I

embarked on this study it was impossible to foresee the 'energy crisis' and the Arab-Israeli war of 1973. I have attempted, rather, to describe in outline the formulation and management of foreign policy in Britain at the beginning of the 1970s, illustrating this outline with case studies drawn from different issue areas, and drawing some conclusions about the characteristic style of British policy-making and the changing context within which foreign policy is made.

This is in no sense an official study. I have had access to no official documents or privileged information. As will be apparent from the footnotes, I have drawn upon what government publications are available, on House of Commons reports, on memoirs and histories, and on a careful reading of the press (here supplementing my own limited surveillance of British newspapers with the extensive resources of the Chatham House press library). For help in interpreting these published materials, for directing my attention to developments I should otherwise have overlooked, and for explaining the intricacies of the policy-making process, I am profoundly indebted to the several hundred people whom I have interviewed in the six years between 1969 and 1974, many on more than one occasion: officials in almost every Department in Whitehall and in nine overseas missions, Members of Parliament and former ministers, parliamentary and party staff, journalists, representatives of interest groups, businessmen and members of foreign embassies. It would have been impossible to carry out this study without their cooperation and forbearance; I hope that they will feel that the completed study has justified the time which they gave me.

Any study of British policy-making is hampered by the secrecy which pervades the whole machinery of government. Nowhere is the veil of secrecy thicker than in foreign policy. With some judicious prompting, I was able to prove the strength of Sir Lewis Namier's dictum that 'A great many profound secrets are somewhere in print, but are most easily detected when one knows what to seek'. In places I have had to rely upon informed surmise, and upon the circulation of drafts to people in a position to correct misconceptions. If any errors of fact or interpretation remain, I offer my apologies and welcome more information; but I am reasonably confident that fuller access to information would not have altered the main lines of my argument, although it would have provided some useful detail to substantiate it. I particularly regret that the publication of Richard Crossman's Diaries, expected for the autumn of 1974, was delayed until after this book went to press.

Any attempt to describe a political process is vulnerable to the continual movement of events, outdating its description even before it is published. When I began to work on this study, a Labour government was preparing to open negotiations to join the European Community. While it was under way, a Conservative government took Britain into the Community; when it was finished, another Labour government was renegotiating terms, and it was uncertain whether Britain would stay in or go out. The consequences of these developments for the whole context of British foreign policy-making are potentially far-reaching. I thought it prudent, however, to refrain from speculating too far about such an undecided, although crucial, future development. In other respects I have endeavoured to take into account changes in the machinery of government and in the management of foreign policy up to the end of 1974.

This study has not been written with any pretensions to contribute to the growing body of theoretical writings on foreign policy. But it will be apparent to those readers familiar with this literature that I have drawn extensively upon it for concepts and insights – most particularly on the work of James Rosenau, Kenneth Waltz, and Karl Deutsch, as well as that of Joseph Frankel, from whose comments I also benefited at Chatham House. I should like too to acknowledge my indebtedness to Theodore Lowi, who first introduced me to the study of the policy-making process and made me apply its concepts to foreign policy, and to Max Beloff for encouraging me in my early attempts to examine British policy-making.

I also acknowledge the help and constructive criticism which I have received throughout this project from officials, politicians, and academics, from the staff at Chatham House and from colleagues at the University of Manchester. Successive members of the Foreign and Commonwealth Office Planning Staff acted as guides and 'door-openers' for me in Whitehall and as critics of my ideas and early drafts. Members of a study group which met at Chatham House in 1972–3 provided invaluable comment and criticism, both for my own and for Joseph Frankel's parallel study (*British Foreign Policy 1945–73*). Roger Morgan encouraged the project from the beginning, and chaired this group. Susan Strange and Andrew Shonfield were particularly helpful in looking at foreign economic policy. Others who helped in the study or commented on particular chapters included Peter Nailor, Kenneth Hunt, Keith Pavitt, Christopher Everett, Sir Frank Roberts, Adam Watson, David Thomas, and Angelika Volle. Christopher Clapham extended my awareness of the management of bilateral relations beyond Western Europe and North America; his contribution appears under his own name in chapter 9.

For financial support for the travel involved in this study I am grateful to the British Social Science Research Council. A preliminary study of interest group involvement in foreign policy, in 1969–70, was supported by a grant from the Nuffield Foundation. An invitation from the University of Iceland enabled me to visit Reykjavik, one from the Deutsch-Englische Gesellschaft to visit Bonn, and one from the Ford Foundation (through the University of Rhode Island Law of the Sea Institute) to visit New York. At Manchester I relied for help, criticism, and occasional assistance with teaching on Dennis Austin and Roger Williams. Maurice Wright read and commented on the final draft.

Marilyn Dunn and Joan Titterton patiently typed and retyped successive drafts. Hermia Oliver tactfully suggested improvements to my most awkward phrases, shortened sentences, checked footnotes and helped to cut unnecessary words from the manuscript. Helen Wallace took part in study group meetings, allowed me to draw upon her own research, encouraged and endured this whole project from start to finish, acted as my most vigorous critic, corrected my punctuation, discovered lost references and pointed out new ones; in short, this book would have been far poorer without her. I am indebted to Peter Mangold for compiling the index.

W.W.

Manchester
April 1975

1: Introduction

A GREATER MYSTIQUE attaches to the making of foreign policy than to the making of domestic policy. In Britain – as elsewhere – the tradition that foreign policy is a matter for the Executive, that the first duty of government is the defence of the realm, still overshadows its treatment both by practitioners and by academics. The greater degree of secrecy surrounding the discussion of foreign policy contributes to the belief that this is a special area, to an extent outside (and perhaps above) the normal processes of domestic politics.

The idea that foreign policy is separate from domestic policy is fundamental to the traditional concept of the nation-state. As John Locke put it, 'the power of war and peace, leagues and alliances, and all the transactions with all persons and communities without the common-wealth' constituted the 'federative' power, which must 'necessarily be left to the prudence and wisdom of those whose hands it is in to be managed for the public good'.[1] In England foreign relations remained a prerogative matter long after Parliament had successfully established its right to be consulted on the good government of the realm; and here the monarch retained a residual influence until the late nineteenth century. The tradition that ambassadors represent the sovereign, not the govern-ment, still reflects something of this prerogative power. As in other democratic countries, there is a long-established parliamentary tradition that foreign policy ought to be insulated from the rough-and-tumble of domestic debate, that both government and opposition ought to seek for bipartisan policies, that politics should stop at the water's edge: honoured as often in the breach as in the observance, but still reasserted in succes-sive Parliaments. Whereas controversy may rage around domestic issues without threatening the safety of the state, in matters of foreign policy issues it is argued, the national interest must come first.

According to this traditional interpretation, therefore, the making of foreign policy *ought* to be distinct from domestic policy; over the last century in British politics this has usually been accepted by all sides except the dissenting minority of the radical left. Most academics have confirmed the view that 'the making of foreign policy . . . is the business of the Executive, and for almost all practical purposes the Executive is unfettered in its exercise of this function'.[2] For the most committed defenders of this traditional line, indeed, 'there is simply not enough to say about how British foreign policy is made to fill a book . . . because the basic constitutional facts are so simple and the nuances communicated by personality so varied and elusive'.[3]

Yet it would be remarkable if the process of foreign policy-making were as simple or straightforward as this would suggest. In contemporary democracies the executive branch is rarely monolithic. Administrative politics, conflicting departmental perspectives, divisions within the Cabinet, all complicate the picture, here as in domestic policy. MPs devote a respectable proportion of their time in debates, at Question Time, and away from the floor of the House in party meetings and other activities, to the discussion of matters related to 'transactions with . . . persons and communities without the commonwealth'. Promotional groups and economic interests are as active in foreign policy issues as they are over questions of transport or educational policy. Foreign affairs topics receive regular and prominent treatment in the mass media. Hence a purpose of this book is to try to discover how far foreign policy-making is in fact distinctive, and to explore the extent to which the traditional distinctions between foreign and domestic concerns have been eroded by international developments in recent years.

A preliminary problem is to define the boundaries of the field. Foreign policy may be defined relatively narrowly in terms of high diplomacy, as concerned primarily with political relations with other states, with international stability and the rules of the international system, and with the promotion of the national interest through the cultivation of good relations with other governments and the negotiation and maintenance of international agreements. The general review of the international situation with which the Foreign Secretary opens each parliamentary foreign affairs debate has traditionally revolved around such matters; so have the references to foreign policy in the annual Queen's Speech. By this definition foreign policy is distinct from the day-to-day management of external relations – negotiations of agreements on aircraft routes, governmental promotion of exports, cultural policy and consular work. Yet all these activities have direct or indirect implications for political relations between states. Export subsidies, preferential treatment for domestic industries, provoke protests from foreign governments whose industries are adversely affected; cultural institutes are closed, or opened, for political reasons. The treatment of British citizens abroad has been a *casus belli* on more than one occasion in British history. Hence it is necessary to adopt a broader definition, to include all those 'decisions and actions which involve to some appreciable extent relations between one state and others'.[4]

This broader definition can accommodate the enormously enlarged and still expanding range of decisions and actions involving relations with other states that are a feature of the last twenty or thirty years – another factor challenging the traditional static interpretation of foreign policy. At the same time the international environment within which the British government operates, and the institutional machinery through which it acts, have altered radically. The classic diplomacy about which

Harold Nicolson wrote in 1939 – bilateral, conducted on the basis of mutual confidence by professional diplomats – has been supplemented and in some ways replaced by the growth of multilateral diplomacy, conducted through permanent international organizations. On the eve of World War II Nicolson wrote confidently that 'the tide is setting against the new system' of diplomacy by conference.[5] Yet within the careers of men then serving in the Foreign Office, Britain, already by the early 50s a leading member of the UN, of NATO, the Council of Europe, and the Organization for European Economic Cooperation (OEEC), had reversed its former antagonism to membership of organizations with extensive executive powers and had applied to join the European Communities.

Not only has the style of diplomacy thus radically altered, but the actors have become much more numerous and diverse. Nicolson could happily confine his study to European countries and the United States, and write approvingly of 'the freemasonry of professional diplomacy', which eased relations among European foreign services.[6] Thirty years later the diplomatic world was far less professional and far less Euro-centred. Diplomacy had been invaded by travelling statesmen, complicated negotiations were now conducted by home civil servants. The international system had already absorbed the newly independent countries of Asia and Africa and was beginning to adjust to the re-emergence of Japan and China as first-rank powers.

The subject matter of diplomacy has also been transformed. Nicolson had noted among 'recent changes' in diplomatic practice 'the increased importance of commerce' and 'of such international problems as currency and finance', the appointment of press attachés to the major embassies, and – more disapprovingly – the growth of propaganda activities by governments, both through broadcasts and through cultural activities.[7] In the international system re-established after the war these 'new' elements rapidly assumed a more central significance. The common concern of governments to avoid a repetition of the international economic chaos of the 30s, aided by advances in economic theory and techniques, led to the acceptance by the British and other governments of a greater degree of responsibility for the concerted management of the international economy. The impetus which wartime research had given to technological development, carried through to the postwar period, brought a new concern with the international political implications of scientific and technological advances; most immediately with atomic energy, in both its military and civil applications, more gradually with other areas of 'high technology'. The impact of these continuing advances in technology, in quickening the pace of international communication, in providing air travel first for elites and then for the mass public, in opening up the sea, the seabed, and space to military and commercial exploitation, successively brought new and more complex matters into the sphere of political relations between states.

These developments have done much to blur the boundaries between foreign and domestic policy. The recognition or non-recognition of foreign governments, representations over the treatment of British citizens abroad, the negotiation of alliances, and the furtherance of good relations with other states are all indisputably foreign policy matters and fall clearly within the responsibilities of the Foreign Office. On many of these newer questions, however, the Foreign Office brings a foreign policy perspective to matters which may from other viewpoints be seen primarily as aspects of domestic policies. The rate of exchange for sterling, incentives to exporters and disincentives for importers are as much a part of domestic economic management as they are of external relations; on occasion the government will consider that domestic imperatives override international obligations, as did the Labour government in the imposition of an import surcharge in 1964 in breach of its obligations to EFTA and GATT. A sharp increase in the fees charged by universities to overseas students seemed fully justified from the point of view of educational policy in 1967, though from the point of view of foreign relations its advantages appeared more doubtful and the manner of its imposition unfortunate. The control of immigration, government subsidies to industry, policy towards foreign investment in Britain, are similarly questions which fall across whatever line one may try to draw between domestic and foreign policy. On these and similar issues the pressures of Britain's international objectives and obligations must be weighed against domestic demands, and foreign policy-makers are of necessity engaged in a dialogue with those concerned with the management of domestic policy to determine and define the national interest.

The alteration in Britain's international position has also affected the definition of foreign policy priorities. An imperial power with global commitments and interests was naturally concerned with the stability of the international system as such: with international order, with disarmament, with relations among the great powers and with the rules governing their behaviour. By 1970, with its troops recalled to concentrate on European defence, with sterling subject to multilateral arrangements, with all but a remnant of the former empire now independent, British policy-makers and observers had alike accepted that Britain could no longer aspire to world status, but was rather a 'major power of the second order'.[8] Their perception of the national interests which foreign policy should pursue reflected the more commercial orientation appropriate to a middle power.

Changes in the institutional machinery for the formulation and management of British foreign policy have been as great. The India Office disappeared in 1947, its remnants combining with the Dominions Office to form the Commonwealth Relations Office (CRO). The responsibilities of the Colonial Office shrank as dependent territories advanced to independence. It lost some responsibilities for economic development to a new Department of Technical Cooperation in 1961, and more when in 1964 this grew into the Ministry of Overseas Development (ODM). In 1966 the Colonial Office was absorbed into the CRO, which in turn merged with the Foreign Office in 1968, to become the Foreign and Commonwealth Office (FCO). Similar major changes in the institutional machinery for defence policy had by the late 60s led to the absorption of the separate service Departments into an integrated Ministry of Defence (MoD). Among other changes in Whitehall, the most significant for foreign policy-making was the slow but steady growth of the Cabinet Office, from a small secretariat to a substantial staff.

The weight of tradition, the continuity of formal procedures, of institutional titles and of parliamentary practice, may have helped to obscure the impact of these changes. There is always a certain time-lag between changes in the international environment and the consequent adjustment of perceptions of that environment. A similar time-lag exists in adjusting perceptions of the process of foreign policy-making, pro- longed by the rhetorical language still used for foreign policy: sovereignty, independence, national interest, security, and the like. Continuing changes both in the international context and in the institutional machinery of British foreign policy, however, present an obstacle to any attempt at description and analysis. Any description of an administrative structure is necessarily static, whereas the scene one is trying to depict is one in which not only the figures but much of the landscape are in constant movement.

This book focuses on the structure and process of foreign policy- making in Britain in the four years from the beginning of 1969 to the end of 1972 – a period of relative stability in the context, content, and organizational structure of foreign policy-making. The merger of the Foreign and Commonwealth Offices had been completed; the process of decolonization had virtually ended; the East of Suez withdrawal was under way, the pound had been devalued, the sterling area was of diminishing importance. The application to join the European Com- munities was made and successfully negotiated; but full membership, with all its implications for the future management, content, and context of foreign policy, had not yet been achieved. While, of course, reference must be made to earlier developments and decisions (for which published material is often far more readily available), and also to the impact of entry into the EEC and of the subsequent oil and energy 'crisis', the 'present' of this study refers where not otherwise stated to the situation up to the end of 1972.

Policy-Making

I have assumed in this study that the process of policy-making is less one of a series of discrete and identifiable decisions than of a continuous flow of policy, in which successive messages received about the international environment, the interpretation given to the information received, the preconceptions of those responsible for policy, their assessment of possible alternatives in terms of their competing and often incompatible objectives, and the organizational context within which they make policy, all combine to shape the direction of that flow. Policy-makers are not individuals or, except in the most exceptional circumstances, small groups acting alone. A specific decision or a specific area of policy, it is true, may be managed by a small number of men; but they depend on others for the information on which they base their policy, and on others again for the implementation of the decisions which they take. Clear and final decisions are as rare in foreign policy-making as in much domestic policy. Important changes in policy evolve out of an accumulation of small decisions, of adjustments to circumstances and reactions to situations, clearer in hindsight than in the making. Foreign policy in Britain, as in other large industrial states, evolves within an organizational framework in which the personalities of those responsible, the roles they are called upon to play, the objectives they pursue, and the domestic and international pressures which they perceive interact to form what the outside observer may see as discrete decisions.

The attraction of a more rational model of policy-making has been strong, especially for those who view the making of foreign policy from the perspective of the international environment: as the purposive actions of governments, holding the boundary between domestic politics and the international system. According to one American writer, 'most analysts' in the United States 'explain (and predict) the behavior of national governments in terms of one basic conceptual model', the 'Rational Actor' model, understanding policy as 'the more or less purposive acts of unified national governments'.[9] But this assumes a degree of simplicity and certainty in the process of decision-making which does not obtain in real-life situations. Governments are rarely unified, objectives rarely entirely clear; information is seldom adequate, and the consequences of a particular line of action are never certain. Perhaps the behaviour of the leaders of a great power during a crisis situation which involves dealing with relatively few foreign actors, where the time for decision is limited and the immediate consequences of the decision seem relatively clear comes nearest to the 'Rational Actor' model – as, for example, studies of the American decisions to give aid to Greece and Turkey in 1947 and to intervene in Korea in 1950, or of US policy-making during the Cuban crisis of 1962 have suggested. Second-rank powers rarely have such a high degree of control over a situation. Characteristically they must deal with circumstances in which a large number of foreign actors are involved, directly or indirectly, whose intentions are not immediately apparent; as a result, future developments are hard to predict. It is worth emphasizing that in the extent to which governmental actors are involved in situations which they neither fully understand nor control, foreign policy-making differs in degree from most areas of domestic policy-making. Shared values and assumptions, long experience of dealing with each other, and a common acceptance of certain written and unwritten rules of the game make it possible for ministers and officials responsible for health services or education to deal with doctors' or teachers' organizations with a reasonable degree of certainty about their reactions to various proposals, and a reasonable expectation that third parties will not directly intrude into this relationship. In foreign policy, even when a clear decision has been taken, unexpected responses from foreign governments, the interaction of a specific relationship with wider international developments, may rapidly outdate the policy decided upon or force the reopening of a settled question. Such a degree of uncertainty, it may be suggested, obtains in domestic matters only in economic and industrial policy.

Some major decisions can certainly be identified as marking turning points in the evolution of British foreign policy over the past twenty years. The successive decisions to apply to join the European Communities, the decision to devalue the pound sterling in November 1967 and the associated decision to withdraw from East of Suez will all be examined in later chapters. Even so, in each case it will be argued that the final decision was, at most, the culmination of a long series of smaller decisions and non-decisions, of considering and foreclosing options, and that this 'final' decision itself was only the beginning of another series of consequential decisions and consequential consideration of further alternatives. More often, however, significant shifts in policy have been clearly evident only when they are completed after a long series of adjustments. For example, by the time of General Gowon's state visit to Britain in June 1973, it was clear that a substantial readjustment of British priorities in Africa had taken place during the previous three years. Whereas at the Singapore Commonwealth Prime Ministers' Meeting in 1970 the new Conservative government had resisted and resented attempts by African governments to influence its handling of negotiations with Rhodesia, by 1973 it was clear that no Rhodesian settlement would be attempted without extensive consultations with the Nigerian government, and perhaps also with the governments of other major African countries. Yet it would be hard to discover any conscious decision to reverse British policy or to identify a single turning point in this process. Rather, a number of converging pressures and objectives, the reassessment of trade prospects, the growing concern for energy supplies, disillusionment with Rhodesia after the failure of further attempts at negotiation, had combined to shift the consensus within the government, gradually but cumulatively, on to a new basis.

This conception of policy as a continuous process implies not only a greater concern with the lower-level decisions which set the context for top-level policy discussions, but also an interest in the interrelationship between the structure of the policy-making machinery and the direction of policy, between organization and output. The structure of the administrative machinery at any point in time reflects to a considerable extent the assumptions and intended priorities of those who command it, or at least the cumulative impact of the assumptions and priorities of past reformers. The demarcation of responsibilities between ministers and Departments reflects, at least implicitly, the accepted divisions between different fields of policy; as those perceived divisions change, so ministerial responsibilities are altered and Departments reorganized. The existence of a separate Commonwealth Relations Office affected the shape of British foreign policy throughout the postwar period; but its status in turn reflected a perception of intra-Commonwealth relations as 'different' from foreign relations, just as its amalgamation with the Foreign Office between 1965 and 1968 reflected the virtual disappearance of the idea. Throughout the 1950s the weakness of planning machinery in Whitehall mirrored the settled antipathy of ministers and civil servants to 'doctrinaire' planning and their preference for 'practical' administration. Conversely, during the 1960s the deliberate strengthening of planning machinery and the creation of new bodies and procedures to coordinate policies that had previously been handled separately indicated a growing awareness of the need for a more integrated foreign policy, for a greater appreciation of long-term trends and a clearer definition of objectives.

In its turn, the size and the performance of the existing administrative apparatus impose a certain inflexibility on the direction of policy. Large-scale organizations display a number of characteristics which reduce their responsiveness to political control: attachment to precedent and continuity, loyalty to the organization as such and to its clients, established routines for handling business and established views of the environment in which they operate. The high morale and prestige of the British civil service, and its successful resistance to the by-passing of its regular procedures by political channels, make the problem of organizational inertia particularly acute for policy-makers in Britain. The existence of a separate Diplomatic Service, with its own norms of behaviour and sense of corporate identity, as well as a consciousness of its elite status in Whitehall and in the country, strengthens this tendency.[10] Both Conservative and Labour politicians have criticized Whitehall for what they see as its imperviousness to political direction and its attachment to its own settled 'views'. Even when formal decisions are successfully reserved for ministers, organizational habit may weigh heavily in the formulation and implementation of foreign policy. One Labour minister noted that from the moment the Labour government took office in 1964, the Foreign Office briefs implicitly assumed a closer relationship with Europe. One of his Conservative successors, after two years in office and a number of ministerial and official reconsiderations of policy, remarked that the implementation of policy decisions by several divisions within the Department of Trade and Industry (DTI) still followed the assumptions laid down by the previous Labour government. Decisions once made must therefore be followed through; where political objectives conflict with organizational habits or objectives, they are likely to gain ground only slowly. 'Policy is not made once and for all, it is made and remade endlessly'.[11]

This is not to say that the British civil service is impervious to political direction, in foreign policy or in general. Rather, what is suggested is that policy evolves in a continuing dialogue between the responsible ministers and their civil servants, a continuing interaction between political direction and the pressures of established practice and administrative interests. Where political direction is clear, it is able to carry the administrative machine with it; in the absence of firm political pressures, however, administrative politics prevail. Nor is it intended to imply in any way that administrative resistance to political direction in Britain stems from any sinister or anti-democratic motives. Officials defend their organizational interests because they believe it is their function to do so and because their professional pride in their own expertise tends to make them trust their own judgement more than that of outsiders. They perceive their role to include protecting the interests of their respective client groups in the Whitehall process. Their judgement of governmental priorities is naturally affected by their particular responsibilities as well as by their own sources of information. Most of all, they see themselves as defending the continuity of British policy vis-à-vis politicians whose perspective is often no longer than the next election. In the ethos of Whitehall, there are two justifications for resisting the full force of ministerial demands: that it is the duty of officials to draw ministers' attention to the weight of external constraints which limit the choices open to them, and that as 'servants of the Crown' they are in a real sense protectors of the national interest against the immediate pressures of party interests, and entitled to ensure that their political masters consider carefully what the national interest may be.[12]

Contrary to the assumption of those political critics who complain of 'Whitehall obstructiveness', the administrative machinery of British policy-making is not monolithic. Whitehall is not Washington; the open conflicts between sections of the administration which characterize bureaucratic politics in America have no exact parallel in Britain. Many British officials indeed deny the relevance of analyses of policy-making in terms of administrative conflict or bureaucratic politics. It is part of the style of Whitehall that differences are muted and as far as possible concealed from the public eye, and that interdepartmental disputes are subject to the acceptance of an overriding common interest. Even so, there are clear departmental interests and clear clashes of interest arising from the very nature of large-scale organizations and of human behaviour. Within Departments and across departmental boundaries there are more complex patterns of disagreement, conflicting views, and prejudices, or of officials defending their own corner.

Officials naturally have their own convictions, principles, prejudices, and blind spots. Most of them succeed to a great extent in separating their personal opinions from their official responsibilities, but the separation can never be absolute. Strong senior officials may impose a 'view' on their Department by the force of their position and personality, preventing the consideration of alternative views as effectively as a ministerial directive. More important than the intrusion of personal preferences is the conviction with which officials play the role assigned to them. In the Foreign Office transfers between posts and between functional and regional specialisms entail a sharper break between the perspectives required in successive roles than is the case with most careers in the Home Civil Service (HCS); yet a diplomat who is, for example, made responsible for representing aid and development questions will do his utmost to defend his 'brief', even if he had argued from an opposing position in his previous post. When he is representing his Department, within which he is likely to have spent his entire career, his advocacy is likely to be even stronger. The disagreement of course remains subject to a shared acceptance of the national interest as over-riding; but it is precisely around the definition of that national interest in a particular situation that discussion revolves. Naturally officials from the DTI tend to view the national interest rather more in industrial terms, those from the MoD in security terms, those from the Foreign Office in political terms. In the British civil service, as in the American, 'Where you stand depends upon where you sit'.[13]

Hence a policy outcome depends partly on which Department first tackles a problem, which takes the lead in defining the question at issue and in providing the background papers and managing the formulation of policy. An interdepartmental problem assigned to (or claimed by) the commercial relations divisions of the DTI is likely to be defined primarily in terms of trade policy; assigned to the FCO, it would be defined more in terms of a 'political' framework; to the Overseas Development Administration (ODA) more in terms of aid and development. The weight given to different factors in the formulation of policy would then depend partly on this initial definition of the problem, partly on the information available to the various Departments involved, partly on the competence and personality of the relevant officials, partly on the strength of the domestic interests concerned and their relations with their sponsoring Departments, and partly on the personalities, competence, and standing in the government of the ministers to whom officials are responsible. The outcome of the policy will in turn be affected by which Department (or Departments) are made responsible for its implementation. The interaction of these political and administrative influences will be examined more fully in later chapters.

A Preliminary Framework

It is customary and for some purposes convenient, to talk of 'foreign policy' as 'an entity, a single field'. Thus James Rosenau, in a widely quoted essay, distinguishes foreign policy as an 'issue area' from domestic issue areas by the distinctive groups of official and non-official elites involved, by the more specialized roles of the interested public it attracts, and by its greater degree of remoteness from the public at large.[14] The assumption of overall cohesiveness within the foreign policy field is evident in the traditional conception of foreign policy already discussed as well as in the practice of parliamentary foreign affairs debates, in which speakers raise topics across the whole range of foreign policy.

Yet this assumption can only hold for a sketchy introductory discussion. If we are to go further, we need to make use of some immediately discernible vertical divisions of the overall field. For example, the officials involved in the management of aid policy and the domestic and foreign interests which work to influence their decisions, as well as the interested public which follows them, are clearly distinguishable from those concerned with defence and security policies, and overlap only marginally with those concerned with foreign economic and commercial policy. (The patterns of policy-making in these several areas are considered in chapters 5–7.)

In addition to these vertical divisions, practitioners and academic writers have commonly, if loosely, distinguished a number of horizontal divisions between different 'levels' of policy. The distinction between 'high policy', or high diplomacy, and 'low policy' is a commonplace of diplomatic discourse and academic writing. It corresponds roughly to the distinction frequently made between foreign policy, narrowly defined, and external relations; as well as to the more novel terminological distinction, established within the European Community, between 'political' questions and 'technical' questions. Academics have added a third layer, 'the middle levels of power', which C. Wright Mills protested attracted too much attention, at the expense of higher and lower levels.[15] It may be helpful to make this horizontal division of foreign policy issues more explicit.

The issues may be broadly divided into three layers: high policy, sectoral policy, and low policy.[16] High policy issues are those which are seen by policy-makers as affecting Britain's fundamental standing in the world: as involving national security or national prestige, as linked to values and symbols important to society as a whole. It is these that form the overall assumptions which underpin British foreign policy. For long periods they may be unquestioned and accepted as given by all 'respected' opinion, part of the consensus on which the day-to-day management of policy rests. When they are questioned, they stimulate sharp and often bitter debate. Major crises, involving the immediate threat of war or of economic deprivation, necessarily become matters of high policy, because they threaten society as a whole. Major challenges to the prevailing assumptions of foreign policy, or major changes in these assumptions – e.g. demands that Britain should renounce its nuclear deterrent, withdraw from East of Suez, devalue the pound, or apply to enter the EEC – are similarly high policy matters. These are what are sometimes called the 'political' issues of foreign policy, the central concerns of foreign offices and of governments as a whole.[17]

Sectoral policy issues are those which are perceived as affecting only certain sections of society, only a limited number of interests and a limited range of concerns. Here what is seen to be at stake are sectoral interests rather than those of the state or of society as a whole. Though governments regularly declare their policies on these issues, it would often be more accurate to describe them in Whitehall terms as departmental rather than as government policies, for in sectoral policy issues vertical divisions between different areas are evident. We commonly refer to aid policy, to defence policy, to commercial policy, or to cultural policy, intending by this to describe a set of assumptions about the general direction of policy within a limited area, of concern to a significant but defined set of actors and interests.

Low policy issues are those in which few political values and few domestic interests are seen to be at stake: detailed and routine transactions between friendly governments, regular conversations with distant countries, technical agreements on matters to which governments attach little political significance, and so on. Policy here is close to administration, although decisions are taken – within the assumptions laid down within the wider frameworks of sectoral and of high policy issues – which may be significant for small and uninfluential groups of British citizens, or for small and uninfluential foreign governments or foreign interests.

What is or is not a matter of high policy is above all a matter of perception, of definition. The valuation of our national currency on the international exchanges might, under a different set of political assumptions, have been treated primarily as a question of economic management and external economic policy. It was the association of sterling with the idea of Britain's international standing which above all made it a high policy issue until the end of the 60s. The procurement of particular types of weapons systems may be defined either as matters of defence policy or as matters of high policy, raised to this highest level either by their association with major political values or by the size of their demands upon the government's budget: threatening the established balance between different sectors of public expenditure, or between public expenditure and private consumption, and so forcing open a debate upon the priorities of government as a whole. It is at this level that the greatest element of mystery clings to foreign policy. Indeed, one might argue that an element of mystery, of association with broad symbolic values, is indispensable in raising an issue to this level for more than a brief moment of crisis. It may have been true in the late 1960s that 'in our present circumstances . . . our entire international standing depends upon our establishing a firm basis for our economy', but it remained difficult to attach symbolic meaning to export promotion sufficient to excite the

Prime Minister and actively involve the Cabinet, or to arouse patriotic feelings in the public at large.[18]

Whether or not a particular issue is defined and managed as a matter of sectoral policy or low policy is mainly a matter of the size and influence of the domestic interests involved and of the government's perception of its domestic political sensitivity. It is unlikely that any question concerning relations with Mongolia, for instance, would be seen as other than a low policy issue, for the extent of public awareness, the number of affected interests, and the significance attached to Anglo-Mongolian relations will in all probability remain minimal. Most questions of commercial, foreign economic, or technological policy are clearly sectoral policy matters, involving a close and continuing relationship between the Departments and the interests immediately concerned. They rise to the level of high policy only when the overall framework of political relations with major foreign governments is seen to be at stake, when fundamental national interests are seen to be threatened, or when national prestige is heavily committed. The question of British relations with the emerging EEC was first treated as a sectoral policy matter, defined conveniently as a foreign trade policy issue and assigned to the care of the Board of Trade – to be redefined, rather painfully, as a matter of high policy when the Treasury, the Foreign Office, the Cabinet, and the leaders of British industry realized that wider questions were involved and that a reassessment of the assumptions underlying British foreign policy might be necessary. On some issues, for instance some aspects of aid policy – say the suspension or restitution of aid to Tanzania – the appropriate level for policy is disputed. Officials may try to confine discussion to technical and legal aspects, so holding the issue down to the level of low policy, while members of the aid lobby, and possibly companies and banks with East African interests, try to intervene to broaden the debate.

In what follows it is argued that the pattern of policy-making on different levels of issues displays a number of distinctive characteristics, the examination of which may help to explain the diversity of governmental and political activity on foreign policy issues. David Vital's statement that foreign policy 'is the business of the Executive' best fits high and low policy-making, even though, except in crisis situations, it would be mistaken to describe the Executive's freedom of decision in high policy matters as 'unfettered' by pressures from party and interest groups. In policy-making on sectoral issues, however, the involvement and influence of groups outside the Executive is considerably greater, the whole pattern of the political process more complex than most observers have allowed.

Different levels of issues are characteristically handled at different levels of policy-making. Strategic questions of high policy closely involve the Prime Minister and the senior members of the Cabinet, as well as the senior officials of the Cabinet Office and the major Departments of State.

The greater the pressure of time in crisis situations, the more likely it is for the matter to be determined by the Prime Minister and his senior ministerial colleagues and official advisers. The decision to invade Suez was taken by a very small group, led by the Prime Minister; the crisis atmosphere in which the Labour government dealt with external economic policy between 1964 and 1967 effectively reserved decisions to a similarly select few. Where time permits, as when consideration is being given to such a major change of direction in foreign policy as the possibility of joining the European Communities or of withdrawing from East of Suez, the debate can widen, spreading from Downing Street to the Departments, the major interests, the parties, and the media. Among the interest groups the peak associations will be drawn in: the Confederation of British Industry (CBI) and the TUC are likely to take up positions, and may well lobby the government. In Parliament and the country the the parties are likely to take up defined positions, even when initial divisions between points of view do not fall along party lines. The question will be widely discussed in the press, thus mobilizing public opinion. Nevertheless the outcome of the debate will be settled in the Cabinet, or at least among the senior members of the government.

But most foreign policy questions fall within the limits of sectoral policy – matters which, while not seen as fundamentally affecting the course of British foreign policy, nevertheless concern substantial British interests. Decisions on, for instance, granting export credits for a major Egyptian project, on the attitude to be taken in the aid consortium to Pakistan during the Bengal famine of 1970–1, on the conclusion of an agreement for the joint development of a nuclear centrifuge plant with the Netherlands and West Germany, or the attitude to be taken to proposals for international monetary reform under discussion with the International Monetary Fund (IMF), would fall within this category. The pattern of policy-making on such issues is again distinctive. Within the Executive it involves senior officials and in most cases departmental ministers; questions involving several Departments will be overseen by a Cabinet committee and by a parallel steering committee of officials. Here the interest groups are the sectoral organizations concerned with the particular area of policy, often bodies which maintain a continuing relationship with the Department or Departments primarily responsible for policy; for example, on a problem concerning South Africa, the competing lobbies of the anti-apartheid groups and the pro-South African commercial and political groups, or on question concerning tariffs and quotas for cotton goods, the various textile associations and some sections of the aid lobby. Parliamentary interest, when raised, is more often at the level of the interested backbench committees than of the parties as a whole; party lines are frequently crossed. With intermittent press coverage and with much interest group activity, a small attentive public may be drawn in, to lobby their MPs, to write to the quality press, or to join in local and national demonstrations of one kind or another. But so

long as the government's prestige is not committed, there is room for
negotiation and bargaining among the affected interests, inside and outside Whitehall; and the outcome may well reflect the balance of pressures
among these interests as much as it does the assumed priorities of high
policy.

Much of the minutiae of external relations – a request for aid from
Gambia or Guyana, the organization of a trade drive in Kuwait, the
conclusion of an agreement for a regular air service between Argentina
and the Falkland Islands – are handled almost entirely within the
Executive, and at that largely at a relatively junior level, senior officials
and ministers being only intermittently involved. Those few interests
affected are in most cases known to the officials concerned and often
share a common outlook and interest, so that formal consultation is
largely superfluous. Parliamentary interest, where it exists, is in most
cases limited to one or two individual MPs; press coverage, if any, rarely
extends beyond specialized journals or occasional articles in the inside
pages of the national press. If the Executive predominates in the determination of policy at this level, as at the highest level, it is because it
remains relatively unchallenged; and by 'the Executive' is here meant not
the Prime Minister and his senior colleagues, but first secretaries and
counsellors in the FCO and principals and assistant secretaries in home
Departments.

This framework, like any other, is clearly too neat to describe the full
complexity and diversity of the field. Its purpose is to outline its most
important features so as to facilitate a critical examination. Studies of
foreign policy-making in Britain or indeed of policy-making in general
have too often assumed that all policies are managed in a similar fashion,
and so have generalized from the more important decisions to the less
important. Thus R. H. S. Crossman, in his introduction to Bagehot's
The English Constitution, cited the decision to develop an independent
nuclear deterrent and the management of the Suez intervention in support of his general argument on the growth of prime ministerial power.[19]
Yet both of these were exceptional decisions, in terms of the symbolic
importance attached to them and of the degree of secrecy with which
they were surrounded. Comparison with the management of other
concurrent policies, such as the renegotiation of the status of British
forces in Germany or the objectives pursued within the OEEC – both
of which carried long-term implications for British relations with
Western Europe and the United States as well as for Britain's
international financial position – might have led to a rather different
conclusion.

The 'great' decisions, the turning points in high policy, the redefinition
of Britain's international objectives, not unnaturally attract the most
attention from politicians and from observers, even though these are,
in the nature of things, exceptional events outside the regular flow of
policy. Yet Crossman assumed, and C. Wright Mills explicitly argued,

that these exceptional decisions are 'crucial' in determining the general line of policy and in understanding the pattern of influence in policy-making. In this study more emphasis is laid on the middle and lower levels of policy-making, in line with the hypothesis that the cumulative weight of decisions at these levels significantly affects the available strategic choices at the higher levels, by foreclosing some options and opening others. What the casual observer notices are the great events: the signature of a treaty, the presidential visit, the rupture of diplomatic relations or the announcement of a new strategy. He is less likely to know about the long process of preparatory meetings and discussions which precede the formal treaty-making conference, the efforts to establish a 'favourable' atmosphere for a top-level visit, the attempts over a period to arrest a deterioration in relations, which set the stage for these major occasions and may largely determine their outcome. If the small change of diplomatic relations is neglected over a long period, the cost in an unanticipated crisis can be very high. If changes in the international environment are not observed and analysed and their implications for British policy assessed, or if the links which important foreign governments draw between separate areas of British external relations – say between the overseas procurement of weapons systems and British negotiations with the EEC – are not appreciated and allowed for, the effects of prime ministerial decisions and presidential conferences may be undone.

Of course this interrelationship between the day-to-day management of diplomacy and high policy objectives has always affected foreign policy-making. But today intergovernmental relations among Western nations are so much more complex that it has become correspondingly more difficult for policy-makers to assess technical relations in the perspective of total foreign policy.

The interesting discovery that has emerged out of the past fifteen years of European history is how important and influential the mass of decisions emerging out of 'low politics' are in our advanced industrial societies. You start out with what seems like a largely technical matter, like the limit on the axle weight of heavy lorries, and you end up with a large number of rules and regulations which, taken together, determine the shape and texture of the environment of millions of people.[20]

One government treats the selection of a system for the transmission of colour television from among competing foreign proposals largely as a matter of technical appraisal and industrial advantage, while another government regards the matter as a test of good relations and as a fit subject for representations between heads of government. Even a government which is clear about its objectives and its priorities risks unintended setbacks if it is not also aware of the differing perceptions and priorities of its partners.

There remain a number of further considerations of relevance to the framework adopted here. The amount of time available for policy-making, as has already been suggested, affects the way in which an issue is handled. In a crisis situation, or where there is a tight deadline for decision-taking, the numbers of those involved is likely to remain small. Studies of American decision-making under crisis have suggested that there is a far greater tendency in such situations for decisions to be taken outside the normal institutional and constitutional framework, and for the personalities and personal relations of the small number of people involved to be crucial in influencing the outcome. This seems as true of crisis decisions in Britain. The late-night decision to close the London gold market in March 1968 was taken by the Prime Minister and a handful of ministers; his Foreign Secretary resigned in protest at not being consulted.[21] The management of the 'Soames affair', the problem of whether to inform the German government about confidential proposals made by the French President to the British ambassador in Paris in February 1969, offers another example. By delaying a week after receiving the report from Paris and pressing it on the Prime Minister for decision just as he was leaving for Bonn, the Foreign Secretary and Foreign Office officials ensured that the Cabinet was prevented from discussing it and that the Prime Minister had only one day for decision, without access to any but diplomatic advice.[22] A calmer atmosphere and a longer time limit allow for, and so demand, a proper respect for regular institutional channels.

A second consideration is the pressure of concurrent problems on policy-makers and on the machinery of policy-making. Those at the top are only capable of handling a limited number of problems at the same time; if a particular foreign policy issue dominates their attention, or if domestic crises distract them, less pressing problems will be put off or decided at a lower level. The constant pressure of other business on ministers also limits the time that a problem remains under discussion at the top level, to push issues on to 'the back burner' when they seem less urgent or when new developments appear unlikely, to reconsider them only when they boil over. Policy towards the EEC, a matter of high policy (and of successive Cabinet meetings) at the time of the Labour government's approach to application, was thus relegated upon the renewed French veto, returning to the Cabinet after de Gaulle's resignation, when it was necessary to reconsider the major foreign policy issues involved. The Rhodesian question similarly shifted up and down from ministerial to senior and middle official levels as new developments loomed or stalemate returned. Yet since ministers operate under so much pressure, a reluctance to reopen questions once they have been decided usually holds issues down at lower levels, thus limiting the reconsideration of alternatives and narrowing the area of debate. Henry Kissinger's comment on the United States applies equally to the United Kingdom:

. . . once the decision-making apparatus has disgorged a policy, it becomes very difficult to change it. The alternative to the status quo is the prospect of repeating the whole agonising process of arriving at decisions. This explains to some extent the curious phenomenon that decisions taken with enormous doubt and perhaps with a close division become practically sacrosanct once adopted. The whole administrative machinery swings behind their implementation as if activity could still all doubts.[23]

This constant effort to reduce the inflow of problems demanding attention to manageable proportions, to parcel them out to different sections of the administrative machine and to select for treatment at a higher level only those problems the novelty, peculiarity, or sensitivity of which demand special attention suggests a third consideration: the continuing tension between coordination and compartmentalization. In an ideal world all incoming problems would be considered in the light of their implications for the whole range of foreign policy objectives and existing policies. In the real world, operating under the constraints of limited time and resources, a considerable degree of compartmentalization of issues, into 'commercial', 'cultural', or 'defence' questions, is clearly essential. More than this, the compartmentalization of problems is a mutually convenient device among governments in international relations, enabling policy-makers to isolate particular issues from the broader questions of bilateral and multilateral relations, and so to negotiate on these specific issues without directly raising issues in a different compartment. However, there is a risk that a foreign government may not respect the boundaries Whitehall has drawn between different sectors of policy, so that its reaction to an initiative in one area may adversely affect its attitude to important objectives in another. Some kind of coordination, some machinery for ordering priorities in foreign relations and for preventing different sections of the policy-making structure working at cross-purposes, is therefore necessary. But coordination involves costs, in terms of raising the consideration of conflicting policies to a higher level, of occupying the time of senior officials and ministers, of delaying the management of business. Not only ministers but also officials therefore prefer instinctively to handle a problem at as low a level as possible, to isolate it as far as possible from wider policy considerations and limit the range of debate.

This being so, this study will take as one measure of the effectiveness of the machinery for foreign policy-making its degree of flexibility in moving problems up and down the administrative ladder, in accordance with shifting priorities and changing circumstances. As has been shown, at the highest level all aspects of foreign policy are likely to be handled on a broadly similar basis. But issues relegated over an extended period to middle or lower levels of policy-making are likely to become more or less isolated from the total foreign policy process, and to develop a distinctive pattern of relations between a relatively undisturbed set of participants.

The chapters that follow first discuss foreign policy as a whole – its formal policy-making machinery, the official and non-official participants, and the flow of policy. Then some specific foreign policy areas and bilateral and multilateral relations are examined to demonstrate the extent to which they have different features and involve distinctive participants. The last chapter attempts a critical assessment. The informed reader may wish to omit the detailed exposition of chapter 2 and focus on the argument developed in chapter 3 and beyond. The less informed are encouraged to persevere through its descriptive passages, as a necessary background to what follows.

Part I: The Policy-Making Process

2: The Whitehall Machinery

To GRASP the formal structure of responsibility and authority in any large and complex organization is to gain no more than a partial account of the way in which policy is made. Even in organizations where the informal process of policy-making differs sharply from the formal hierarchy a knowledge of this structure is necessary for any full appreciation of the process of policy-making. In Britain the informal channels which foreign policy-makers use to supplement the formal structure in practice correspond more closely to that structure than in most other countries – far more closely, say, than in the United States or France.

Formal responsibility for the conduct of British foreign policy rests with the Secretary of State for Foreign Affairs and under him the FCO. According to the conventions of the British constitution, the Foreign Secretary's actions are subject to the approval of the Cabinet and of the Prime Minister as its chairman. Where questions of foreign policy involve matters within the sphere of responsibility of other Departments of State, the Foreign Secretary or his officials formulate policy in consultation with those Departments. These policies are implemented by the FCO, either directly or through the agency of British embassies and missions abroad.

The strength of the formal structure rests partly in its recognized efficiency in operation, partly on the high prestige and high morale of the Diplomatic Service, and partly on the recollection of past events. The two major occasions within living memory when the formal structure was deliberately by-passed became the two most widely regretted actions in British foreign policy: the period of appeasement of Germany leading up to and including the Munich crisis, and the Suez intervention. Part of the remembered shame of Munich and Suez, among politicians and commentators as well as among officials, is specifically attached to the clandestine way in which the Foreign Office and foreign missions were ignored – and in the Suez case actively misled – in preference for informal advisers and extraordinary channels of communication with other governments. Though seldom referred to explicitly, this recollection combines with a certain respect for the efficiency of the machine in handling day-to-day business to counterbalance the frustrations which ministers and others occasionally express at what they see as the FCO's solidarity and immovability.

As might be expected, the actual process of policy-making in any specific case corresponds to the formal structure to a much greater extent in lower-level than in higher policy-making. Junior officials in any hierarchy pay particular attention to the rules by which routine decisions should be made, leaving it to their superiors or to their political masters to accept responsibility for idiosyncratic decisions or for short-circuiting the proper channels. At the level of high policy, the formal structure is far less controlling: among those who share the formal responsibility for the direction of foreign policy, personal relationships, prejudices, and interests play a considerable part in shaping both the informal channels of communications and the output of policy, as in other small groups. Even here, however, formal relationships, awareness of roles and acceptance of those roles, exert a certain pressure. Except in situations of acute crisis, decisions are at least confirmed through formal channels, even when they are effectively made outside them; and confirmation is not always a matter of course.

This formal description applies most accurately to the traditional concerns of foreign policy, narrowly defined: the management of intergovernmental relations, the negotiation of treaties, representation abroad. It has never been the case that the Foreign Office or the Foreign Secretary were responsible for the direction or conduct of international economic policy, which is the preserve of the Treasury and the Bank of England. Yet economic relations have never been entirely separable from political relations between states, and are now close to the heart of intergovernmental diplomacy. External commercial policy has always been shared, through varying instititial arrangements, between the Board of Trade and the Foreign Office. The growth of intergovernmental concerns and of economic interdependence between states, increasing governmental intervention in the economy, and the revolution in communications and transportation, have brought more and more home Departments into a cooperative relationship with the Foreign Office. The intrusion of technological questions into high policy has added another sector in which the role of the Foreign Office is more accessory than decisive. It is emphatically not true that foreign policy is what the Foreign Office does; rather, what the Foreign Office takes the main responsibility for nowadays constitutes a relatively small proportion of the issues of foreign policy. Over most important issues of intergovernmental relations, certainly between Britain and the governments of the industrialized countries of Western Europe and North America, the Foreign Office shares responsibility for the formulation and implementation of policy with one or more other Departments of State.

The succession of institutional changes in Whitehall between 1964 and 1974 presents some difficulties in discussing the structure of Departments. The FCO was still commonly referred to as the Foreign Office, long after the completion of the merger in 1968; hence the two titles are used interchangeably in this discussion. The Board of Trade and the Ministry of Technology became the DTI in 1970, to reappear in altered form as the Department of Trade and the Department of Industry in 1974. The ODM became the ODA in 1970, and a ministry again in 1974. The Ministries of Transport, Housing, and Public Building and Works were united in the Department of the Environment in 1970. In what follows, Departments are referred to by their titles at the time. The reader should remember that changes in name and in ministerial responsibility do not always affect the administrative pattern of policy-making below the senior official level. Underneath the succession of reshuffles, divisions within Departments continued to exercise the same continuing functions, and often to implement the same continuing policy.

A further potential source of confusion is the Foreign Office's distinctive practice of referring to its internal divisions as 'departments', in contrast to all other Departments in Whitehall. To avoid confusion between these internal departments and the major ministries, or Departments of State, the Foreign Office divisions will be referred to in lower case throughout, and Whitehall Departments will retain a capital. Thus 'departments' are those sections of the Diplomatic Service within the Foreign Office; home Departments are all those Departments in Whitehall which are primarily concerned with domestic policy, as opposed to the FCO, the ODM, and upon occasion the MoD.

The Foreign and Commonwealth Office

In 1968 the newly-created FCO could look back to one of the most disturbed histories of any Whitehall Department. For several decades the common situation for its members had been one of continual readjustment to developments in an international environment over which Britain exercised declining influence, which meant consequent administrative reorganization, constant pressure of work, and an almost permanent shortage of manpower. The 1943 *Proposals for the Reform of the Foreign Service* (Cmd 6240, paras 20-2) had included the recommendation for a substantial period of initial training for recruits to the new Foreign Service, based upon a more flexible use of manpower. But the postwar expansion of Foreign Office concerns, the emergence of a succession of newly independent states and the consequent increase in the number of overseas missions, as well as the Treasury's continuous pressure on expenditure, effectively prevented the creation of a margin of manpower sufficient to make such a scheme practicable. The Plowden and the Duncan Reports both returned to the theme; but their recommendations for more flexible use of manpower and the provision of adequate facilities for training were overtaken by the renewed search for economies at home and abroad, and by the multiplication of diplomatic tasks as Britain approached the European Communities.[1]

The overseas Departments which now merged into the FCO had not, of course, been alone in facing the expansion of tasks and the consequent succession of reorganizations. The transformation of the role and functions of the Foreign Office were, however, as rapid and as far-reaching as any. In the 50s a Permanent Under-Secretary could still write that 'it was within the lifetime of men still employed in the Foreign Service' that the office 'emerged fully from clerkly bondage into its present status as an advisory body'.[2] Yet the Foreign Office, like the Treasury, had escaped the wide range of managerial tasks which most other Whitehall Departments were assuming – although the burden of self-administration had increased in parallel with the larger number of overseas posts and the growing size of the Foreign Service. Like the Treasury, the Foreign Office remained primarily a policy advisory and policy-making ministry, with a number of executive tasks performed on its behalf by associated agencies. It therefore remained a relatively small Department, but with a claim to play something of a strategic role in Whitehall.

Criticism of the Foreign Service's slowness to adapt to postwar conditions, often reinforced by objections to the 'traditional standards of entertainment' maintained in British embassies during a time of austerity at home, was supplemented from the 1950s onwards by attacks on the Foreign Office's commitment to 'pragmatism', its failure either to plan ahead or to develop a coherent strategy, or to anticipate major international trends.[3] Similar criticisms had also, of course, been made of the HCS and home Departments, in the late 50s and early 60s, culminating in the appointment of the Fulton Committee and the admonitory comments in the first chapter of its report.[4]

In 1964 the acceptance of the Plowden Report's recommendations that the separate Foreign and Commonwealth Services should be merged instituted a period of major reform. A single Diplomatic Service was established in 1965, members of the separate Trade Commissioner Service which had operated in Commonwealth countries being given the option of transferring into the new Service or of returning to the Board of Trade. The completion of the institutional merger, in October 1968, did not mean the end of the process of change. It took some time to absorb the Commonwealth Office and reduce the overhang of ministers and senior officials which the merger had left behind. In 1970 the ODM formally became part of the FCO, though retaining much of its separate status. The approach to membership of the EEC brought further adjustments in internal organization and in ministerial responsibilities. The Duncan Committee, which reported in July 1969, had been asked to investigate the scope for economies in overseas representation. As a result there were some further readjustments: some senior staff were

Departments

		Departments
		Historical Adviser | Library & Records | Research
		Planning Staff
	AUS	Central & Southern Africa | E. African | Rhodesian | W. African
DUS		
	AUS	Middle East | Near East & N. Africa | UN
		Arms Control & Disarmament | Defence
DUS	AUS	Overseas Police Adviser | Republic of Ireland
		Permanent Under Secretary's Department
		} Western Organizations*
	AUS	S.E. European | S.W. European | W. European
DUS	AUS	N. America
		Eastern European & Soviet
		Overseas Labour Adviser
	AUS	Financial Relations | Trade Relations &
DUS		Exports
	AUS	Economists
	(Chief Economic Adviser)	
	AUS	Energy | Marine & Transport | Science & Technology
	AUS	Protocol & Conference
	AUS	Personnel Operations | Personnel Policy
	(Deputy Chief Clerk)	Personnel Services | Security | Training
		Accommodation & Services | Claims | Consular
DUS (Chief Clerk)	AUS	Finance | Migration & Visa | Nationality & Treaty | Passport Office
	AUS	Inspectorate
		Communications Administration
		Communications Engineering
	AUS	Communications Operations
		Communications Planning Staff
		Communications Technical Services
	AUS	Latin America
DUS		} Caribbean*
	AUS	Commonwealth Co-ordination | Gibraltar & General
		Pacific Dependent Territories
		West Indian & Atlantic
		} Hong Kong & Indian Ocean*
	AUS	Far Eastern | India Office Library & Records
		S. Asian | S.E. Asian | S.W. Pacific
		Cultural Exchange | Cultural Relations
	AUS	European Integration (Information Subjects)
DUS		Guidance & Information Policy
		Information Administration | Information Research
		Parliamentary Commissioner & Committees Unit
		News
DUS	AUS	European Integration (External)
		European Integration (Internal)

PERMANENT UNDER SECRETARY

DUS – Deputy Under Secretary; AUS – Assistant Under Secretary.

* Western Organizations Department and Hong Kong & Indian Ocean Department report to *two* Assistant Under Secretaries and *two* Deputy Under Secretaries; Caribbean Department reports to two Assistant Under Secretaries but to the same Deputy Under Secretary.

retired early; a small number of overseas posts were closed and others were reduced in size.

The contrasting assumptions of the Plowden and the Duncan Reports, five years apart, also reflected a sea change in the environment of British foreign policy-making. The Duncan Report (p. 23) explicitly abandoned the aim to which Plowden had clung, of a Diplomatic Service and a Foreign Office machine capable of serving the global needs of a world power, and replaced it with the more modest machinery required by 'a major power of the second order'. Developments within the Foreign Office and the Diplomatic Service during the 1960s – the turnover of staff, the emergence of new functional specializations and departments and of new planning procedures – had perhaps already outdated earlier criticisms. By 1972 the last officials with career experience of the Foreign Office before World War II were approaching retirement; the Permanent Under-Secretary and five of the ten deputy under-secretaries were post-war recruits. But older members of the Service passed on to younger ones something of the traditions of the interwar and postwar periods, which they also absorbed as they read through the wealth of diplomatic diaries and memoirs. This was still evident in the mistrustful relations with the Treasury during the 60s, as it was too in the revival of the ancient title of Chief Clerk for the head of administration in 1970. The FCO was still, recognizably, the Foreign Office, absorbing other Departments and Services without losing its character, as it was still physically recognizable in the splendours and miseries of the old Foreign Office building, with its marble staircase and poky offices – even though the FCO had long since spilled over into the equally splendid and miserable India Office next door, into the Commonwealth Office in the same range of buildings, across Clive Steps to occupy a section of the Treasury range and into about a dozen other buildings, some more than a mile away.

The Foreign Office in 1972 had some 68 departments, each headed by a counsellor, the Diplomatic Service equivalent of an assistant secretary, reporting through 15 assistant under-secretaries and 9 deputy under-secretaries to the Permanent Under-Secretary and the Foreign Secretary. The traditional core of the Foreign Office, its expert knowledge of and advice upon developments in foreign countries, rested in the twenty-two geographical departments: each consisting of some six to a dozen administrative grade personnel, organized into country desks (many of which, of course, are responsible for more than one country), with one or more senior first secretaries to supervise and to assist the head of department. Five more departments dealt with information and cultural policy, providing guidance to overseas posts on British policy, liaising with the Central Office of Information (COI), the BBC, and the British Council; a sixth, the News department, was responsible for relations with the press. A further fifteen departments, reporting to the Chief Clerk, managed the executive responsibilities of the Foreign Office and administered the Office and the Diplomatic Service. The Research

Diplomatic Service Ranks and their Home Civil Service Equivalents

Diplomatic Service	Types of job	Home Civil Service
Grade 1	Permanent Under-Secretary or senior Head of Mission	Permanent Secretary
Grade 2	Deputy Under-Secretary or Head of Grade 2 Post	Deputy Secretary
Grade 3	Assistant Under-Secretary, Head of Grade 3 Post, Minister or senior Consul-General	Under-Secretary
Grade 4	Counsellor, Consul-General, Head of Foreign and Commonwealth Office Department or Head of Grade 4 Post	Assistant Secretary (Administrative Class) Principal Executive Officer (Executive Class)
Grade 5A	First Secretary or Consul	Principal
Grade 5E	First Secretary or Consul	Chief Executive Officer
Grade 6	First Secretary or Consul	Senior Executive Officer
Grade 7A	Second Secretary	Assistant Principal
Grade 7E	Second Secretary	Higher Executive Officer
Grade 8	Third Secretary or Vice-Consul	Assistant Principal
Grade 9	Junior Attaché or Vice-Consul	Executive Officer

department, Library and Records, the Legal Advisers, the Economists, and the India Office Library and Records serviced the rest of the Department and were largely staffed by specialized personnel. The remaining departments represented the main growth area within the Foreign Office during the 60s: the functional departments, organized in subject desks dealing with specific fields of policy.

Much of the work of the FCO still centred upon the collection and interpretation of information on developments in foreign countries. This is the source of advice and policy proposals tendered to their ministers and of briefings for other Departments and for ministers preparing for visits abroad or for discussions with foreign visitors, drafts for parliamentary questions and for speeches, and so on. This represents the core expertise of the Foreign Office and its most distinctive function in Whitehall. 'The special contribution of the Foreign and Commonwealth Office to the national effort lies in its amassed and living knowledge of overseas countries. This knowledge is called upon constantly by home Departments, by British industry and commerce, and by the general public.'[5] The range of work at higher levels within the Office otherwise differs little from that within home Departments: servicing their minister, representing him to other Departments, formulating major policy for ministerial decision and implementing it after decision, deciding minor policy, and managing the Department's executive responsibilities.[6] The growth of the functional departments reflects the growth of the 'representational' role in Whitehall, the extent to which the FCO has been drawn into areas of policy which overlap the spheres of responsibility of other Departments and which require extensive liaison with officials from those Departments.

Low-level questions occupy a good deal of the time of desk officers – requests for information about British domestic or foreign policies from foreign governments, regular contacts with embassies in London and with overseas posts. Such questions do not rise above the departmental level unless a parliamentary question forces them on to the attention of a minister. A considerable amount of routine intergovernmental work is also handled at this level: arrangements for foreign visitors (from journalists to parliamentarians to prime ministers), briefings and introductions for a similar range of British visitors going abroad, handling requests from foreign newspapers for interviews with British ministers, and the like – the small change of international relations, unexciting in itself but capable of disturbing good relations between governments if not carefully attended to. Increasingly in the early 70s personal contacts with opposite numbers in the foreign ministries of other states, membership of intergovernmental working parties and committees, institutionalized exchanges of views were becoming a part of Foreign Office routine, not only with the United States and West European countries during the approach to Community membership but also with such countries as Japan. At the middle and higher levels of policy and policy-makers such contacts had become much more frequent. Involvement in intergovernmental exchanges and in direct intergovernmental negotiations was complemented at home by extensive contacts with interest groups and informed opinion, as well as with other Departments.

The FCO has direct managerial responsibilities for self-administration, for assistance to British citizens abroad, for the administration of Britain's remaining dependent territories, and for a number of 'grants-in-aid' to public and private organizations within its sphere of responsibility. As a separate entity from the HCS, staffing and servicing not only the FCO but a large number of overseas posts, the Diplomatic Service is responsible for its own personnel management and for much of its own security and accommodation arrangements, which are covered by six administrative departments.[7] In addition, its own inspectors regularly visit and report on overseas posts. The work of the Claims, Consular, Nationality and Treaty, and Migration and Visa departments is largely routine, but can easily become politically sensitive either in domestic terms or in bilateral relations. The internment of British subjects in Egypt and the sequestration of their property was one of the complicating factors in the Suez intervention and the later negotiations for withdrawal; fifteen years later the problem of compensation for confiscated property remained to bedevil Anglo-Egyptian negotiations on commercial and financial relations. Four of the Parliamentary Commissioners for Administration's first fifty-seven cases of maladministration concerned the FCO, including perhaps the most celebrated: the FCO's refusal to acknowledge the claims for compensation of twelve survivors of the Sachsenhausen concentration camps, in spite of a determined parliamentary campaign.[8]

The FCO prides itself upon the flexibility of its working methods and internal organization. There are still not too many administrative personnel for informal contacts between members of different departments, based upon mutual acquaintance, to be the rule rather than the exception – even though the steady expansion of the Office through the series of amalgamations has made this a little more difficult than in the past.[9] Easy contact between senior and junior officials is fostered by the 'cameraderie' of the Diplomatic Service and the shared experience of serving in posts abroad. Departments within the Foreign Office are created, divided, merged, and disbanded as needs require, in sharp contrast with many other foreign ministries. Two problems of internal organization have however proved intractable: to contain the growth of the functional departments, and to reduce the number of supervisory under-secretaries.

The Plowden Report (para. 212) had reluctantly accepted that 'there must be specialist functional departments', though it added that 'care must be taken throughout to avoid extending the sphere of specialized departments in such a way as to diminish the responsibility and effectiveness of geographical departments'. However, the pressures of dealing with other Whitehall Departments and with multilateral negotiations led rather to an expansion in the size and numbers of the functional departments, so that by the early 70s it was these departments that were in effect playing the main part in handling relations with 'inner area' countries, with the geographical departments managing more routine bilateral work. The reorganization of departments which accompanied entry into the EEC in early 1973 reduced the total number of functional departments, but not their workload or their staffs. Those concerned with the European Community, moreover, looked to a further expansion of these specialist departments, as the Community extended common policy in new directions and as multilateral negotiations between it and the other developed countries extended into new areas. Some idea of the balance of work within the FCO may be gathered from the figures for total staff (administrative, executive, and secretarial) given in the 1972–3 Estimates: geographical departments 347; functional departments 850; information, cultural and news 126; administration 707.[10]

Similar pressures had prevented the reduction in senior staff which had been hoped for as a result of the merger of the Foreign and Commonwealth Offices, despite agreement within the Diplomatic Service that the new FCO had inherited 'far too many Under-Secretaries'. The Duncan Committee (p. 56) considered it 'clear' that 'the present number of supervising Under-Secretaries is too large'; it was glad to hear that some reductions were in train and others anticipated. Yet after an initial reduction from a total of 26 assistant and deputy under-secretaries in 1969 to some 22 in 1971, in 1972 there were 24, in 1974 27. The reasons were similar to those which failed to prevent proliferation of the functional departments: that the pressure of multilateral consultation and negotiations along functional lines, covering fields which directly involved the interests of home Departments, pushed in the direction of increasing staff. Interdepartmental committees in Whitehall, Foreign Office representation at multilateral meetings, and preparations for these meetings, imposed a heavier workload on the senior officials than a smaller number could manage.

In contrast, the number of ministers in the FCO was sharply reduced between 1968 and 1972.[11] In 1967 the separate Departments commanded a total of 12 ministers, 7 in the Foreign Office and 5 responsible for the Commonwealth and the Colonies (though one of these, Lord Caradon, as Britain's representative at the UN, spent little time in the Department or at Westminster). There were in addition 6 unpaid parliamentary private secretaries, and a separate Minister of Overseas Development with his own unpaid p.p.s. By 1969 there were only 8 ministers and in 1970, 7, with 2 parliamentary private secretaries in attendance: still sufficient for the Foreign Secretary to devolve geographical and functional responsibilities to particular ministers, working alongside undersecretaries. The Conservative government reduced the FCO's ministerial strength still further – to 6 in 1971 and, with the transfer of the responsibility for ministerial coordination on European Community questions to the Cabinet, to 5 in 1972, plus one p.p.s. The Minister for Overseas Development was also now formally part of the Foreign Office, though his other duties did not allow him to relieve his colleagues of many of their ministerial burdens. Organizationally, the senior minister of state acted as a deputy to the Foreign Secretary across the whole range of departmental responsibilities, while his three colleagues were delegated particularly sensitive areas of policy and shared the burden of ministerial representation at foreign conferences, receptions, and the like. The system of assigning geographical and functional responsibilities to junior ministers, introduced by the Labour government during the process of merging the Departments, was continued by the Conservatives: however, with a much smaller number of departmental ministers the scope for the devolution of responsibility was necessarily limited.[12] The Labour government returned in March 1974 followed the Conservatives in appointing a total of five ministers to the FCO (the Foreign Secretary, two ministers of state, and two parliamentary under-secretaries).

If it was correct to say in the early 50s that 'no democratic system yet devised has ever attempted to solve the problem of the crushing responsibility borne by foreign ministers', the nature of the problem twenty years later was still more intractable.[13] Besides his responsibilities as a member of the Cabinet and his parliamentary duties at Westminster, the Foreign Secretary faced an ever increasing burden of political work and formal duties arising from the growth of multilateral organizations, the greater ease of international travel, and the multiplication of independent states. By the late 50s it had already become customary for the Foreign Secretary to visit New York for an extended period during sessions of the UN General Assembly; as well as regular NATO meetings, there were the less regular demands of British involvement in great power diplomacy. In 1959–60 he was abroad for a total of 125 days in one calendar year on a succession of foreign visits and conferences, provoking criticism of a consequent neglect of his parliamentary duties.[14] Increasing British involvement in intergovernmental consultation in Western Europe during the 60s, culminating in the successful conclusion of negotiations for Community entry, compounded the strain. And the requirements of protocol sent him out to London Airport to welcome foreign dignitaries and engaged him in formal luncheons and dinners, many of which could not be delegated to junior ministers without giving offence. Yet no Foreign Secretary can totally neglect domestic policies, his party or constituency. Sir Alec Douglas-Home, as an elder statesman of the Conservative Party, was not infrequently called upon between 1970 and 1973 to pronounce authoritatively on such matters as Enoch Powell's economic arguments or the weaknesses of Liberal policy. The Foreign Secretary, then, can only himself deal with the broad outline of foreign policy, selecting from the mass of Foreign Office business those few issues which his personal interest, his awareness of high policy implications, inter-ministerial differences, or parliamentary pressures bring to the forefront of his attention. Less urgent or less sensitive matters, given the severe constraints imposed by time and human capabilities, must necessarily be left to the management of the Foreign Office machine and its supervising officials.[15]

Besides its role in the formulation and management of foreign policy the FCO acts as the main channel of communication between Whitehall and overseas posts, as the supervisory Department – and representative in the Cabinet – of a number of associated agencies, and (as has already been noted) as the home base and administrative centre for the Diplomatic Service.

In 1972 the British Diplomatic Service had a staff of rather more than 6,000, over half of whom belong to the subordinate secretarial, security, and communications branches. Before the merging of the administrative and executive branches (in accordance with the recommendations of the Duncan Committee), the administrative grade totalled 1,100: a considerable figure when compared with the total of 2,600 administrative-grade personnel throughout the entire HCS, supervising the work of a far larger number of executive personnel. The 1943 Proposals under which the Foreign Service was separately established had envisaged a fully 'generalist' service, to replace the specialized consular and commercial services whose functions it was to assume; though the degree of non-specialization within the Foreign Service was often overestimated by outside critics, as indeed it was also of the similarly 'generalist' administrative grade of the HCS. The core specialization of the Diplomatic Service was and remains linguistic and regional. Half the administrative grade entrants to the Service are assigned to learn a 'hard' language, acquiring in the process a regional specialization. The largest group, and the only one with a separate training centre (the Middle East Centre for Arab Studies), are the Arabists, who staff some twenty posts in North Africa and the Middle East; next come specialists in Russian and Slav languages, the East Europeanists, and a slowly growing group of Japanese and Chinese specialists. During the 60s a recognizable group of specialists on Western Europe emerged; perhaps surprisingly, in view of the large number of Spanish-speaking overseas posts, there seems to be no similar group of Latin American specialists.[16] Specialists can expect to spend up to half of their careers in positions directly related to their areas, including two or three overseas postings and periods in the relevant geographical departments at home.

Functional specialization within the Diplomatic Service has been slower to develop, and has so far been largely confined to expertise acquired 'on the job'. The policy-formulating levels of the Service had, until the mid-60s, only two separately recruited groups of specialists: the Research Department, and the Legal Advisers, both of whose members spend most of their careers in London, with limited periods abroad.[17] Amalgamation with the CRO also brought a small group of economists into the FCO. Some of the administrative grade staff specialized to a degree in information, commercial, or consular work, though during the 60s there was a tendency to rely more on executive personnel in these specialisms. The combination of new demands on the Diplomatic Service and of a feeling of unease among junior staff at their lack of functional skills in an increasingly specialized environment led during the same period to the beginnings of recognizable and recognized specializations in economic and technological subjects, though as yet without extended periods of training outside the job. In 1972 the most regular form of training in any functionally specialized field remained the year-long secondments to the Royal College of Defence Studies or to the NATO Defence College in Rome. The three or four men so seconded each year were counsellors in mid-career.

Criticism of the Diplomatic Service in recent years has focused less on its calibre or competence than on its character as a self-conscious and close-knit elite, its lack of contact with Whitehall, with domestic interests and with domestic opinion, and its high career mobility. The Duncan Committee (p. 23), indeed, thought it proper to consider whether the Diplomatic Service was 'extravagant' in its consumption and utilization of some of the most talented products of British universities. The pattern of recruitment, and even more the process of socialization within a relatively small service sharing responsibilities in overseas posts, has generated both a high service morale and an elite consciousness.[18]

Certainly, the high proportion of their careers spent abroad, and the moderate difficulty of regular visits to London during overseas postings, did make it difficult to keep in close touch with developments in Whitehall or with domestic interests and opinions. However, criticisms of the too rapid transfer of British diplomats from post to post and from subject to subject were by the late 60s often overstated (as they were, similarly, of the HCS). At least one of the senior FCO officials responsible for European Community questions in 1972 had been concerned with the Community, in London or in Brussels, since 1958; individual postings now averaged between three and four years each, and some stretched to five or six.

Of the Whitehall agencies with whose work the FCO has been associated, the most difficult relationship to describe is that between it and the ODA. The intention of the incoming Conservative government in 1970 to integrate the ODM into the Foreign Office, as part of their creation of several 'giant' Departments in Whitehall, was weakened during the summer of 1970 by the efforts of the substantial 'aid lobby' to protect 'their' ministry from absorption. The form of words adopted in the 1970 White Paper on *The Reorganization of Central Government* indicated a careful compromise: giving 'ultimate responsibility' for overseas aid to the Foreign Secretary, delegated to a Minister for Overseas Development whose 'status' (though not his legal position) would be equivalent to that of a minister in charge of a separate Department not represented in the Cabinet, who was to have 'full charge' of his functional unit of the FCO, which would continue to be staffed by home civil servants.[19] In 1973 the continuing looseness of the link was indicated by the maintenance of the minister's private office, with the rest of the ODA, in a separate range of buildings a considerable distance from the FCO, although relations had gradually grown closer in the previous two years. Part of the FCO's willingness to accept so loose an arrangement may well have been a feeling that aid questions were sufficiently distant from foreign policy to be dealt with in a separate compartment; possibly there was also a sense of misgiving about the dilution of the Diplomatic Service involved in the incorporation of so many home civil servants into its ranks. As a separate Whitehall Department, the ODA maintained representation on a number of interdepartmental committees, but in most instances its position was fairly close to that of the FCO. The renewed separation of the ODA from the FCO in March 1974, under its own minister, did not immediately seem to have affected this established relationship.

The formal relationship between the FCO and the three bodies responsible for the management of informational and cultural activities is more straightforward. The Information departments of the FCO liaise with the COI and BBC External Services, the Cultural Relations department with the British Council. Nearly half the COI's expenditure, and three-quarters of its staff time, are committed to the overseas information services; here, as a non-ministerial Department, it operates entirely as an agency for the FCO and for overseas missions, producing material to order. With the BBC and the British Council, as incorporated bodies with a degree of independence from governmental direction, the FCO is responsible for the general outlines of policy, the overall allocations of the budget between activities and countries, and the defence of that budget in the Whitehall process. The details of implementation, and the content of particular programmes and activities, are reserved to the agencies themselves.

Overseas Missions

In formal terms, embassies and overseas missions represent and report through the Foreign Office to the British government as a whole. Ambassadors represent 'the Crown' in person, a function which envelops them in the complications of diplomatic protocol. In practice overseas missions relate far more closely to the FCO than to any other part of Whitehall, for a number of reasons: they are predominantly, though not exclusively, staffed by members of the Diplomatic Service, their communications are in most instances routed through the FCO and the tasks they perform on its behalf remain among the most important of their functions.

The major British embassies perform a very wide range of tasks. The Duncan Committee (pp. 18–19) distinguished seven broadly defined categories of work involved in overseas representation: the handling of intergovernmental relations, the provision of advice on foreign policy, assistance to British subjects and British companies, political reporting, influencing overseas opinion, processing potential travellers to Britain, and self-administration.[20] Of these the most directly related to policy-making are the handling of intergovernmental relations, the provision of advice, and the preparation and sending of reports.

The volume of reporting, that is the provision of background papers on a country's foreign policy or domestic political situation, has declined to some extent in recent years, in response to official and unofficial criticisms that 'there are far too many people at home and abroad, writing memoranda to each other'.[21] The main beneficiary of such reports is the Foreign Office, since they provide information on, for instance, the balance of opinion within a foreign government on an issue coming up for international negotiations, to supplement what is available from other sources. But some reports, for instance on personnel or policy changes in the host country's economics ministry or central bank, are of direct interest to other Whitehall Departments, and are intended primarily for them.

The Duncan Committee (p. 18) described the handling of intergovernmental relations as 'the basic and indispensable diplomatic function', involving casual meetings and contacts, informal conversations, formal representations, and full negotiations. Traditionally this work fell almost entirely on the embassy staff alone, who might on occasion conduct lengthy bilateral negotiations on behalf of their government. The revolution in international travel has now placed the conduct of negotiations more often in the hands of ministers or officials from Whitehall, from the home Departments most directly concerned or from the Foreign Office. The role of the embassy has become much more one of establishing and maintaining contacts with the ministers and officials of foreign governments before and between such visits, of providing 'the essential "door opening" function' for 'experts flown over from London for short meetings', of providing an element of continuity.[22] In an age of large governmental organizations and wide-ranging intergovernmental concerns, this involves rather more in the way of knowing whom best to approach in the host government's transport ministry on a particular question, and of being sufficiently well acquainted with him to be able to contact him by 'phone without offence, than the traditional 'well-directed hospitality' intended to 'create the right atmosphere for explaining British policies and outlooks'.[23] Yet the much criticized and ridiculed role of the diplomat as 'a soft buffer between hard substances', as a cultivator of good personal relations with the political and governmental elite, remains important:[24] a significant factor in the changing degrees of understanding and misunderstanding, of confidence and lack of confidence, between London and Washington and between London and Paris within the last decade.

Delegations to international organizations play a rather different role. They are unencumbered by the detail of consular work and export promotion, and in most cases are less caught up in the social niceties of the diplomatic round. Several include a much greater proportion of home civil servants – over a third in the NATO delegation and half in the small OECD delegation. They are chiefly concerned with the exchange of information, reporting, and negotiation: a narrower range of activities, though often requiring a longer working day. On occasions British embassies have themselves become responsible for the conduct of multilateral as well as bilateral negotiation; as in the Bonn embassy's responsibilities for the four-power agreements over Berlin, or the role of the British ambassador in Helsinki as British representative in the preparatory negotiations for the Conference on Security and Co-operation in Europe in 1972 and early 1973. There are as many differences between the major embassies, with an array of specialized staff organized into different sections, and the minor embassies, with a handful of diplomats each covering a number of tasks, as there are between embassies and delegations to international organizations. The Duncan Committee (pp. 48–50) distinguished between the 'Comprehensive Mission' required in developed countries and in a few major developing states, and the 'Selective Post', concerned primarily with consular work, commerce, and aid, which it saw as sufficient elsewhere.[25] In larger countries a number of consular posts subordinate to the British embassy were also maintained (nineteen in the United States in 1972, including several trade development offices, and eight in France). During the 1960s their functions became increasingly commercial; but they retained their consular functions, made more time-consuming by the development of mass international travel, and to some extent also performed representational and reporting functions.

The importance attached to advice from overseas missions and from ambassadors has not so much declined as altered in its character as travel and intergovernmental communication have become easier. Nowadays no Prime Minister or Cabinet is likely to repeat the mistake of the Chamberlain government in the late 30s of relying heavily on the judgement of Sir Nevile Henderson in Berlin, or even (if that is considered an exceptional case) on that of Lord Perth in Rome. There are abundant alternative sources of information about major foreign countries and ministers and officials have become increasingly familiar with foreign countries. However, a capable ambassador or head of delegation can in compensation play a much more direct part in the formulation of policy at home. The revolution in communications that has reduced his freedom of action by bringing him detailed and up-to-the minute instructions from Whitehall, has also given him the opportunity of seeing and commenting on drafts under discussion in Whitehall, even at short notice. He now has 'the chance to make his views known before important decisions are taken'.[26] Furthermore, he and his subordinates have become less remote figures to Downing Street and Whitehall. Even if diplomats stationed abroad do not yet regularly return to London for consultations, ministers and home-based officials more frequently pass through foreign capitals, pausing for consultations and striking up personal relations with their resident representatives; and in consequence are able more adequately to assess the quality of incoming advice. Senior officials in the major delegations, to the UN, to NATO, and to the EEC, have effectively become part of the process of policy-making in their areas. Christopher Soames, no doubt an exceptional political ambassador, 'became a regular visitor to Downing Street' during the negotiations for European entry in 1970 and 1971.[27]

Other categories of representational work largely involve more routine, low-level administration; although the volume of work and the proportion of diplomatic staff devoted to it have steadily grown. From the mid-50s the growing preoccupation with Britain's overseas trade position had the effect of raising the status of commercial diplomacy and export promotion. By the late 60s it had become accepted Foreign Office doctrine that commercial work was one of the most important functions of the Diplomatic Service, and a spell in the commercial section of an embassy was considered an advantageous career experience for 'high flyers'. In this, overseas posts worked in close touch with the industrial and commercial Departments, the Ministry of Technology and the

Board of Trade, and later the DTI. Except when political pressures were directly involved, in such cases as arms sales or major governmental contracts, this work rarely required the attention of ministers or senior officials at home; though a minister might use a foreign visit to display a new British aircraft or to add prestige to a trade drive. While mass travel and tourism have swelled consular work in assisting British nationals abroad and dealing with applications to visit or work in Britain, these are mainly routine matters most of which can be delegated to locally engaged staff. In regard to applications to work in Britain, the Diplomatic Service acts in effect as an agent of the Home Office: a task which the operation of strict controls on immigration has made more demanding. In carrying out their duties under the Merchant Shipping Acts, consular staff and the small number of shipping attachés similarly act as the agents of the Ministry of Transport (since 1970 the Department of Environment), and correspond direct with that Department. Information work is in some ways a less routine activity, requiring the ambassador upon occasion to lend his prestige to the presentation of the British viewpoint; but here again much embassy work is effectively acting as the local agent for services directed from Whitehall.

The larger British missions abroad are usually organized in a way that reflects this compartmentalization of routine work. The chancery, or political section – the main channel of communication with the Foreign Office in reporting and in the provision of advice – also coordinates the work of the embassy. It is staffed almost exclusively with home-based Diplomatic Service personnel. The commercial section has a much bigger staff, many of them recruited locally. During the 60s economic work in the largest embassies was hived off from commercial work in another, if smaller, section. Other sections deal with consular matters and information. A number of military attachés handle relations with the armed services and, increasingly, promote the sale of British weapons systems. Members of these sections often report direct to the Whitehall Departments to which they relate, normally sending copies to the chancery and the FCO. In Western Europe, if time is short, they may well 'phone direct. Coherence within the embassy is maintained through daily meetings of heads of sections with the ambassador and with the one or more 'ministers', officials at under-secretary level who oversee particular sensitive areas; an old established procedure universally known as 'morning prayers'.

There has long been a proportion of non-Diplomatic Service personnel in overseas posts, in the form of military attachés. Commercial work in embassies between the wars was handled by a separate Commerical Diplomatic Service, and in high commissions until the amalgamation of 1965–8 by the Trade Commission Service, drawn largely from the Board of Trade. The expansion of intergovernmental relations since World War II has however enormously increased the number of home civil servants attached to overseas missions or seconded to the Diplomatic

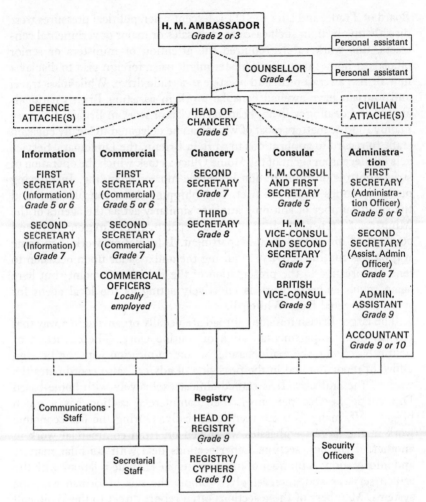

Typical Embassy Structure

Service. Ernest Bevin's enthusiasm for broader contacts than the traditional Foreign Service ones brought a large number of 'labour attachés' into embassies. They were still in 1969 the largest single category, amounting, the Duncan Committee noted, to over a quarter of all the attachés (see table, p. 39).

Besides these civilian attachés, a number of other home civil servants were directly seconded to the Diplomatic Service to fill posts which would otherwise have been held by Diplomatic Service staff; in a few posts, as in the UK Delegation to NATO, the substantial HCS contingent served on regular HCS terms. For reasons of professional and departmental interest the Diplomatic Service has tended to resist claims by home Departments for having 'their own men' in overseas posts. The Duncan Committee was particularly scathing, arguing (p. 127) that such posts come to be regarded 'as perquisites of certain Departments', that their occupants frequently do not carry a full load of work, and that their functions would be more effectively performed by regular officials of the missions, supplemented by visits of specialists from Whitehall. Many diplomats would add that the presence of a substantial number of attachés who regard themselves first as representing their home Departments and only second as members of the mission, and who correspond directly and regularly with their own Departments, would threaten to destroy the coherence and consistency of overseas representation.[28] The counter-argument made by home Departments – perhaps most vigorously in recent years by the External Relations divisions of the Ministry of Agriculture – is that regular members of the mission have neither the commitment to supply them with the particular information they need, nor the expertise to be accepted by the foreign officials and advisers with whom they must deal, as valuable and trusted contacts.

Civilian Attachés in Overseas Posts, 1964–69[1]

	1964	1969
Labour	20	20
Scientific and Atomic Energy	14	11
Civil Air	9	10
Defence Supply	3	9
Defence Research	3	5
Financial and Economic	10	7
Agricultural	8	8
Shipping	4	3
Others	8[1]	3
Total	79	76

[1] These include 3 colonial attachés, 3 veterinary attachés, a petroleum attaché (in Washington), and a pensions attaché. Only the petroleum attaché remained five years later, joined by two new industrial development attachés.

Sources: Plowden Report, para. 381; Duncan Report, p. 125. Comparable figures for later years are not available because of the more general adoption of secondment to the Diplomatic Service for home civil servants in overseas posts.

The number of civilian attachés in overseas posts had tended to decline during the 60s, despite some resistance from the Ministries of Agriculture and Technology; but the growth of intergovernmental relations, and in particular entry into the EEC, reversed this tendency. For instance, in the post-Duncan retrenchment the agricultural attaché in Washington was withdrawn; but early in 1973 new agricultural attaché posts were created, for cogent reasons, in Bonn and Paris. The ODA, for rather different reasons, resisted the Duncan Committee's arguments for using more Diplomatic Service officers to supervise aid and technical assistance overseas, after a month's initial training to familiarize themselves with the work. Because the ODA insisted on the need for expertise

in aid management and administration, the number of regional Development divisions abroad, operating alongside the local embassies, was
raised from two to five between 1969 and 1972.

The steady growth of contacts between home Departments and overseas missions, and of overseas travel and involvement in negotiations by
home civil servants, might have been expected to call into question the
continued need for a separate Diplomatic Service. One or two outside
critics argued the logic of closer integration with the HCS, even if 'the
most obvious remedy' of full integration was considered too shattering
to administrative morale: 'the very ferocity with which the proposal is so
often resisted shows how near the bone it reaches'.[29] Administrative
conservatism on the part of both Services, and concern for organizational
survival and career prospects, have certainly played a part in preventing
more interchange between them, in spite of the firm recommendations
of successive reports.[30] The comparative rarity of foreign language skills
within the HCS, even within the external relations divisions of some
Departments in the late 60s, as well as the reluctance of home officials to
uproot their families and disturb their careers by accepting a foreign
posting, have also hindered progress; sometimes home Departments
have found it difficult to fill 'their' attaché posts from their ranks. The
pride of the Diplomatic Service in its professionalism as a separate
service is another obstacle to integration. Paradoxically, the disappearance of the Trade Commissioner Service and the reduction in the number
of attaché posts were working to reduce the level of overseas experience
(as against overseas travel) within the HCS just as its involvement in
intergovernmental relations was increasing with the approach of Community membership. Conversely, as the role of the FCO within Whitehall
was becoming more and more closely linked to other Departments, the
proportion of Diplomatic Service careers spent at home remained around
only one-third.

The involvement of home Departments

If it is still true that in most areas of foreign policy 'the central core or
central column of the policy-making machine' extends from overseas
missions through the Foreign Office up to the Foreign Secretary, the
Prime Minister, and the Cabinet,[31] it will already be clear that a number
of home Departments are at times crucially involved in the process of
foreign policy-making. No Department in Whitehall is now entirely uninvolved in relations with foreign governments. In the late 60s and early
70s those most actively concerned were the Treasury, the MoD, and the
DTI. All three had responsibilities which overlapped with significant
areas of high policy as well as low-level external relations.

The Treasury's involvement is the most direct, the most ancient, and
the least amenable to Foreign Office direction. Its involvement stems
from two fields of its responsibilities. Its control over public expenditure

of course includes the oversight of expenditure on overseas policy, with a particular concern for the control of governmental expenditure 'across the exchanges'. Its responsibility for the direction and management of economic policy necessarily extends to external monetary and economic policy: from the viewpoint of the Treasury 'economic policy is a seamless robe', in which the management of the exchange rates, negotiations over international currency arrangements, and concerted multilateral efforts to mitigate interest rate competition have direct bearing on the domestic economy and domestic rates of growth and unemployment.[32]

The formulation and implementation of foreign economic policy is one of the main responsibilities of the Finance Group – one of the Treasury's three sections, headed by a second Permanent Under-Secretary. A Treasury division to handle overseas finance was first established at the end of 1914, its first head being the temporary war-time civil servant, J. M. Keynes. Its concern with questions of high policy and with international negotiations began with the Paris Peace Conference and the protracted discussion over reparations, and continued throughout the interwar years. World War II, the creation of the sterling area, the intricate negotiations with the Americans and others over the framework for a re-established international monetary system, exchange controls and the dollar gap, all enormously increased its workload. The symbolic importance of sterling for the government also increased the weight of the Overseas Finance division in the management of the domestic economy and in the formulation of foreign policy, some would argue to the detriment of both.

Considering the range of its responsibilities and the calls upon its staff, the Finance Group remained remarkably small, totalling less than 50 administrative personnel. In 1972 its 10 divisions were grouped into 3 blocs. The largest, Home and General, dealt with domestic monetary policy, with export and import policy, information on monetary flows and external balances in foreign countries, international payments problems and the international monetary system as a whole. Finance Overseas covered financial aspects of British relations with Western Europe, the Soviet bloc, the oil-producing countries, and Latin America; it had been particularly closely concerned with the negotiations to enter the EEC. Finance Development was concerned with relations with the developing countries; for reasons of convenience, it was also responsible for control of expenditure on aid and development and for the FCO Vote, on which it also reported to the second Permanent Under-Secretary in charge of the Public Sector Group.[33] During the 50s regular and close multinational consultations between officials of national finance ministries began to develop, expanding rapidly during the following decade. This provided the Treasury with its own sources of information about attitudes and policy positions in other major capitals and involved its officials in delicate and continuing negotiations both about British economic interests and about the structure of the international monetary system. These were to a considerable extent insulated from Foreign Office participation by the closeness of the network and the technicality of the content and language of the discussions.

The Treasury's Public Sector and National Economy Groups have only rarely been involved in high policy matters; but increasing economic interdependence has meant that they too have been dealing with external relations. The former oversees FCO expenditure; its Defence (Policy and Materiel) divisions perform such policy-related functions as taking the lead in offset negotiations for the British Army of the Rhine, and participate in discussions on joint procurement. The expenditure divisions of the National Economy Group responsible for Agriculture, Trade and Technology, and for Public Enterprises are likewise drawn into sensitive areas of intergovernmental relations. Moreover, exchange of economic information and forecasts within the framework of the OECD and, from late 1972, the EEC has drawn officials from this group into intergovernmental contacts in a slightly less sensitive but traditionally highly secretive area.

In managing overseas financial relations the Treasury works in partnership with the Bank of England. The *official* relationship is that the Treasury formulates policy and the Banks acts as its agent in its implementation; but, as one Bank official *informally* admitted, 'as agents we do make suggestions about policy'. In practice relations between the Treasury and the Bank are extraordinarily complex. Evidence to the Select Committee on Nationalized Industries in 1969–70 showed that 'there is no complete agreement among politicians and distinguished senior administrators in the Bank and the Treasury on a definition of the sort of institution the Bank is'.[34] Part of the Bank's strength vis-à-vis the Treasury rests on its more generous staffing and resources, so that the Treasury frequently relies on it for information and advice. The Governor of the Bank is appointed for five years with security of tenure. He has direct access to the Prime Minister and the Chancellor but little or no contact with the Foreign Secretary. Until the end of the 60s, indeed, direct contacts between the Bank and the FCO had been minimal, communications being channelled through the Treasury; although visits to overseas posts in their 'parishes' made for some personal contacts between Bank officials and diplomats. The Bank is also represented on a number of Whitehall committees concerned with the coordination of foreign economy policy.

Given the extent of Britain's involvement in international trade, few of the responsibilities of the industrial and commercial Departments in Whitehall do not in some way overstep national boundaries. The range of international interests of the DTI, which between 1970 and 1974 grouped this whole field together under one senior Cabinet minister, was enormous. As the successor Department to the Board of Trade it was responsible for external commercial policy, export promotion, and overseas trade. As the sponsoring Department for most of British industry, it represented industrial interests in discussions of overseas policy and defended the interests of British companies operating in foreign countries. Its responsibilities for competition and the control of monopolies involved it in relations with international companies operating in Britain, whose answerability to the requirements of British company legislation might be in question, and whose interests their home governments would naturally defend. Through its direction of government research and development and of policy for the high technology industries it was drawn into an exceptionally sensitive area of intergovernmental relations, and it participated in multilateral discussions through its responsibility for shipping and airline landing rights. Energy policy, the exploitation of North Sea oil and gas, the balance between coal, nuclear energy, and oil, had similarly become multinational questions. Hence most of the divisions of the DTI were in regular communication with overseas posts and with the functional and geographical departments of the FCO, and many officials had to travel overseas for consultations and for the management of joint intergovernmental projects. The core divisions of the old Board of Trade, Commercial Relations and Exports, had of course been closely engaged in international tariff negotiations since World War II. The dismantlement of the DTI into four separate ministries began with the creation of the Department of Energy in January 1974 – a ministry with a direct and vital interest in foreign policy, in close contact with the new Energy department of the FCO. Of the three established by the new Labour government in March 1974, the Ministry of Trade regrouped the commercial divisions of its predecessor Board of Trade, while the Ministry of Industry took over responsibility for representing industry. Both were immediately involved in the question of renegotiations with the EEC. Only the Ministry of Consumer Protection lacked significant international interests.

The MoD works closely with the FCO over a rather narrower range of concerns. The central Defence Secretariat maintains contacts with the relevant overseas posts and FCO departments about cooperation with NATO, courtesy visits of ships to foreign countries, overflying rights, forces training overseas, and so on. Other sections of the ministry are drawn in on questions of military procurement, and there is a close and intimate relationship between the two ministries on intelligence questions. The MoD has its own 'foreign service' in the 150 or so service attachés and their substantial staffs stationed in overseas missions in nearly seventy foreign countries. The Duncan Committee (p. 139) noted that in October 1968 the defence staff in Washington alone totalled 67 servicemen and 132 civilians. Their functions include some intelligence work, the exchange of information, and the promotion of arms sales; they form part of another international network among armed services which is strengthened by cross-postings, service with international organizations, and formal consultative procedures.

Several other Whitehall Departments also contain separate external relations divisions. Of these the one most actively concerned with international relations since World War II has been the Ministry of Agriculture, Fisheries and Food (MAFF), which represents the UK on a number of international commodity agreements and commissions. While this ministry's status in the Whitehall 'pecking order' has been relatively low, the morale of its External Relations personnel has been high, and their negotiating ability is respected in both the Treasury and the Foreign Office. Their negotiating experience has been as great as that of the Commercial Relations and Exports divisions of the Board of Trade and has arguably surpassed that of many sections of the Foreign Office. During most of the 50s and 60s the ministry's two External Relations divisions (with some eight to a dozen administrative officials and a large number of executive staff) roughly divided their responsibilities between temperate commodities and the developed world, and tropical commodities. Each time the question of entry into the EEC came alive a third division was created, which by 1972 had itself divided into two divisions. These divisions acted as a channel of communication for the commodity divisions with the Foreign Office, overseas posts, and international organizations, and conversely as a point of first contact for Foreign Office departments, for the ODA, the DTI, overseas posts, foreign embassies in London, and international organizations with the Ministry of Agriculture as a whole. A secondary function of the divisions is to represent the international dimension within the ministry as a whole, alerting it to international developments affecting its responsibilities. Negotiating delegations are staffed from commodity divisions as well as from the external relations divisions themselves. The Fisheries department has maintained a degree of autonomy in handling its own external relations, relating to the Marine and Transport department of the FCO and to a distinctive group of international organizations and agreements.

Much of the work of the Ministry of Agriculture, and more of some other Whitehall Departments, is low-level intergovernmental relations; rarely involving politically sensitive questions, often confined to exchanges of information, consultations, or discussions of highly technical matters in which the British government has a merely passive interest. Their activities represent the least exciting aspects of the 'new diplomacy' born of industrial modernization, economic interdependence, and the multiplication of global and regional international organizations: the OECD, the Council of Europe (both with extensive networks of committees and working parties), the WHO, the ILO, and so on. Through such technical consultations, bilateral agreements, and multilateral conventions Britain has contributed to the harmonization of international industrial standards and safety regulations, the movement of students, cars, and freight containers through European countries, and the mutual recognition of social security contributions and benefits between Britain and a number of foreign states. The Departments of Education and Science, of Employment, and of Health and Social Security handle this dimension of their work through small international relations divisions, similar to those within the Ministry of Agriculture; which also act for the Scottish and Welsh Offices on international questions which overlap their responsibilities. The Home Office's direct concern with the highly sensitive questions of immigration control and citizenship dispenses with the need for an intermediary division to liaise with the Foreign Office and posts abroad. The Department of the Environment, like the DTI, represents so wide a spectrum of policy areas that in 1972 twelve of its divisions listed international matters among their responsibilities, ranging from the management of British diplomatic and defence property overseas (which one of its predecessor ministries had assumed in 1874), to international aspects of environmental pollution and European road haulage questions.[35]

These technical external relations, however, often threaten political embarrassment. A fisheries disagreement may blow up into a dispute, a concession on the harmonization of food standards or of axle weights into a domestic row. Occasionally, as with the Channel Tunnel, the size and cost of a project and the prestige attached to it by the British or foreign government raise discussion and decision to the highest level; hence neither the Department which is functionally responsible, nor the Foreign Office and overseas posts, can manage policy in isolation.

From all this it is clear that foreign policy-making is a shared concern, an interdepartmental process in low-level issues, even more so in middle and high-level issues. Geographical desks responsible for monitoring relations with other countries operate not only within the FCO but also in the ex-Board of Trade divisions responsible for commercial relations and exports, in the ODA and in the Bank of England, and, on a more rudimentary regional basis, in the Treasury and the Ministries of Defence and Agriculture. The differing perspectives of these and other divisions within Whitehall interact with each other as well as with foreign governments to form the changing pattern of policy. Where it is necessary to pull together the different strands, issues are referred upwards through the central coordinating structure of Whitehall, from the Cabinet and the Prime Minister to the network of interdepartmental committees which clusters round the central column of the policy-making machine.

The Centre

The ultimate responsibility for the conduct of overseas policy, as for the whole range of government policy, rests with the Cabinet. Constitutionally the full Cabinet represents the last point for resolution of interdepartmental differences and the forum for approving decisions taken by the Foreign Secretary, the Prime Minister, or groups of senior ministers. It is a long-established Cabinet practice to include on the regular weekly agenda a verbal report from the Foreign Secretary surveying international developments and his attitude to them, and answering questions; this follows consideration of parliamentary business for the coming week at the top of the agenda.[36] Major questions of external policy are raised as a separate item. FCO telegrams are distributed to members of the Cabinet 'on a selective basis'; papers on important questions are circulated beforehand to all Cabinet ministers.[37] Strategic questions of external policy may occupy whole meetings of the Cabinet, or even a succession of meetings.

Within the Cabinet, the relationship between the Prime Minister and the Foreign Secretary is crucial in determining external policy. All Prime Ministers since Eden have had some previous ministerial experience of foreign affairs, though Mr Heath's experience was mainly confined to the first EEC negotiations and Mr Wilson's to external commercial relations. In any Cabinet the Foreign Secretary is among the handful of senior ministers on whom the Prime Minister depends for advice, often on questions far beyond their formal responsibility. Consultation between Prime Minister and Foreign Secretary on foreign policy questions outside the Cabinet is as intimate as between Prime Minister and Chancellor on economic policy; the Foreign Secretary's office is only a minute's walk across Downing Street from No. 10. But it is not a relationship between equals. To be effective – to be able to carry the Cabinet, to maintain influence with the other major Departments of State, and so to pursue a coherent foreign policy – the Foreign Secretary must either receive the Prime Minister's trust or else accept his prior authority.

Prime ministerial involvement in foreign policy is nothing new. Lloyd George at the end of World War I largely conducted his own foreign policy; Neville Chamberlain disregarded both the Foreign Office and his Foreign Secretary. 'That passion for foreign affairs which has gripped so many Premiers' has led successive Prime Ministers to devote a great deal of their time to summit conferences and foreign tours, often at the expense of other pressing matters.[38] Mr Wilson, for instance, had left for a visit to Moscow just as the economic crisis of July 1966 broke, and major decisions had to await his return. The illustrations in Mr Wilson's memoirs – nineteen of them depicting him with Commonwealth or foreign statesmen and only seven as involved in domestic concerns – seem to underline the allure of the international scene. Mr Macmillan in the 1959 election made his recent conversations in Washington and Moscow a major campaign image. Even if a Prime Minister were disinclined to play a part on the European or the global stage, the changing conventions of international diplomacy and the practice of other governments would constrain him to do so. Protocol as well as diplomacy required Mr Macmillan rather than his Foreign Secretary to negotiate with President de Gaulle and Mr Heath to visit President Nixon and Chancellor Brandt. Presidential and prime ministerial diplomacy by major foreign states, the whole apparatus of 'summitry', has unavoidably involved British Prime Ministers in their turn, whether they like it or not. The necessities of foreign travel impose heavy burdens upon the Prime Minister's time, while at home he must also receive a steady stream of visiting heads of state and of government, each expecting an hour or two of conversation as their due.

A Prime Minister's relative freedom of choice in selecting ministers allows him a certain leeway in determining the relationship between the two sides of Downing Street. R. A. Butler recalls that in December 1955 Anthony Eden told him 'that he had never had the idea that I should go to the Foreign Office, since I would be under him and that he would not like. He fancied Selwyn Lloyd for the Foreign Office and said he would be the best subordinate.'[39] The relationship between Sir Alec Douglas-Home and Mr Heath was one of trust rather than subordination, based partly upon Sir Alec's acceptance of Mr Heath's role in some areas of foreign policy, partly upon Mr Heath's acceptance of Sir Alec's experience in other areas, and partly upon an affinity of views between the two men. The difficulties of a situation in which an activist Prime Minister and an energetic Foreign Secretary do not share a common outlook or a mutual understanding were well illustrated during George Brown's tenure of the Foreign Office. The Foreign Office and the Foreign Secretary have, however, one strong line of defence against complete prime ministerial domination of foreign policy – the competing calls on the Prime Minister's time. Even if a Prime Minister could devote as much of a quarter of his time to foreign affairs, he must still leave a good deal of the formulation and management of policy to the established Foreign Office machinery.

The Chancellor and the Secretary of State for Defence are the other senior ministers most frequently involved in foreign affairs. Lord Carrington as Minister of Defence shared something of the burden of international travel and international negotiation, not only on defence matters. If this group of senior ministers is agreed, the Cabinet may in effect be by-passed; an 'inner Cabinet' or a 'partial Cabinet' may oversee a line of decision without referring it to the whole body.[40] The Prime Minister's control of the agenda enables him when he wishes to exclude a question from Cabinet discussion; consideration of devaluation was excluded for two and a half years. On at least one occasion Mr Wilson as Prime Minister successfully prevented a paper from one minister from being circulated to the Cabinet, as contrary to the line he wished it to accept.[41] Pressure of business has forced an increasing proportion of matters to be dealt with in Cabinet committees rather than in full Cabinet. From 1967 on, moreover, Mr Wilson laid it down that matters could only be taken from a committee to the Cabinet with the agreement of that committee's chairman. As a result some observers argue that 'the Cabinet seems to have disintegrated' as the central decision-making body both in domestic and foreign affairs, though it is probably more accurate to conclude that

decisions by Ministers are taken by procedures and in groups that vary according to the constantly changing patterns of political personalities and events in
Cabinet Committees, inner Cabinets, partial Cabinets, *ad hoc* meetings
between Prime Ministers and one or two individuals in the Departments, and
in the full Cabinet itself.[42]

A Prime Minister and his Foreign Secretary need not bring every important shift of policy to the Cabinet, provided they are confident enough of
their overall position and of arousing little positive disquiet from busy
ministers. But if they fail to carry the majority of the Cabinet along with
their general lines of their foreign policy, they will in time undermine
their own position, and disquiet will spread from the Cabinet to junior
ministers, the civil service, the parliamentary party, and the press.

The first reported regular Cabinet committee was the 'War Committee'
of 1855–6 which concerted the government's prosecution of the Crimean
War. Its first standing committee, from 1903, was the Committee of
Imperial Defence, whose secretary was a Foreign Office clerk.[43] At
present the Defence and Overseas Policy Committee (DOPC) remains the
only publicly recorded Cabinet committee.[44] Under the Labour government of 1964–70 this committee normally met weekly, with the Prime
Minister in the chair, the Foreign Secretary, the Minister of Defence,
and the Chancellor (or the Chief Secretary to the Treasury) among its
regular members, and the Chiefs of Staff often in attendance. Under the
flexible arrangements which characterize the procedures of British
government at this level, a varying number of ad hoc committees meet
as often as is necessary, under the chairmanship of the Prime Minister or
of another senior minister, to discuss problems which require ministerial
attention or interdepartmental resolution. During the first Wilson government these included committees on Rhodesia and Europe. Less crucial
or sensitive problems are discussed in sub-committees or in subordinate
committees of junior ministers, which effectively prepare the way for
approval at higher level or handle less vital matters. These in turn are
'shadowed' by official committees, which meet at differing levels. A
committee of permanent secretaries agreed the papers for the discussion
in full Cabinet of the approaches to Europe in 1967; deputy secretaries
or under-secretaries shadow Cabinet committees and sub-committees.
The central policy-making machinery in Whitehall, in foreign affairs as
elsewhere, is less a machine than a network of well understood procedures.

What restricts the influence of domestic ministers over foreign affairs
is less their exclusion from the process of policy-making than their continual preoccupation with their own departmental business, their constant efforts to keep abreast of more immediate concerns. The telegrams
and FCO or Cabinet papers they receive can rarely be given priority
except when they directly concern their own Department. Most ministers
now find themselves drawn, one way or another, into intergovernmental
matters, representing their Department at international conferences or
demonstrating their interest at a foreign exhibition or trade fair.[45] But

these necessarily revolve around their departmental concerns; their interest and involvement in external policy is usually limited and rarely extends to an active interest in the direction of foreign policy as a whole. This compartmentalization of course also works in reverse, restricting the attention which the Foreign Secretary can give even to the less 'political' aspects of external relations. For much of the 60s, for instance, the Foreign Secretary did not regularly attend the Cabinet's Economic Policy Committee.

The Cabinet itself and its subordinate ministerial and official committees are serviced by the Cabinet Office. Partly in response to the increasingly interdepartmental character of governmental business, this grew rapidly in the 60s; at the end of 1972 it had a staff or 400, 90 of them at the administrative level.[46] The core of the Office remained the Cabinet Secretariat, one wing of which serviced the DOPC, which called for and circulated papers and provided the secretariat for ministerial committees and the chairmen of their subordinate groups. In the late 60s a number of small separate 'units' emerged to deal with particularly important areas of overlapping departmental concern, two of them primarily concerned with foreign affairs: the Assessments Staff, created in 1968 to coordinate the intelligence and information analysis functions of a number of major Departments, and the European Unit, dating from the successful negotiations of 1970 onwards, which by 1972 had become an established part of the Cabinet Office. A third unit, the Central Policy Review Staff (CPRS), created in 1970 by the incoming Conservative government, during its first three years of operation was not involved in any matters concerning major foreign policy considerations, although its members included one seconded member of the Diplomatic Service and many of its reviews impinged on international concerns. The seconded staff of the Cabinet Office included at the end of 1972 14 members of the Diplomatic Service, 7 officials from the MoD, and 9 serving military officers. The small separate Office of the Prime Minister, in No. 10, included (as for many years earlier) one private secretary drawn from the Foreign Office, whose function it was to service and advise the Prime Minister on foreign policy, and to maintain close contact between the two sides of Downing Street.[47]

The expansion of summitry and the exercise of presidential diplomacy by two of Britain's leading partners, the United States and France, have involved the Cabinet Office still more closely in foreign policy matters. The Prime Minister, on a foreign visit to discuss a range of problems which cut across the departmental divisions of Whitehall, naturally includes senior Cabinet advisers, as well as his private secretaries, in his entourage. Presidential advisers on foreign policy, visiting London for discussions, expect to deal with their 'opposite numbers' in the Cabinet Office at least as much as with officials in Departments. Hence it is the Cabinet Office rather than the FCO, the Treasury, or the DTI which calls for papers and prepares the final brief for these discussions, thus further diminishing the role of the major Departments in determining final policy.

More loosely connected with the Cabinet Office structure, more or less formally organized, meeting either regularly or irregularly as circumstance require, a network of interdepartmental committees and consultations on matters of external relations extends throughout Whitehall. About half the subordinate committees within the Cabinet Office structure were in the early 70s chaired by Cabinet Office personnel; the remainder were chaired and serviced by the Department responsible for 'taking the lead' on that question. In such cases that Department's minister would similarly chair the supervising ministerial committee. Interdepartmental working parties are set up, as required, to review policies which overlap the responsibilities of more than one Department. Less formal procedures include extensive telephoning between officials at all levels, the circulation of papers for consultation and comment, interdepartmental representations by formal official or ministerial letter and where necessary informal or semi-formal ministerial meetings. The informality and flexibility of these procedures disguise the strength of the conventions which guide the transaction of business in Whitehall.

Interdepartmental differences rarely involve bitter disputes and often cut across departmental boundaries. Official role-playing, a natural belief that the subject of their responsibility deserves a higher place in the hierarchy of national interests, the standing of ministerial figures and of the Departments which they head in the Cabinet and its subordinate committees, affect both the pattern of bargaining and the outcome. One may perhaps note, however, a further difference of perspective between the Foreign Office and domestic Departments which complicates relations and the resolution of disputes on foreign policy issues. The role of the Foreign Office is to represent the external dimension across the whole range of policy-making: 'to act', as one FCO official rather pompously put it, 'as the Council of Abroad in the affairs of the nation'. Home civil servants tend in return to see the Foreign Office as half-hearted in defending national interests, as 'always trying to avoid rows with other countries'. It is a widely held Whitehall view that 'the Foreign Office does not represent the national interest: in a way it represents the interests of foreign governments'.[48] Home civil servants easily equate the national interest in any specific instance with the interests of the industries their Department sponsors or of the domestic constituency with which they deal. They suffer the interventions of the FCO – so often explaining why something cannot be done or why such apparently imprecise considerations as the maintenance of good relations must override departmental interests – with some occasional impatience.

This ambivalent attitude to the Foreign Office is not unlike the attitude of Departments to the Treasury on public expenditure questions. Both the FCO and the Treasury are only indirectly related to particular domestic interests; both regularly have to argue the untimeliness or impracticability of proposals from other Departments; both have acquired a certain reputation for imposing their 'views' on their ministers, and for insisting on the constraining logic of 'the facts' of economic or international life. In part, this relates to the separation of the Diplomatic Service from the rest of Whitehall, with home civil servants viewing FCO officials as a little extraneous to the life of Whitehall and so less familiar with the complexities of domestic politics. In part it relates to the assumption, still strongly held within the HCS in the late 60s, that foreign policy lies outside the normal domestic political process, even when that process has come to involve for instance the Ministry of Technology (and its successor Departments) in such boundary-crossing activities as technological agreements with state trading countries. Such differences of perspective are mitigated by regular interdepartmental contacts and collaboration between the functional departments of the Foreign Office and the related divisions of other ministries, as well as by the increasing involvement of home civil servants in intergovernmental relations. But the assumption that foreign policy is a separate and distinctive area, above and outside the external relations of home Departments, is still strong enough to buttress the natural tendency for domestic officials to insist that their external responsibilities fall within their own sphere of responsibility, and to resist the efforts of the Foreign Office to impose its own perspective and priorities.

Ministers and Officials

So far it has been assumed that the official machinery feeds smoothly into the ministerial, as policy rises for decision or approval. The Whitehall structure is an official machine with a political layer on top. It remains to consider how and how easily the official and the political elements fit together.

The formal line of distinction between the two 'sides' is supported by a number of unwritten but well understood conventions. Officials do their best to ensure that they 'know their minister's mind' and to take his assumed preferences into account in formulating and implementing policy. In the Foreign Office, as elsewhere, the manifestos of incoming governments are widely read, the opposition commitments and previous speeches of the new Foreign Secretary carefully noted. But the minister is debarred from seeing the political papers of his predecessor, and is discouraged from intervening too actively in the internal life of the Diplomatic Service. George Brown's interference in the process of official promotions and appointments, for instance, was sharply resented.

All Whitehall Departments to some extent believe that they represent the continuity of public policy; in contrast with the alternating views of successive ministers and governments, they are 'the guardians of some form of public interest' extending beyond the life of any single government.[49] The self-image of the civil service, the concept of loyalty to the Crown as wider than that to the government in power, is bound up with this distinction between the perspective of permanent official and temporary minister. The Diplomatic Service, a separate elite with its own corporate loyalty, may be expected to hold particularly strongly to this belief because of the widely held conviction among diplomats that 'there is or should be a continuity to the foreign policy of a country which there needn't be, or shouldn't be, in its domestic policy': that foreign policy should be insulated to a degree from the ebb and flow of domestic politics. It is not only that the national interest is peculiarly at stake in foreign affairs, but also for many officials that 'the events of international life are seen to be very compelling'.[50] 'Whatever politicians may say when they're in opposition', one retired diplomat retorted to George Brown's post-resignation criticisms, 'they soon find out when they get into office and read the confidential papers that they can't possibly do what they said they would do and must instead follow the line of their predecessors in office, because there's just no other line any Government can follow'.[51] Such possibly extreme expressions are matched by the criticisms of Labour and Conservative politicians of the Foreign Office's alleged imperviousness to political direction. They maintain that the conservatism of the machine swallows independent-minded ministers, converting them through a process of 'psychological indoctrination', into mouthpieces for the 'immutable aims' of official policy.[52] While Labour ministers tend to regard the Foreign Office as inherently conservative, Conservative ministers, at least in 1970, considered it distressingly imbued with progressive mythology.[53] Academics have supported the charge that the collective influence of the official machine is such as to reduce 'the contribution of successive Cabinets, let alone Foreign Secretaries, to an order of magnitude that is rarely more than marginal'.[54]

It is very difficult to assess the relative impact of official advice and political direction on external policy, because of the complexity and intractability of the international environment. Of course there is a difference in outlook between the official, whose professional career is foreign policy, and the minister, who must be more concerned with domestic politics, his constituency, his standing in his party, and the next election. It was said of Herbert Morrison as Foreign Secretary that it was hard for officials to catch his ear because he kept it so close to the ground. The relative unfamiliarity of Foreign Office officials with the constraints of Parliament and domestic politics, because they spend so much time abroad, no doubt sharpens this difference in outlook. The politician, frustrated by a more limited freedom of manoeuvre than he has in domestic policy, is tempted to project his frustration on to the machine itself: to blame 'the Foreign Office view' – anti-European in the 50s, pro-European in the 60s, allegedly pro-Arab (for many critics) throughout – for his inability to effect great changes in Britain's foreign policy. Comparisons may here again be made with the Treasury, similarly suspected by politicians and outside critics of successfully resisting ministerial efforts to change the settled 'Treasury view'.[55] It is possible that the politician's view carries most weight when a new government enters office, armed with the commitments made in opposition and outlined in its manifesto, and that ministerial and official views converge during its period of office. This may well have been the case with the Conservative commitment to supply arms to South Africa in 1970 and to impose a new interpretation on the Commonwealth relationship. On the other hand the rapid reversal of policy on the nuclear deterrent force by the incoming Labour government in 1964 argues the converse. It would in any case be difficult to maintain that external policy becomes steadily more dependent on official rather than on ministerial initiative as governments stay in office. The pro-European consensus within the Foreign Office ensured that the Labour government's reorientation towards Europe in late 1966 and early 1967 did not meet with disapproval from officials, but the impetus for the change clearly came as much or more from political discussion as from official advice.

The bridge between the politicians and officials is provided primarily by ministers' private offices. In 1972 the Foreign Secretary's private office contained four members of the Diplomatic Service and his personal secretary, headed by an official of counsellor rank. These officials arrange the Foreign Secretary's diary and appointments and also select from the mass of incoming material those papers he most needs to see, either for decision or to keep abreast of developments within the official machine, to alert him to differences of opinion which might otherwise be filtered out as papers rise through the hierarchy, and in return to keep officials aware of their minister's attitudes and interests, and to provide access to him when decisions are needed. They also act as a bridge between their ministers and the political heads of other Departments. They keep in particularly close touch with the Prime Minister's second private secretary, who is responsible for advising him on foreign policy. From 1970 until 1974 the Foreign Secretary's private office also included a 'political secretary', a former member of the Conservative Party Research Department, whose salary was met by the Conservative Party. His specific function was to mediate between the official advice tendered to the Foreign Secretary and opinion within the Conservative Party; he paid special attention to Rhodesian questions.[56] Mr Callaghan in March 1974 brought with him the Labour Party's International Secretary (from Transport House), whose functions within the FCO were similar, but whose salary was met from public funds.

How far a minister accepts the role outlined for him by his officials and the advice they give him depends upon his personality, his preferred style of work, and his relations with his senior officials. Some ministers, faced with the relentless press of appointments and paper work, want their Permanent Secretary to protect them from unsettled disputes and official differences. Some Permanent Secretaries, in turn, have seen it as their duty to maintain a united departmental front, to avoid 'the Secretary of State umpiring between two of his officials', to aim 'always to give him an agreed recommendation'.[57] A good minister, aided by his private office, avoids such a development by cultivating relations with a wider number of officials. Bevin, for instance, would frequently summon the officials responsible for a particular policy to his office, down to the head of department or below; he actively encouraged the expression of dissenting views, and 'never minded his subordinates speaking up'.[58] Both Michael Stewart and George Brown, as Foreign Secretaries under the Labour government of 1964–70, held similar meetings, the differing degrees of formality and informality in their 'office meetings' reflecting the different personalities of the two men.[59]

At the highest levels, relations between officials and ministers are affected as much by personal factors as by formal structure. At times their roles may be almost indistinguishable. A Permanent Under-Secretary who has the trust and respect of his minister may act in effect as an additional junior minister; he will certainly tender his advice candidly and freely and will attend ministerial meetings and committees at which he may be invited to speak. The standing of a Department's minister in the Cabinet, the span of his interests, his energy, his previous experience or expertise, will all affect the response he gets from his officials and the atmosphere and morale of his Department as a whole. A senior minister with years of experience is likely to have struck up and maintained personal friendships with a number of officials, which cut across formal boundaries. Ministerial travel brings them into contact with members of overseas missions, and relations with their private secretaries are often very close; though the size even of the Diplomatic Service and the Treasury, let alone of the larger Whitehall Departments, and the constant pressure on ministerial time severely limits the range of personal contacts.[60] The concentration of work within the Foreign Office (as within other Departments) and the way in which junior ministers are drawn into the policy-making process are all affected by the personality and preferences of the Department's political head. To a lesser but not negligible extent, the personality and preferences of the Permanent Under-Secretary, over whose appointment the minister may well have exercised little or no influence, will also affect the style and pattern of administration within a Department.

A good example of the continuity and political neutrality of the civil service in foreign policy (as in domestic policy) is provided by the change of government in 1970. The interdepartmental team which had prepared the Labour government's negotiating position for entry to the EEC continued unchanged to service, and negotiate for, the new government; the FCO hierarchy, if not without severe misgivings, adjusted established policy on Southern Africa and East of Suez. Even so, very occasionally the political neutrality of officials may slip. In the aftermath of the Suez invasion there was a good deal of talk of resignation within the Foreign Service, though in the outcome only a handful of officials resigned.[61]

The head of the Foreign Office Disarmament department allowed his dissent to become known when in 1970 the Labour government decided to change its attitude to CS gas.[62] Unattributed 'leaks' to the press or to MPs, lesser and less visible breaches of official neutrality are a little more frequent, though ministerial displeasure is a powerful disincentive to the official who takes the risk. But on the whole official neutrality is steadily maintained.

It would be an over-simplification to portray ministers and officials as solidly ranged against each other. Differences of opinion and attitude within Departments and between Departments are matched by differences within the government. During a major Whitehall debate cross-cutting 'alliances' of ministers and officials may well take shape. During the Labour government's reorientation of policy towards Europe, pro-European ministers informally consulted with like-minded officials in a number of Departments, and were in turn faced by a temporary alliance of anti-European ministers and officials. The strength of the formal structure of Whitehall, the degree to which both ministers and officials accept the limits of their roles, do, however, impose a pattern on the flow of policy. It is to that pattern which we now turn.

Appendix: The External Budget

Cost is always one of the main constraints on policy. In external policy there is the additional constraint that expenditure often involves transactions across the exchanges. Net government services and transfers across the exchanges in 1972 amounted to £548m: a significant total for a country which has suffered from persistent balance-of-payments deficits since 1945.

The external budget as defined for purposes of the public expenditure scrutiny process includes defence, overseas aid, overseas representation, information and cultural activities, and contributions to international organizations. The 1972–3 public expenditure programme included also, for the first time, contributions to the European Communities. The Defence budget accounts for by far the largest proportion of this. Expenditure under the DTI budget on export promotion may also be considered part of the British government's external effort; so also may the increasing costs to home Departments of foreign travel for their officials – less easy to separate out from the global expenditure figure.

The size of the defence budget ensures it close attention in the process of public expenditure scrutiny and review. The Defence (Policy and Materiel) division is one of the largest divisions of the Treasury Public Sector Group, relating to the financial divisions of the MoD, the Procurement Executive, and the other Departments involved. The interaction between defence costs and defence strategy, forces and equipment will be examined in chapter 5. Naturally any reconsideration of the total resources allocated to defence has implications for the overall objectives of British foreign policy. Between 1965 and 1968 the long series of expenditure reviews and consequent defence reviews brought about a redefinition of Britain's whole international position.

The External Budget 1972–3

	£m
Defence Budget	2,842·0
Other military expenditure[1]	74·8
Overseas aid	274·6
Overseas representation	80·2
Overseas information	38·0
Contributions to international organizations etc.	40·0
	3,349·6[2]

[1] This includes recruitment and publicity expenditure and a number of head-quarters and civilian staff costs, and military aid, (such as payments under the new defence agreement with Malta), counterbalanced by accounting adjustments in respect of purchases of US military aircraft.

[2] This does not include a further £7·8m allocated for export promotion, nor the costs of foreign travel by home civil servants; nor does it include an item which appeared in the estimates of public expenditure for the first time in 1972–3, £40·0m for net contributions to the European Communities.

Source: Cmnd 5178, Dec 1972.

Expenditure across the Exchanges, 1972

	£m
Military expenditure	359·0
Diplomatic, administrative etc.	75·0
Economic grants	90·0
Military grants	6·0
Subscriptions and contributions to international organizations	36·0
Multilateral economic assistance	25·0
Other government transfers	32·0
	623·0

Note. The difference between gross and net expenditure is accounted for by the offsetting official expenditure of other governments in the UK, amounting to £75m. This represents the expenditure of American and Canadian forces stationed in this country (£19m), of other states' forces training in Britain and payments for British military facilities (£27m), and of overseas representation in Britain (£29m). Net expenditure is thus calculated at £548m.

Source: UK Balance of Payments, 1973, table II.

The ODA, with a separate Finance division, is responsible for the politically sensitive aid budget. The existence both of an active aid lobby and of substantial public scepticism about overseas aid has been such as to provoke political debate on the proper definition of aid expenditure, on consequent varying calculations of its current size and future growth, and on its net impact on the balance of payments. These will be examined further in chapter 7. One-third of the British Council's expenditure is included in the aid budget, to cover those of its activities which are carried out on the ODA's behalf in developing countries.

The remaining items of overseas expenditure come under the authority of the FCO. They are handled administratively by its Finance department, responsible through the Chief Clerk to the Permanent Under-Secretary as accounting officer. 'Overseas representation' as defined for the purpose of public expenditure programmes covers: the cost of the FCO in London, including the ODA, the Passport Office and its regional branches, and the Diplomatic Service communications network; overseas posts and missions; staff costs, except for those engaged in information work, and official travel. 'Overseas Information' includes two-thirds of the British Council's budget, formally a grant-in-aid from the Foreign Office, the costs of the BBC's External Services (including a substantial contribution to the BBC Monitoring Service), the cost of FCO information staff and activities, and the operations of the COI and the Stationery Office on their behalf.[63]

Exact definition of the costs of overseas representation is difficult, given the degree of overlap which now exists between domestic and foreign policies and between the activities of home Departments and the FCO. The Duncan Committee's own definition included, with the items already mentioned under overseas representation and information, Ministry of Works (now Department of the Environment) expenditure on accommodation overseas, civilian and military attachés, costs of promoting exports and defence sales and of the External Relations divisions of home Departments. These it calculated, for 1968-9, to amount to £105·8m, of which £46·4m fell across the foreign exchanges. It noted, separately, the overseas travelling costs of home Departments, as 'over £2 million' (Annex C, pp. 166-8).

However calculated, the total cost of overseas representation and information amounts to a very small proportion of British government expenditure. The Duncan Committee assessed it as 1 per cent of the total government budget, though nearly 10 per cent (gross) of government foreign exchange expenditure (p. 9). Even so, the small size of the total budget has not preserved it from being squeezed in periods of cutbacks in government expenditure. Although the Plowden Committee (para. 605) had concluded, at a time when public expenditure was not such a cause of immediate concern, that 'the present cost' of overseas representation 'is not unreasonable', the Duncan Committee was asked only five years later 'to bear in mind, in the light of the current need for the strictest economy, the importance of obtaining the maximum value for all British Government expenditure and the consequent desirability of providing British overseas representation at lesser cost' (p. 5). Given that some 80 per cent of the expenditure for which the FCO is directly responsible relates to manpower and its associated costs, the only way to make significant reductions was by reducing staff and the size and number of posts abroad. Amalgamation of the Commonwealth and Colonial Offices with the Foreign Office allowed a reduction of over 10 per cent in headquarters staff between 1965 and 1971, and a number of overseas posts were closed in the post-Duncan review. But scope for further reductions was limited both by the pressure of business falling on many overseas posts and the offence given to foreign governments by the withdrawal of resident representation.[64] The new Conservative government in 1970 reduced net costs by increasing charges for passports and consular fees. The most attractive target for expenditure cuts during the late 60s was the information budget, noticeably larger than those of France and Germany and relatively open to planned reductions in services without offending either foreign governments or domestic opinion. The overseas information services accordingly suffered a succession of reviews and reductions in this period. Overall, the FCO proportion of total public expenditure fell slowly from the late 60s onwards.

As a relatively small item of the total budget, the FCO budget does not attract a great deal of attention within the regular process of public expenditure scrutiny and review. By the end of 1972 only one Policy Analysis and Review exercise had been conducted on a programme within the FCO's sphere of responsibility – on expenditure on the Dependent Territories. The Defence and External Affairs Sub-Committee of the new House of Commons Expenditure Committee turned its attention to the FCO for the first time during the 1971–2 parliamentary session, briefly examining the management of property owned or rented overseas. Between such larger investigations, FCO expenditure was governed by the operations of the system of Treasury control and Treasury authorization.

Much of the mutual suspicion between the Treasury and the Foreign Office in the 1930s and in the postwar period arose from FCO resentment of the Treasury's detailed control of its expenditure and constraints on its manpower, and the Treasury's suspicion of what it saw as diplomatic extravagance abroad in a period of austerity and of the Foreign Office's apparent unconcern with the costs of foreign policy. Evidence to the Estimates Committee in 1957–8 suggested a remarkable lack of confidence on both sides. A separate 'Imperial and Foreign' division of the Treasury supervised the establishment and supply expenditure of the three overseas departments. The relatively small total expenditure encouraged Treasury officials to concern themselves with very small sums; it was revealed, for instance, that there were Treasury guidelines and cost-limits on soft furnishings and electrical fittings in overseas accommodation, requiring individual references to the Treasury, and a delegated financial authority 'to provide up to two bicycles to a consulate abroad'.[65] The position by the late 60s was far more flexible, though lingering doubts within the Treasury about diplomatic consideration for the financial implications of the proposals they put forward made for some continuing caution. Awareness of the overall costs of external policy within the Treasury was improved by grouping supervision of the FCO budget with aid in the Finance Development division; in 1972 for the first time a Diplomatic Service counsellor was seconded to this division, to oversee FCO expenditure.

Overseas expenditure suffers from two particular constraints: its regular commitments are highly inflexible, often almost automatic, and unexpected calls for additional expenditure are not infrequent, yet difficult to anticipate within the framework of five-year public expenditure programmes. The requirements of overseas representation in over 120 countries are not easily adjusted. The 'marginal Embassy', as defined by the Duncan Committee, of three or four home-based staff plus locally recruited personnel, already existed as an irreducible minimum in a number of countries. Continuing concern with export promotion, and the demands which mass travel and tourism placed upon the consular services of a growing number of posts, outpaced the economies gained by reductions in political reporting. The time taken to train officials in foreign languages and other skills adds another inflexible element in allocating manpower. While it is relatively easy to reduce or expand information services in the short term, the more long-term work of cultural activities can only be jeopardized by short-term chopping and changing. Again, Britain's contributions to international organizations are largely automatic. The established style of British foreign policy, with its commitment to good relations and international order, makes it difficult for a British government to decline to contribute its share to each new aid consortium or to pay its subscription to each new international organization or committee, even if it has opposed its creation in the intergovernmental bargaining beforehand. With the small size of the total budget, these factors mean that there can be very little financial flexibility. For example, *The Times* reported on 1 June 1971 that the FCO claimed that 'they could not find' the £3,000 requested for an international conference on disaster relief despite their 'high regard' for its aims and sponsors.

If the regular FCO budget and the regular aid budget are very fully committed, unanticipated demands for additional expenditure may be both sudden and large. The Maltese demand for an additional £10m per year for British base facilities involved both the FCO and the MoD in hurried consultations with the Treasury. The overthrow of a friendly regime and the subsequent suspension or cancellation of aid sometimes releases funds previously committed; but more often a request from a friendly regime or a new government, such as the post-Nkrumah Ghanaian regime, for massive and immediate assistance runs up against the difficulties of reordering Whitehall priorities and bypassing its procedures. A major international disaster such as the Bengal floods of 1971 threatens to disrupt the whole external budget by the size of its demands. Successive Foreign Office pleas for a contingency fund to meet such unexpected foreign requests for assistance have predictably run up against Treasury resistance, and are further hampered by the difficulty of gauging the size of such demands.[66]

The Foreign Office's main method of resource control and reallocation consists of regular reviews of the staffing and balance both of its overseas posts and of its headquarters departments by its Corps of Inspectors. In the mid-60s the normal interval between inspections was three years, but following the publication of the Duncan Report the number of inspectors was increased and special inspections were made of particular posts abroad. Regular assessments of British interests in relation to the diplomatic effort deployed, on a country and a regional basis, are now compiled as part of the process of review.[67] The allocation of resources within the information budget is reassessed by an annual review process conducted within the FCO among the various departments concerned. Review of the aid budget is a more complex process, carried out by the ODA, a number of FCO departments, and representatives of the Treasury, the DTI, and on occasions the MoD.

The Treasury plays a prominent role in assessing, and attempting to control, Britain's contributions to international organizations. A Treasury official, seconded to the British Mission to the UN, serves on the budgetary committees of the UN and of a number of its agencies, so playing a part in the process of reviewing their staffing and expenditure. British membership of the European Communities enormously enlarged the problem of automatic British contributions to international organizations; by the beginning of 1973 Treasury officials were attempting in Brussels to exert their traditional pressure for economy both in staffing and in overall expenditure.

To some extent the Treasury's Finance Development division is in a position to assess in general terms the balance of expenditure on external relations, beyond the defence budget itself. The Foreign Office's Economists' department may now be in a position to do the same. Yet there is no absolute standard by which to measure either the size or the balance of overseas expenditure. The Duncan Committee's comparisons (p. 17) with French and German expenditure could only serve as a very crude yardstick, unless one were to assume a greater rationality about the balance of French or German overseas representation and information and cultural efforts. A Foreign Office exercise to compare the pattern of British exports with the pattern of overseas representation demonstrated only that such a simple measure was not helpful.[68] Experimentation in overseas output budgeting has been limited by the difficulties both of delimiting the different programmes and of more narrowly defining the objectives they are intended to fulfil.[69] The size of British expenditure on foreign relations and the balance between different countries and different activities depend in the long run upon the political assumptions of those responsible for foreign policy-making and on their conception of the priorities of British interests. There is no more certain guide.

3: The Flow of Policy

THE BUSINESS OF FORMULATING, deciding and implementing policy is a continuous process, unavoidably distorted in attempting an analysis. But it may be helpful to abstract the various stages in this process from the jumble of competing problems and responsibilities. The first pre-condition for effective foreign policy-making is the collection of informa-tion: the selection from the mass of incoming material of those reports which seem most significantly to affect Britain's interests, and the inter-pretation of these reports in the light of previous experience and present expectations. Some foreign policy actions stem primarily from initiatives within the government, or respond to domestic pressure; but the regular pattern of British foreign policy is one of reaction to international develop-ments. Determination of the appropriate response to a particular reported event – the central process of making policy – will then depend upon consideration within Whitehall of the balance among interests involved and among domestic or international political constraints, and the re-sources for influence at the disposal of the government. Behind the official and ministerial response to a single event lies a consensus of received opinion – about the behaviour to be expected from particular foreign governments, the priorities of British external interests, and the preferred pattern of international relations which British actions should aim to promote. These provide both a set of concepts for interpreting information and a set of doctrines about appropriate patterns of response: essential devices for reducing the chaos of incoming information and the clash of competing domestic demands to order, but in need of regular reassessment if they are not to lose their explanatory value.

Decisions taken must then be implemented, by bringing the necessary resources – diplomatic, financial, military, and so on – into play. Lines of policy determined upon must be set out by confidential instructions, by statements in Parliament, by releasing information to foreign govern-ments or to the domestic and foreign press. The British government's output of policy in turn forms part of the policy input of other govern-ments and international actors. Their interpretation, assessment, decis-ion, and response are in their turn fed back to London, through their own channels of communication as well as through the British govern-ment's, and so the process flows on.

The Collection and Interpretation of Information

The volume of information available to a government largely reflects the size and energy of the machine for gathering it and the efficiency of the channels for its transmission. In 1972 Britain still ranked third, after the United States and the Soviet Union, and a little ahead of France, in the number of diplomats it sent abroad, and ranked among the top six nations in the number of countries in which it maintained diplomatic representation. Its diplomatic communications network was acknowledged to be one of the most efficient and secure maintained by any government. Its core was the Diplomatic Wireless Service, staffed in Britain and in overseas posts by the Communications branch of the Diplomatic Service, handling a steady flood of coded and uncoded telegrams. Less urgent or more bulky non-confidential communications are sent by post; confidential ones travel by Diplomatic Bag, a courier service provided by a separate corps of Queen's Messengers – fortnightly or weekly for the smaller or more remote posts, up to five times a week for the most important foreign missions. Between the wars the spread of international telephone lines provided a direct and immediate, if insecure, alternative channel of communication, use of which grew rapidly despite some Foreign Office disapproval.[1] By 1970 the FCO maintained secure telephone lines, or commercially rented private lines, to the most important missions and embassies. and during the 60s Telex facilities were installed in the majority of embassies and missions and in some subordinate posts.

The volume of official information flowing through this network is enormous. Around 2,000 items a day came into the FCO during 1972. Over a quarter of these were telegrams, the most urgent and immediate communications; the remainder included letters, despatches through the Diplomatic Bag, and minutes of confidential intergovernmental meetings. This total excludes telephone conversations, many of which are as a matter of record confirmed by telegram or letter. Many items were non-confidential and of only indirect political significance: information on export opportunities or economic trends, requests for a ministerial interview with a foreign newspaper or television company or for support for a cultural project. Others made detailed and potentially embarrassing comments on foreign political personalities and developments, or called for immediate action on urgent business. Not all were directly or primarily addressed to the FCO; a number were exchanges between overseas posts and other Whitehall Departments, and some were primarily exchanges of information between posts, both relayed through the FCO as a matter of convenience and of record.

Telegraphic Traffic through the Foreign Office, 1939–72

	Inward	Outward
1939	25,088	18,351
1962	75,391	155,020
1969	166,000	271,000
1972	231,269	391,859

Source: Plowden Report, para. 27; FCO statistics.

The steady increase in the volume of traffic throughout the 1960s, when Britain's global commitments were contracting, reflected not only the weight of bureaucratic inertia and diplomatic habit, as critics at times suggested, but also the wider range of matters on which the Foreign Office and other Departments demanded information, as intergovernmental cooperation extended into new fields.

Both the Plowden and the Duncan Committees criticized the volume of political reporting from overseas posts, and the level of requests for political information from London. 'Sometimes', the Plowden Report remarked (paras 195, 197):

it seemed to us, work in the overseas services was being undertaken . . . because as part of a ritualised diplomatic or bureaucratic process it was difficult to refuse', and reports were being called for 'simply because the subject is historically or academically interesting or because similar work has been undertaken in similar circumstances in the past.

The Duncan Report (p. 56) saw 'a certain danger of duplication and circularity', in which the desk officers in the FCO and the members of the chancery in overseas posts, as able and energetic men, 'may make more work for each other than the intrinsic importance of Anglo-Ruritanian relations really justifies'; it further suggested that Whitehall officials, MPs, 'and other public figures' expected to obtain a fuller provision of 'non-essential information' from the Foreign Office than Britain's interests required or the overseas budget should support. In response to these criticisms, the volume and coverage of political reporting on domestic developments in foreign countries was substantially reduced; yet this was more than compensated for by the growth in commercial and economic traffic and increasing requests for information on such untraditional subjects as agricultural, transport, or social policy. In an attempt to check the flow, all overseas posts were ordered early in 1973 to cut their telegraphic traffic by 10 per cent (assessed against the monthly totals for the previous year), and to justify specifically any failure to do so; but measures such as these were likely to have only a temporary effect.[2]

Embassies and missions collect information from various sources. One official accredited to a major West European country estimated that 75 per cent of the information accumulated by his embassy came from overt sources: from the national press and from specialized journals, from watching TV programmes, from conversations with journalists and businessmen, from using the opportunities available to learn about a country by living there. The remaining 25 per cent was gathered by more active diplomacy, by cultivating relations with members of the political parties, by exchanging classified information with government officials, and by maintaining close contact with them. It included a very small proportion which could be considered 'clandestine' – highly valuable on occasion, but only to confirm a suspicion or alter an interpretation;

not as the regular basis of intelligence and information-gathering itself. In all democratic and industrialized states the press is an important and immediate source of embassy information. Officials in the FCO will themselves follow the main national newspapers of Britain's most important partners; but they rarely have time to read them carefully, and often receive them late, so that they still depend on embassies to alert them to important developments and to fill in the background. Informal methods of collecting information have frequently been criticized as generating 'conspicuously superficial' reports based largely upon 'cocktail party gossip'.[3] Yet while there remain few capitals, even in Europe, where political influence and the social elite are synonymous, entertainment does help to win confidences or a sympathetic hearing. Informal relations with 'proximate policy-makers' provide a useful source of information and influence; influential men and women expect and appreciate a pleasant environment for conversation. The problem of cultivating contacts with a wider range of the actually or potentially influential than the social elite is met in the larger posts by assigning different officials to 'cover' and report on different political parties or groups. It is, for instance, a natural part of the functions of a first secretary, labour, in a foreign post to maintain contact with and report on the labour movement and on the relevant political attitudes of its leaders.

In non-democratic countries the problems of information-gathering are far greater and the balance among the various sources is rather different. In post-1967 Greece, for example, it was important to have some indication of how much support the Colonels' regime had throughout the country and of how seriously to take the exiled and domestic clandestine opposition groups. Thus embassy staff had continually to weigh the advantages of maintaining contacts with groups opposed to the regime against the danger of offending those then in power, and so damaging immediate political (and commercial) interests. Similar problems face diplomats in a large number of other non-democratic states. In the Soviet Union and Eastern Europe it is often hard to obtain reliable economic information. One of the functions of the 'Russian secretariat' in the Moscow embassy, whose members were expelled in retaliation for the British expulsion of 105 Soviet officials in 1971, was to watch prices in the shops and to report on unannounced rises and reductions, as indicators of the state of the Soviet economy otherwise unavailable to analysts in Britain. It seems that the Russians found this activity particularly objectionable. In such countries travel around the provinces, casual conversations, café gossip, and what can be gleaned by clandestine contacts must therefore rank as important sources alongside the more limited contacts with the official elite and the less reliable information drawn from the media.

In almost all overseas posts information and interpretation of information is exchanged between the British and their closest partners. In 1946

British embassy staff in Moscow saw all the first four drafts of George Kennan's famous paper on 'The Sources of Soviet Conduct', and commented on it as it took shape; in the mid-50s the American, British, and French ambassadors there met at weekly dinners to compare notes on the internal situation and to discuss the reports they sent back to their governments. During the 60s, as Britain drew closer to the EEC, cooperation with officials of other embassies extended from the United States (and occasionally France) to other West European states, encouraged and to an extent institutionalized from 1972 under the 'Davignon' framework for political cooperation set up in parallel to the European Community. The permanent missions to the UN and NATO have long been important links in the information exchange network among friendly governments, especially within the framework of NATO. From the beginning of 1973 institutionalized political cooperation among the member states of the European Community added another important channel of information. Information-gathering is of course inseparable from interpretation and assessment; what is exchanged is rarely simply 'information'as such, but information linked to differing interpretations of its context or its significance.[4]

The reduction of political reporting to the Foreign Office from overseas posts during the 60s has given more importance to the archives maintained by these posts as sources of information in a crisis. In many countries of no real continuing political interest to Britain but where British interests or prestige might be jeopardized in a crisis situation – such as the Philippines or Peru, Chile or Argentina – the information gathered over the years in the embassy files has become an invaluable source of background material, transferred to the Foreign Office Library after a number of years. In countries where Britain still has major and continuing interests such archives are likely to be a fuller and more easily accessible source than those in London.[5] The maintenance of such an institutionalized 'memory', supplemented continually by background reports entered by officials in the course of their regular work, to an extent compensates for the limited expertise on local developments imposed by the regular turnover of diplomatic staff.

The information and opinions flowing in through official channels are supplemented from other sources. Reports from foreign correspondents in the press and on radio and television provide one alternative source, all the more important for officials to keep abreast of because it ranks as the most regular source of information not only for opposition spokesmen but also for many ministers. The FCO, like a number of other Whitehall Departments, maintains its own press clippings service, covering the British press and selected foreign papers. Outside experts and those involved in the affairs of particular foreign countries, in the universities, the churches, business, and voluntary societies, are listened to, particularly on their return from more remote or more 'difficult' countries. Officials with previous service in the countries for which they are now responsible in the Foreign Office have often kept in touch with some of the academics, missionaries, representatives of oil companies or overseas banks, or even groups investigating the treatment of prisoners or of minorities or the survival of slavery, which form part of the fairly close community revolving around the more remote embassies. This more informal exchange of information is of value to both sides, especially in situations where overseas officials are inhibited by their official position from obtaining the information themselves. During the Nigerian civil war, for instance, the only first-hand reports of conditions behind the Biafran lines available to the FCO came from returning clergymen and aid officials; during the 1971 crisis in Bengal the staff of the deputy high commission in Calcutta was refused permission to visit the disaster areas, and it and the Foreign Office had perforce to rely 'on reports from journalists, refugee workers, and from Oxfam officials'.[6]

The Foreign Office can also draw where necessary upon the resources of the Secret Intelligence Service and on its exchanges of information with the intelligence services of friendly governments. For most of the 60s the head of the Secret Intelligence Service was a senior FCO official, supplementing the regular pattern of liaison through a Foreign Office adviser at counsellor level.[7] But information-gathering intelligence, as opposed to analytical intelligence work in London, has declined in value with the growth of electronic surveillance by satellite and by other means. Occasional conferences in London of ambassadors to regional groups of countries allow for an assessment of the overall pattern of regional developments, or of British interests in that area.[8] Foreign embassies in London are themselves a regular source of information and self-analysis, supplemented by the steady flow of ministers and prime ministers of foreign governments through London for talks with British ministers and officials.[9]

The Foreign Office's own 'memory' is provided by its Research Department: a separately recruited body of some fifty specialists, who 'normally devote their career to the study of a single region of the world', and who are 'organized into sections on regional lines'.[10] The origins of the Research Department are closely linked with Arnold Toynbee and Chatham House. During World War I Toynbee worked in the newly-established Political Intelligence department of the Foreign Office, from which he went to Chatham House. At the outset of World War II he converted the Chatham House research effort into the 'Foreign Research and Press Service', originally housed in Oxford. In 1943 it was taken over directly by the Foreign Office and merged with the old Political Intelligence department to form the new Research department, of which Toynbee remained director until 1946.[11] Reorganized in 1957 as part of the heart-searching which followed the Suez débâcle, its functions in the 60s included providing the background information requested by geographical and functional departments, undertaking historical research, and compiling and circulating background papers on trends and developments abroad. Most of this 'reflective' work naturally relates to developments within the previous two years, or at the most five or ten. But for some Central European questions it has been necessary to refer back to World War II, and for the Gibraltar dispute to the early eighteenth century. The Research department draws upon the FCO's archives, as well as on its own extensive files, on academic studies and the publications of other governments. Its expertise is concentrated on those international regions less familiar to British officials but which are important to British interests (as traditionally defined); in 1972 nearly half its staff were concerned with Eastern Europe, the Soviet Union, and China.[12] The Foreign Office also contains three other specialized units for the provision of information and advice: the Legal Advisers, who also advise the whole of Whitehall on international law, the small Arms Control and Disarmament Unit, and the recently established Economists' department.

Compared with some other capitals, the exchange of information between Departments in London is relatively open and effectively organized. The FCO Communications department selects the distribution of each incoming telegram, if not already indicated by the sender, according to standardized procedures and nearly fifty different distribution lists. Those government offices closest to the Foreign Office building, the Cabinet Office, No. 10, the Treasury, and the MoD, can receive their copies immediately, and other Departments where necessary by special delivery in addition to the regular delivery of 'boxes' around Whitehall three times a day. Although in the first months of EEC membership there were occasional complaints from other Departments about being 'left off' the distribution list, this system appears in general to work well. The constant problem, as within the FCO itself, is to maintain a balance between the desirability of keeping all those affected informed of developments and the need to keep down the bulk of paper in circulation, to avoid overloading civil servants with unnecessary material.

These other Departments also have their own direct sources of information about international developments. As has already been noted, specialists in overseas posts correspond directly with 'their' home Departments; home civil servants communicate direct with their opposite numbers in other capitals, and exchange information and views with them in bilateral and multilateral conversations. The interests, industries, and groups which form their clientele provide alternative perspectives derived from their own international activities. A great many of these now belong to international federations, which also serve as channels for the exchange of unofficial information, and which in their turn hold consultative status with international organizations. The Treasury and the DTI, as well as the Bank of England, collect economic statistics of other countries; analysts in the MoD concern themselves with economic as well as with military and technological intelligence. When they are of wider concern, reports flowing in to home Departments are duly circulated to the Foreign Office and the rest of Whitehall and become part of the mass of documentation on which assessment and policy-making are based.[13] Overseas posts are themselves included in this system, receiving copies of relevant reports and of the comments on them, enabling them not only to keep abreast of thinking at home but also through their own comments to take part in the process of assessment and decision which follow.

Often relatively few people within Whitehall are concerned with a particular issue, and the circulation of paper is therefore limited. But when a wide-ranging discussion of issues is in prospect, as in the preparations for a major international conference or a summit meeting, the sheer mass of paper, the problems of absorbing and collating information into briefs and formulating proposals for discussion, are enormous.[14] The capacity of any administration to absorb, interpret and act upon incoming information is not unlimited, and the costs of attempting to absorb too rich a flow of information is that the machinery becomes clogged and slow to respond.

Nor does the academic separation of information from interpretation or policy-making hold good in practice. Information is called for and provided on the basis of existing expectations, and incoming reports contain explicit or implicit interpretations, and often suggested courses of action as well. The collection and selection of information is itself a part of policy-making, reflecting established assumptions and drawing attention to preferred alternatives. The higher a question rises within the Whitehall hierarchy, the more it must compete for attention with other matters: busy men demand summaries of lengthy reports, ministers are unlikely to read more than a page or two on all but the most vital subjects. One may therefore visualize the flow of information through Whitehall, gathering comments and proposals as it moves, as a funnel with a wide mouth and a very narrow neck. At successive stages particular points are selected from of the mass of incoming material according to their perceived importance, while others are choked off for assessment and decision at lower levels.

Interpretation of the significance of incoming reports, and assessments of their bearing on existing policy and interests, are part of the regular responsibilities of officials of the FCO and other Departments. The interdepartmental nature of so many international issues, and the differing perspectives of the various Departments involved, however, require a considerable degree of discussion and comparison of assessments, conducted primarily through the structure of interdepartmental committees, with analysts from different departments meeting to compare, and if possible agree on, interpretations and recommendations. Cooperation between the Foreign Office and the service ministries, conspicuous for its absence during much of the 30s, has since World War II been carried out within the framework of the Cabinet Defence Committee and the

Chiefs of Staff Committee, assimilated during the 60s to the DOPC structure. The Joint Intelligence Committee, with officials and service-men meeting regularly under a Foreign Office chairman, has remained the most important forum for consultation; assisted since the late 60s by the Cabinet Office Assessments Staff, with personnel drawn from the main Departments concerned.[15]

Interpretation shades into contingency planning, the assessment of feasible alternatives and of the consequences of each suggested course of action, and so to recommendations for decision. In most of these debates, the crux turns on an analysis of the factors bearing on the problem and on predictions about the consequences of alternative ways of dealing with it.[16] Information is never complete; assessment of the situation or of the likely reaction to any British move can never be certain. These preliminaries to decision affect the way in which a decision is presented and the perception of those responsible for taking it; thus in practice they form part of the process of decision itself.

Policy-Making

In formal and constitutional terms the official machinery stops short at this point. Selected and summarized reports, draft recommendations, are forwarded for ministerial consideration and decision; once given, the civil service takes over again and carries out the minister's wishes.

It is the job of the staff of the Foreign and Commonwealth Office in London to collate and analyse reports received from Her Majesty's representatives abroad and to advise the Foreign and Commonwealth Secretary on all matters of policy. They also assist in the execution of policy by drafting instructions and guidance to Her Majesty's representatives abroad.[17]

The formal position of other Departments is similar.

In practice low-level matters, and many middle-level matters, are decided and implemented below the ministerial level. The pressure on ministerial time and attention is such that their attention must be reserved for the most urgent, sensitive, novel or complex questions. One of the firmest principles of Whitehall administration, in foreign policy as elsewhere, is that matters should be decided at as low a level as possible; resisting the perennial bureaucratic tendency to refer questions to higher authority, 'the drift upwards of the level of decision-taking', in the hope of giving those at the top an opportunity to consider the larger issues without being submerged in day-to-day detail.[18]

Officials must therefore constantly bear in mind the competing desirabilities of clearing action with higher authority and of avoiding overburdening the small number of ministers and senior officials. 'Part of the professional skill of the diplomat', as of the home civil servant, 'lies in judging which decision he may take on his own account within the overall policy of the government and which need to be put to Ministers for their personal decision'.[19] 'Judgement' is a quality much valued in the Diplomatic Service: the ability to decide when to choke off a question at first secretary or counsellor level, and when to refer to under-secretaries or ministers for advice.[20] Two crude criteria appear to be used by officials in determining at what level a question should be handled: its novelty, and its political sensitivity. 'Obviously the more a problem lies outside, or casts doubt on, established lines of policy, the closer it will need to come to Ministers';[21] routine matters, or problems which can be decided within what officials understand to be their ministers' previously stated preferences, can safely be decided at a lower level. Knowing their ministers' mind means being able to assess what courses of action would or would not be acceptable to them. When in doubt, informal consultation with the minister's private office may circumvent the need for formal reference up through the hierarchy. For most officials the working definition of political sensitivity – the second criterion – is whether an issue is likely to raise a storm, or at least a question in Parliament, which might embarrass or commit the minister. Reactions from affected interests or from the media are in effect considered as a part of this, since they may bring pressure to bear on the minister or raise interest and support in Parliament. A running check on such lower-level decisions is maintained by circulating copies of the relevant reports and instructions to under-secretaries and private offices. Here again, the pressure of time and the resistance to unnecessary duplication acts as a limiting factor.

Given that few foreign policy questions are of interest only to one division or even one Department, informal and formal consultations are needed among officials at all levels: adding a series of lateral networks to the pyramidal structure of the official hierarchy. If an incoming problem affects the interests of more than one Department, but not to the extent of warranting reference to under-secretaries or ministers, consultation may begin and end at the level of principals and first secretaries, or possibly with assistant secretaries and heads of department. A routine matter will prompt a 'phone call or an informal meeting, resulting in a minute to the head of department on the lines of: 'I have discussed this question provisionally with Mr A of the X Division of the Y Department, in view of its implications for British economic interests in Z, and we both recommend that the following action should be taken. . .'.[22] The recommendation is then approved and implemented. Lord Strang estimated that in the Foreign Office in the mid-50s 'as much as eighty per cent of all incoming papers are dealt with by the heads of departments without reference to higher authority'.[23] If officials at this level cannot agree, or if their superiors judge that the matter raises wider issues or has awkward political implications, the item rises up the hierarchy, gathering comments and recommendations as it goes, until agreement between the parties involved is reached or until more senior officials exert their authority to decide it.

Policy issues go up through the Whitehall structure by two routes. A question which was defined as being important but primarily the responsibility of one Department will rise within that Department to ministerial level, and if accepted by the minister will be taken by him to the Cabinet or the Prime Minister, or cleared on his own authority. Such matters as Britain's vote on Chinese representation in the UN, which had numerous implications for relations with the United States but few direct ones for British domestic policy or immediate economic or military interests, are when necessary discussed by the Foreign Secretary and the Prime Minister, but at most reported to the Cabinet for formal ratification. Where ministers raise objections or the Cabinet fails to agree, the matter is then referred to a ministerial committee for resolution. The proposal to expel a large number of Soviet officials, as primarily a 'political' question, would have been settled in a similar fashion. But far more often an issue important enough to demand ministerial time and attention will immediately involve the interests of a number of different Departments, and so stimulate activity in several parts of Whitehall. Initial informal consultation at a low level here serves as the prelude to formal coordination by means of interdepartmental committees. If differences cannot be resolved at under-secretary level, the issue will again be referred upwards, to a committee of junior ministers, to a Cabinet committee, and if necessary in the last resort to the Cabinet itself. This procedure operates as 'a process of sieving', with fewer issues being referred up from each level, and with those so referred normally receiving at each stage less detailed discussion. In this way a problem which has preoccupied an official committee for months may occupy an hour in a Cabinet committee, and perhaps ten minutes in full Cabinet.[24] Since few issues are simple enough to be resolved by a single discussion or decision, but demand successive discussions and decisions as negotiations proceed or as the situation develops, reference up to ministerial level for general guidance or for final agreement is often only an interval between continuing management of policy at the middle levels of officialdom.

The burdensome and time-consuming process of coordination is necessary for a number of reasons. For issues involving relations with the same foreign government (or governments), consultation among those responsible for them helps to avoid crossed lines or an appearance of incoherence. It is often sufficient to circulate the papers within Whitehall, when necessary supplemented by informal discussions. Embassies to the countries concerned, through their communications with different Whitehall Departments, can help here, and the geographical departments of the Foreign Office hold a 'watching brief'. If a particular issue or negotiation involves the responsibilities and interests of several Departments, the interdepartmental committee provides a well-established procedure for deciding policy on a cooperative basis, with the chairman and the secretariat provided by the Department most actively concerned, or where more than one major Department is closely concerned, by the Cabinet Office. Whitehall is never short of such committees: when necessary a moribund committee is revived or a new one is created. The negotiations with Malta over the British and NATO base in 1972 naturally required such a committee, involving as they did not only questions of diplomacy and defence but also of an increased financial contribution, industrial and commercial relations, and potentially also questions of civil aviation. So did preparations for the UN Conference on the Environment in Stockholm in 1972. The delegation to the Conference itself was drawn from a number of Departments and backed up by a continuing committee in Whitehall. Where the parties involved in the determination of Whitehall policy sharply disagree, co-ordination becomes a mechanism for the resolution of conflict and the ordering of priorities. This is particularly needed in relations with Britain's major partners, where important interests may be at stake. Their importance, the competing domestic groups which they affect, and the resulting sharpness of the differences between Departments, ensure that these most often rise to the ministerial level and may be handled for extended periods by ministerial committees. During the mid-60s, for instance, the delicacy of Britain's relations with the United States, their enormous economic, political, and security importance, and the resulting conflicting pressures – from economic advisers not to jeopardize American support for sterling, from government supporters to condemn the American position in Vietnam or American intervention in the Dominican Republic – necessitated careful and high-level consideration of the balance of interests, of where pressure might be applied and where not. But so long as the Prime Minister and the Foreign Secretary held to a firm line, the general direction of British policy remained unquestioned within Whitehall.

Coordination in Whitehall also serves a fourth function: to feed into consideration of foreign policy issues the full significance of domestic interests and constraints. Competing priorities which need to be resolved in foreign policy-making arise because all too often the desirability of making a concession in negotiations or the decision to adhere to an international treaty have to be weighed against domestic interests or expected adverse reactions. As the Foreign Office role represents the external dimension, so home Departments represent the domestic context of foreign policy-making. It is over this that some of the sharpest interdepartmental disputes take place. This is partly because home civil servants perceive it as their role to represent the views of the interests they sponsor. Partly it is because they regard themselves as representing their ministers, and the convention of Cabinet responsibility leads them to reserve their minister's position on contentious points (even when their Department is not primarily responsible) until they are sure that they are not sacrificing either his departmental or his political interests.

All these consultative and coordinating activities however carry costs, in terms of increasing the burden of work in Whitehall and of reducing the amount of time available to administrators to deal with their direct responsibilities: the circulation of telegrams and of informative memoranda adds to the weight of paper which bears down on officials. While informal collaboration is primarily the work of junior officials, and is fairly easily carried, it is the interdepartmental committees, attended by those sufficiently respected and senior to protect their Department's interests and give authority to its decisions, which consume the most time and energy of officials who, from another perspective, might be more constructively occupied in other activities. A recently retired Permanent Under-Secretary recalled that the chief role of the Foreign Office under-secretaries was intended to be consideration of longer-term policy matters; instead they were constantly preoccupied with representing the FCO viewpoint on immediate problems in interdepartment committees.[25] Much duplication of work among different Departments is necessary to represent various interests in these committees, perhaps nowhere more than in the Foreign Office, where functional departments are primarily engaged in covering the work of other ministries.

Hence the importance of restricting the rise of policy questions to higher levels. The Labour government of 1964–70 introduced a similar restriction at the ministerial level, through the prime ministerial ruling that a Cabinet member overruled in committee could appeal to the full Cabinet only with the consent of that committee's chairman.[26] The series of amalgamations in Whitehall during the 60s were partly intended to reduce the need for interdepartmental negotiation by containing more overlapping areas of policy within the new 'giant' Departments, so delegating wherever possible the responsibility for resolving conflicting policies to departmental ministers and to senior civil servants within single ministries. Yet these procedures in their turn give rise to fresh problems. Agreement at lower levels avoids discussion at higher, with the consequent danger of suppressing debate on matters which would benefit from wider examination and of treating as established policy questions which would merit review. In the Defence Reviews of 1956–7 and 1965–7, for instance, the Minister of Defence prevented conflict between the services on strategy and force structure from rising to the Cabinet; it is arguable that on both occasions a wider discussion would have exposed inconsistencies in foreign policy which thus remained unexplored. Ministerial amalgamations have further reinforced the tendency to restrict debate. For example, conflicts between the European and the Commonwealth perspectives, which would formerly have reached the Cabinet through the persons of the Commonwealth and Foreign Secretaries, are now settled within a single Department, just as conflicts between external commercial policy and industrial policy were (from 1970–4) settled within the DTI. What might some years ago have been the focus of ministerial discussion is now more likely to emerge at Cabinet level as the settled 'view' of a major Department, unless ministers take care to discover differences of view at an early stage.

To sum up, the flow of foreign policy through the Whitehall structure in a 'normal' case follows well-established paths through well-worn procedures. Only major innovations or changes in direction rise to the Cabinet; the regular management of policy is conducted by officials. The number of men directly and actively involved in the management of a particular issue, writing briefs and instructions, initiating decisions, is likely to be small, perhaps ten or a dozen; but the number drawn in less actively on any complicated issue – reading the files, commenting on proposals, attending interdepartmental meetings – will often be very considerable. The pressure of business at the higher levels operates to hold down less 'urgent' matters to a lower level, to define incoming problems as falling within established guidelines and to manage them according to routine. But increasing awareness of the interdependence of different areas of foreign policy, as well as of domestic and foreign policy considerations, in effect limits this compartmentalization and forces choice between priorities. It forces the FCO to concern itself with a widening field of governmental business, and involves the Cabinet Office, the interdepartmental committee structure, and the Cabinet and its committees themselves, in the consideration of continuing questions of policy.

This model of foreign policy-making, necessarily, has so far assumed that there is a normal pattern of policy-making which the observer can discern. In practice, of course, a number of intervening factors disturb, or on occasion disrupt, the smooth and regular flow of policy. The most disruptive one is urgency, or acute crisis, demanding the immediate attention of key policy-makers without allowing time for preliminary work at lower levels – a far more common occurrence in foreign policy than in domestic policy. Some of the foreign policy problems faced by the Labour government of 1964–70 were, 'so to speak, blown on to the Cabinet by their suddenness and importance', without the opportunity for full official discussion or the preparation of papers, sometimes without even a formal Cabinet agenda.[27] Such were the lengthy discussions on whether or how to intervene in the Gulf of Aqaba in the hope of preventing war in the Middle East in June 1967, or on how to react to the Soviet invasion of Czechoslovakia in August 1968. The decision to proclaim a Bank Holiday in the face of international financial uncertainty in March 1968 (over which George Brown resigned), and the decision in February 1969 to inform the German Chancellor of President de Gaulle's proposals for secret Anglo-French discussions (the 'Soames affair'), were taken in such haste that the Prime Minister could only consult one or two senior ministers.[28] There are, however, crisis procedures within the FCO and Cabinet Office structure to speed official reaction when needed. Copies of incoming telegrams go to under-secretaries, the FCO private office, and selectively to the Cabinet Office and No. 10; an urgent matter will thus spur activity on several levels at once. The Foreign Office is equipped with an 'Emergency Room' – in reality, a number of rooms –

which can be manned around the clock in crisis situations. This draws upon staff from the relevant Departments when needed, and the Cabinet Office will similarly borrow extra staff as required.[29]

Ministerial initiatives or whims may vary the pattern of policy. Officials within the Cabinet Office and the FCO pride themselves on their ability to react immediately to 'the Prime Minister's night thoughts' or to a query or proposal from the Foreign Secretary, though by the time a minister's rudimentary ideas have been developed and tempered through the Whitehall structure the report which comes back to him is likely to have lost some of its sharper edges. Ministers if they wish may prefer advice from unofficial rather than official sources or may occasionally ignore the official machinery altogether. Recent years have witnessed nothing so extreme as Neville Chamberlain's reliance on Sir Horace Wilson, whose position as Chief Industrial Adviser gave him no official standing in making external policy, his use of his sister as a channel of communication with the Italian government or his preference for Sir Neville Henderson's opinion against those of the rest of the Foreign Office; but all Prime Ministers naturally turn to particularly trusted advisers, official and non-official, from time to time. In early 1970 Mr Wilson sent Lord Hunt as his 'personal representative' to Nigeria. Lord Goodman played a larger role, in London and abroad, in the evolution of policy towards Rhodesia. While the extreme case of by-passing almost the entire Foreign Office over the Suez war is unlikely to recur, less dramatically, the Conservative government disregarded the advice of its officials on the Singapore Commonwealth Prime Minister's Meeting in December 1970, and Mr Wilson's Cabinet is said to have overruled the Foreign Office in agreeing to exchange the British teacher, Gerald Brooke, for the two Russian agents, the Krögers, in June 1969.

By one means or another, however, settled policies emerge. Decisions once made are passed back down the official structure for implementation; if, as happens even in the Cabinet, discussion has not led to an immediate or a clear decision, interim instructions are given. Where the appropriate response is a telegram, a draft reply will have been attached to the action file as it circulated within Whitehall, and suitably amended will go out to the delegation or overseas post concerned for action. Major changes of policy will emerge as ministerial pronouncements, to Parliament or to some convenient public audience, after careful drafting within the private office. When it is not the Foreign Office but other Departments that are responsible for implementing policy, the Cabinet Office and the interdepartmental committee network follow the decision through: the troops are moved, the necessary financial resources transferred, the subordinate officials informed of what is expected of them.

The output of foreign policy calls into play an extensive apparatus of communication. Even if the policy decision is not intended to become public knowledge, action is needed to ensure that all those sections of the government machine affected by it are aware of its implications.

Outgoing telegrams are copied to other overseas posts, according to regular procedures. The Foreign Office Guidance and Information Policy department supplements these with the daily provision 'to posts overseas of background and guidance on matters of general concern affecting Government policy', so as to keep embassies fully in the picture and maintain a coherent presentation of British policy.[30] At home the FCO News department daily briefs the British and foreign press on developments. Background material for publication is prepared for the Foreign Office by the COI, and is circulated by information officers abroad. Ministers inform foreign statesmen, confidentially talk to selected backbenchers or a party committee, chat privately to favoured journalists or publicly tell the House of Commons; officials brief members of foreign embassies. The presentation of policy, like policy-making, is a continuing activity, in Whitehall, Westminster and abroad.

Concepts and Objectives
Effective foreign policy-making for managing immediate problems requires more than efficient machinery if it is to achieve more than rapid reaction to international events as they take place. To be able to anticipate events, it is necessary to question fixed ideas about the behaviour of other governments and about significant international trends. Governments also need to re-examine their objectives in the light of their capabilities and their understanding of international developments, in order to be able to influence these developments. To a limited extent the day-to-day process of policy-making allows for such reconsideration. Interpretation of information, in overseas posts and in Whitehall, shades into re-interpretation, contingency planning into reassessment of objectives. But studies of many large-scale organizations, governmental and non-governmental, have concluded that the responsibilities and pressures of administration do not fit easily with the formulation of long-term objectives, that there is a 'Gresham's Law of planning: daily routine drives out planning'.[31]

In contrast to the general acceptance by outsiders of the efficiency and reliability of the British foreign policy-making structure in handling immediate problems, there has been widespread and continued criticism of what are seen as its shortcomings in anticipating international developments and in providing a coherent and realistic overall set of objectives. Nicholas Kaldor, writing in 1959, and A. H. Birch, writing in 1967, listed a number of examples of 'a certain lack of foresight in foreign policy' since World War II: first, the failure to adjust to, or correctly interpret, developments in the Middle East before the Suez invasion; second, the acceptance from 1950 on in the NATO negotiations on rearmament of a British contribution 'wholly out of line' with its capacity to bear the burden; third, the absence of any safeguard clause in the 1955 Bonn Agreements on the cost of maintaining British forces in Germany (compounding the problems inherent in Eden's 1954 pledge to maintain a substantial army in Germany for an indefinite period); fourth, the failure between 1956 and 1958 to appreciate the commitment of Continental governments to European integration; fifth, the short-sightedness of developing major bases in Kenya and Aden in the early 60s; sixth, the overemphasis of successive governments on the significance of both the Commonwealth relationship and the 'special relationship'; and lastly, the failure to expect and to plan for Rhodesian UDI.[32] On planning, Ernest Davies's conclusion in 1955 that 'inadequate provision for consideration of long-term policy is probably the main fault of the present organization of the Foreign Office'[33] was echoed in the understated prose of the Plowden Committee, in 1964, that 'some of the more intractable international issues in which we have been involved in the last two decades could, in our view, have been handled better if their implications had been explored more fully in advance. . .'. (para. 217). David Vital, in 1968, was more forthright: he saw 'the long-established tradition of the pragmatic approach' as still the natural posture of British foreign policy-makers,

the adoption of the line of least intellectual resistance . . . , geared, essentially, to the handling of problems as they arise, rather than to the definition of goals and objectives in terms of which such problems as arise are to be dealt with.[34]

Others have maintained that not only the structure and style of policy-making but also the attitudes and assumptions of the officials responsible for policy – and, some have added, of their ministers as well – have been at fault.[35]

Certainly, the structure and style of Whitehall policy-making do inhibit strategic thinking. Extensive use of interdepartmental committees in which civil servants must arrive at compromise positions means that proposals too often lose their bite long before they reach their final form. Insistence that consideration of policy must begin at the lowest level, for good practical reasons, often means that 'advice originates at the bottom and mellows as it goes upwards'.[36] It may also mean that differences of opinion, within Departments as well as among Departments, are suppressed as discussion rises; so that the minister concerned or the Cabinet are presented with firm views rather than with a choice of alternatives, unless they take particular care to keep in touch with thinking at lower levels. The attempted review in 1958–60 of Britain's role ten years ahead, a rare exercise by a high-level group, was perhaps a classic example of this. The working party included 'some stark proposals' in its recommendations, but these 'were greatly watered down by the steering committee' of permanent secretaries, so that the final report 'made very little impact upon the government's thinking' when it reached the Cabinet.[37] The consensual style of Whitehall officials, who view their role as reinforcing Cabinet agreement 'by bringing together the differing views of Ministers' operates against the reopening of agreed questions or the re-examination of received doctrine.[38] If 'one of the principal values of the dominant central group in the British civil service' is 'that competing bureaucracies and competition within the administrative system are to be minimized', then it is hard even for innovators to build in to the structure mechanisms to promote the re-examination of accepted concepts and assumed objectives.[39]

The Foreign Office Research department has not been able to re-examine assumptions about international developments, because its status has been too low and its main function has been to provide background material for policy departments. Even after the 1957 reorganization it remained physically separated from the policy departments, its different sections scattered on either side of the Thames, and the morale of its staff low.[40] Only towards the end of 1972 did it begin to move into the main Foreign Office complex, so as to bring its members more actively into the consideration and reconsideration of policy. The much larger research effort within the MoD benefited greatly from the unification of the service departments in 1963–4, although the Plowden Report's recommendation (paras 230–1) that the Cabinet Office committee which was to be established to keep 'the military plans of the Ministry of Defence in line with the planning of the overseas and economic Departments . . . would need staff of its own' did not emerge fully, as the Assessments Staff, until 1968. By the 60s contacts with outside experts, occasional seminars with academics, and participation by officials in the work of research institutes in London had also begun to provide opportunities for those responsible for the interpretation of information and advice on policy to examine their assumptions before a select audience and to exchange views.

The growth of planning staffs specifically intended to promote discussion and re-examination of long-term objectives within Whitehall has been a slow and painful process. The Foreign Office Economic and Reconstruction department, established in 1943 to anticipate postwar problems, is said by one of its members to have become 'a machine for thinking out an entire long-term foreign policy'.[41] It was, however, disbanded at the end of the war. In 1949 Ernest Bevin set up a Permanent Under-Secretary's Committee within the Foreign Office, briefed 'to identify the longer-term trends in international affairs and to prepare studies on their implications for the formulation of British policy'; but, without any staff permanently attached, this failed to maintain its initial burst of activity, and had ceased to meet by 1955.[42] Reaction within Whitehall to the implications of the Suez invasion, particularly from the Chiefs of Staff, led to the creation of a small policy planning department in 1957, headed by a first secretary; from 1961 it was formally attached to Western Organizations department, and the Plowden Committee found that 'in practice priority is given to current work' (para. 221). In accordance with Plowden's recommendations, this was therefore established as a separate department in 1964, with a counsellor at its head.

Nine years after Plowden had doubted 'whether the present planning staff will prove large enough' and after the subsequent merger with the Commonwealth Office Planning Unit, its staff had risen only from three to four.[43] But it had benefited from the general change of attitude in Whitehall towards planning and from contacts with similar planning units in other Departments. Its standing in the FCO appeared to be high; its first head, Michael Palliser, had gone on to be private secretary to the Prime Minister (and later to be the first UK Permanent Representative to the European Communities) and his successors had become the first two heads of the Cabinet Office Assessments Staff. In 1973, quite exceptionally, the head of Planning Staff was made an assistant under-secretary.

These developments had by the end of the 60s built into the structure of Whitehall a number of mechanisms for re-examining both doctrine and objectives. But some outside observers and ministers still continued to criticize what they saw as the conservative and unimaginative character of official foreign policy recommendations. One senior member of the 1964–70 Labour government, for instance, remarked that he knew of no single initiative in British foreign policy since 1957 which had come from the Foreign Office Planning Staff. Such continuing criticisms raise three further questions: whether there are more obstacles to long-term planning in foreign policy than in domestic policy; whether the structure of Whitehall still severely inhibits the planning of foreign policy; and where one should best look for fresh sources of initiative.

Foreign policy has several characteristics that make it peculiarly difficult to formulate long-term objectives and to assess trends. The time-scale of forward planning is limited by the uncertainty of the international environment. In the Foreign Office, 'long-term' planning has come to mean looking three to five years ahead, 'medium term' a year or so ahead, and 'short term' a matter of two or three months; FCO planners rarely attempt to predict developments more than five years in advance, not only because of the anticipated scepticism of their colleagues but also because the number of plausible political futures has by then become so large that prediction loses all claim to scientific credibility. In 1967 no one could have predicted how much longer President de Gaulle would remain in office, let alone the manner of his going, or could have anticipated either the 1968 'Prague Spring' or the subsequent invasion. In 1971 the collapse of the Democratic campaign in the American presidential elections could not have been foreseen; nor could the subsequent emergence of the Watergate scandal which undermined Mr Nixon's sweeping victory. Yet all of these developments had far-reaching implications for British foreign policy. Defence planners, in contrast, have no choice but to plan further ahead. The lead-time for development and production of new weapons, and the relative predictability of future costs, necessitate assumptions about the military and technological environment in ten years' time—although that does not prevent new weapons systems from being outdated by changes in the political environment in the intervening period. Foreign policy planners can probably be faulted for not paying enough attention to long-term economic and social trends in recent years; but the frequency with which projections of political developments have proved mistaken may partly excuse a reluctance to venture too far with them.

The problem of defining foreign policy objectives sufficiently precisely to measure progress towards their achievement is suggested by the generality of the objectives outlined in an early study of overseas output of budgeting.[44] The characteristics of the overseas budget make it peculiarly difficult to assess the costs and to weigh objectives against capabilities. Some items fundamental to the aims of British foreign policy incur few direct costs; others, less important, seem disproportionately costly.[45] Nevertheless, there remain grounds for suspecting that a reluctance by ministers and officials to define foreign policy objectives precisely makes clear thinking and planning more difficult than it need be. Suspicion that this remains true of the FCO is strengthened by evidence of its continuing resistance to strategic rethinking on its own organization, severely criticized by the Duncan Committee yet still evident in its adjustment to entry into the European Community.[46]

Two factors have limited the impact of planning staffs on policy-making in Whitehall: their relatively 'junior' status, and their departmental basis. For Foreign Office or MoD planners, strong support from senior officials is needed if their intentionally iconoclastic ideas are to reach ministerial level without dilution. Within the FCO in 1972 the planning staff reported to the Planning Committee, composed of the Permanent Under-Secretary and the deputy under-secretaries, with the head of the planning staff in attendance. This gave the planners access to, and a hearing from, the most important officials within the Office; but depending upon the personalities involved, the pressure of other concerns, and the openness of senior officials to alternative views, it could also serve as a filter which sieved out proposals considered impractical or unacceptable to ministers. The relatively informal FCO working style gives planners easy access to the ministerial private office and the opportunity to participate in discussions with ministers; but it is arguable that a closer institutional link with ministers, perhaps by formally associating the planning staff with the private office, would do more to ensure that ministers regularly hear opposing viewpoints.

It would be easier to formulate and reformulate foreign policy objectives if the Foreign Office were still unambiguously the sole Whitehall Department responsible for the direction and coordination of overseas policy. If it was never accurate to say that the Foreign Office was solely responsible for foreign policy, it is fair to conclude that thirty or forty years ago it had the major say in the direction and management of high policy, challenged only by the Treasury in foreign economic policy. By 1972 too much was at stake for home Departments in major problems of foreign policy for them or their ministers to accept unquestioned FCO leadership. Just as in home policy the focus of coordination had by then shifted from the Treasury to the Cabinet Office and its network of committees, so the coordination of foreign policy was no longer the prerogative of the Foreign Office. But, as the Plowden Committee noted (para. 230), the difficulty of formulating objectives and planning on an interdepartment basis is that the committee easily becomes 'simply a forum where Departments arrive, with the help of a neutral chairman, at the highest common factor of interdepartmental agreement and no more'. Since then it has become still clearer

that the structure of inter-departmental committees, each concerned with a separate area of policy, needs to be reinforced by a clear and comprehensive definition of government strategy which can be systematically developed to take account of changing circumstances and can provide a framework within which the Government's policies as a whole may be more effectively formulated.[47]

The Conservative government's response to this criticism, in 1970, was to establish the CPRS withing the Cabinet Office, to provide a sufficiently powerful spur to the reconsideration of policy outside the departmental structure. But this dealt almost entirely with domestic policy. The Assessments Staff, which fulfilled some of the Plowden Committee's recommendations in its function of focusing Whitehall reconsideration of assumptions and forecasts in foreign policy, had neither the authority nor the standing to play a similarly active role.

The early experience of the CPRS, which reportedly frequently discovered that ministers held views which their Departments were unaware of and were receptive to alternatives which their civil servants had ruled out as impractical, suggests some of the consequences of this situation in foreign affairs. The established pattern of Whitehall policy-making in unavoidably conservative. Civil servants are constantly forced to consider, as they formulate proposals or as they defend their Department's position in interdepartmental committees, what is and is not likely to be acceptable to their minister. For the best reasons they tend to be cautious in interpreting 'the minister's mind', and try to avoid wasting their minister's valuable time with proposals which he might well reject; which pushes their proposals back towards consensus and continuity. Yet the fundamental difficulty about any further centralization of planning within the Cabinet Office is that it would threaten to weaken the collective responsibility of the Cabinet; it is precisely this that the whole structure of interdepartmental committees, official and ministerial, reflects. However, since with British entry in the European Communities the 'political' dimension of external policy (the traditional responsibility of the Foreign Office) has become even more intermixed with the economic, industrial, and even social dimensions, it is difficult to see how such a development can be avoided.

Hence it may be that ministers will look in vain to the proliferation of planning staffs to provide the initiatives, the sense of direction, and the criticisms which they feel are needed. Nor are they more likely to find these qualities in senior officials. Their role as advisers on policy was intended to include a broad overview of objectives, but they are unavoidably too much caught up with immediate and urgent matters to have enough time for long-term thinking. Sometimes discussions in Whitehall will throw up new initiatives or move the weight of official opinion behind a new consensus; but this only happens irregularly and informally.

According to the traditional interpretation of the British constitution, officials were not expected to be responsible for formulating or reconsidering the strategic direction of policy. Ministers made policy, or at least laid down its general direction, and officials executed it. One cannot escape the impression that successive ministers have blamed their civil servants for lack of foresight and strategic thinking in foreign policy in rather the same way as bad workmen blame their tools; that it has been their reluctance to consider the possibility of choice, or to demand and decide upon clear alternatives, which has been the fundamental failing in British foreign policy over the last twenty years. Too often they, as well as their officials, have preferred to wait upon events, to cling to established assumptions and objectives until they are plainly untenable, and to present their decisions, once made, as the only alternative.[48] The absence of a thorough reconsideration of Britain's world role after Suez may owe much to the working practices of Whitehall; but there are no grounds to believe that senior officials, in moderating the starkness of the alternatives they proposed, misinterpreted what their political masters would stand. On the first and second approaches to Europe, a substantial body of officials put up thoroughly researched papers to their ministers. On the East of Suez role, there were sceptics in Whitehall from 1964, and by 1966 these included some junior ministers, whose alternative views did not reach the Cabinet, in part at least because the leading members of the Cabinet did not want to hear them. On devaluation, officials prepared papers listing this as an alternative from 1964 onwards but were left in no doubt that ministers did not want to see them.[49]

Once in office, senior ministers in any event are subject to much the same pressures of immediate and urgent business as their senior advisers, and carry the additional burden of their political responsibilities. The heads of the major Departments in Whitehall who are also members of the Cabinet could never find the time or inclination for original thought, at least without considerable assistance from elsewhere. Some senior members of the Labour government of 1964–70 looked to their junior ministers, less weighed down by administration, for new initiatives, even as junior ministers were being more closely integrated into the decision-making structure of large Departments. Successive parties, in opposition, have argued for a larger number of political advisers for the Prime Minister and also for heads of major Departments, and a few advisers have been introduced in recent years. These provide the hope of a more critical examination of current policy in the light of longer-term objectives, from within the government if not from within the administration. But for wider criticism, for the sort of debate which can throw up contrasting perspectives and provoke rethinking, ministers must look outside Whitehall: to their party, to Parliament, and to the unofficial but informed debate among the interested and the expert which goes to make up the shifting consensus of domestic opinion. These form the subject of the next chapter.

Policy-making in Practice

Some examples of developing policy and changes in policy will be examined in more detail in Part II. Here it may be useful to illustrate the arguments developed in this chapter by briefly examining two cases which fall into that hazy residual category of external relations, the 'political' – the management of the Rhodesian problem in 1964–5, and the approaches to Europe by the Conservative government in 1960–61 and by the Labour government in 1967.

The illegal unilateral declaration of independence (UDI) by the Rhodesian government in October 1965 did not burst on the British government without prior warning. A unilateral declaration of independence was already in the air in April 1964, when Winston Field resigned as Prime Minister rather than accept the Conservative conditions for legal independence or break with Britain. It was widely expected in October 1964, when the general commanding the Rhodesian forces was retired because Ian Smith's government doubted his loyalty if UDI was declared. There was therefore plenty of time for Whitehall to gather information and make contingency plans, and for the Labour government to prepare policy. From the time Labour took office in October 1964, senior ministers and the Prime Minister himself had devoted much thought to the problem; it was discussed at length in full Cabinet and in special Cabinet committees set up for the purpose. On the official side, a number of Departments were involved in planning and policy-making, and missions abroad provided detailed assessments of the likely reactions of other countries.

No single decision determined the government's handling of UDI, but a number of earlier decisions had effectively foreclosed other options. The decision not to use force in any circumstances, publicly announced by the Commonwealth Secretary in the summer of 1965, precluded such a response; which would in any case have required substantial preparations beforehand, given Rhodesia's geographical position. The Cabinet had similarly decided, or at least accepted, that it was not possible to gain the support of public opinion against the Rhodesian government. Its acceptance of optimistic advice on the effectiveness of economic sanctions had encouraged it not to make preparations for international action through the UN, but to rely solely on British dominance over the Rhodesian economy.

Even so, the declaration when it came seemed to catch the British government off balance. Confident predictions that the imposition of sanctions by Britain would bring the rebellion to an end in a matter of weeks gave way to renewed attempts at negotiation, the eventual involvement of the UN in the imposition of sanctions, still further negotiations, and eventual stalemate.

It can be argued from the succession of events 'that Britain relied on sanctions to bring down the Rhodesian regime, not because it was a second-class power, but because it depended on second-class advice'.[50] Yet the government was provided with a range of different assessments from different Departments. It chose to prefer the more optimistic advice offered from the Department of Economic Affairs (DEA) to 'the different opinions' prevailing in the ODM. The government's faith in sanctions was 'unduly sanguine', one critic adds, 'when so much scepticism about their efficacy was expressed within and outside official circles'.[51] There were strong political arguments for wanting to believe the DEA. The government had the narrowest possible majority in the House of Commons; it expected that the Conservative opposition would not support stronger action (though it is not clear how far, if at all, bipartisan conversations were attempted), and that public opinion would be behind the Conservatives on this issue. Faced with varying advice from officials, ministers chose that which best fitted their preferred course of action. The official who later told an official committee that he had prepared these optimistic predictions about the effect of sanctions 'because this was the picture he thought ministers wanted' confirms the conclusion that the Cabinet had agreed that what was the most the domestic political context would stand was also the most that was needed.[52] The concentration of domestic debate in the months before UDI on partisan conflict, with the strongest criticism coming from the Conservatives, further restricted consideration of any but the preferred alternative.

The Conservative government's approach to the European Community began shortly after the 1959 general election. Indications are that the initiative for a change of policy came partly from within the civil service and partly from influential Conservatives with links in the 'City', and met a favourable response from a Prime Minister actively looking for ideas on new policies. Within Whitehall the strongest support for an application came from within the Foreign Office. The Treasury, which had previously been very reluctant, was becoming more favourable; some other Departments, notably the Board of Trade, contained substantial opposition opinion, not unconnected with their departmental roles. In January 1960 a high-level committee began reviewing the possibilities of a British application, and by the late spring detailed investigations were under way in several Departments. Their resulting reports were discussed by a still-reluctant Cabinet in June and July, against the background of exploratory debates in Parliament. In July Mr Macmillan extensively reshuffled his Cabinet, putting 'pro-Europeans' in charge of the 'delicate' Ministry of Agriculture and CRO, and appointing a Cabinet minister with special responsibilities for Europe. During the autumn and winter, Mr Macmillan and other ministers travelled to the Continent, and began to try to prepare opinion in the Commonwealth for a shift in policy. More cautious attempts were made to prepare opinion within the Conservative Party, and only indirectly to prepare public opinion for such a major change. The decision to open negotiations was announced to the House of Commons on 31 July 1961; even then a number of Conservative MPs were unpersuaded and failed to support their government in the debate which followed.

In this slow and gradual shift in policy a number of contingent decisions can be identified, though few were made, in the most positive sense, by the Cabinet; they were, rather, accepted by the Cabinet in response to prime ministerial initiative. For much of the 'period of decision' the Cabinet was divided, and it retained a number of sceptical ministers throughout the subsequent negotiations. The Conservative Party was similarly uncertain, and was similarly managed by the Prime Minister, with some assistance from the party's Research Department. Public opinion was not prepared for a momentous shift in British policy; rather, the tactics of party management required the playing down of the significance of negotiations to domestic opinion. To a certain extent the government deliberately obscured the issues involved, to avoid disturbing public opinion, finding itself in consequence uncomfortably placed between the rousing speeches its ministers made on the Continent and the dampening remarks they made at home. But if this discouraged a wide public debate, the decision itself was clearly political, the Prime Minister and his senior colleagues drawing on diverse advice from within the civil service and from outside, setting the Whitehall machinery in train, and carrying the Cabinet with them, at least as far as agreeing to open negotiations – though in the event no final decision on entry had to be made.

The Labour Party's approach to Europe followed a similarly winding path. A number of ministers, both in the Cabinet and at junior level, had been in favour of Community entry since the first application; some influential officials, particularly within the Foreign Office, also favoured entry. Board of Trade and the Ministry of Agriculture officials were more inclined, from their position, to oppose entry, and in 1966 both Departments had ministers who shared their officials' predisposition. In the 1966 election the Labour leadership had seemed more opposed than the Conservatives to another attempt. In reality, both parties were divided on the issue, and in the summer and autumn of 1966 shifting coalitions of ministers and officials debated the pros and cons of entry. One deciding factor was the move of the most committed pro-European, George Brown, to the Foreign Office in July 1966; but the most important one was the conversion of the Prime Minister, who by late 1966 had come to see a new initiative as valuable and the European Community as less of a threat to national sovereignty than he had feared. The Prime Minister's change of attitude gave the pro-Europeans the advantage in swaying the Cabinet; but it did not immediately bring either the rest of the Cabinet or the Parliamentary Labour Party (PLP) round.

The strategy adopted by the Prime Minister was therefore one of a succession of small steps, none of which would be finally 'decisive', but which were intended to carry the dissenters along until they were past the point of fundamental disagreement. An enormous amount of preparatory investigation was undertaken by officials throughout Whitehall, leading up to the series of lengthy briefs which Mr Wilson put before the Cabinet. But the conclusion of the official studies, after much interdepartmental discussion, was that the economic arguments were finely balanced; it was the political arguments which might be seen as compelling, if the Cabinet accepted them. Preparation of opinion in the Cabinet, party, and country began with Mr Wilson's announcement of an exploratory exercise in November 1966, and a series of exploratory visits to continental capitals in January and February 1967. The PLP did not debate the question of entry specifically until April; the Cabinet was brought round gradually through a series of meetings, culminating in a week-end at Chequers in late April at which by a very narrow majority it accepted the proposals to apply for entry, without at that time committing itself specifically to accept the terms when negotiated. During the spring, further to prepare public opinion, ministers had conducted a number of background briefings for journalists, and selected political correspondents had been invited down to Chequers for conversations.[53] In the event, the renewed opposition of the French President prevented the opening of negotiations and the application had to be laid aside; to be taken up again by the Cabinet, on a similarly conditional basis, after de Gaulle's resignation in 1969.

There was no lack of information or of policy planning at the official level in this application. One official afterwards commented that investigations in Whitehall amounted to the largest policy exercise, and the greatest weight of paper, that he had ever witnessed. Yet no decisive conclusions on the advantages of entry or clear estimates of the chances of success emerged. Official opinion within Whitehall remained divided. At the political level, the Cabinet's eventual commitment to negotiation left those of its members who were still sceptical of the Common Market sufficiently free to be able to claim later that they had at no point accepted the principle of membership. In contrast to the situation over Rhodesia in 1964—5, domestic opinion and pressure strengthened the Prime Minister's hand. The opposition leadership was already committed to entry, and could be counted on to support the government even against its own dissidents. Elite opinion was predominantly in favour, as was the press; the CBI was actively lobbying for entry in Westminister and

Whitehall, and the leadership of the TUC was not openly opposed. The government's careful management of the media, and its presentation of the issue in terms of high-level policy, succeeded in swinging Labour supporters towards accepting the idea of entry. The most difficult obstacle for the government was its own party, both in Parliament and in the country; a considerable part of its efforts in the months leading up to the formal application was therefore devoted to converting its own party.

All three of these examples emphasize the difficulty of identifying clear decisions, the uncertain nature of information available for those responsible for policy, the non-monolithic character of Whitehall and of the government itself, and the importance of the domestic context for foreign policy. If in all cases the Prime Minister and his leading colleagues played the decisive roles in determining policy, they also paid close attention to the balance of opinion within Parliament, within the informed elite, and within the wider public. Government activity itself can do much to set the tone of domestic debate on foreign policy, but there are a great many other participants in that debate.

4: The Domestic Context

IN SPITE OF the convergence of foreign and domestic policy issues, it has been a commonplace of academic writing that the formulation and management of foreign policy remains relatively free from the domestic political constraints which hem in the government in other fields. Foreign policy matters, for instance, rarely require legislation, so that most proposals are spared the process of detailed discussion and possible amendment involved in a bill's passage through Parliament. No domestic interests can wield the direct sanctions over the government's foreign policy that, for example, doctors can over health, or teachers over education. The cooperation of interest groups to achieve the government's aims is needed only in foreign commercial, and to some extent international financial, policy.

Yet no government can afford to ignore the domestic context of foreign policy. Domestic opinion, and the occasional swelling of public interest and public pressure, are as important as the international environment: setting limits to what policies are feasible, providing or denying support for the government. Mass opinion may be relatively uninterested and uninvolved in foreign policy issues – as will be argued below. But governments must bear in mind the importance of carrying opinion with them, of explaining significant shifts in policy and so avoiding arousing opposition or giving the impression of uncertainty or confusion at the top. Only a very small section of the public, geographically concentrated and closely inter-knit, maintains an active interest in foreign policy questions. But this 'informed public' is important both as a constraint on the government's freedom of action and as a source of constructive criticism. It not only exerts a direct influence upon the government but also acts as an intermediary between it and the general public, putting a gloss on official interpretations of policy and setting the tone of the public debate – indeed, largely conducting the public debate.

The members of this informed public are drawn from Parliament, the press, the universities and research institutes, those sections of business, finance, and commerce most concerned with international trade, and the leadership of the many organized groups which focus on foreign policy issues. Although for convenience of exposition these various bodies will now be examined separately, the degree to which they interrelate must be stressed. MPs assist promotional groups and advise companies and trade associations. Journalists cultivate MPs and meet them and academics at conferences and study group meetings; some also have links with particular lobbies. Businessmen and bankers may well attend the same conferences, and many support groups lobbying to further the interests of the countries with which they trade. Foreign interests and foreign governments are also closely involved in this informal debate, cultivating MPs and journalists in their turn, briefing the press. cooperating with business, and on occasion supporting or even sponsoring interest group activity.

There is naturally a correlation between public influence on foreign policy and the level at which that policy is defined and managed. On low-level issues the number of those who are interested or expert is likely to be very small. Most may well know each other, and unless there is any deep division of attitude amongst them (which would itself be likely to raise the level of discussion and decision), their influence is likely to be direct and continuous. The principals and first secretaries responsible for, say, trade with Central American countries know their interested public and are in regular contact with its members; many of them will represent those minor 'national interests' on behalf of which the civil servants are working. The widest room for interest group manoeuvre comes at the middle levels of policy, where party lines on issues are often not sharply drawn but where public and political interest is enough to effect the exertion of influence. Organizations supporting or condemning the military regime in Greece, demanding the recognition of Bangladesh or of East Germany, above all supporting one side or the other in the continuing Middle East conflict, or working for innumerable other causes, are paralleled by commercial associations defending or promoting the interests of foreign investors, bondholders, bankers, exporters and importers. Ministers and civil servants are lobbied, parliamentary questions are tabled, letters written to newspapers, all the paraphernalia of interest group activity are deployed. But high policy is to some extent protected from the hubbub of these activities. Where party lines are drawn, the formal clash of party leaderships resolves and clarifies the confused debate below. Where the front benches are united, as they most often are, the tradition of bipartisanship in foreign policy serves to damp down debate, to lend the respectability of the national interest to the accepted consensus and to label criticism as somehow extreme, if not also disloyal. Here critics of government policy must fall back on attempts to arouse mass opinion, by demonstrations and rallies, or else to try to capture one of the peak associations, the CBI, the TUC, or even one of the parties themselves. These were the only paths open for the Campaign for Nuclear Disarmament (CND), or for the later critics of government policy on Vietnam.

But informed debate and the exercise of influence are limited by the government's relative freedom from the need to gain parliamentary sanction or to ensure the cooperation of affected groups. The peculiar secrecy in which foreign policy matters are discussed and decided in Britain is another obstacle. While there is sufficient non-confidential information available to support intelligent discussion among experts (though even they are often handicapped in debating policy issues by their ignorance of government intentions), wider public interest is discouraged by the poverty of explanation and justification which has characterized British foreign policy over the last twenty years. It will be argued that successive governments have failed to enlighten the general public and to provide adequate information to support a critical debate; it is this that has left public opinion so far behind the government and that has contributed to the frequent failure of the informed public to provide convincing alternatives to the policy proposals of the government's official advisers.

Parliament and the Parties

Parliament provides the most immediate focus for the justification and criticism of government policy. Formally both Houses have a number of regular devices which enable them to come to grips with the government on foreign policy questions. In the Commons one day of the opening debate on the Address each session is by custom devoted to foreign affairs. General debates on foreign affairs take place roughly once each session: two days' discussion on a technical motion to adjourn, often ending without a division. More specific debates – on the situation in the Middle East or relations with Eastern Europe – are allotted one or two days of parliamentary time by either the government or the opposition, as the need arises or as party interest is felt to demand it. Ministerial statements and the questions and answers which follow them allow further opportunities for brief debate. Parliamentary Questions, to the Foreign Secretary or to other ministers with external responsibilities, above all to the Prime Minister, focus attention on issues of public concern and elicit statements of policy from ministers.[1]

Other opportunities for exerting influence and publicizing criticism exist off the floor of the House. Over the past decade the slow growth of specialist parliamentary committees has brought some foreign policy issues within the range of committee scrutiny. Early Day Motions (EDMs), statements of opinion circulated by Members to attract signatures, are an accepted form of signalling to both front benches and to the press the strength of parliamentary opinion on particular issues; rarely themselves selected for debate, they are printed on the Order Paper, and those which attract a substantial number of Members may provoke a ministerial statement, even on occasion a formal debate. Ministers and opposition spokesmen may be buttonholed in the corridors and made aware of the strength of feeling on an issue; their parliamentary private secretaries keep them informed of the currents of parliamentary opinion and the discontents of particular groups of Members. Much of the toughest debate on foreign policy matters takes place off the floor of the House, in the party committees on foreign affairs and in meetings of the

PLP and the 1922 Committee. In the relative privacy of these meetings critics of party or government policy can let fly, uninhibited by the presence of Members of opposing parties or of the press but in the presence of one of their ministers or at least of a p.p.s. when the party is in government. The party machinery for discussing and developing policy on foreign affairs includes as well the research department at party headquarters, the advisory committees, the ginger groups, and the formal procedure of resolutions submitted to and debated at party conferences. In much of these MPs are themselves engaged, and they take account of them in determining their attitude to party policy.

Various sources of information on foreign affairs are open to interested MPs to supplement what is provided by the government and through the press. Foreign embassies supply them with a wealth of literature (not all of great value); foreign diplomats are active in giving sympathetic MPs their interpretation of international developments.[2] Many MPs have business connections with companies involved in overseas trade. They have a wide range of opportunities for travel. Most MPs are members of the British branches of the Inter-Parliamentary Union (IPU) and the Commonwealth Parliamentary Association (CPA), bodies which receive Exchequer grants-in-aid to promote contacts between parliamentarians – entertaining visiting groups of foreign MPs and sponsoring visits abroad for groups of British parliamentarians from both Houses.[3] Parliamentary committees now send sub-committees abroad at government expense. Foreign governments invite MPs, sometimes in large numbers, to make sponsored visits to their countries – one unofficial estimate was that over a quarter of the House of Commons had visited Israel in the three years before the 1967 Middle East war. Some MPs travel abroad fairly regularly on behalf of companies with which they are associated, occasionally combining such business with parliamentary duties.[4] Others travel on behalf of organized groups, carrying out investigations or representing libertarian organizations at 'political' trials.[5] Even before British entry to the EEC added the European Parliament to their number, delegations to parliamentary assemblies – the Council of Europe Consultative Assembly, the WEU and North Atlantic Assemblies, each with subordinate committees and working parties attached to them – took MPs regularly to the European continent and the United States.[6] Two MPs each year form part of the British delegation to the UN General Assembly, and others are occasionally invited to sit on UN committees.[7]

At the end of 1972 there were 68 all-party bilateral 'Anglo-Ruritanian' Parliamentary Groups, most of them affiliated to the IPU or the CPA – each with three or four MPs as officers and a minimum membership of twelve needed to gain recognition and the right to have their meetings advertised on the weekly Non-Party Whip.[8] Their degree of activity varied enormously. Most convened at least two or three times a year to hear talk by 'their' ambassador or by a distinguished visitor from that country; the most active held fairly regular meetings, showing films, discussing recent visits abroad, meeting visiting delegations. They also served as a point of parliamentary contact for organized groups and foreign embassies, and for MPs as a link with the network of groups and interests outside the House.[9] Another thirteen all-party groups, several of them very active, were primarily concerned with international questions, from the United Nations Group to the Parliamentary Committee for Soviet Jewry and the Parliamentary Group for World Government.[10] Previous career experience, military, diplomatic, or colonial, also provided a minority of MPs with a degree of expertise and with particular links with foreign countries.[11]

Whitehall Departments relate to this parliamentary activity primarily through their Parliamentary Units, responsible for handling each Department's parliamentary business, through their responses to parliamentary questions, through dealing with parliamentary committees, and through correspondence with and deputations from MPs. Because it is responsible for a very small amount of legislation, the FCO's Parliamentary Unit is one of the smallest in Whitehall. (In 1972 it had a staff of four executive grade officials attached to the Parliamentary Secretary's Private Office, and was primarily concerned with orchestrating the FCO response to parliamentary questions.) Increasing overseas travel by parliamentary committees had led in 1968-9 to the addition of an equally small Parliamentary Commissioner and Committees Unit, responsible for Foreign Office assistance with overseas visits, for liaising with parliamentary committees which take evidence from FCO officials or request memoranda, and for handling their Department's response to individual complaints referred by MPs to the 'Ombudsman'. Five or six deputations a week which included MPs visited the FCO in the early 70s, all of which would be received by a minister and a number of officials; less often, similar deputations made representations to other Departments on international matters. When requested the FCO and the DTI provide briefings for MPs going abroad; official deputations are briefed as a matter of course and are accompanied by an embassy official while abroad. When foreign affairs are being questioned or debated at Westminster up to ten officials squeeze into the box provided for them behind the Speaker's chair, to take note of parliamentary opinion and where necessary to give information and advice to their minister.

Such extensive parliamentary activity might seem to indicate wide parliamentary involvement and influence in foreign policy. Yet the appearance of debate and activity often serves to mask the ineffectiveness of Parliament in holding the government to account in foreign policy matters or in influencing policy. Foreign affairs debates are among the most unsatisfactory in the House of Commons, beginning with a general *tour d'horizon* by the Foreign Secretary and a similar speech by his opposition 'Shadow', continuing with a long series of unrelated contributions by backbenchers, wound up by the Leader of the Opposition and the Prime Minister without much reference to the intervening speeches.

Backbench speakers tend to use the opportunity to forward their particular causes, notably the Middle East, or else to recount their impressions of recent overseas travel. There is no statement of policy comparable to the annual Statement on Defence round which to focus debate. A period of thirteen months elapsed between general debates on foreign affairs in 1971–2; press comment on that of December 1972 and on the next one in June 1973 noted the inconclusive nature of the exchanges.[12]

Part of the difficulty for the two front benches in foreign affairs debates is that the spread of opinion and the strength of the bipartisan tradition in foreign policy often put both party leaderships in the uncomfortable position of supporting each other against their respective foreign policy oppositions. The Conservative Party throughout the long process of decolonization has carried within it a group of MPs who have resisted what they saw as the too rapid retreat from Empire and from Britain's traditional alliances, focusing in the mid-50s on the Suez 'surrender', in the mid-60s on Rhodesia and southern Africa. The Labour Party has similarly carried within it a number of overlapping groups of pacifically-inclined or even pacifist MPs, of believers in a 'Socialist' foreign policy, and of anti-colonialists, coalescing around a similar succession of issues – opposition to German rearmament, to the British nuclear deterrent, to the Labour government's attitude to the Vietnam war, to American bases in Britain. Both groups appeal to strands in their party's traditions which command wide sympathy within each party, and thus occasionally require considerable efforts by the leadership to prevent them carrying the party. What seems to the front benches to be a responsible attitude to their country's international position often looks to these groups a sordid compromise of party principles; and the vigour with which they criticize their leaders makes reasoned debate between the two front benches more difficult. Conversely, debates on specific topics have tended to take place on issues on which the party initiating the debate feels more confident that it can present a united front in criticizing its opponents, thus creating a formal confrontation between the two parties which does not encourage concessions or re-thinking. Such occasions as the two-day debate on the principle of British entry into the European Communities at the end of October 1971 have been rare; the strength of party discipline, and the dominant style of Commons debates drives real discussion into the party meetings upstairs. Formerly an increasingly restrictive interpretation of the House of Commons Standing Order governing the admissibility of motions to discuss matters of urgency had made it almost impossible for the House to discuss immediate international emergencies without the agreement of both front benches. Fortunately the substantial revision of the definition of this ruling in 1967 has 'added an element of surprise together with vigour and immediacy to the Commons' discussions on foreign affairs'; all but one of the twelve emergency debates in the next three sessions were on topics with international implications.[13]

The effectiveness of Parliamentary Questions as a means of drawing the government out and of holding it to account for its policies is open to doubt. In the 1972–3 session questions to the Foreign Secretary headed the list only every third Wednesday in the House of Commons. Questions to the Prime Minister, which were taken in the last fifteen minutes of Question Time every Tuesday and Thursday, often concerned international issues: but during this session Prime Ministers' Questions had developed into a somewhat stylized clash between the two front benches, not easily amenable to penetrating questioning. Successive governments have refused to answer questions on a number of important issues, including the supply of arms, the details of arms sales, the numbers of foreign forces training in the UK, future forecasts of overseas aid, and elections in the UN Security Council.[14]

Questions are asked for many reasons other than to elicit information. A number are 'planted' from within the Foreign Office, sometimes to provide an opportunity for a minister to make an announcement, sometimes to ensure that ministers can respond to friendly questions; during the Labour government's approach to Europe in 1967, for instance, suggested questions were fed to selected MPs. Or a series of hostile questions may be put down as part of a political campaign, with the objective of occupying the whole of Question Time on one subject.[15] Labour MPs admitted to the Select Committee on Parliamentary Questions in 1972 that they had pursued this tactic in harrying their own government on Vietnam. Not surprisingly, therefore, the attitude of FCO officials to Parliamentary Questions is generally defensive; Sir Ivone Kirkpatrick's mild rebuke in his office memorandum of 1949 that 'there is a tendency in drafting answers to withhold information' would not be too unkind today.[16] The attitude of members of the Diplomatic Service to Parliament, possibly reflecting their relative lack of contact with domestic politics and their experience of parliamentary interventions as an additional complication in the already difficult conduct of diplomacy, still appears to be one of resigned but reluctant tolerance. One official regretted that parliamentary and political factors meant 'that decisions were not taken on the sort of objective criteria that are available in the Foreign Office'; another commented that 'the Foreign Office can manage very well without Parliament, and would rather it weren't there at all'.

The pervasiveness of this attitude among British diplomats results partly from the dominance, in their view, of parliamentary discussions by the respective foreign policy oppositions of the two main parties, and the active concern of these opposition groups with matters which, while not among the most important or highest level issues in British foreign policy, are among the most sensitive for the responsible officials to handle: relations with Dr Caetano's Portugal, with post-1967 Greece, post-1968 Czechoslovakia, or Chile before and after the 1973 coup. Certainly members of these groups have tended to dominate foreign affairs questions, debates, and party discussions upstairs, out of proportion to their numbers in each party.[17] For MPs without an emotional or ideological commitment or a particular expertise in foreign policy, there is little incentive to devote much effort to pressing the government on international issues, since it is difficult to exert influence. A more powerful disincentive is that foreign policy does not win votes – and MPs in all but the safest constituencies are concerned to maintain their support at the next election. George Jeger's explanation, in an adjournment debate in late 1957, of his parliamentary priorities in speaking may still be representative, coming as it did from a Member with a number of international connections:

When I was in my constituency last weekend I asked my constituents who are concerned with this matter which they would rather I did – endeavour to catch Mr Speaker's eye in the grand foreign affairs debate tomorrow or raise the question of their bus shelter, which is only a local problem. They told me that any fool can speak on foreign affairs and no doubt several would, but that if I did not speak about their local bus shelter, then nobody else would.[18]

The ability of parliamentary committees to provide either an effective check or a stimulus to the government in overseas policy was also doubtful, at least until the early 70s. Throughout the 50s and 60s calls for specialized select committees on overseas issues were made by opposition Members, but were denied by successive governments. In the debate on the Nassau Agreement in January 1963, for instance, Richard Crossman protested that 'we are the most diddled Parliament in the Western world . . . because we are the only Parliament without a Defence Committee'; yet differences of opinion within his party on this issue were indicated by the failure of Denis Healey as Shadow Minister of Defence to support him.[19] The history of the Select Committee on Agriculture, appointed in December 1966 and disbanded, after much dispute, in February 1969, illustrates the strength of administrative and governmental resistance to parliamentary involvement in foreign policy issues. The first subject it chose to investigate was 'The scope and adequacy of the inquiries made by the Ministry of Agriculture, Fisheries and Food concerning the effects of possible entry into the European Economic Community on Britain's agriculture, fisheries and food', and it announced its intention of visiting Brussels to assist its task.[20] The Foreign Office immediately took issue with the opportuneness of such a visit, maintaining that it trespassed on its own sphere of responsibility, and it was only after a delay of some months that a brief visit by five Members was arranged. Supporters of the expansion of select committees argued that this initial dispute was responsible for the government's apparent determination to disband the Committee at the end of the following session, though other MPs have denied this.[21] A 'departmental' Select Committee on Overseas Aid was appointed in the 1969–70 session, but was not reappointed by the incoming Conservative government. The weight of parliamentary scrutiny therefore fell on the Select

Committee on Estimates. In the twenty years from 1945 to 1965 the Estimates Committee published 34 reports on aspects of defence expenditure – more than on any other field of policy – though few of these dealt with questions directly related to strategic policy. In two reports in 1963 and 1964 on military expenditure overseas, however, the Committee severely criticized the inability of the armed services to relate costs to strategy, and suggested that there was room for a more thorough review of overseas commitments than had yet been made.[22] During these two decades the Committee produced two reports on overseas aid and one on the British Council; it twice attempted to investigate the Foreign Office in the early 50s, but met with such resistance from the FO that it thereafter desisted. It was further handicapped by its inability to travel abroad in pursuing its investigations.[23] It is hard to escape the conclusion that in external relations (as elsewhere) 'Government Departments did not always treat the recommendations of the Committee with the seriousness they deserved, and its painstaking examinations and conclusions were not infrequently without result.[24]

It was not only that MPs lacked both the opportunity to subject government policy to detailed examination and much of the information required to conduct such an examination; they also lacked the staff to absorb what information was available. In 1966 the total number of House of Commons clerks was thirty-six, one fewer than in 1900. A small Overseas Office, with a staff of three clerks, had been established as a separate unit in 1964, with the primary task of assisting Members attending international assemblies and dealing with the growing number of requests for advice from Commonwealth legislatures. The House of Commons Library had a similarly small staff. The situation had improved a little by the early 70s, with a gradual expansion in the numbers of clerks and library staff; but entry into the EEC found the Overseas Office inadequately staffed to service the delegation to the European Parliament, let alone to answer queries from other MPs on Strasbourg and on the European Communities, and without authorization to do so.

The research departments of the political parties were hardly better placed to service MPs. The handful of full-time researchers in the Conservative Research Department concerned with overseas questions between 1964 and 1970 were responsible for publishing a monthly *Overseas Review*, for servicing the Shadow Cabinet committee on foreign policy matters as well as the weekly meetings of the 1922 Committee's Foreign Affairs and Commonwealth Sub-Committee, for drafting speeches for party spokesmen on foreign affairs, and for providing the detail to support the party's developing policies on Europe and defence East of Suez. A separate Overseas Bureau, with one full-time administrator, serviced the extra-parliamentary party's foreign policy body, the Conservative Commonwealth and Overseas Council, and developed contacts with conservative parties abroad. The small Overseas Department in the Labour Party headquarters combined all these functions. The

Liberal Party between 1965 and 1969 had one member of its Research Department working on defence and foreign policy matters; after his departure it was completely dependent on voluntary advice. Both the Labour and Liberal Parties made extensive and profitable use of advisory groups of sympathetic 'experts' during this period. This was less easy for the Conservative Party, faced with a larger number of members interested in and knowledgeable about foreign policy from long service in the armed services or abroad, many of whom were, however, inclined to resist new policies. The hardening of Conservative policy on retaining a 'presence' East of Suez between 1967 and 1968 owed a great deal to vigorous representations from interested party members outside Parliament. The various 'ginger groups' within all parties – the Bow Group, the Fabian Society, and so on – complemented the more official advisory groups as a stimulus towards new policy and a provider of often detailed and expert proposals, with MPs often participating in their study groups.

The amount of time spent by MPs in foreign travel and in inter-nationally-related activities has not been closely linked to involvement in discussions on policy. There is considerable cynicism among MPs of all parties about the purposes of all-party parliamentary groups and about MPs' susceptibility to invitations for overseas visits at the expense of foreign governments. Arthur Lewis informed the Select Committee on Members' Interests in 1969 that one Member had been 'heard to declare that he wanted to secure election' to the CPA Executive 'because it would help his hotel business in one of the Commonwealth countries'. Andrew Roth, in giving evidence to the same committee, was sure that 'experienced parliamentarians like yourself know there are certain of your colleagues who live for this, who do not seem to do anything else but work up to the next trip abroad'.[25] Several MPs remarked upon the large membership of those all-party groups which promoted good relations with countries with warm climates whose governments habitually invite parties of MPs and their wives to pay a visit during the spring or summer recess. But if they have no resources of their own for overseas travel, serious-minded and other MPs alike remain dependent on interested bodies for assistance in travelling abroad. A review body of MPs pay and conditions in 1971 recommended that an annual grant of £20,000, to be administered by an all-party committee, should be made to assist MPs to make investigatory visits abroad; but the opposition of a small number of Labour MPs was sufficient for the government to withdraw the proposal when it came up for parliamentary approval.[26]

Yet the influence of Parliament, and of the political parties through their representation in Parliament, on the evolution of foreign policy is not negligible. It is rare for initiatives and new proposals on high-level policy to come from within either the government or the opposition party, given the pressures of other business on MPs and the shortage of resources at their disposal; though the party 'ginger groups' often throw up valuable prosals at the middle level, on say the pattern of overseas aid or British relations with Commonwealth African countries, and within both parties groups were active in the debates on Europe and on southern Africa. But Parliament acts as a powerful constraint, a negative if not a positive force of considerable strength. The difference in the pace and atmosphere of Whitehall when Parliament is in recess is a clear indicator of this, though then ministers and officials habitually weigh in their minds the likely reaction of party conference and parliamentary backbenchers in deciding upon the lines of foreign policy. During parliamentary sessions, the flow of questions tabled, the number of signatures appended to EDMs, reports of party meetings upstairs in the House of Commons and of the reaction of leading party members outside are all monitored as indicators of likely trouble ahead. Civil servants refer policy matters upwards according to their estimate of the degree of trouble they may arouse; and ministers consider how far they can risk offending parliamentary supporters on a particular issue, in the light not only of their need for continuing support on foreign policy in general but also of their domestic policy objectives.

The amount of energy the Labour government devoted in February 1967 to an attempt to mediate between the United States and the Soviet Union on Vietnam, at the cost of reducing its chances of achieving a number of other foreign policy objectives and of distracting its attention from pressing economic and industrial difficulties, directly reflected the strength of pressure from within the Labour Party to modify the government's policy on this issue. In December 1969 the collection of over 100 signatures from all parties in support of an EDM opposing the further sale of arms to Nigeria led to the simultaneous departure of Mr Maurice Foley (then parliamentary Under-Secretary at the FCO) and Lord Carrington for Lagos for urgent talks. Pressure from all sides of the House played a major, quite probably a crucial, part in persuading the Conservative government to alter its initial cautious response to the civil war in Pakistan in 1971 and to offer a major aid contribution to Bangladesh. The number of MPs who had visited Bangladesh on fact-finding visits for aid organizations or other bodies substantially affected the developing debate. A series of EDMs on the situation in East Bengal, signed by up to 328 MPs, were further indicators of the strength of parliamentary opinion, to which the government felt it necessary to respond.

There is some justification in the criticism often made by officials that parliamentary activity on foreign policy issues focuses disproportionately upon questions which are neither central to British overseas interests nor of widespread public concern. The 328 signatures gathered for one EDM on Bangladesh represented the largest total appended to any EDM on domestic or foreign topics during the 1971–2 parliamentary session. Several EDMs on southern Africa attracted well over 100 names, as did a Labour resolution on the withdrawal of American forces from Vietnam; a large number of EDMs on the treatment of Jewish citizens in the USSR, Syria, and elsewhere attracted 50–60 signatures, while a resolution on the situation in Burundi attracted 65. The distribution of Parliamentary Questions on foreign policy matters shows a similar lack of identity with the government's own definition of foreign policy priorities. This partly reflects the extent to which the activities of back-benchers and backbench groups cluster around the middle level of policy, where party divisions are less tightly defined; it also reflects the greater degree of manoeuvre which organized groups and 'lobbies' have at this level, and their relative success in recruiting MPs to support their causes. Partly, too, it reflects the importance within the traditions of the separate parties of the symbolic issues and principles mentioned earlier. Parliamentary pressure on these peculiarly sensitive issues is not how-ever entirely dysfunctional. It does represent the deeply-held feelings of particular groups within the political parties; and it keeps before the attention of the government a range of issues which, though perhaps not of the first importance to policy-makers, do raise major questions of the values at stake in the pursuit of foreign policy.

Since the mid-60s various changes in the powers and the working patterns of parliamentary committees have made it much easier for members of both Houses to investigate foreign policy questions. Administrative resistance has given way to official assistance to com-mittees or sub-committees wanting to conduct hearings abroad.[27] During the 1972–3 session sub-committees drawn from the Commons made fifteen overseas visits, and several sub-committees from the Lords also took evidence overseas. Members of the Select Committee on Science and Technology, for instance, visited the Woomera rocket base and had talks in Washington with White House staff, National Aero-nautics and Space Administration officials, and Congressmen during their investigation of Britain's activities in space research in 1971.[28] The replacement of the Estimates Committee by a new Expenditure Com-mittee in early 1971, with expanded terms of reference and a larger membership, was a major advance. Its trade and industry sub-committee visited Brussels in February 1973 and established a precedent by hearing evidence from two members of the European Commission. Although the Conservative government's original proposal that the Expenditure Committee should include separate sub-committees on defence and on external affairs was turned down, partly on the grounds that too many sub-committees would make unacceptable demands on MPs' time, the combined defence and external affairs sub-committee did not confine itself solely to defence and by 1973 was pressing for a change of ministerial policy whereby classified information would be released to form 'a basis for stimulating informed parliamentary and public debate in this country'.[29] The trade and industry sub-committee held a series of public hearings from May to July 1973 on the wages and conditions of

African employees of British companies operating in South Africa, taking oral evidence from representatives of twenty-eight companies as well as from civil servants and journalists, and receiving written memoranda from a further 100 companies, extending parliamentary investigation well beyond the actions of the government itself.[30] In December 1972 another Select Committee on Overseas Development was created, in response to a sustained campaign by the aid lobby and a substantial group of MPs. The activities of these committees, and the gradual expansion of Commons staff to service them, offered the prospect of enlarging the number of parliamentarians with detailed knowledge on aspects of foreign affairs.

British entry into the EEC added a further impetus to the development of specialized committees and to the involvement of MPs in matters previously considered outside their proper concern. The turn-over of Members, with the progressive retirement of MPs whose attitudes to foreign policy had been shaped in the emotional atmosphere of the 30s, and their replacement by a generation with an often more inter-ventionist idea of a backbencher's role, seemed likely to support a con-tinued increase in parliamentary investigation into foreign affairs matters. Such a development would not necessarily clarify the grand debate on the great issues of foreign policy between the two front benches; but it promises to raise the standard of informed debate and discussion on middle-level questions by backbenchers on all sides of the House.

Informed Opinion

Parliamentary activity, articles and letters in periodicals and in the quality press represent the public expression of a continuing debate on foreign policy questions among interested and expert opinion. The elite nature of British political debate, its social homogeneity and geographical concentration, and the close network of channels for formal and informal communications among its members, have often been noted. A survey of the 'active British elite' carried out in the spring of 1963, based upon a sample of entries in *Who's Who*, noted that half of those included had been to either Oxford or Cambridge; 60 per cent had attended a public school, 15 per cent the four leading schools. Nearly three-quarters of them lived within a 65-mile radius of London, an area which contains only a third of the population of the United Kingdom. Forty per cent belonged to one or more London club, nearly 15 per cent to one of the four clubs which cluster around Waterloo Place and Pall Mall – the Travellers', the Reform, the Athenaeum, and the Oxford and Cambridge. Three-quarters of them read *The Times* regularly, and nearly two-thirds said they regarded it 'as the most useful of all daily newspapers for keeping in touch with international news'; among businessmen and civil servants the proportion regularly reading *The Times* was above 80 per cent. Not surprisingly, at a time when public opinion was divided on the desirability of EEC entry and the speed of withdrawal from empire, there was a high degree of consensus among the elite on the main assumptions underlying British foreign policy. There was overwhelming agreement on the value of NATO and of the special relationship with the United States, as on the continuing importance of Britain's Common-wealth links; a minority of 10 per cent expressed scepticism about the UN, while on EEC entry a slightly larger minority, 13 per cent, were positively opposed and another 17 per cent expressed themselves as undecided.[31]

The compactness of the political elite and its high degree of consensus are even more marked among the still smaller group which represents what we may call 'the foreign policy elite'. One writer in the early 60s distinguished between what he called the 'official elite', which included among its potential members only senior officials within the Foreign Office and within those other Departments of State now drawn in-creasingly into foreign policy discussions, senior officers of the armed services and members of their intelligence staffs, members of the govern-ment and leading members of the opposition party, and the 'unofficial elite'-party discussion groups and ginger groups inside and outside Parliament, newspaper editors, leader-writers and foreign correspon-dents. The few hundred active participants in general discussion of foreign policy drawn from these groups exchanged views 'either in private or in the semi-private organs of communication' represented by the correspondence columns of the quality press and the publications of the institutes and organized bodies of London intellectual political society.[32] The hallmark of all these channels of communication was the degree to which access to them depended upon the approval of the exist-ing elite, operating therefore to exclude the maverick and the persistent non-conformer and to maintain the established consensus.

This portrait of informed opinion on foreign policy would have fitted the London of 1935 almost as closely as the London of 1960; but within the last ten or fifteen years a number of changes have widened its membership and lessened its solidarity. The activities, expertise, and number of research institutes in the foreign policy field have all grown, the most notable addition being the International Institute of Strategic Studies (IISS), founded in 1958. The interest and involvement of business and commercial elites in foreign policy questions, not negligible even in the 50s, has continued to grow. The enormous expansion of the universities, with a more than proportionate expansion in the social sciences and in studies of extra-European countries, have considerably increased the level and the geographical spread of academic expertise. Generational turnover, and the efforts made to widen recruitment to the home civil service and to the diplomatic service, have modified its social homogeneity. Whitehall attitudes, most particularly within the MoD and the Foreign Office, to non-official opinion and outside advice have shifted markedly. The greater number of those now interested, and the greater complexity of the questions which interest them, has made it less accurate to talk of a single coherent elite. Informed opinion on foreign policy matters in the early 70s was represented by a series of inter-connecting groups, focusing around particular interests – in the different regions of the world and in military, economic, or cultural aspects of foreign policy.

Participants in this continuing debate included not only the 'official' and 'unofficial' elite (as defined) and the staffs of the main institutes and university departments, but also leading members and staffs of a number of organized groups – with the staff of foreign embassies in London, foreign journalists, and foreign academic experts and researchers on its fringes. The close links between the various bodies from which they are drawn is suggested by the ease with which participants move from one occupational base to another, and by the extent of interlocking member-ships among the differing groups. Specialist journalists move on to posts in research institutes, and occasionally to university chairs. Diplomats, retiring relatively early, become active in advising companies, interest groups and political parties. Policy advisory committees of such respected groups as the United Nations Association (UNA) or the British Council of Churches include MPs, academics, journalists, and former officials, and the full-time staff who service them have regular contacts with Whitehall. Members of one committee of the British Council of Churches in 1966 included not only churchmen, academics, and politicians, but also official 'observers' from three Whitehall Departments.[33] Journalists, academics, the staff of research institutes, and ex-officials advise the political parties and join in the activities of their various societies and research groups.

In the early 70s retired diplomats were among the most active 'influentials' linking the various groups and meeting points of informed opinion. Lord Trevelyan, a former ambassador to Egypt, Iraq, and the Soviet Union, was in 1970 a director of British Petroleum, the British Bank of the Middle East, and Matheson & Company, a trading company prominent in Hong Kong and the Far East. He was also president of the Council of the Corporation of Foreign Bondholders, and chairman of the Council of Chatham House (the Royal Institute of International Affairs).[34] Another diplomatic life peer, Lord Gladwyn, had become spokesman on foreign affairs to the Liberal Party and the Liberal member of the parliamentary delegation to the Council of Europe, as well as vice-president of the Atlantic Treaty Association, chairman of Britain in Europe, and author of several books promoting the cause of Community entry. Sir Frank Roberts, a former ambassador to Yugoslavia, the USSR, and West Germany, was an advisory director of Unilever and adviser on international affairs to Lloyds, the president of the British Atlantic Committee, vice-president of the Anglo-German Association, and a member of the Council of Chatham House; in 1969 he had served as one of the three members of the Ducan Committee (with Andrew

Shonfield and Sir Val Duncan, of Rio Tinto Zinc). Some leading businessmen had similarly wide-ranging commitments. Lord Campbell of Eskan was in 1970 president both of Booker Brothers McConnell and of the West India Committee, chairman of the *New Statesman* and of the Commonwealth Sugar Exporters' Group, a sponsor of the Movement for Colonial Freedom, an executive member of the Africa Bureau, and a Labour life peer. J. H. Keswick, the chairman of Matheson and Co., was a council member of the Corporation of Foreign Bondholders, a director of Barclays Bank, the chairman of the China Association and the president of the Sino-British Trade Council; in 1972 he was given a knighthood, exceptionally, in the *Diplomatic Service List* of the New Year Honours for 'services to British interests in the Far East'. A number of MPs had a similarly broad range of commitments, from advisory committees to business to research institutes.

Much of the small change of opinion-swapping and of diplomatic discourse takes place at the innumerable social gatherings which mark London diplomatic, commercial, and political life.[35] Dinner meetings of such bodies as the Foreign Affairs Club, the members of which include journalists, retired officials, MPs, and businessmen, provide opportunities to hear foreign and British statesmen and to ask questions informally. They also give ministers an opportunity to guide or respond to elite opinion; Sir Alec Douglas-Home, for instance, used the occasion of a meeting of the South Africa Club in 1973 to make a major speech on British policy in Africa, reported in the quality press.[36] Open meetings at Chatham House draw audiences of businessmen, journalists, academics, parliamentarians, party research staff, and officials to hear foreign visitors and British experts on international topics, to fire questions at them and to state their views.

More privately and more thoroughly, the various research institutes sponsor conferences and study groups on particular aspects of inter-national relations, with a more select but similarly mixed membership of officials, experts, journalists and businessmen. The oldest of these, the Royal United Services Institution (RUSI), has in recent years become somewhat less of a professional body for members of the armed services and more of a focus for conferences and seminars on questions of defence and defence policy, with serving military officers, officials, journalists, and academics as participants. Its slender financial resources were strengthened a little during the 60s by a number of grants from the MoD and from foreign sources. While not employing any research staff, it published, apart from the *RUSI Journal*, a number of pamphlets, which circulated among the services, Whitehall, and other interested students; the MoD itself in 1970 ordered 1,000 copies of a critical study by Michael Howard of *The Central Organisation of Defence*.

Chatham House was founded in 1920, to 'encourage and facilitate the scientific study of international questions, and to publish or arrange for the publication of works with these objects'.[37] With a small full-time research staff, a Council which represented a cross-section of foreign policy 'influentials', and a series of study groups and research programmes covering aspects of international affairs relevant to British foreign policy, it had the reputation of representing the foreign policy 'establishment'. During the 60s it was supported by substantial grants for research projects from the Ford Foundation. In 1972 the costs of maintaining its activities and research libraries led it to accept for the first time a non-recurrent grant of £20,000 from the FCO. Its financial resources, however, remained, apart from the income from a substantial endowment, primarily dependent upon the subscriptions of its individual and corporate members, which included a large number of banks and companies with international interests, newspapers, several trade unions, universities, and government Departments. Its director until the end of 1971 was Sir Kenneth Younger, a former Labour MP and Foreign Office minister; his successor, Andrew Shonfield, had previously served as chairman of the Social Science Research Council, and earlier as economic editor of the *Observer* and as Director of Studies at Chatham House. A number of other smaller institutes covered particular areas of international interest, similarly initiating research, sponsoring conferences, and setting up study groups. Some of these also received limited assistance from the Whitehall Departments to which they most directly related. The Federal Trust for Education and Research, focusing primarily on European questions, was receiving in the early 70s a regular grant-in-aid of £10,000 from the FCO; the Overseas Development Institute was receiving a rising contribution from the ODA.[38]

The establishment of the IISS in 1958 was itself an interesting example of communication and cooperation amongst various sections of informed opinion. The proposal for such a body came originally from the Commission on International Affairs of the British Council of Churches, a group which included among its lay members a number of retired officials and a former Director of Naval Intelligence. Gaining support from a number of defence journalists and Labour MPs, they were able to persuade the Ford Foundation to provide an initial grant of $150,000. Under its first director, Alastair Buchan, formerly the *Observer* defence correspondent, the institute won the confidence of the MoD and of students of defence policy in other European countries. Its role as 'an educative force of some consequence among members of the political and official hierarchies' was widely accepted as having informed and extended the debate on defence policy.[39]

The journalists who participate in the informed debate include foreign editors and leader-writers of a number of newspapers, who attend institute meetings and conferences and see it as part of their job to keep abreast of expert opinion, and defence correspondents from the quality papers, who have established a close relationship with the MoD and participate actively in discussions within the RUSI and the IISS.[40] As questions of international trade and finance have become more directly political a number of economic correspondents have also become involved in discussions of foreign policy. Diplomatic correspondents, despite their privileged status vis-à-vis the Foreign Office, are perhaps at a certain disadvantage compared with other specialist correspondents, from the breadth of the field that they have to cover. Newspaper economics have brought about a reduction in the size of their diplomatic staffs while the number of independent states and the importance of extra-European developments have grown; the resulting scramble from, for instance, a briefing from the relevant FCO department on Middle East developments to rapid reference to newspaper files and interviews with press attachés of Middle East embassies, and then to a story on Anglo-Chinese relations, leaves little time for relaxed consideration.[41] One continuing effect of the close relationship between the Foreign Office and diplomatic correspondents is to maintain some degree of insulation between press coverage of foreign and domestic political issues. It remained in 1972 unusual for the Foreign Secretary to meet the 'Lobby', the corps of political correspondents; for him to have met them regularly would have been considered a slight to the diplomatic correspondents.[42]

The foreign press corps in London remains on the fringes of informed opinion. It has its own organization, the Foreign Press Association, which hears British and foreign politicians at its regular dinners. Respected foreign journalists receive more than formal cooperation from the FCO News department, and have access to many of the informal discussions and conferences described above. Their reports, read within the FCO and by other official and non-official students of foreign newspapers, also contribute at the margin to the consensus of received opinion. Their opposite numbers abroad, the foreign correspondents of the British news media, contribute significantly to the focus of London discussion by their selection and interpretation of foreign news. The overwhelming majority of full-time correspondents are stationed in Western Europe and North America.[43] Elsewhere freelance or part-time correspondents are employed, normally supplemented by the British foreign news agency, Reuter's, and other sources, and during crises by teams of visiting 'firemen' flown out from Britain; Independent Television News, with only one permanently-based correspondent abroad, relies almost entirely upon this method. This makes for an unavoidable 'threshold' effect in the coverage of extra-European news. The East Bengal crisis of 1971 and the Ethiopian famine of 1973 exhibited a similar pattern in British news coverage, of initial neglect followed by efforts to arouse editorial interest from the aid organizations, visits by MPs and correspondents, culminating in extended coverage by TV teams.

In some circumstances, common reliance on each other's newspapers and news agencies can lead to a certain circularity both in the definition of newsworthiness and in the interrelation of news, well exemplified in 'the procession of television reporters in the early 1960s to Switzerland to interview Swiss private bankers on their views about the British economy – views which were in fact mostly derived from the British press'.[44] Particular foreign correspondents or home-based journalists, with the help of sympathetic editors, can however materially affect the pattern of debate. Adam Raphael's reports on working conditions in South Africa, worked up into a campaign by the *Guardian* in early 1973, provoked the Expenditure Committee's trade and industry sub-committee into a parliamentary investigation; welcomed by the anti-apartheid lobby as strengthening their case, they also led the CBI to consider the social responsibilities of British companies operating in South Africa.

While 'contacts with unofficial opinion on international problems (including Chatham House and the Institute for Strategic Studies)' were in the first place the responsibility of the Planning Staff, by 1970 most FCO departments accepted the need for contacts with non-official experts within their area.[45] A number of seminars on different regional and functional topics had also been arranged, with non-official participants. The traditional civil service attitude to contacts with universities and to sabbaticals for officials, according to one diplomat, had been 'that any civil servant worth his salt should be a Fellow of All Souls anyway'. But by the early 70s up to twelve FCO officials a year were taking sabbaticals in universities and institutes, and a much smaller number of academics had served for a period in the Foreign Office. Exchanges of personnel between the civil service and industry and the City had also made for closer communication with opinion outside. A limited number of respected academics, MPs, and party research staff received regular but unattributable surveys of developments in Asia, Africa, and the communist countries from the FCO. Foreign Office personnel were often active participants in seminars and conferences outside Whitehall. Two advisory panels to the Foreign Office, on disarmament and on UN questions, established by the Labour Government in the first flush of enthusiasm in 1964, continued to meet under the succeeding Conservative government at roughly six-monthly intervals, bringing together half-a-dozen MPs, a few academics, and influential members of the most respected groups. But although ministers and officials continued to regard these as valuable, outside participants were generally sceptical, seeing them as opportunities for the exposition of governmental policy rather than for an open exchange of views.[46]

The degree to which this wider circle can offer Whitehall and Westminster alternative perspectives on foreign policy issues is more generally limited by two factors. First, the difficulty which even the most expert outsider experiences in discovering the terms of debate within Whitehall on his own field unavoidably limits his own ability to contribute and his usefulness as an alternative source of opinion to officials or ministers. Secondly, the very closeness of the interconnecting establishment of official and non-official informed opinion and the advantage which official access to privileged information gives reinforces the tendency for the consensus of informed opinion to reflect the consensus of Whitehall. 'The result is that, while Whitehall continues to respect Chatham House' (and the other institutes and organizations) as centres of information and learning, 'it does not find it exactly a hotbed of new and inspiring ideas'.[47] The conventions of the informed debate, as well as the problems of acess to official debate and information, do not perhaps encourage novelty or inspiration.

Organized Opinion

A large though constantly changing network of non-official organizations is concerned to a greater or lesser extent with foreign policy questions.[48] The most respected groups maintain regular and close contacts with particular Whitehall Departments; a handful of voluntary organizations receive grants-in-aid from 'their' Departments. The more radical or revolutionary have little or no foothold in established political society, and must necessarily focus their attention on the party conferences or the general public. Some organizations represent economic interests abroad; others are purely promotional groups, while yet others blend idealism and interest. Many have close contacts with foreign organizations and governments and some receive financial assistance from them. Foreign governments and non-governmental foreign organizations thus also help to shape the domestic context of British foreign policy-making.

Economic interests have organized themselves to influence the government's foreign commercial and economic policy for over 200 years. The 'peak' organizations, the CBI and the TUC, operate primarily at the middle and higher levels of foreign policy, leaving more specialized associations to lobby the government on less central issues. The CBI's organization for foreign policy issues includes an overseas directorate and a number of committees of businessmen.[49] CBI representatives participate in the activities of the OECD through its Business and Industry Advisory Committee, and form part of the British delegation to the ILO. Close links have been established with employers' organizations throughout the EEC. The CBI was particularly active in lobbying for the Labour government to renew Britain's application to join the European Community. It published an industrial appraisal of *Britain in Europe* in late 1966, and a revised edition in January 1970, circulating copies to a wide range of ministers, senior civil servants, and MPs. There followed invitations to meet CBI members over lunch and discuss the report's implications. In response to a number of Parliamentary Questions, in January 1970 the Prime Minister announced that the government's White Paper on Community entry would take account of the CBI report.[50]

The Association of British Chambers of Commerce, and the larger

Chambers of Commerce themselves, maintained a not dissimilar network of committees concerned with overseas questions, of links with parallel organizations in Western Europe and elsewhere, and of regular contacts with Whitehall Departments. When British entry to the EEC was in prospect, the major trade associations, covering such sectors of industry as motor manufacture or electrical goods, similarly moved closer to their Continental colleagues. By the end of 1972 the National Farmers' Union (NFU) had an office in Brussels, and many other associations had begun to play an active role in the many parallel Community-wide organizations. Representations to the government on international matters and contacts with their counterparts in other countries are part of the close and continuing relationship between government and industry – made primarily to their sponsoring Whitehall Departments rather than to the FCO. The closeness of this relationship is suggested by the not infrequent inclusion of interest group representatives on government delegations to international conferences and negotiations.[51]

Groups concerned specifically with international trade and the interests of British business and investment abroad cut across the overseas responsibilities of the industrial associations: the West Africa and West India Committees, the Malaysia-Singapore Commercial Association, the Middle East Association, and so on. The oldest of these date from the eighteenth and nineteenth centuries – the West India Committee from 1750, the Corporation of Foreign Bondholders from 1873, the China Association from 1889; many more were set up with the expansion of international trade in the 50s. Some serve as meeting places for businessmen, bankers, and officials with interests in a particular region, as a point of contact with the embassies concerned and with visiting foreign statesmen. The chairman of the China Association frequently pressed the government during the Cultural Revolution to make stronger representations to Peking about the treatment of British ships and sailors in Shanghai. The West Africa Committee's salaried 'adviser', Sir Evelyn Hone, a former Governor of Northern Rhodesia, took part in discussions with the Nigerian government during the civil war, both directly and through the Committee's representative in Lagos. During the 60s growing governmental attempts to boost exports resulted in committees financed by the government but composed of businessmen, with the object of promoting exports to various regions, grouped (until its abolition in May 1971) under the British National Export Council (BNEC). Most of these associations and committees were mainly concerned with economic relations with 'their' particular region, although these interests tended to include also the promotion of cultural and educational links or the direction of British aid policy.

Promotional groups relate more directly to the Foreign Office since most of them are concerned with aspects of political relations with other countries. The great exception is the aid lobby, which established close contacts with the ODM soon after it was established in 1964. In 1972 in many ways the ODA was acting as an ally and a sponsor of the voluntary organizations; one of their main coordinating bodies, the Voluntary Committee on Overseas Aid and Development (VCOAD), received a £20,000 grant-in-aid towards the cost of its secretariat. A rather smaller number of promotional groups with primarily domestic aims and interests concern themselves with international issues on more than the peripheral basis of passing resolutions which are rapidly forgotten and sending delegations to occasional meetings with like-minded groups in other countries. The British Council of Churches is one of the most active of these: concerned, through its international department and through its association with Christian Aid, with a wide range of foreign policy issues, from disarmament to the sugar trade, and actively engaged in promoting these causes throughout the country. The relatively small degree of over-lap between promotional groups concerned with foreign policy and groups promoting domestic issues reflects the continuing separation of foreign policy issues from domestic, except in the sphere of industrial and economic interests.

The range of interest, scale of activity, size of membership, and degree of acceptability to Whitehall and to informed opinion of the innumerable voluntary organizations primarily concerned with international questions all vary enormously. The UNA, for instance, would be included with the British Council of Churches in any list of respected organizations with general foreign policy interests; with a professional staff in London, the leaders of the three main political parties as its honorary presidents, a number of committees responsible for its activities in human rights, disarmament, aid, and education, and a network of branches throughout Britain. More specialized groups, with smaller active memberships, pro-mote the interests of foreign minorities, political prisoners, and other disadvantaged groups. Several of these are associated with similar groups in other countries, and many hold consultative status with the UN or one of the international organizations associated with it. Nearly 100 societies exist to promote good relations between Britain and one or more foreign countries, with activities which range from social and cultural to representational and propagandistic.[52]

The organizations whose objectives are largely acceptable to informed opinion and whose activities respect the conventional limits of British politics in effect act as a bridge between informed opinion and the wider public. MPs who sit on their committees, academics and journalists who advise them, improve their access to the national media and their aware-ness of informed and expert thinking; contacts with officials, who may on occasion attend conferences or even agree to speak on 'safe' subjects, bring the most respected groups effectively into the informed debate. Through their attempts to raise public awareness about international issues they widen communication between the elite and at least some sections of the broader public, whether their efforts are aimed at providing documentation for those already interested (as in the case of Amnesty International and the Minority Rights Group), or at educating the uninterested public or even working through the schools (as in the case of the World Development Movement or the Council for Education in World Citizenship). Some groups represent opposing causes, each with supporters among informed opinion, such as the competing anti-apartheid and pro-South Africa lobbies or the pro-Israeli and pro-Palestinian groups. Here Whitehall officials tread very cautiously – though MPs and publicists are to be found in the front ranks on either side. But there are very few groups with enough public support not to value the respect and sympathy of Westminster and Whitehall, if these can be won, and to feel a certain pressure to confine their activities within conventional limits. The strongest such groups are those which promote good relations with Israel, with a base in the Jewish vote and Anglo-Jewish society firm enough to ensure respect for their opinions. Groups whose objectives clearly lie outside the informed consensus look for support from a wider public: for the peace movement, through efforts at persuasion, for CND also through efforts to capture, if not the PLP, at least the Labour Party Conference, for the Vietnam Solidarity Campaign and similar campaigning groups through mass demonstrations and public meetings. The way in which the informed consensus disadvantages dissenting groups was illustrated by the difficulties which anti-Common Market groups experienced between 1969 and 1971 in obtaining detailed information from the government or in getting publicity in the national media.

The attempts of foreign governments to influence the domestic debate on foreign policy in Britain focus around their relationship with sympathetic groups, their cultivation of informed opinion and the press, and their efforts to reach the wider public. Most of their activities are in no sense subversive of British sovereignty, or underhand. Indeed, they form part of the accepted pattern of diplomatic representation and are mirrored by the activities of British missions abroad. Certain levels of acceptability are however immediately apparent, reflecting the British government's view of the state of relations with particular foreign governments and of the friendliness or unfriendliness of their intentions towards this country.

Most Anglo-'Ruritanian' societies maintain close links with 'their' embassies, as do the parallel parliamentary groups. Embassy officials attend their functions and speak at their meetings; embassy receptions are often among the highlights of their activities. They often receive material assistance, in kind or in cash, to help with administration or to support particular efforts. The Brazilian government, for instance, during the 60s provided a grant to the Anglo-Brazilian Society to enable it to employ a full-time secretary; the Danish embassy lent its staff to help with the secretarial side of the Anglo-Danish Society.[53]

Many of the Anglo-'Ruritanian' societies attract the informed and influential, and so act as a forum through which representatives of foreign governments can hope to exert influence. There are, of course, many other points of contact and channels of influence. Parliamentary groups provide opportunities for the ambassador or visiting ministers to address groups of MPs, the usefulness of such meetings varying according to the standing of the MPs attending. Officers of these groups may assist by writing sympathetic newspaper articles or letters to *The Times*, or even by tabling Parliamentary Questions. Invitations to MPs, journalists, publicists, even academics and student leaders, to make sponsored visits to their countries may bring returns in the shape of more favourable press comment and a friendlier atmosphere. The Israeli and South African governments, among the most generous in their invitations, have also aroused the most public controversy; but the West German and the United States governments and a number of East European and Arab governments are also active.[54] Private dinner parties and receptions cultivate good personal relations and provide opportunities for foreign diplomats to inform their governments of received opinion towards their countries' interests and to work to influence it. At ambassadorial dinners British officials, politicians, businessmen, and journalists meet visiting statesmen in a congenial atmosphere; and such groups of specialist embassy staff as the Association of Economic Representatives or the Military Attachés' Association invite corresponding British specialists to regular luncheons.

Relations between foreign missions and Whitehall Departments are governed by established conventions. Formally, missions must approach the British government initially through the Foreign Office, even if the subject they wish to raise is primarily about civil aviation or double taxation agreements. In 1959 Commonwealth high commissioners had the distinctive right 'to deal direct with other departments of Government', so that 'the High Commissioner and his staff at appropriate levels have contacts of an informal sort throughout the machinery of Government'.[55] In practice in the late 50s those non-Commonwealth governments most closely aligned to Britain had just as easy access to Whitehall as a whole. The United States government cooperated at all levels with its opposite numbers in several Whitehall Departments on an intimate basis. By the early 70s all distinction between Commonwealth and non-Commonwealth governments had disappeared, and officials from the governments of European Community members were in direct and regular contact with their opposite numbers in Whitehall, not only through specialist attachés in London embassies but also through shared membership of intergovernmental committees and by telephone; able therefore to exchange views and to seek each other's support in bargaining with the other Departments of their own government. Less friendly governments attempting to contact the DTI or the Ministry of Agriculture would, however, be referred back to the Foreign Office for clearance; anticipating such a response, most would therefore approach the FCO in the first place. Ostracism of a foreign mission from all contacts with

Whitehall is a gesture of extreme displeasure, imposed only after approval from the Cabinet.

Direct intervention in British policy-making is open only to those governments recognized as British allies or confident of support from within the elite. For example, during the long series of interdepartmental discussions on defence policy East of Suez in 1966–7, the US and Australian governments made sustained efforts to strengthen the hands of the Foreign Office and the MoD by pressing their views at both official and ministerial level. Lee Kuan Yew, the Prime Minister of Singapore, additionally used his links within the PLP to mobilize support. On his second visit in one year, in December 1968, he succeeded in postponing the deadline for withdrawal from Singapore by a crucial six months, after discussions with senior ministers.[56] Less successfully, the South African government attempted in 1970 to push the incoming Conservative government into a premature confirmation of its pre-election pledge on arms sales, by arranging for its Foreign Minister to arrive in London immediately after the election, and by giving their 'shopping list' to the British press.[57]

Relations with the press are cultivated primarily through embassy press attachés and the 'social lobby'. Ambassadors and their staffs often participate in the public debate by writing letters to the quality papers or by seeking out journalists and editors to press their side of the case. A number of foreign governments also advertise extensively in the British press, to publicize statements of policy, present a favourable image of their country, or correct what they see as distorted reports. Not all of this activity is aimed at the British public. A series of full-page advertisements in *The Times* and the *New York Times* promoting the official biography of Kim Il Sung, for instance, were followed by claims in North Korean newspapers that the world press was publishing laudatory articles on their national hero.[58] The scale of advertisements by Arab governments in the quality press in the early 70s reflected the view of their missions in Britain that this was the only avenue open to them to publicize their case, because of pro-Israeli pressures on the media. Such pro-Israeli pressure is largely informal; the South African government, in contrast, withdrew thirteen columns of advertising from *The Times* in 1970 in protest against a decision to allow advertisements from anti-apartheid organizations in a supplement on South Africa.[59]

Efforts to reach the wider public extend beyond the national press, to provision of articles to local newspapers, circulation of official literature and magazines, and promotion of films and exhibitions In the first six months of 1972 the author saw in Manchester cinemas subsidiary feature films describing the forward-looking development programme in Saudi Arabia, the dependence of New Zealand on trade with Britain, and the rebuilding of Munich and its symbolic importance as demonstrating the reshaping of German society. For these and other purposes foreign governments employ public relations agencies – for most of the time without arousing controversy, though the activities of Voice and Vision on behalf of the Central African Federation in 1961–2, of Markpress on behalf of the Biafran government during the Nigerian civil war, and of Maurice Fraser and Associates on behalf of the Greek government in 1969 all became minor *causes célèbres*.[60] Members of foreign missions in London also receive a large number of requests for information and speakers from schools and societies, which they strive to meet in the hope of increasing understanding of their countries.

Non-governmental actors also indirectly affect the domestic debate on foreign policy. The Ford Foundation, as we have noted, has provided substantial financial support for studies of defence policy and of European integration, which have fed back into the government's perception of policy alternatives. Members of foreign political parties linked to British parties have intervened in party discussions, not always with great effect. The offices of international organizations in Britain, above all the European Communities Information Office, provide speakers, circulate literature, and sponsor meetings and conferences. Most of these activities are aimed at informed opinion rather than the wider public; for them, as for most other organizations attempting to influence domestic opinion on foreign policy in Britain, it is informed opinion which counts above all.

The Wider Public

International issues appear remote from the day-to-day problems which preoccupy most people, except when acute crisis forces say the imposition of petrol rationing or the mobilization of military reserves. The idea that the government is responsible for foreign policy tends to make the public hold the government responsible for international developments outside its control, for example for the rising cost of imported foodstuffs or the declining international competitiveness of British textiles or of the shipbuilding industry. Opinion poll evidence over the last ten years and more has consistently confirmed the low salience of international issues in comparison with the staple issues of the cost of living, housing, taxation, and the domestic economy.

It is arguable that the level of public interest in international questions has been lower since World War II than before. The half million members which the League of Nations Union achieved between the wars has, for instance, never been matched by its successor, the UNA, whose membership has only briefly risen above a tenth of that. The organization which has come closest to creating mass interest and involvement in a major issue of foreign policy since 1945 was probably CND: approximately 100,000 people took part in its Easter marches in 1960 and 1961, and groups of supporters held demonstrations and worked to arouse public interest throughout the country.[61] Foreign policy matters have not been a major issue at any general election since 1945.

Public opinion might be enlightened and educated, and popular interest raised, through the medium of the press or the efforts of organized groups, of the political parties or of the government itself. Newspaper, radio, and TV reports on international developments are the main sources of information and interpretation for the vast majority of the public. Over the last decade coverage of foreign news, particularly of developments in the United States and Western Europe, has improved considerably, most markedly within the 'quality' press – though among popular newspapers only the *Daily Mirror* has made any sustained attempt to educate its readers on international issues. Some promotional groups have attempted to widen the circle of active debate on foreign policy. Through mass lobbies of MPs, the organization of national petitions, and letters in the national and local press, the groups concerned with aid and development have helped to keep interest in the developing world alive, despite the decline in interest in Commonwealth affairs. During the Nigerian civil war a brief upsurge of public sympathy for Biafra had some influence on Parliament and on the government, aroused and encouraged by campaigning journalists and supported by a number of Catholic groups. On such middle-level issues, where party lines are not tightly drawn or the government's prestige so firmly committed, it is easier for wider public opinion to have some effect. Where 'special publics' exist with an interest in particular issues – Jewish voters on the Middle East, Bengali voters on Bangladesh – their influence, exerted through their MPs as well as through voluntary associations, is likely to be greater. But on most issues those responsible for making policy are well aware that the groups which lobby them do not have the backing of public at large.

The role of the political parties in explaining and interpreting policy to their supporters has been inhibited by their internal differences on foreign policy issues. Bipartisan support for NATO and for a defence policy based upon the nuclear deterrent helped to limit the spread of unilateralist attitudes among Labour supporters at the end of the 50s, just as bipartisan support for German rearmament had helped to carry the electorate with the Conservative government some years before. But on the two applications to join the EEC internal divisions in both the major parties helped to dampen down debate, so that the United Kingdom entered the European Communities at the beginning of 1973 without the advantages or the implications being made clear to the general public. Successive Labour and Conservative governments had claimed that it would be premature to mobilize public opinion in favour of entry while they were still negotiating, for fear either of weakening their negotiating position or of losing political support if their efforts should fail. Yet government efforts to carry public opinion with it once entry had been achieved hardly extended beyond the provision of a series of small leaflets in post offices and support for a cultural festival to celebrate entry, 'Fanfare for Europe', which concentrated its activities predominantly on London.[62] The Labour Party in opposition between 1970 and

1974 was too much preoccupied with maintaining a façade of unity on this divisive issue to give any public lead.

Successive governments appear to have regarded public opinion as a negative constraint upon their freedom of action in foreign policy, without drawing the conclusion that the public needs therefore to be informed and led. The difficulty of persuading voters to accept major changes or particular deprivations has often been taken by ministers to exclude alternatives from 'practical' politics, from the 1930s to the present day. It was generally accepted within both parties in 1956 that the unpopularity of national service necessitated its abolition, in spite of the difficulties this would make for meeting continuing defence commitments. In 1965 Labour ministers were convinced that public opinion would not support the use of force in meeting the unilateral Rhodesian declaration of independence; though little effort had been made during the previous year to prepare public opinion to accept such a possibility. In 1973 ministers and officials were arguing in private that public hesitancy over the EEC made it impossible for the government to pursue more than a minimalist policy within the Community.

Successive governments have given financial support on a small scale to a few promotional groups working to educate public opinion on accepted issues, such as the UN or NATO. Government attitudes to Parliament and to the press on foreign policy issues, however, have reflected a belief in the desirability of restricting public information and public debate. The relationship between the Foreign Office and diplomatic correspondents is one in which journalists are very heavily dependent upon FCO approval for continued access, and are open to 'the subtle but very powerful pressure put on journalists who cause "embarrassment" (i.e. adopt a critical attitude to the conduct of British foreign policy or draw heavily on other sources of information beyond the FO and a handful of Western embassies)'.[63]

Government management of the press is reinforced by the Official Secrets Act and the 'D'-notice system, whereby a form of self-censorship on sensitive issues is operated by a committee composed of journalists and Whitehall officials, serviced by a full-time secretary and chaired by the Permanent Under-Secretary of State of the MoD.[64] The 'D'-notice system, which was established in 1912 under the 1911 Official Secrets Act, was the focus of a major parliamentary and press dispute in 1967, over which its secretary resigned, and was again publicly questioned in 1973 when, ironically, influence was exerted to remove parts of the text of a TV programme questioning the continued usefulness of the Official Secrets Acts.[65] These Acts themselves came into question over the prosecution of a journalist in 1970 for unauthorized publication of a report to the government on the war in Nigeria.[66] This case led to another committee of inquiry, into section 2 of the 1911 Official Secrets Act. The Conservative government accepted in principle the committee's recommendation that section 2, which deals with the wrongful communication of information, should be repealed, but added that 'the complexity of the problem is bound to mean that the process of preparing legislation will take a lot of time'.[67]

This restrictive attitude to the provision of information on foreign policy also restricts informed attempts to discuss and criticize the alternatives facing the government. One academic, writing in 1963, described 'the gradual throttling of the flow of information to the public on the background of British foreign policy . . . over the last five decades' as crippling to informed discussion; deploring the demise of the diplomatic blue book, and the government's failure to provide any substitute for this detailed publication of diplomatic despatches.[68] The relaxation of the fifty-year rule restricting access to official files to thirty years has now eased the problems of historians, but there has been little easing in government attitudes to the release of explanation or documentation on current policy. One of the British government's first initiatives in the EEC was to press its partners for a tightening of security on discussions of policy.

If some degree of secrecy is clearly necessary, particularly in defence policy and matters relating to military intelligence, it is hard not to conclude that Whitehall's insistence on secrecy and its concern to keep information out of the press are somewhat exaggerated. The American government's regular publication of the *Department of State Bulletin*, for instance, and its support for such informative journals as *Problems of Communism* contrasts sharply with the practice of the FCO, which in the early 70s distributed three-monthly reviews of developments in different international regions to select list of recipients in conditions of great secrecy and complete nonattributability.[69] Some officials believe that the restrictive attitude to the press is due to ministerial insistence on secrecy; even suggesting that ministerial displeasure at official 'leaks' had sharpened in the last decade. But the attitude of some senior officials is suggested by the proposal from one retired Permanent Under-Secretary that the Defence White Paper – one of the few regular reviews of international policy – should be discontinued 'because first of all it is certainly a very elaborate document which must take a great deal of time and effort to produce'.[70]

This attitude is not, of course, confined to foreign policy matters. The publication by the *Sunday Times* in October 1972 of a discussion document prepared within the Department of the Environment on the future shape of the railway network led to a vigorous police investigation of possible breaches of the Official Secrets Act. Treasury ministers were resisting pressure from the Expenditure Committee to publish the economic assessments on which their expenditure forecasts were based, as their colleagues were resisting the demands of its Defence and External Affairs Sub-committee.[71] Some comfort may be taken from the increasing pressure from parliamentary committees for the provision of fuller explanations of government policy. In the meanwhile the obstacles put in the way of the interested observer, academic critic, journalist, or MP in following, understanding, and criticizing the evolution of government policy in foreign affairs have impoverished informed debate and helped to minimize public interest. At a time when international and domestic issues are becoming more and more closely intertwined, it has helped to perpetuate the myth that foreign policy is a separate field, a 'mystery' outside domestic politics.

Part II: Patterns of Policy-Making

5: Defence and Technology

THE RELATIONSHIP between foreign policy and defence, between the maintenance and exercise of sovereignty and the defence of the realm, has been for centuries at the heart of British overseas policy. In traditional terms, defence should be the servant of foreign policy. The balance of forces at home, the deployment of troops abroad, the whole size and shape of the defence effort, should reflect the fundamental assumptions and objectives of foreign policy, and when necessary provide the means to achieve those objectives. Conversely, foreign policy objectives should reflect, and be limited by, the potential ability of the armed forces to supply the means for their achievement.

Such a balance between defence and foreign policy has not obtained in Britain for much of the period since World War II. Certainly, close military cooperation with the American armed forces, in intelligence, training, strategy, and equipment in the twenty years after the war reflected (and reinforced) the assumption that the 'special relationship' was central to British foreign policy; just as the move towards closer military cooperation within Western Europe in 1968–9, and the British initiative to establish the Eurogroup, reflected and reinforced the Labour government's reorientation of foreign policy towards a European commitment. Certainly too, at the outbreak of the Korean war, a government which had only just adjusted its force structure and strategy to postwar conditions and to the loss of India made a strenuous attempt to bring Britain's forces and equipment up to the level which the extent of foreign commitments and the immediacy of the external threat appeared to demand. But from then on the size of the defence effort was reduced far more rapidly than any corresponding reductions in commitments or declared objectives, and for a decade and a half until the final withdrawal from East of Suez, Britain's defence capabilities remained embarassingly out of balance with successive governments' declared objectives and commitments. Perhaps the classic case of a commitment made without considering the consequences in terms of defence policy was Eden's pledge in 1954 permanently to maintain four divisions and a tactical air force on the Continent, made as a diplomatic initiative after the collapse of the scheme for a European Defence Community. The process of colonial withdrawal saw a succession of further pledges of military support, too often without any readily apparent means for their fulfilment. In both the 1956–7 and the 1965–6 Defence Reviews, substantial reorientations in the balance of Britain's defence effort were made without significant parallel adjustments in the declared objectives of foreign policy; and in both cases the adjustment in these objectives followed, rather painfully, later.

A 'rational' model of policy-making for defence would postulate a process of feedback in which the severity of the perceived external threats to existing British commitments and objectives, the level of expenditure which policy-makers were prepared to accept and to maintain public support for, the forces and equipment which this level of expenditure would provide, and the ability of those forces to meet the demands placed upon them, would be balanced against those commitments and objectives – changes in one being reflected in consequent adjustments in the others. That such a process of adjustment operated so imperfectly in the fifteen years before the final withdrawal from East of Suez in 1968 is related, first, to the association of defence with some of the most powerful symbols of national sovereignty and self-esteem, second to the machinery within which policy was made, and third, to the distinctive constraints which bear upon defence policy.

Defence issues are particularly close to the mystique which attaches to foreign policy. Memories of wartime exploits and half-forgotten ceremonies, images of national pride and national standing, cloud the vision of politicians and of the public. The emotional appeal of defence questions offered political leaders a powerful instrument for swaying public opinion: associating government actions in this field with images 'above' the political debate, with considerations of national status and memories of 'Britain's finest hour'. Such symbolic and emotional associations were most firmly attached, for twenty five years or more after World War II, to the nuclear deterrent and to the East of Suez role: twin symbols of Britain's continuing great power status and global interests.[1] At a lower level, however, they also attached to particular services, to particular armaments, even to particular regiments. For a politician to suggest that the navy's role must be reduced was to risk an upsurge of opposing sentiment, not only in dockyard towns but throughout the country. Proposals to amalgamate regiments, to make possible more flexible distribution of shrinking manpower, created successive protests, which reached their peak in the campaign against disbanding the Argyll and Sutherland Highlanders in 1969–70. The obstacles to rational planning, at different levels, were therefore formidable. In defence debates in Parliament in the 50s and 60s repeated calls for a bipartisan approach to defence policy from both sides of the House, as well as nostalgic references to the bipartisan consultations institutionalized before 1914 and between the wars in the Committee of Imperial Defence, testify to the strength of these associations for the opposition as well as for the government of the day.

The framework within which defence policy has been made since World War II will be examined in greater detail below. It may be noted here that, until the defence reorganization of 1963–4, the distribution of resources within the total defence budget was decided as much by a process of inter-service bargaining as by the imposition of an overall strategy, and that even after this reorganization political constraints inhibited a wider reconsideration of the balance between expenditure, forces in being, overseas commitments, and declared objectives. The relative insulation from other political considerations of the network of interests, of interested commentators, of parliamentarians, servicemen, and civil servants which provided the context within which defence policy was made, and the secrecy in which that policy was made, also helped to inhibit a reconsideration of existing assumptions. A brief examination of the slow process of withdrawal from East of Suez, between 1964 and 1968, may help to illustrate these points, and provide a basis for discussing how far the structure and context of policy-making for defence has altered since then.

The most powerful and distinctive constraint on defence policy is cost. Defence is overwhelmingly the most expensive aspect of external policy, a direct and major competitor with domestic programmes of public expenditure.[2] Defence is accordingly closely bound by the disciplines of the budgetary process, subjected to a regular and detailed scrutiny which many other areas of external policy hardly justify. The difference of perspective which this gives to officials within the Defence Secretariat from those within the Foreign Office is suggested by one official's comment: 'in the Ministry of Defence we cost foreign policy'. A second distinctive constraint derives from the services' demand for manpower. Given the exclusion on political grounds of any form of compulsory service, the successful maintenance of voluntary recruitment and re-engagement depends on the public image of the services and on forces' morale: making it imperative in decisions on training and stationing troops overseas, on re-equipment and on redefinition of service roles, for Defence Ministers to consider the implications of the alternatives offered for morale. These two constraints tie defence policy more closely to domestic politics than most other areas of external policy, requiring policy-makers to pay careful attention to carrying party and public opinion with them.

A third constraint is that of Britain's alliance commitments: more sharply limiting since the abandonment of British efforts to maintain a capacity for independent military action, in the course of the withdrawal from East of Suez, and the concentration of its forces within the NATO area. The interpenetration of governmental planning and policy-making in the defence field, within NATO, had by the early 70s gone further than in any other area of external relations, except perhaps international monetary policy.[3] Strategic doctrine, tactics, deployment of forces and equipment are all matters on which Whitehall can no longer make decisions on its own, without considering the likely reaction of Britain's allies, and in almost all cases consulting them beforehand – to such an extent that the MoD has found in the support of other NATO-member defence ministries a powerful protection against Treasury assaults on the defence budget.

A fourth distinctive constraint is equipment, which imposes its own imperatives on defence capabilities and planning. The lengthening lead time from definition and design of major equipment to production and deployment necessitates attempts to plan up to ten years ahead, in spite of the unavoidable pitfalls involved. The increasing costs of such equipment, and the repeated tendency for costs to escalate far beyond initial estimates have led to extensive collaboration with foreign governments in defence procurement and to a greater emphaisis on arms sales overseas, in the hope of recouping development costs through an extended production line. Decisions on equipment – the cancellation of weapons essential to major commitments, collaboration versus independent development, major arms sales to foreign governments – may have direct implications for foreign policy as a whole; but they cannot be determined simply by their foreign policy implications. Apart from their significance in terms of public expenditure, major procurement projects are important consumers of skilled manpower and engineering production, and important providers of domestic employment; so that considerations of regional policy or of priorities in domestic economic growth necessarily enter the argument over re-equipping the navy or supplying the RAF with new aircraft.

The extent to which military and civil procurement of high technology equipment has since the end of the 1950s overlapped national boundaries, and become a factor in British external relations, will be examined in the third section of this chapter. The significance of high technology for British foreign policy in the last fifteen years or so has not been due only to its immediate implications for defence, or to the size of the financial transfers across the exchanges involved in the procurement of, say, military or civilian aircraft. The way in which technological progress became identified in the minds of political leaders, in Britain and elsewhere, with the symbols of national prestige and sovereignty has elevated technological policy, like defence, to the status of high foreign policy. In the 1960s 'the products of its science and technology [had] become, for better or worse, the source of a nation's pride, as pig-iron production statistics were in the late nineteenth century or figures of dreadnought launchings in the early twentieth'.[4] It will therefore be of interest to consider how far considerations of technological policy were integrated with other considerations of external relations during this period, or how far they constituted a separate area of policy.

Apart from the strategic issues – the size, balance, commitment, and major equipment of the armed services – the day-to-day conduct of defence policy involves a great many decisions on matters which, while of less long-term importance, may touch potentially sensitive areas of external relations. Facilities for training British troops abroad, for instance, can for most purposes be agreed with foreign governments by officials and serving officers, subject only to ultimate ministerial approval. Within the NATO area it is unlikely that any serious problems will arise of a kind that would raise such questions above the normal pattern of low-level decisions. Nevertheless, the ten-year agreement signed with the Canadian government in 1971, giving British troops access to a large training area in Western Alberta, brought British servicemen up against demonstrating groups of Canadian conservationists, and British participation in allied army exercises in Greece and in naval celebrations in Portugal in 1973 aroused domestic protests.[5] Withdrawal from East of Suez still left residual commitments to British dependencies and to CENTO and SEATO, while both the maintenance of a general peace-keeping capability and considerations of service morale reinforced arguments for regular training outside the NATO area. The Jungle Warfare School in Malaya was handed over at the end of 1971, but British troops continued to train there under an agreement with the Malaysian government. In 1972 army units also took part in exercises in Australia, New Zealand, Brunei, Fiji, Hong Kong, Kenya, the Persian Gulf, Cyprus, and Jamacia. RAF and army personnel continued to see active service in Oman, while naval vessels exercised in the Caribbean, in the Persian Gulf and with a number of South American navies, and maintained the Beira patrol to enforce the UN sanctions against Rhodesia.[6] Except for the Omani involvement, most of these exercises aroused little or no controversy. A MoD announcement about a battalion exercise in British Honduras at the end of 1971, however (intended to assist recruiting by emphasizing the continued opportunities for travel in the armed forces), provoked a succession of protests from Guatemala, which was satisfied only after an official 'inspection' by an observer nominated by the Organization of American States.[7]

The small change of defence policy also includes such matters as reciprocal facilities for German or Ghanaian troops to train in Britain, the secondment of British servicemen to training posts in other countries' forces, arrangements for transit facilities for naval vessels and over-flight rights for aircraft, military assistance in civil disasters and road building, and the promotion of arms sales. Management of policy on disarmament and arms control represents a rather separate area, with a rather different constituency in terms of interested opinion at home. In the 1970s evolution of policy towards the connected series of negotiations on European security, within the context of the CSCE, the mutual force reduction talks, and the US-Soviet Strategic Arms Limitation Talks (SALT) required another distinctive network of policy-making: drawing together senior officials in the MoD, the FCO, and the Cabinet Office and involving a great deal of multilateral consultation with Britain's allies. Of these various middle-and lower-level issues, the management of arms sales, in many ways one of the most sensitive areas of defence-related external relations, will be explored further below.

Policy-Making in Defence

The most immediate problem in attempting to describe the policy-making process in defence is to discover a 'normal' pattern. To one degree or another British defence policy operated under abnormal circumstances from 1937 or 1938 to 1968 or perhaps even 1970. Externally the long process of decolonization and imperial withdrawal kept British forces on active service from the end of World War II until the withdrawal from Aden in November 1967. In Whitehall, a succession of reorganizations among the service ministries culminated in the creation of a unified Ministry of Defence in 1964, progressively integrated during Denis Healey's long tenure of the Secretaryship of State; to which the Conservatives added the Ministry of Aviation Supply in 1971, in a further reorganization. There were nine Statements of Defence Policy in the six years from 1965–70, reflecting the three major reviews undertaken by the Labour government and the partial reversal of policy by their Conservative successors. The major watershed, clearly, was the decision to end the East of Suez role; from which followed, in 1968 and 1969, the consequent reinforcement of naval and military forces in the European area, and the British initiative to establish the Eurogroup within NATO. Nevertheless, the last two years of Healey's long tenure of office, together with the three and a half years of Lord Carrington's tenure from 1970 to early 1974, do represent a period of relative stability, in which one may discern a stable pattern of policy-making. It may be helpful, therefore, to distinguish between the pre- and post-1968 periods in the discussion below.

The development in institutional machinery for the coordination of defence policy reflected both its close association with high policy and the particular involvement of the Prime Minister in this field. 'Defence', Anthony Eden considered, 'is very much a Prime Minister's special subject'.[8] The Defence Committee of the Cabinet, which was merged with the Foreign Affairs Committee in 1963 to become the DOPC, has been chaired by the Prime Minister since its creation in 1940, except for a period under the Labour government immediately after the war. The origins of the Cabinet Office itself are closely linked with the development of the Committee of Imperial Defence from 1904 on.[9] The beginnings of the current structure, however, can most clearly be traced from Winston Churchill's appointment of himself as Minister of Defence in 1940, and the establishment during World War II of a network of civilian and joint civilian-service committees which carried their activities and pattern of interdepartmental cooperation over into peacetime. The chief weakness of the machinery which emerged after 1945 was the lack of authority and of departmental support for successive Ministers of Defence in their attempts to impose a coherent strategy on the three separate service ministries and on the Ministry of Supply. Coherence was not furthered by the rapid succession of ministers who held that office. Of the nine Conservative Ministers of Defence between 1951 and 1964, only Duncan Sandys, Harold Watkinson, and Peter Thorneycroft remained in office long enough to present more than one annual review. The powers of the Minister of Defence and the size of his staff were substantially increased by Mr Macmillan at the beginning of 1957; but the weight of service interests and of the service ministries still out-balanced the central machinery, so that defence policy-making was still dominated by the endless tug-of-war among the services.[10]

Until 1964, therefore, there existed in the defence field 'not one civil service concerned with administering the Armed Forces, but four, whose mutual relations were not invariably ones of confidence'.[11] The reorganization of 1963–4 at last subordinated the service ministries to central control, represented by the (primarily civilian) Defence Secret-ariat and by the more loosely integrated Defence Staff. The appointment of Denis Healey as Labour's Minister of Defence in 1964 – a man whose familiarity with strategy and defence policy had already won respect among servicemen, civil servants, and academics in Britain and abroad – and his five and a half year tenure of that office, helped to confirm the new pattern. The subordinate status of the service ministers was emphasized by their exclusion from the new government's DOPC, thus making the Minister of Defence their sole spokesman. In 1967 the ministerial representation of the separate services was further down-graded, to the level of parliamentary under-secretaries, and ministerial (and, later, official) responsibilities under the Minister of Defence were divided along functional lines between Ministers of State for Adminis-tration and for Equipment. The advantages of this progressive integration were already apparent by the time of the 1965 Defence Review, when for the first time in may years 'departments were required to work out jointly what longer-term policy variations existed, rather than to cobble together whatever could be represented as agreement from the sum of individual departments' preconceptions and appreciations'.[12] The disadvantage was that continuing adjustments kept the organization of the Ministry in flux until after the return of the Conservatives in 1970, who halted the trend towards functional integration by providing for a single deputy to the Minister of Defence, with under-secretaries of state for each armed service.[13] It was not surprising that the 1970 RUSI pamphlet on *The Central Organization of Defence* enjoyed such a large sale among civil servants; some MoD officials commented that it provided them for the first time with an understanding of how their own ministry was now organized.

The establishment of the DOPC, in late 1963, was intended to provide an institutional framework within which 'major questions of defence policy' could be 'examined in relation to foreign and economic policy'.[14] Its original membership was publicly laid down – uniquely for a Cabinet committee – as 'normally' including, under the chairmanship of the Prime Minister, the Foreign Secretary, the Chancellor or the Chief Secretary to the Treasury, the Home Secretary, the Commonwealth Secretary, and the Secretary of State for Defence, with the Chief of the Defence Staff, the Chiefs of Staff, Permanent Under-Secretaries (to the MoD, the Foreign Office, and on occasion the Treasury) and the Chief Scientific Adviser to the MoD in attendance as required. We may assume that its membership was not dissimilar ten years later, with other Cabinet ministers attending as the Prime Minister's preferences and the subjects to be discussed suggested. The interdepartmental committee of senior officials which was established at the same time to prepare its agenda and to follow through its decisions was rapidly supplemented by a network of subordinate committees and working groups, as well as by committees of second-rank ministers, to handle issues which were of importance to more than one Department but for which room could not be found on the DOPC agenda. Under the Labour government of 1964–70 the DOPC met roughly once a week.

At this highest level, the operation in practice of institutional machinery depends above all upon the personalities of the ministers concerned. Neither Wilson nor Heath as Prime Ministers displayed as close an interest in defence policy as their Conservative predecessors; though Mr Wilson decisively influenced the course of the successive Defence Reviews of 1965–8 and both he and Mr Heath preferred to take personal control in an acute crisis. The style and preferences of Denis Healey and Lord Carrington, both strong ministers who held office for long enough to stamp their character on their Department, were therefore of crucial importance.

It was Denis Healey who made the most decisive impact on a Department which was just beginning to take shape when he took over, imposing his own ideas on the structure outlined in the 1963 White Paper, *Central Organization for Defence*. He largely ignored the body which the reformers had intended to be the central decision-making forum, the Defence Council, preferring to take decisions more rapidly and informally. When he first took office in 1964, 'in order to lighten the burden which the new system imposes on the Secretary of State', his Deputy Secretary of State was given special responsibility for 'matters of international policy relating to defence', in addition to his role as Minister for the Army;[15] his first Deputy, Fred Mulley, indeed had considerable expertise in NATO questions. But after Mulley's transfer to the Ministry of Aviation, in 1965, Healey himself increasingly took personal charge of this international dimension, becoming in effect 'Minister for National Security' as well as 'Minister for the Armed Forces'.[16] With the lessened pressure of major defence decisions after the withdrawal from East of Suez and the reorientation of forces towards Europe, Carrington expanded this national security role, becoming in his ministerial visits abroad something of a second Foreign Secretary, discussing topics which ranged far beyond his strictly departmental responsibilities with, for instance, the Greek, Nigerian, or Kenyan governments. The mutual confidence of his relations with Sir Alec Douglas-Home, as Foreign Secretary, removed any dangers of friction between their overlapping interests.

The central nexus of what would, in the United States, be called national security policy clearly by the early 70s lay within the DOPC structure. At the ministerial level, the key relationships were those between the Minister of Defence and the Foreign Secretary and between both and the Chancellor, with the Prime Minister intervening as other responsibilities permitted. The nature of their responsibilities and the orientation of their Departments tended to throw the Minister of Defence and the Foreign Secretary together into a common resistance to the Chancellor, under both the Labour and Conservative governments; reinforced in both administrations by the personal outlooks of the ministers concerned. The extensive network of ministerial and official committees within the framework of the DOPC were serviced by a section of the Cabinet Secretariat, headed by a deputy under-secretary from the Diplomatic Service and including three or four military officers. The Assessments Staff and the Joint Intelligence Committee to which it reported were not formally part of the DOPC machinery; but the intimacy and informality of the Cabinet Office ensured the closest effective cooperation. Like the DOPC Secretariat, the Assessments Staff included upwards of a dozen officials seconded from the MoD, the FCO, and the Treasury, and a handful of military officers, with a Foreign Office under-secretary at its head. Except under conditions of international or economic crisis, the management of defence policy followed a fairly regular seasonal cycle. The annual Defence White Paper rose through the DOPC structure to the Cabinet for final approval; meetings of NATO defence ministers and of the NATO Council (of foreign ministers) similarly required predictable and regular interdepartmental preparation. Characteristically of Whitehall policy-making, defence policy in its widest aspects is decided not by any single minister but by a series of committees.

Below the ministerial level, the roles of the FCO and the MoD were central, and the relations between the two Departments close. The integrated Ministry of Defence was the largest Department in Whitehall; in 1973 it had over 10,000 staff in its main headquarters, and another 7,000 in the headquarters of the Procurement Executive.[17] Many of its civilian and military divisions related, directly or indirectly, to departments of the Foreign Office. At the middle and lower levels of policy, however, the points of first contact between the two Departments were two sections of the central Defence Secretariat, responsible for NATO and extra-NATO matters respectively, and the Western Organizations and Defence departments of the FCO: two pairs of 'mirror-image' departments, the relationship between which was described by one official as one in which 'we're in each other's pockets'. Other sections of the Defence Secretariat, responsible for East-West security talks in Europe and for arms sales, similarly dealt continuously with departments of the FCO. These small divisions in turn linked the FCO with the (military) Defence Policy and Defence Operations Staffs. Another, overlapping, network of formal and informal contacts linked those responsible for intelligence in the FCO, the MoD, and the services. Cross-representation on departmental committees aided mutual understanding. The deputy under-secretary in the Foreign Office responsible for international security matters was, for instance, a member of the Chiefs of Staff Committee. The pattern of work between the two Departments was similar to that within the FCO, already described: to settle differences and agree policy wherever possible by informal consultation at low level, raising matters to under-secretaries or to ministers only when major decisions were required or where differences proved irreconcilable.

The contrast between this relatively harmonious relationship and the tension which has so often characterized contacts between foreign and defence ministries, most of all between the State Department and the Pentagon, calls for some explanation. The immediate situation of the years before 1970, when Foreign Office and MoD officials had conducted a long rearguard action, in support of their ministers and their departmental interests, against repeated attempts to cut back British forces both East of Suez and in Europe, had built up a pattern of shared perceptions. The preparation of agreed papers for intergovernmental discussions within the NATO framework required regular consultation among sections of the Defence Staff, the Defence Secretariat, and the Foreign Office; given the administrative traditions of the British civil service, the practical requirements of managing decisions accustomed those involved to working together. The experience of successful cooperation in managing relations with our alliance partners created a greater sense of common purpose, reinforced by the contrast which officers and officials observed between the easy give-and-take which marked British delegations and the suspicion and intrigue displayed by those of some other countries. Interdepartmental harmony was also promoted by the familiarity with defence problems and strategic studies which many FCO officials had acquired during the 60s. Diplomatic Service members attended the year-long course at the Royal College of Defence Studies, alongside senior military officers and officials from the MoD. Others were seconded to the IISS, or studied defence-related questions at British or American universities. FCO officials regularly participated in discussions and meetings at IISS and the RUSI, and MoD officials similarly took part in Chatham House discussions. Officials within the two Departments therefore shared a common vocabulary and a common outlook which, while not eliminating differences of view, enormously assisted mutual understanding.[18]

Probably the most important difference between Britain and the United States, however, was that in Whitehall the dictum that defence should be the servant of foreign policy was reflected institutionally in the Foreign Office's formal and informal relations with the MoD. Diplomatic Service personnel headed the Cabinet Office sections concerned with international security questions; FCO officials were accepted participants in a range of internal MoD committees, often relating to MoD officials one or two levels above them in the Whitehall hierarchy.

Reinforcing the good relations between civil servants was the relative absence of tension in civil-military relations within the MoD. The tradition of the service ministries before 1964 had been one of shared and 'intensive group loyalties among military and civil servants alike, which seemed in some cases to border on the fanatical'.[19] This tradition, transferred after some transitional difficulties to the integrated MoD, carried with it an acceptance by serving officers that civilian officials had their interests at heart, and a consequent acceptance (strengthened by the long-established traditions of the British armed services) of the supremacy of civilian control. It was rare for senior military officers to criticize political or administrative decisions in public, even in periods of sharp retrenchment, or to speak out along lines which did not match MoD doctrine. In the wake of the major 1957 Defence Review there was a certain amount of service lobbying and some leaks to the press, and in November 1959 General Sir John Cowley publicly criticized the doctrine of strategic deterrence at a RUSI lecture.[20] In 1966 the First Sea Lord, Admiral Sir David Luce, resigned in protest at the outcome of another major Defence Review; but he left it to the Navy Minister, Christopher Mayhew, who resigned simultaneously, to state the navy's case. There was some disquiet in 1972 about public statements on counter-insurgency operations made by the Commandant of the School of Infantry, Brigadier Frank Kitson, which led to demands in the House of Commons for his resignation.[21] But these were exceptional instances, over a long period – one in which, although the armed services were under considerable strain, the principle of civilian control and the practice of cooperation and understanding between military officers and civil servants became still more firmly established.

The Treasury's involvement in defence policy was on a different level, casting it in a posture of opposition to the informal alliance between the Foreign Office and the MoD. The Treasury division most directly concerned was the Defence (Policy and Materiel) section of the Public Sector Group, comprising less than a dozen administrative-grade civil servants whose responsibilities covered the whole defence and military procurement budget. The size and shape of the defence budget was determined, not within the DOPC framework, but within the annual review process of the Public Expenditure Scrutiny Committee, to which the Finance and Budgets section of the Defence Secretariat directly related. Formally, the Treasury role in the defence process was to consider the economic consequences of particular strategies, commitments, and re-equipment programmes. Necessarily, in view of the small number of officials concerned, the Treasury's influence on the shape of the defence budget throughout the 60s had been in effect a negative one: resisting proposals for new programmes which would generate major demands for additional expenditure, imposing an overall ceiling on the defence budget, and encouraging the MoD to decide its allocation between the different services and force requirements. In an ideal world, perhaps, Treasury officials should also have considered the relationship between the resources provided and the commitments which Britain was attempting to maintain, intervening more actively in the dialogue between the MoD, and the Foreign Office on security policy – but the pressures of immediate concerns and of detail on a small staff largely precluded this.[22]

The Foreign Office views defence policy within a time-scale which ranges from the immediate to some three or four years ahead: oriented as it is to considerations of immediate threats, of diplomatic necessities, of existing commitments and obligations. The Treasury operates within the rolling framework of five-year forward projections of public expenditure. The MoD, in contrast, is forced by the necessities of designing and developing new equipment to make assumptions about the international environment for up to ten years ahead. The pressures which major equipment programmes have placed upon a budget already subject to a tight ceiling also enforced careful planning and costing within the MoD. One of Mr Healey's greatest successes as Minister of Defence was the encouragement he gave to the development of rigorous costing techniques within his Department, producing ten-year forecasts for defence planners and those responsible for the defence budget to discuss and amend. The influence of American experience here was considerable. In 1963 a party of Whitehall officials had visited the Pentagon to examine their new budgetary methods; Healey himself was familiar with the advantages of the Planning, Programming, and Budget System in cutting through the entrenched positions of inter-service bargaining.

By 1970 the MoD had thus developed an extensive and efficient machinery for rational internal planning, within the boundaries imposed by such political decisions as the incoming Conservative government's commitment to retain forces in the Far East. This did not always fit easily with the different time-scale of the FCO, or with the political imperatives of new governments. Not unnaturally, defence planners were frustrated by the Foreign Office's inability to 'write on one sheet of paper the country's foreign policy for the next ten years', and tended to see such political imperatives as the residual Far Eastern commitment as unfortunate incursions into a rational long-term process.[23]

This distinctive outlook on defence policy and planning was shared, outside Whitehall, by a small but expert body of non-official opinion, the growth of which during the 60s also owed much to the MoD and to Denis Healey. British universities had been much slower to accept strategic studies as an academic subject than universities in the United States, though from 1958 the IISS had acted as a focus for research and study outside the universities. The 1966 Defence Review announced a number of proposals 'to encourage the universities to play a more active role in higher defence studies and to stimulate academic awareness of defence problems', including the establishment of sponsored lectureships at a number of universities and the provision of fellowships for senior officers and civil servants to 'pursue some appropriate course of advanced study or research'.[24] By 1972 there were seven such lectureships, at five universities, and the special relationship between the MoD and the academic world was marked by ministry briefings and regular conferences at which servicemen, civil servants, and academics exchanged ideas. The RUSI's standing and its level of activities had also been upgraded, thanks to a major appeal for funds from industry in 1968, for which the MoD offered proportional contributions to those raised from corporate subscribers.

By the early 70s, therefore, there existed a framework for informed debate on defence matters between the MoD and expert opinion from outside, largely created during the previous decade.[25] It is less clear that there yet existed a fulcrum for bringing informed criticism to bear upon the government at ministerial level, through parliamentary questioning and debate. Throughout the 60s the annual defence debates remained ill attended, and marked by repeated backbench and opposition protests at the difficulties of obtaining relevant information; though one Conservative MP claimed not to be 'too upset that the debates are so poorly attended if only because it does, to some extent, insulate the thing from party politics. . .'.[26] In this respect the creation by the new Commons Expenditure Committee, in 1971, of a Defence and External Affairs Sub-Committee was a major advance. Sceptical civil servants found its attitude in its first year of operation 'a rather pleasant surprise', and went some way to meet its repeated requests for more information. While some of its early investigations were confined to safe subjects closely related to expenditure (such as the administration of HM Dockyards, land used for military purposes in Britain and abroad, and financial control procedures within the MoD) it dared in the 1972–3 session to examine the nuclear deterrent programme, calling the Minister of Defence himself as a witness, and reiterating in its report the Committee's 'need to have all the relevant information put before them as early as possible'.[27] Even more ambitiously, after examining the facilities available to parallel committees in Ottawa and Washington, another report in this session called not only for 'greater access, when there is a clear need, to a higher grade of classified material and to commercially confidential information', but also for fuller directly published information in Defence White Papers and for substantial increases in committee staff.[28] In response to this request, two members of the Exchequer and Audit Department were assigned to the committee for a two-year period, to assist in interpreting the statistics and papers which the MoD was now providing. They acted, in practice, as extra clerks – giving this sub-committee a marked advantage in staffing over its fellows, still relying on one clerk each.

During the withdrawal from East of Suez, party pressure inside and outside Parliament had a significant influence on both government and opposition, not only in the timing of the Labour government's withdrawal but also in the reversal of official Conservative policy between 1966 and 1968. After 1970, with the acceptance of second-rank status as a military power and of a largely symbolic commitment in the Far East, defence questions became a less active subject of controversy within the Conservative Party; though within the Labour Party the left wing continued to criticize the overall size of the defence budget and to press for sharp reductions. The first serious revolt against the majority Labour government elected in October 1974 came over their defence proposals. In December fifty left-wingers divided the House of Commons against their own government to demonstrate their discontent at the moderation of the cuts proposed.

Beyond these, the domestic constituency for defence policy in Britain in the early 70s was not large – unless one includes the services themselves as a constituency. It is difficult to discern anything resembling a military-industrial complex in Britain in the sense of a powerful lobby linking the armed services with defence industries, pressing for a larger defence effort and a security-oriented foreign policy. In procurement, certainly, the relationship between government and industry was close, with defence suppliers organized into such bodies as the Warship Supply Group and the Society of British Aerospace Constructors; but the MoD clearly had the decisive say, reinforced by the parliamentary criticisms which followed the Ferranti affair.[29] Old-established organizations, the Navy League, the Army League, continued to promote the interests of 'their' services, but with only a shadow of their past influence. Wider public opinion seemed little interested in defence questions once the East of Suez question had been settled. Even the nuclear deterrent, the focus of mass campaigns in 1960–1, now attracted little concern. A small number of defence correspondents, attached to the national newspapers, tried to keep the public informed on defence questions, with varying degrees of cooperation from the MoD.

The long and slow withdrawal from East of Suez dominated discussions of defence policy, inside and outside Whitehall, from 1964 to 1968, though it was not until a very late stage in the process that the decision was squarely faced at ministerial level.[30] To a considerable extent the eventual acceptance of withdrawal had been pre-determined before 1964 by decisions on strategy, on bases, and on equipment. Heavy investment in bases in Kenya, on which £7·5m was spent before the withdrawal in early 1964, and in Aden, on which nearly £30m was spent between 1962 and 1966, had committed funds that with hindsight could far better have been spent on island bases in the Indian Ocean, or on creating facilities in Australia – which, in consequence, were unavailable without substantial further investment as Aden became increasingly untenable, from 1966 on. Several years' delay in placing an order for the first of the new aircraft carriers which the navy would need in order to maintain its East of Suez role into the 1970s brought the cost of the new carrier into the defence budget at the same time as the Polaris fleet (necessitated by the Conservative government's determination to retain the nuclear deterrent after the American cancellation of Skybolt). New equipment for the army and the navy was also a major concern in 1962–4, complicated for both by the divergent needs of Europe and of the East of Suez role.

The foreign policy objectives which the military presence East of Suez served, though never clearly defined, were unquestioned by both Conservative and Labour front benches in 1964. British defence policy, like British foreign policy, was still based on Churchill's belief that the 'three circles' of British influence, the 'special relationship' with the United States, the links with Europe and the Commonwealth, together guaranteed Britain great power status. Peter Thorneycroft as Minister of Defence maintained that the nuclear deterrent, the commitment to Europe, and the military presence East of Suez 'have markedly increased our influence in the world and enabled us to play an important part in the world'.[31] The Labour Party leadership different from the Conservatives only in their greater commitment to the Commonwealth, in their more sceptical view of the nuclear deterrent, and in their willingness if necessary to cut back on forces in Europe to meet the needs of the wider world.

Overwhelmingly our most important and worthwhile job in the ten or twenty years we can foresee [Mr Healey declared as opposition spokesman in the 1964 defence debate] will be not so much the protection of specific national interests overseas as the prevention of anarchy and war in those areas of the world, many of them newly independent, in Asia, the Middle East and Africa, and perhaps in Central America, where we and we alone have at present the political right and the physical capacity to intervene effectively . . . a role and a responsibility which challenges all that is best in our national tradition and our national character.[32]

That role had been fulfilled with considerable success in the Kuwait crisis of 1961, the Brunei rebellion of 1962, and the East African mutinies of January 1964, and was still being tested in the Aden emergency and the developing Malaysian-Indonesian 'confrontation' – successes which diverted political attention away from the consequent overstrain on service manpower and the escalating foreign exchange burden. In the years since the major 1957 Defence Review the three services had developed coherent rationales for their role East of Suez. The navy saw its limited-war capability in the Indian Ocean as its most distinctive role, its importance reflected in the commando carriers and assault ships on order or coming into service. With the cancellation of Skybolt in 1962 and the approaching end of its strategic bomber force, the RAF was coming to see in the East of Suez commitment a guarantee of its future status, developing a concept of island bases in competition with the navy's concept of afloat support.

The new Labour government in 1964 was also committed to maintaining the closest possible relationship with the United States government in defence and foreign policy. The message from Washington, conveyed during a visit by the new Prime Minister, the Foreign Secretary, and the Minister of Defence in December 1964, was clear: the British contribution in the Far East was warmly approved. The pressures on the new government to reconsider the scale of its commitment did not therefore come from its allies, from the Foreign Office, or from the service ministries: they came from the Treasury, prompted first by the huge balance-of-payments deficit and the need for sharper restraints on public expenditure, and secondly by its concern at the spiralling costs of military R & D and equipment. A major review of the defence programme was therefore undertaken during 1965, profiting for the first time from the more unified MoD machine to examine and cost the requirements of each service and each major commitment. It was not open to the defence planners, however, to question the commitments themselves, not only because these were matters for the Foreign Office but, more powerfully, because the government's determination to maintain those commitments was unambiguously clear. The Treasury's interests were met by the acceptance of a ceiling of £2,000m on the defence budget: a provisional target which rapidly hardened into a firm figure, unrelated to the number of commitments the defence forces were expected to meet.[33]

Economies began with the cancellation of the RAF's main strike aircraft for the next ten years, the TSR-2 – announced, significantly, by the Chancellor in his 1965 Budget speech –, of several other aircraft projects and of the fifth Polaris submarine. There were also cuts in the reserve forces. The TSR-2 was to be replaced by the American F-111, the Americans agreeing to substantial purchases of British equipment to offset the balance-of-payments cost: another example of intervention in the British policy-making process by a foreign government, and by no means the last in this case.[34]

Within the Ministry of Defence, the review resolved itself into a traumatic struggle between the navy and the RAF, with the RAF claiming that the more versatile F-111, with an island base strategy, could replace the enormous cost of a new aircraft carrier. Cost-effectiveness studies supported the RAF; and on the announcement that the carrier force would be phased out in the 1966 White Paper, which concluded the review, the Minister for the Navy, Christopher Mayhew, and the First Sea Lord resigned.

This first review took place almost entirely within Whitehall. It was primarily an internal exercise in the MoD, within the limits set by the Treasury and by the government's declared foreign policy. Mr Mayhew attempted to raise the increasing imbalance between capabilities and commitments at various stages in the review but was prevented by Mr Healey from putting his case to the DOPC or to the Cabinet. The debate did not actively engage Parliament. The opposition of the Labour Party's left wing could to some extent be discounted as ideologically based; the reasoned criticisms of Enoch Powell, the Shadow Conservative spokesman on defence, were muted by dissensions within his own party. By 1966 informed opinion had become sceptical of the military value and political rationale of the East of Suez role;[35] but there was no way in which their criticisms could be brought to bear upon the Cabinet. The doubtful utility of British defence expenditure outside Europe had been illustrated, for some, by the Defence Minister's outright resistance to any suggestion of military intervention in Rhodesia after UDI; its continued value, for others, was demonstrated by the success of operations in Malaysia and by continued American gratitude for the Far Eastern commitment. The government's lack of clarity in defining the purposes which the commitment should fulfil was demonstrated both by suggestions that the Polaris submarine force should be stationed in the Indian Ocean (presumably to deter another Chinese attack on India, though their range was inadequate to reach the industrial centres of China from there), and by the acceptance of American participation in the development of the network of island bases – without first agreeing any common definition of military and political objectives with the US government. In short, the review was a classic example of handling policy at the wrong level: rational within its own terms, but inadequate because of the failure to re-examine high-level assumptions, and because there was no way within the secretive processes of Whitehall policy-making to force the Cabinet to question those assumptions. The outcome, as Christopher Mayhew pointed out in his resignation statement, was an irrational compromise. The forces retained were too weak to meet the commitments the government now reiterated, but were larger (and more expensive) than would be needed if those commitments were cut.

The economic crisis of July 1966 reopened the question of the size of the defence budget and precipitated a second major defence review. Although this began less than six months after the conclusion of its predecessor, a number of important factors had altered. Criticism within the Labour Party had now become open, strengthened by an alliance between Mr Mayhew and the left wing. But divisions of opinion within the Conservative leadership to some extent neutralized Labour hostility, creating a curious 'four-party' situation in Parliament in which the Conservative defence spokesman, Mr Enoch Powell, was closer in attitude to Labour backbench critics than to many of his own backbenchers, who in turn strongly supported the globalist views of the Labour front bench. In June 1966 a rowdy PLP meeting heard Mr Wilson deliver an impassioned and emotional defence of the East of Suez role. But in October the Labour Party Conference carried a motion for withdrawal against the leadership; moreover Mr Wilson's dominance of the Cabinet had been considerably weakened by his handling of the July crisis, and the ministerial reshuffle which followed had strengthened the position of those in the Cabinet who were becoming sceptical. The replacement of Michael Stewart by George Brown at the Foreign Office was of particular importance, bringing into the debate on overseas policy a committed 'European' without strong emotional attachments to the Commonwealth and without too sober a respect for the established views of his Department. The Foreign Office's ability to provide a thorough reconsideration of objectives East of Suez, however, was limited by the continued existence of a separate Commonwealth Office and by preoccupation with the slow process of merging the two ministries, which was not completed until October 1968.

Shifts of attitude within the government towards the Commonwealth and towards the desirability of Anglo-American cooperation in the Far East therefore remained relatively unarticulated, background factors rather than explicit arguments for change. The lack of sympathy which many Commonwealth governments displayed for Britain's predicament over Rhodesia had begun to disillusion Labour ministers, as well as many Conservatives, about the value of the Commonwealth to Britain. Growing US difficulties in Vietnam were beginning to cast doubt upon the wisdom of too close an identification with American policy in the Far East, as well as on the practicality of open-ended British commitments there. The ending of the Malaysian-Indonesian confrontation, in June 1966, opened the prospect of substantial military withdrawals from the Far East as a means of saving foreign exchange; and at the same time increased American pressure for a more positive gesture of military support in Vietnam.

The second defence review thus got under way in the autumn of 1966, as part of another reduction in proposed public expenditure. Once again, the bulk of the work was conducted within the MoD, within financial limits fixed by the Treasury, with frequent reference on policy to the Foreign Office. It was now clear within the MoD that further cuts in expenditure implied eventual withdrawal. In late October Denis Healey obtained the approval of the Prime Minister and other interested senior ministers for this official view.[36] But there now opened a gap between declared government policy and the lines along which MoD planners were working. Only a week earlier, on 15 October, Mr Wilson had told the Labour Party that Britain's frontier was on the Himalayas; and when in March 1967 sixty-three Labour MPs voted against the annual Defence White Paper he made a savage speech which one of his ministers considered 'the high point in the justification of the Cabinet's East of Suez policy'.[37]

A working party of senior officials within the DOPC framework had completed a review of the proposed changes by the end of March 1967, and forwarded them to the full Committee for final decision. In April the decision was taken in principle to reduce the level of forces in the Far East to about half their present strength by 1970–1, and to withdraw them altogether at an unspecified date in the mid-70s. The next three months were occupied in extensive consultations with foreign governments and active lobbying by those governments, with the support of the Foreign Office and of Mr Healey, to prevent any firm public announcement of the date for withdrawal. The US government exerted considerable pressure; the Prime Ministers of Australia, Malaysia, and Singapore – the last of whom (Lee Kuan Yew) enjoyed close relations with the Labour Party, as heading what Labour MPs saw as the only Social Democratic government in Asia – visited London to talk to the government, the opposition, the press, and MPs. Opinion within the Cabinet was swayed at a late stage, in May 1967, by the heated debate over a proposed British intervention in the Gulf of Aqaba, in the run-up to the third Arab-Israeli war – a prime ministerial proposal resisted by the Defence Minister and effectively vetoed by the Chancellor which caused several Cabinet ministers to question the value of maintaining troops for 'peacekeeping' purposes at all. The Supplementary Statement on Defence Policy, published in July, set out the main conclusions agreed by the Cabinet, announcing that this was 'the end' of a 'continuous' process of major review over the previous three years.[38]

Any expectations which the services and the defence planners may have had of a period of stability in which to apply the plans and proposals so painfully worked out were, however, rudely shattered by the renewed economic crisis of November 1967. Devaluation automatically increased the foreign exchange costs of maintaining forces in the Far East (and in Germany), and of procuring the F-111, by now the lynch-pin of the East of Suez role, from the United States. Post-devaluation expenditure cuts threatened many of the Labour government's most cherished social programmes, and the battle within the Cabinet and the party resolved itself into a contest between further reductions in the defence budget or sharp cuts in education, health, and the social services. The argument was now more over equipment than over commitments, focusing on the F-111 order. The US government again intervened to offer a more generous offset agreement. At a late stage in the review, when the principle of earlier withdrawal had been accepted, Lee Kuan Yew flew to London and persuaded the government to postpone the date of withdrawal by six months. The decision to withdraw at a definite date, by the end of 1971, and to cancel the F-111 order was announced by the

Prime Minister as part of the post-devaluation package of cuts in public expenditure on 16 January 1968.

As a postscript, it should be added that the Labour government's gradual conversion to withdrawal was matched by a parallel Conservative movement towards a commitment to stay. Mr Powell's departure from the Shadow Cabinet meant that Sir Alec Douglas-Home dominated overseas policy, and opinion within all sections of the party actively interested in defence, inside and outside Parliament, favoured retaining a presence East of Suez. By now this attitude had little to do with the Commonwealth, with which most Conservatives were thoroughly disillusioned. It was much more a matter of loosely-defined ideas about maintaining international order and resisting the communist menace, which in an opposition party are neither subject to the questioning and closer definition of official Whitehall nor so directly affected by the pressure of outside events. The incoming Conservative government was in time in 1970 to reverse the last stages of withdrawal (as Lee Kuan Yew had intended). Officials within the FCO, intent on resisting the new government's proposals to sell arms to South Africa, did not feel strong enough to resist this policy as well; officials and officers within the MoD accepted as a political decision a residual commitment which few regarded as rational.

This lengthy process of withdrawal illustrates the way in which distinctive constraints bear on defence policy. The element of mystique, the identification of defence with national status, was evident both in Mr Wilson's romantic attachment to a global role and in the reorientation of Conservative policy. Economic considerations, though powerful throughout, were never dominating, imposing ever tighter limits on the options available but not completely dictating them. The cost and availability of equipment was crucial at several points in the debate; indeed, one former Labour minister argued in 1972 that if the Australian government had ordered the TSR-2 in 1964 instead of the F-111, thus opening up the prospect of a longer production run and weakening the arguments for cancellation, 'we'd still have a presence in the Pacific'. This illustrates another significant factor throughout the process of withdrawal: the active influence exerted by foreign governments, through one means or another, over British policy-making.

The tendency to put defence issues in a separate compartment from other important issues of overseas policy is also evident in the failure to link the East of Suez debate with the parallel high-level discussions, in different Cabinet committees, of foreign economic policy and of policy towards the European Community. Certainly, the darkening balance-of-payments position weakened the case for the Far East role, and devaluation effectively ended it; yet at no point were the two issues discussed together in Cabinet or in ministerial or official committee. Certainly too the emerging consensus in favour of Community entry coincided with diminishing support for Britain's global role; but, again, the connection between the two was subconscious rather than conscious. Mr Healey himself admitted that 'in those days I wasn't particularly interested in economics' and that in 1967 he was too much preoccupied with the practicalities of defence 'to worry about the metaphysics of the Treaty of Rome'.[39] Even for such a fundamental decision, discussion was almost entirely confined within the separate machinery for defence policy-making.

Discussion was likewise for most purposes confined within the Executive. Even when the consensus of expert opinion outside was joined by considerable forces within the Labour Party, the Cabinet resisted outside criticism. This was partly because it was so difficult for outsiders to bring their criticisms to bear on the government in any but the most general way, and partly because the majority of government ministers, preoccupied with their departmental responsibilities, had insufficient time to absorb arguments on subjects outside their immediate sphere. A leading critic within the Labour Party later estimated that the combined effect of the platform's defeat at the 1966 Labour Conference, the parliamentary revolt of March 1967, and extensive private lobbying accounted for perhaps some 25 per cent of the pressure for final withdrawal, scarcely achieving more than to counterbalance the pressures from foreign governments.

Most of all, this process illustrates the argument made in chapter 3, that the pattern of British policy-making lends itself to the avoidance of choice rather than to the choice of decisions. Patrick Gordon Walker's conclusion that 'the Cabinet came to the decision to withdraw from East of Suez at the earliest moment when such a policy became practical' ignores the number of earlier occasions on which the Cabinet or its committees discussed the East of Suez role without considering what by the beginning of 1966 had become a chorus of informed criticisms.[40] It likewise ignores the continuing expenditure on Indian Ocean and Persian Gulf bases during 1967 and the maintenance by Mr Wilson of a declared global policy months after the effective decision for withdrawal had been taken. The insulation of the Cabinet from outside opinion is evident also in the continued ministerial emphasis on the need to protect British investment and oil supplies, during 1966 and 1967, by which time the CBI and the oil industry both substantially agreed that a military presence was more likely to arouse local antagonisms than to protect existing investment.[41] The Conservative opposition too, in redefining its policy on East of Suez (worked out in considerable detail between 1968 and 1970) paid far less attention to the prevailing scepticism of informed opinion and, by then, of serving military officers than to the dominant perceptions of the Shadow Cabinet and of the foreign policy lobby within the party.

One may, finally, ask whether improvements in the machinery of policy-making and of policy debate since 1968 have made it less likely that such a crab-wise process of decision would recur. In one sense, it is unlikely that it would, since the termination of the East of Suez role weakened the association of defence policy with the emotional mystique of national status and standing. Future decisions on defence policy, it may be argued, will be made on a much more reasoned basis, taking into account the cost-effectiveness of different alternatives and the importance attached to particular objectives. One awaits with interest the decision on whether and how to replace the Polaris system, Britain's nuclear deterrent force. Certainly, the integration of the Foreign and Commonwealth Offices has made it easier to re-examine the priorities of foreign policy outside the North Atlantic area; certainly too the strengthening of the Cabinet Office has made it easier to prepare papers covering differing aspects of foreign policy for ministers to consider. It is hard to believe that some of the accepted arguments for maintaining forces East of Suez could long have survived questioning in the new Defence and External Affairs Sub-Committee. Even so, the root of the problem may have lain in the committee system, from interdepartmental committees to Cabinet, which continues to impose a pattern of compromise on British policy-making, not in defence alone.

The Technological Dimension

British involvement in intergovernmental cooperation in matters of science and technology began in the nineteenth century. Britain became, for instance, a founder member of the International Meteorological Organization in 1878, and of the International Council for the Exploration of the Sea in 1902, both non-controversial technical bodies concerned with the exchange of scientific information, and had joined a number of similar organizations before World War II. The first collaborative project in an area of high political and military significance was the wartime Anglo-American Manhattan Project, which built the first atomic bomb – and which also provided, in the subsequent Congressional abrogation of Anglo-American nuclear cooperation under the McMahon Act, an early lesson in the pitfalls of international collaboration. Postwar policy and practice re-established national self-sufficiency as the pattern of research, development, and production. Wartime industrial mobilization had created a large and highly skilled aircraft industry and also a number of governmental and private research teams in nuclear energy, electronics, and associated fields. It was natural to assume that a great power should maintain the industrial base for supplying its own armed forces without having to depend on the uncertain approval of foreign governments. There were also high hopes that these advanced technologies would make a major contribution to the increased exports needed to ensure economic recovery, through civil and military sales abroad. Questions of science and technology therefore remained primarily a matter of domestic concern until the late 50s. Membership of several technical intergovernmental organizations promoting research and the exchange of information served a useful but limited function, costing little and threatening few political complications.

A number of factors combined to make technological questions more politically sensitive, in both domestic and foreign policy terms, from the mid-50s onwards. In Britain, as in France and in the United States, the cost of R & D was rising sharply with each generation of aircraft and of electronic equipment. Private companies were forced to depend more and more upon the government for funds; the government, already struggling to contain the growth of public expenditure, above all the defence budget, was forced to cut the number of projects it financed and to consider ways of spreading the burden. In the early 50s the British aircraft industry had considerably expanded in response to the rearmament programme and a range of successful export orders, but then encountered difficulties in financing and selling the next generation of aircraft. Output and employment began to fall in 1957, and by 1960 the situation was serious enough for the government to intervene directly to reorganize the industry and provide additional finance.

To considerations of cost, of the balance of payments, of domestic employment, and of the maintenance of an industrial base for defence procurement must be added two other factors which were becoming important in public minds at this time. The first was the association of high technology with economic growth: the belief that the 'spin-off' from research and development in advanced technology, as well as the direct economic benefits from production and sales, benefited other spheres of industrial activity, so stimulating further economic advance. The second was the association of high technology with ideas of national independence and status, sparked off most sharply by the Soviet Union's successful launching of Sputnik in 1957 but evident also in the reaction of many Conservative MPs to what they saw as Russia's 'nuclear black-mail' at Suez. During the next decade such images coloured the whole political debate about technology. A government report on the future of the aircraft industry thought it proper to emphasize in its conclusions

the part played by the aircraft industry in the nation's view of itself. The traditions of the industry, especially its role in the last war; the penetration of scientific frontiers that it involves; the tangible way in which it spreads the nation's name across the world; and, quite simply, the inherent glamour of aeroplanes; all these combine to make the industry a symbol of Britain's aspirations.[42]

Mr Wilson spoke of the dangers of 'an industrial helotry', 'my favourite theme' during his exploratory tour of EEC capitals in the early months of 1967.[43] Mr Heath warned that if Europe accustomed itself to importing technology its best brains would 'become flaccid and dispirited'.[44]

A further argument linked advanced technology to considerations of high-level foreign policy.

The aircraft industry [the Plowden Report on the industry argued] is one in which governments can readily promote cooperative international ventures, because they take the major share of the industry's products. At the present stage of United Kingdom foreign policy the aircraft industry has a role to play for which few other industries are so well fitted.[45]

This role, the Labour government soon made clear, was to act as the technological trump card which would win Britain entry into Europe, by offering to the European Communities the benefits of British advanced technology and at the same time demonstrating, through our willingness to cooperate, Britain's bona fides as a European partner.

We are concerned here with what has come, significantly, to be known as 'high' technology – aviation above all, space, nuclear energy, and, increasingly in the late 60s, computers – rather than with the whole range of British technological relations with other governments. It may be noted that the range and intensity of British involvement in intergovernmental technological relations at lower levels also increased markedly during this period. Progress towards harnessing atomic energy for civil purposes, with a consequent demand for some form of international control, led to the establishment in 1957 of the International Atomic Energy Agency (IAEA), of Euratom and of the European Nuclear Energy Agency. The conclusion of the Nuclear Non-Proliferation Treaty in 1968 and the spread of civil nuclear power stations correspondingly increased diplomatic activity. It remained deliberate government policy to manage civil nuclear issues on a technical level, to avoid the incursion of 'political' quarrels into such delicate negotiations; partly for this reason, the atomic energy division of the DTI, not the FCO, took the lead within Whitehall. With increasingly complex international scientific cooperation, several new intergovernmental organizations, such as the European Molecular Biology Organization, were established, raising the costs of British subscriptions to their activities. The Labour government's refusal in 1969 to contribute to the 300 GEV accelerator proposed by the European Centre for Nuclear Research (CERN), and the Conservatives' subsequent agreement to participate, provoked a major dispute within the scientific community in Britain and on the Continent. But unless sizeable commitments were incurred, or unless ministers promoted particular policies (as both Harold Wilson and Anthony Wedgwood-Benn, the Minister of Technology, promoted a series of technological agreements with East European governments in the late 60s), these issues were managed at official level, in collaboration with the small groups of scientists concerned.

The experience of technological collaboration between 1960 and 1970 is perhaps best seen as a process of learning – both about the need to be clear about the divergent objectives pursued and about the problems of managing an untidy complex of policies. It was not only that no coherent strategy for technological collaboration was ever developed. It was also that there was no single national technological policy as such. Policies towards the aircraft industry, towards nuclear energy, space, and the computer industry were dealt with piecemeal, sector by sector. As a result in 1964–5 the Labour government was struggling to save 'the indigenous computer industry' at the same time as it pressed for collaboration in military aircraft projects with the French, and in 1966–7 was extolling 'a strong and independent European computer industry' shortly after provoking a major crisis within the European Launcher Development Organization (ELDO).[46] Part of the reason for this sector-by-sector approach was that in each sector the government was dealing with major industrial interests; partly, too, the intractability of technical and industrial problems did not lend themselves to an imposed identity of treatment. The difficulty of separating defence from civilian considerations when dealing with the aircraft and electronics industries further complicated the issues at stake.

By the late 50s the doctrine of self-sufficiency had given way, at least as a matter of declared policy, to the acceptance of 'interdependence' in military procurement. In practice this meant continued independence from European suppliers but the acceptance of limited dependence on the United States; a dependence that became pivotal after the cancellation first of Blue Streak and then of the American Skybolt project. The desirability of cooperation with European partners appears to have been accepted first by those ministers responsible for defence and for the aircraft industry, without entirely convincing the Prime Minister or the Cabinet.[47] The first major step towards collaboration was taken in 1961, with the British initiative to establish ELDO, thus providing a continued role for the Blue Streak rocket as the basis of a European satellite-launcher. The ELDO Convention was signed in April 1962 by the Minister of Aviation and the Lord Privy Seal, representing respectively the interests of the British aerospace industry and the government's concern to emphasize its new-found commitment to Europe. In the same year it was decided to combine British studies of a supersonic civil transport aircraft with a parallel French project, on the basis of a formal inter-governmental agreement signed in November by the Minister of Aviation. A separate European Space Research Organization (ESRO) was also established during 1962 by an agreement signed by the Minister for Science. The lack of a clear technological strategy was, however, emphasized by the Prime Minister's negotiation of the Nassau Agreement in December 1962, committing the most symbolic British weapon system, the nuclear deterrent, to an American vehicle.

The Labour opposition made great play with the need for a 'scientific revolution' in the long run-up to the 1964 general election. Their emphasis on this theme reflected a belief that more efficient exploitation of high technology provided the answer to Britain's continuing economic weakness (and carried a powerful appeal to electoral imaginations). It also reflected Harold Wilson's personal identification with technology, as the son of an industrial chemist and the minister responsible in 1948 for the formation of the National Research and Development Council (NRDC).

However, Labour's preparations before the election seem to have given little attention to international collaboration as part of a new policy for technology; their proposals were focused on national activities, and were measured by their ability to stand up to American competition.[48] On coming into office, the new government's request to the French government to re-examine the Concorde supersonic aircraft project preceded a substantial commitment to Anglo-French collaboration in aircraft development, represented by the Anglo-French variable geometry (AFVG) project, the Jaguar, and three types of helicopter. For immediate replacement of cancelled military aircraft, the government turned to American suppliers; concerned primarily to procure the most advanced aircraft available at the lowest possible price.

A new political dimension to British external technological relations opened in January 1967, with the succession of exploratory visits to European capitals and Mr Wilson's proposals for a European technological community. The exact shape of this community and its relation to the existing Communities was not spelt out. An outsider's impression is that the impetus for this initiative came from Transport House, and that there was very little detailed work on its implications within the civil service.

In June 1967, a few days after Mr Wilson had made a two-day visit to Paris, the French government cancelled the AFVG. Its eventual replacement in the summer of 1968 by a major collaborative project with Germany and Italy, the Multi-Role Combat Aircraft (MRCA), contributed to a shift in the balance of Britain's external cooperation from France to Germany. This shift was also reflected in a number of shared developments in the defence field, from artillery to electronics. By early 1969 discussions had begun with the Dutch and the Germans on possible collaboration in the development of a nuclear centrifuge. The establishment of the Eurogroup within NATO, with Britain, the Netherlands, and Germany as its core, and of a substantial number of consultative groups on procurement, helped to reinforce the move away from France. But in industrial policy Britain continued to pursue national concentration rather than international collaboration. The Industrial Reorganization Corporation supported the amalgamation of AEI and English Electric, and the GEC takeover, in late 1968, 'to form a company capable of fighting the European giants on equal terms',[49] while the Ministry of Technology sponsored a major reconstruction of the British nuclear plant industry.

By 1969 the Labour government had fewer illusions about the advantages of European technological collaboration. It had announced its intended withdrawal from ELDO the previous year; it had supported an ambitious Anglo-American aircraft project by underwriting development of the RB-211 jet engine; it refused to join in the European Airbus. Yet collaboration continued on a wide range of activities, if without so clear a political rationale. Discussions continued on a number of politically sensitive joint ventures, including the proposed Channel Tunnel.

The new Conservative government in 1970 did not markedly alter this posture. Mr Heath in opposition had accepted as one of the motive forces for European unity the same belief in technological cooperation on a scale which could challenge the Americans; to which he had added the highly sensitive suggestion that Anglo-French cooperation on nuclear deterrence would help to strengthen the sense of European identity. Between 1970 and the end of 1972, however, an added political constraint affected the whole question of technological collaboration: that during the negotiations for and subsequent run up to membership of the EEC the British government must be seen to be behaving as 'a good European', and in particular must avoid giving unnecessary offence to the French government. Here, at least, an overall strategy was imposed upon the entire range of technological relations: though perhaps not entirely without ill effects.[50] What had changed, gradually but cumulatively over the previous decade, was the whole context of British management of advanced technology. With the MRCA, with Jaguar and Concorde, the Centrifuge project, and other collaborative developments, Britain was now engaged in a multilateral process of procurement, an integrated process that constrained yet further the government's freedom of choice.

The succession of reorganizations within Whitehall during the course of the 60s reflected uncertainty over the management of technological policy as a whole rather than simply with its external dimensions. The Ministry of Aviation, which replaced the Ministry of Supply in 1959, attracted much criticism for its failure to control or monitor costs in development programmes, most spectacularly over the Bloodhound missile. It escaped the defence reorganization in 1963 and was left out of the newly-established Ministry of Technology in 1964, but was eventually integrated with that ministry in 1967. Indeed, the expansion of the Ministry of Technology to cover the sponsorship of almost all major industries somewhat simplified the allocation of responsibilities, though it created an internal conflict between its responsibilities for promoting the interests of sponsored industries and the need critically to evaluate proposals for national and international projects. It did not attempt to develop an external technological strategy; its international divisions lacked the authority within Whitehall, and its minister (never one of the Labour government's enthusiasts for European unity) saw his role primarily in domestic terns.

Here again, the Treasury was not organized or equipped to promote a clear definition of objectives or priorities at the point of financial control. Within the public expenditure scrutiny process, Treasury divisions dealt with policy questions according to established departmental categories. Defence (Policy and Material) dealt with military procurement, Agriculture, Trade, and Technology with most aspects of civil technology, though in 1972–3 the British subscription to Euratom was assigned to the Public Enterprises division, as an extension of its responsibilities for atomic energy. The inability of the Treasury to control or coordinate technological policy early in the 60s is suggested by its admission in 1964 that it had not yet given formal authorization to the Concorde project.[51] In 1970 a parliamentary committee discovered that the Treasury still examined proposals for expenditure on related space developments under their separate departmental categories.[52]

Foreign Office involvement in external technological relations was relatively limited before 1964, and concerned mainly with the military and civil implications of nuclear energy. 'The Foreign Office interest' in the negotiation and signing of the ELDO Convention, official witnesses explained to a parliamentary committee, 'was simply limited to providing services to other departments who were engaged in negotiating with the other ELDO partners'.[53] A new Scientific Relations department emerged out of the old General department in 1965, reflecting the growing burden of this work. Yet this department was responsible only for outer space questions, civil applications of atomic energy, and scientific research, leaving civil aviation matters and cooperation in military procurement within the remit of two other departments. By 1969 the internal organization of the Foreign Office reflected a clearer definition of objectives, with Science and Technology, Defence Supply, and European Economic Integration departments grouped under a single under-secretary, and with the FCO claiming and playing a much more active role in technological relations. Its evidence to a Commons committee inquiring into space policy in 1971 contrasts sharply with that of 1966, in claiming as its function 'to relate UK space policy to our wider international interests' and 'also to ensure that the interests of the British aerospace industry are taken into account by other countries whenever possible'.[54] Its use of embassies and scientific attachés had also expanded considerably; the assistance and advice the Paris embassy provided for Whitehall discussions on the future of the computer industry in 1971–2 marked a radical change from its passive role in the ELDO negotiations.

Yet the FCO was inadequately equipped, in a number of ways, to play a central role in relating the growing network of external technological agreements to overall national interests and foreign policy objectives. The small number of officials responsible for this extensive field were necessarily much occupied with the complications of the Non-Proliferation Treaty and with other detailed international responsibilities, at the expense of watching for and noting, for instance, the potential implications for Anglo-French relations of a proposal for a company merger or a foreign takeover bid. Their technical expertise was, in the nature of the case, small. Furthermore, their function in Whitehall terms was to argue the case for considering the potential damage to relations with one or more foreign governments involved in abandoning or not entering any technological project rather than to argue for a careful examination of the potential costs and benefits involved. What had been most needed in the years between the launching of Mr Wilson's technological community proposal and the approach to EEC membership was a hard-headed attempt to balance the quantifiable elements, direct costs, prospects of future sales, and so on, against the unquantifiable elements of hoped-for foreign policy gains. The Foreign Office was not competent to conduct such an exercise; nor was it its proper role.

The incoming Conservative government in 1970 merged the Ministry of Technology into the Department of Trade and Industry, but without its responsibilities for civil and military aviation. After a government inquiry, military aviation and all other aspects of defence equipment were regrouped into a new Procurement Executive, a separately accountable agency within the MoD. Civil aviation, including the Concorde project, were transferred to the DTI, with a Ministerial Aerospace Board, in effect a ministerial committee, to coordinate between the two Departments, on which the Secretary of State for Education and Science and the Minister for Posts and Telecommunications also served for the purpose of coordinating space policy.[55] The widespread involvement of the Procurement Executive in joint procurement, bilaterally, trilaterally, and multilaterally, within the NATO framework and within a number of ad hoc organizations, ensured a thoroughgoing consideration of the advantages and disadvantages of particular projects; the accumulated experience of the past decade provided a useful guide.

Nevertheless, there was still a gap between official management and ministerial perceptions. In 1972 Conservative ministers could still talk in symbolic terms about the value of collaboration, as if it were an end in itself: 'the great lesson of Concorde . . . is that collaboration does work . . . Concorde will be remembered as one of the first and one of the greatest symbols of [Europe's] joint endeavours'.[56] The mixture of motives, the uncertainty over objectives, were still evident. Here, as in other areas of policy, officials in Whitehall did not see it as their function to pull the various strands of policy together, except through the consensual framework of interdepartmental committees, in which they did their best to defend what they saw as their ministers' wishes. Ministers were too preoccupied with political considerations, or in some cases too dazzled by the glamour of advanced technology, to devote enough attention to the compatibility of decisions on individual projects with wider or longer-term objectives, or consciously to balance conflicting considerations of domestic employment, of industrial policy, of the potential impact on the balance of payments, and of hoped-for benefits in foreign policy. Stronger critics might also argue that the dominant styles of debate both in Whitehall and Westminister inhibited clear definition of choices and of objectives, preferring to manage policy on a 'practical', which is to say a day-to-day basis.

To some extent pressure from outside the administration had by the late 60s encouraged sharper questioning of the assumed advantages of collaboration and clearer definition of government objectives. In the technological field domestic interests were concentrated and organized in a relatively small number of associations, such as the Society of British

Aerospace Constructors or the National Industrial Space Committee. In the civil nuclear energy sector, by 1972–3 the interests of industry were in effect represented by Sir Arnold Weinstock, as chairman of GEC. Relations between these interests and Departments were close and regular. Industrial disillusionment with the experience of technological collaboration in aviation under the Labour government, set out for instance in the Elstub Report on the aircraft industry in 1969, fed directly into Whitehall, questioning as it did much of what had earlier been conventional wisdom in this sector; though it is less clear that its criticisms were absorbed fully either by government ministers or by the opposition.[57] A compact group of industrialists in associated companies and journalists with specialist publications completed the network of informed and interested opinion in this field: small enough for critical attitudes rapidly to make themselves known to responsible officials in Whitehall, but relatively highly insulated from the general political debate.

Parliamentary committees provided a secondary source of outside criticism, strengthened in the early 60s by the election to Parliament of a small number of MPs with experience and expertise in technological matters, and by the creation of a new Select Committee on Science and Technology. The Estimates Committee and the Public Accounts Committee had already produced some searching reports on aspects of technological policy, and continued to do so. The Science and Technology Committee was one of the most successful of the new Select Committees, establishing a good relationship with Departments in Whitehall and producing, with the help of several sub-committees, a wide range of reports. Yet none of these committees succeeded in criticizing government policy as it developed. The Conservative government of 1970–4, like its predecessors, refused to give Parliament information about government intentions or about current calculations of costs and benefits of technological projects, so that parliamentary criticism was for the most part confined to retrospective comment. The Public Accounts Committee's criticism in 1969 of the failure publicly to re-examine the assumptions behind the Concorde programme apply to many other ventures as well. The Committee concluded that: 'Parliament should have been made aware at more frequent intervals of the escalating estimates and of the slippage in the programme, so that informed debate could take place on the justification for continuing with the project.'[58]

There remains the question of whether the different strands of policy within Whitehall might better have been pulled together at the centre. The Cabinet Office Secretariat, it must be reiterated, had no standing to impose its own perspective on departmental views; its role was limited to coordination, the preparation of papers, and the servicing of committees. The appointment of a Chief Scientific Adviser in 1966 improved the quality of advice available to the Prime Minister and the Cabinet, though his staff in 1971 amounted only to eight, four of whom were physicists.[59] The CPRS had the authority, indeed the aim, of questioning accepted assumptions and investigating areas of policy which fell across the responsibilities of several Departments, though it too was limited by the small size of its staff and the range of its other responsibilities. In 1971–2 the CPRS conducted an investigation into government policy on computers, primarily in terms of the domestic industry, but necessarily overlapping onto international considerations. But time and other priorities had not yet permitted a parallel investigation of other sectors of technology. Beyond this the established pattern of interdepartmental relations in Whitehall, strengthened by the close cooperation established by the early 70s, between the relevant divisions of the DTI and the FCO and by their links with the Procurement Executive, provided a regular forum for reviewing competing policies, both informally and through a number of committees.

The same pressures which pushed the British government towards greater and greater involvement in technological collaboration pushed in towards a more positive approach to arms sales. Joint procurement with other governments presented one means of spreading the cost of development and lengthening production runs; sales to foreign governments presented another. A third option, buying major weapons systems from foreign suppliers, had a damaging impact on the balance of payments – apart from the potential restrictions on freedom of use threatened by foreign control over the supply of spares and replacements – whereas sales abroad directly benefited the balance of payments. Moreover the construction of naval vessels and military aircraft provided substantial employment for skilled labour, often in shipyards where work was short. Nevertheless, foreign policy considerations cut across these defence, domestic, and industrial arguments. For the Labour Party in particular, the sale of arms to many foreign governments carried major political, or for some moral, implications, which more than counterbalanced the arguments in favour. For governments of whatever complexion, sales of arms may offer foreign policy pay-offs in terms of prestige, of cementing alliance ties or of creating good relations. Once arms have been supplied, provision of spares, replacements and ammunition provide a useful lever for political influence. The factor which distinguished arms sales from other technological issues, above all, was the political sensitivity, in domestic terms, of sales to countries which did not share the British system of government or the British perspective on international relations. This brought Parliament, political parties, and organized public opinion into the considerations which policy-makers must take into account.

Exports of British-built armaments had begun well before World War I. Vickers had supplied battleships to South American navies and other weapons to a range of countries; their arms salesman, Basil Zaharoff, was knighted for his achievements, though in the reaction of the 1920s he became a model for the 'merchants of death' who were blamed for fomenting war. The level of government involvement rose after World War II, partly because of the closer relationship between government and industry, partly because of the need for government-guaranteed export credits, partly because the North Atlantic alliance instituted a strategic embargo on defence-related exports to hostile countries, requiring a system of export licensing. The emergence of a succession of new states, as decolonization proceeded, each seeking to equip and expand its armed forces, widened the international market for sales of armaments as the Korean war rearmament effort slowed, leaving spare industrial capacity to fill. Yet until the early 60s the British government appears to have been more concerned with the political and strategic aspects of arms sales agreements than with the economic and industrial aspects, contracting to supply former dependent territories with weapons as part of the pattern of post-independence defence agreements. There was no conscious effort to promote arms exports. The permanent head of the Foreign Office, asked by a parliamentary committee in 1957 to describe the organization 'for soliciting or eliciting purchases of arms in respect of foreign countries', replied 'My knowledge is that there is no organization; the whole thing is done on a haphazard basis.'[60]

The impetus for a more direct approach to sales promotion came from three main developments. The aircraft industry failed to secure overseas sales for the next generation of military aircraft; after the success of the Hawker Hunter and the Canberra, the Lightning interceptor, designed too narrowly for distinctively British defence requirements, and the TSR-2 failed to attract foreign interest. At the same time growing concern at the continuing balance-of-payments deficit made politicians and officials anxious to exploit all export opportunities. Most significantly, the creation by the US government in 1961 of a specific arms sales organization, and the success of this organization in raising American arms exports and in displacing the British from some of their traditional markets, led to discussion of the need for a British response.[61]

In July 1965 the Labour government therefore asked the managing director of British Leyland, Sir Donald Stokes, to advise them on the most appropriate means of promoting exports of defence equipment. In the following year a new Defence Sales Organization was set up, within the MoD, headed by a prominent industrialist seconded to Whitehall.[62] The aim of ensuring as close cooperation between government and industry as had already been achieved in America was apparent in this appointment, confirmed in the appointment of another seconded businessman as his successor, in 1969. Service attachés in overseas missions were now expected to investigate sales possibilities and report back regularly; in 1967 there were, in addition, specialized defence supply staffs in posts in Washington, Bonn, Paris, Ottawa, and Canberra. In 1971 the Defence Sales Organization was transferred to the new Procurement Executive, its head now made responsible both to the Chief Executive and to the Permanent Under-Secretary in the MoD. The work of the new organization was remarkably successful; from a position in which Britain had fallen far behind France as well as the United States in terms of arms exports, overseas sales in the early 70s were increasingly rapidly and beginning to regain ground lost to French and American competition. In 1969–70 total British export sales were estimated at around £170m, of which some £55m were made by Royal Ordnance Factories and the rest by private industry. By 1971–2 this had risen to £270m at current prices, by 1973–4 to £405m.[63] As with so many other aspects of British external relations, the multilateral dimension had by now become important. Joint procurement projects, with the French, German, Dutch, and Italian governments, necessitated joint sales efforts – and threatened additional political complications about the acceptability of customers. Offset agreements with the German government now included consultation with the Americans; the 'package deal' negotiated with Saudi Arabia in 1965, worth over £100m, was part of a complicated agreement with the Americans to offset the costs of purchasing the F-111.[64]

The political sensitivity and security risks of arms sales to many countries naturally required an extensive structure for considering proposed contracts in Whitehall. Three of the twelve Commons emergency debates between 1967 and 1970, after all, had been on particular proposals for arms sales, to South Africa, to Nigeria, and to Libya. Expressions of interest by foreign governments might embarrass the British government, changes of regime throw doubt on the wisdom of existing contracts. In 1973 the Chinese government raised the possibility of buying some 300 Harrier jet fighters for defence on its western frontiers. Later that year the left-wing government of Chile, one of Britain's oldest arms customers, which had contracted to buy several naval vessels, was overthrown by a right-wing junta. In Whitehall an Arms Working Party, chaired by the FCO, considered the political expediency of selling arms to particular governments, and referred difficult cases upwards. A Military Information Policy Committee, mainly composed of MoD personnel, considered the desirability of allowing particular items of advanced equipment to pass into the hands of non-allied governments. Most decisions were taken effectively at the middle level, with little more than a final reference to Cabinet or Cabinet committee for approval, though experience of parliamentary storms over arms sales encouraged ministers to give more than perfunctory consideration to all large contracts. Underneath the network of committees responsible for monitoring and limiting arms sales, the services themselves were establishing special units to promote them. In 1973 a Royal Fleet Auxiliary was sailing round foreign ports carrying a floating exhibition of armoured vehicles, while the Royal Armoured Corps maintained a Sales Troop and the Royal Navy was forming a Foreign Training Unit to assist helicopter sales.

The peculiar sensitivity of arms sales to South Africa stemmed from the close historical relationship between the two countries. On the one hand was the repugnance which progressive politicians in Britain expressed for South Africa's racial policies, particularly after the 1961 Sharpeville massacre, on the other the internal divisions within the Conservative Party about what some saw as Harold Macmillan's abandonment of the white Commonwealth and over South Africa's withdrawal from the Commonwealth in 1961. Until 1964 Britain had been the dominant arms supplier to South Africa. In 1964 a UN resolution called for a boycott on arms supplies to South Africa, and the new Labour government announced that it would observe the resolution after the fulfilment of existing contracts, in spite of British obligations to South Africa under the Simonstown naval base agreement. By the end of 1966 most outstanding orders had been delivered, and the supply of new armaments (though not of spares) had ceased.

Why then did a majority of the DOPC, and perhaps of the Cabinet, appear to favour renewing arms exports to South Africa in December 1967? The South African government had been discussing the possibility of renewal for about a year beforehand, reportedly asking for up to £200m of purchases, all clearly intended for external defence rather than for internal repression. They wanted frigates, Buccaneer bombers, Nimrod naval reconnaissance aircraft, and air defence missiles. Judging the circumstances to be favourable in the immediate aftermath of devaluation, the South African government now set a deadline for decision. Official opinion within the Foreign Office was divided, primarily according to departmental perspectives and responsibilities. The Foreign Secretary himself, who had been directly involved in the discussions with the South Africans, was in favour of renewing supplies. He hoped, in return, for South African 'good offices' in any renewed attempts to reach a Rhodesian settlement; he was concerned about the increased strategic importance of South Africa since the closing of the Suez canal in July 1967 and in the light of rising Russian naval activity in the Indian Ocean, and he believed that a British refusal would not deprive South Africa of the arms but would merely lead to the French arms industry taking over a traditionally British market.[65] Officials within the MoD naturally emphasized the strategic argument. Still fighting in the post-devaluation review of public expenditure to save the F-111 order and the East of Suez presence, they were unlikely to support a negative decision which would depress the balance of payments and so increase the pressure to reduce overseas military expenditure. Their minister clearly supported the Foreign Secretary.[66] The new Chancellor of the Exchequer was fully occupied with the programme of expenditure cuts and with proposals to divert domestic production to increased exports. Ministers of spending Departments were struggling to defend items to which their party was firmly committed from the Treasury review, such as free prescriptions within the Health Service or the raising of the school leaving age. The arms order, details of which leaked out to the press early in December, offered the prospect of extending aircraft production lines which might otherwise soon be closed, of providing work for shipyards already short of orders. The argument was made, on at least one occasion, that the Labour government had not been elected to put Labour voters out of work.

Rumours of the Cabinet's impending decision, however, reached backbenchers and activists within the Labour Party – according to some accounts, inadvertently, according to others, by the efforts of a Prime Minister who had earlier approved the Foreign Secretary's discussions with the South Africans but who, scenting trouble, was now encouraging opposition from outside the government. An EDM put down by Labour MPs rapidly attracted 140 signatures, a majority of the party's backbenchers; questions were tabled in the House of Commons, and some furious lobbying took place within the party. Both sides gave different stories to the press, thus widening the dispute further. Faced with such pressure from its own party, the Cabinet reluctantly reaffirmed the ban. Mr Wilson announced its decision in a statement which began,' . . . no area of expenditure can be regarded as sacrosanct for the purposes of the searching examination we are making', in effect affirming that the strength of Labour Party feeling on an issue of great symbolic importance, if not of the highest importance to overall British foreign policy, had retained as sacrosanct a principle of foreign policy at the potential expense of some cherished principles of domestic policy.

The issue in 1970 was rather different. Very little official opinion within Whitehall by now strongly favoured resumed sales, though awareness of the economic and industrial benefits remained, and opinion within the MoD still placed some weight on the strategic importance of South Africa. The FCO was now firmly opposed to a resumption of exports, from consideration of the likely adverse reaction of the rest of Africa, of the importance to Britain of African trade and of oil imports from Nigeria; and perhaps also from a suspicion of South African motives. The crucial factors in this case were the development of Conservative opinion in opposition and the attempted intervention of the South African government in the British debate.[67] With some difficulty, the Conservative front bench had held to a broadly bipartisan line on Rhodesia over the past five years of opposition, containing imcipient revolts from its right wing, the section of the party most actively interested in foreign policy. To some extent the resulting discontent was deflected into a greater insistence on the importance of ties with South Africa, and on the need to ally more closely with those who were prepared to resist communist expansionism – clearly identified with increasing Soviet influence and naval activity in the Indian Ocean, and magnified by rumours of new Soviet naval bases and of subversive plans. The party had therefore committed itself in opposition to resuming sales of arms which were intended for external defence, if the South African government should ask for them.

The South African government's interest was not only in armaments (which were, after all, available from elsewhere) but in the gains in an increasingly isolated international position to be had from the demonstration of British support for South Africa which a major arms contract would provide. However, it overplayed its hand, perhaps from over-optimistic expectations of the strength of party and business influence on the new government. The South African Foreign Minister was, conveniently, in Geneva when the result of the election was announced; his arrival in London, as the government's first and uninvited foreign visitor, attracted wide press publicity and aroused a storm of protest. The new Foreign Secretary, Sir Alec Douglas-Home, received him four days later, after some hurried discussions within the FCO. Sir Alec's apparent initial willingness to lift the arms embargo was tempered by the comments of several ministers within the DOPC.[68] The reaction of other African governments, and of a number of Britain's allies, reinforced the arguments for caution. Opinion within the CBI was divided; the pro-South African lobby, organized within the UK-South Africa Trade Association, was countered by companies with investments or trading interests in the rest of Africa and by the scruples of some CBI officials. A small group of Conservative MPs emerged who were opposed to lifting the embargo, partly counterbalancing pressure from the party's right wing. The decision was postponed through the summer, then postponed again until after the Commonwealth Prime Ministers' Meeting in January 1971. The decision which finally emerged, in February, was an agreement to sell seven naval helicopters: a far cry from the 'shopping list' which the South Africans had detailed in June 1970 and little more than a gesture to opinion in the party. Although further discussions between South African representatives and British shipbuilding companies and aircraft manufacturers continued for some months afterwards, the issue was in effect shelved. Given divided opinions in industry and in the country, the combined influence of official opinion and of foreign governments, reinforced as the debate dragged on by a growing number of Cabinet ministers, was sufficient to push back the party pressure which had built up in opposition, when such other constraints were less compelling.[69]

These two examples briefly demonstrate the differing patterns of domestic and international constraints on different areas of policy within the broad defence field. Policy-making on arms sales differs from aspects of external relations related to technology in the involvement of organized public opinion, most directly through the political parties but also (as in the case of arms supplies during the Nigerian civil war) through the churches and through other organized groups concerned with foreign policy.

This emotive dimension attached to British involvement in the international arms trade before governmental participation had become so direct, and before the high cost of advanced technology and the desperate need for exports had added their imperatives. Technological policy has to an extent taken over from defence policy the aura of national prestige.

It shared with defence a heavy demand on public expenditure, but in the last decade has been distinguished from defence policy, strictly defined, by the much greater emphasis placed upon intergovernmental collaboration – and by the confusion displayed both in the objectives pursued and in the Whitehall policy-making machinery. None of these issue areas are dominated alone by foreign policy considerations; in each of them domestic pressures and domestic objectives intervene. It is all very well to declare that 'defence research and development is a part of defence and foreign policy', or that 'defence must be the servant of foreign policy'.[70] The relationship between commercial, industrial, military, emotional, and external considerations is far more complex than that. The distinctive network of interests and constraints in each area imposes its own pattern of policy.

6: Economic and Commercial Policy

BY THE EARLY 70s the overwhelming importance of economic considerations in foreign policy had become part of the conventional wisdom
of Whitehall – repeatedly stated, even if not always accepted in practice.
The inhibiting effect of economic weakness on Britain's freedom of
action in foreign affairs had profoundly impressed officials within the
Foreign Office during the Labour government of 1964–70. Consciousness
of Britain's dependence on the United States for support for sterling
(which forced the government to suppress its doubts about American
policy in Vietnam and in the Dominican Republic), the enforced withdrawal from East of Suez, the acrimony which accompanied successive
offset negotiations with the Germans, the economic necessity which cut
expenditure on overseas aid, on cultural policy, and on diplomatic
representation abroad, all these emphasized the impossibility of pursuing
an independent foreign policy without a firm base in a sound economy.

Increasing instability in the international monetary and trading
systems also brought economic issues more and more to the centre of
ministerial and prime ministerial concern. The succession of currency
crises, the long disputes about the role of gold and the creation of new
forms of international reserves, the rumbling dispute over trade discrimination between the United States and the European Community,
culminated in the 'Nixon initiative' of August 1971, when the American
administration suspended the convertibility of the dollar and deliberately
linked issues of trade and of defence with its conditions for international
monetary reform. The emergence of a cartel of oil producers, first
threatening and then in 1973 successfully imposing restrictions on oil
supplies and sharp and rapid increases in price, added to the sense of
international economic crisis. By the end of 1973 it was evident to all that
economic issues would be at the heart of Britain's foreign policy for the
foreseeable future.

The separation of foreign economic policy from the traditional diplomatic and security concerns of foreign policy has, however, been deeply
embedded in British policy and practice. The reasons for this separation
are to be found partly in the dominant economic ideology of British
policy-makers both before and after World War II, partly in the distinctive institutional framework within which economic policy was handled
both at the national and at the international level for twenty years after
the war, partly in the direct link between domestic economic management and foreign economic policy, and partly in the distinctive and highly

influential domestic interests which are involved in the field of economic policy.

The predominant orientation of policy-makers – and of economists – to matters of international economic policy throughout the interwar years represented one which identified Britain's interests with the maximum possible degree of free trade and with sound money. Even when the near collapse of the international economic order had forced the British government to take the pound off the gold standard and to abandon free trade for imperial preference, many attitudes associated with these principles persisted: including the belief that political considerations should not be encouraged to distort the international economy, and that the government should intervene in the operations of the international market as little as possible. In May 1938, for instance, Treasury officials, and some ministers, opposed proposals from the Foreign Office and the Board of Trade for positive efforts to expand British economic influence in the Balkans, as a counter to German economic and political penetration, because they were not consonant with the principle of non-intervention in the free market.[1] In spite of the changed attitude of postwar governments to governmental intervention in the domestic economy, such attitudes tended to persist into the postwar world: evident in the predominant attitude to sterling and to the maintenance of a stable exchange rate, and in the identification of Britain's interests with those of a liberal international economic order. Large areas of foreign economic policy were therefore taken as given: not closely linked with foreign policy because they were not seen as proper or as available instruments of foreign policy. This conceptual separation of economic from political considerations was reinforced by the predominant orientation of academic economists towards the international economy. The economic advice which successive governments received about foreign economic policy, throughout the 50s and for much of the 60s, reflected the academic perception of economic problems as more technical than political, as well as the divorce of economics from politics which obtained in the universities.[2]

To some extent this compartmentalization of foreign economic policy disguised the unquestioned association of existing economic policies with the overall high policy objectives of postwar British foreign policy: the maintenance of great power status, the 'special relationship' with the United States, and continued British leadership of the Commonwealth. Britain did, after all, have a political stake in the re-established economic order, apart from the economic interest dictated by its dependence on imports of raw materials, its income from overseas investment and from the management of international finance, insurance, and shipping. With the United States, Britain played a key role in the management of the international economy. The IMF, for many years, was in effect 'an Anglo-Saxon institution'.[3] Sterling and the dollar were the twin pillars around which the international monetary system revolved, giving the British a special position in American international economic relations which reinforced the political special relationship. The sterling area was seen less as an economic liability left over from the war than as a political asset which helped to bind the Commonwealth together under British leadership, with the annual conferences of Commonwealth finance ministers as one of its most tangible economic and political ties. Sterling, indeed, came to symbolize more than this. The maintenance of the existing parity of sterling held a place in the imagination of many British politicians, bankers, and commentators comparable to that of the Stars and Stripes in American patriotism: a symbol of the country's pride, of all that was best in the British tradition.

A further factor which helped to separate debate on foreign economic policy from other fields of foreign policy was the technical language in which policy was so often discussed. The expertise needed to follow international economic discussions, most particularly in monetary policy, less so in commercial negotiations, operated to some extent to exclude the technically unversed from participation in the formulation of policy. At its worst, this led to the dismissal of opinions from representatives of non-economic Departments as unworthy of respect, and to suspicion on the part of those attempting to intervene that technical language was used to baffle them. At best, it nevertheless represented a barrier to the exercise of influence on the direction of policy by the non-expert.

The institutional framework in Whitehall will be examined in detail below. Here it is worth emphasizing the distinctive international context within which those responsible for the management of Britain's financial and commercial relations mixed with their opposite numbers from other countries. The establishment at the end of the Second World War of a stable international monetary system and an acceptable set of rules for international trade, together with the firm support the United States provided for the institutions which embodied them, succeeded in insulating international economic relations from high foreign policy for some twenty years afterwards. Most successfully in the ten years from the mid-50s to the mid-60s, international monetary management was handled by a select group of national and international officials, with ministers of finance and governors of central banks playing a supervisory role. A similar club of international officials, with its own private language and its own set of shared assumptions, was responsible for the conduct of successive tariff and trade negotiations. As during the 60s the problems of managing the international economic system became gradually more acute, and the system itself gradually less stable, the intensity of contacts within this multinational network sharply increased – till by the end of the decade the significance of the political differences which underlay the problems of technical adjustment had become apparent to all. The United States was moving from its established position as the custodian of the existing system to one of demanding major reforms, the developing countries were pressing for more consideration of their interests. Not only foreign offices, but prime ministers and presidents were becoming directly involved in international economic discussions, and it was less possible to keep international economic relations in a separate compartment.

Perhaps the most compelling reason for the separation of foreign economic policy-making from other aspects of foreign policy is the inseparability of foreign economic policy from domestic economic management. From the point of view of a Foreign Office planner, Britain's relations with, for instance, Japan or the United States may form a pattern in which considerations of monetary policy, trade barriers, investment, security, attitudes towards third countries, and shared views about the shape of the international policial system, all fall into place. But planners in the Treasury, the Bank of England, or the DTI (and its successor ministries) will have a different perspective, linking international monetary policy with domestic monetary priorities and international trade policy with domestic industrial interests. The very success of the postwar international economic order in reducing the barriers between domestic economies has meant that very few aspects of domestic economic management do not now contain significant international implications, and conversely that changes in the rules governing international economic cooperation carry direct domestic consequences, and are likely to arouse direct domestic protests.

The enlargement of governmental activity in the economy since World War II has contributed to the difficulty of disentangling domestic considerations from international ones. 'Managed economies and balance of payment problems . . . go hand in hand.'[4] Countries with fully convertible currencies must pay attention, in determining the level of interest rates, not only to their effect on domestic economic activity but also to the level of interest rates in other countries, the degree of international confidence in the national currency, and the consequent implications of a rise or fall in domestic interest rates on foreign currency reserves. Other potential instruments of domestic economic management, import controls and export incentives, are subject to international rules and restrictions; though government assistance to exporters, through the underwriting (and on occasion subsidization) of export credit and through official promotion of exports, has developed into a not very well controlled intergovernmental competition. Regional incentives for industrial investment attract foreign companies to the less prosperous regions of Britain, while the encouragement of industrial mergers through governmental intervention and the provision of government finance shields domestic companies from foreign competition. Subsidies by foreign governments to such industries as shipbuilding force the British government to extend tax concessions and grants to domestic industries, even when (as under the Conservatives between 1970 and 1973) such actions fit uneasily with declared government policy, in order to maintain full employment and to prevent an additional burden on the import bill. The interdependence of domestic and international economic policy was brought home most starkly to the British government and to the British public by the succession of conditions which foreign creditors, first the United States bilaterally and then the IMF multilaterally, imposed on the provision of support for sterling between 1964 and 1969. They demanded first the re-examination of major technological projects, then looked for reductions in public expenditure and for a stricter incomes policy, and finally, in the 1969 IMF Letter of Intent, imposed tight limits on the expansion of domestic credit.

The pursuit of a coherent economic policy cannot easily be combined with the pursuit of a coherent foreign policy. Priorities, as well as perspectives, differ. Where international obligations conflict with domestic economic objectives the former may well appear less binding, as in the imposition of import quotas in 1964, in breach of Britain's EFTA and GATT obligations, or in the postponement of British adherence to the European Community's monetary arrangements throughout 1973. Economic management is at the centre of the domestic political debate. Governments win elections by their success or failure in managing the economy, in holding down the rate of inflation, in stimulating growth or in reducing unemployment. It is one of the paradoxes of contemporary politics that national governments stand or fall by their performance in a sector over which, given the interdependence of national economies, they exert only partial control: a paradox which pushes the British and other governments towards contradictory international policies, towards both an insistence on the necessity of cooperative intergovernmental management and a willingness to jettison international obligations and to by-pass international machinery when domestic politics seem to demand it. They are moved by the most powerful of domestic constraints – the urge above all to ensure their political survival at the hands of an electorate which cares little and knows less about the intricate regulations of international trade or the finer points of proposals for new forms of international reserves, but which expects from its government full employment, low interest rates, stable prices, and rising incomes.

Much of the subject matter of foreign economic policy is close to the heart of the relationship between government and industry. The importance which governments must attach to private interests is thus much greater in this field than in defence and security policy: to a considerable extent, the 'national interests' which the British government is promoting and defending abroad *are* those of British finance and industry. The pattern of consultation established over the past fifty years between government and industry has therefore extended from matters of domestic economic policy to international questions. In some sectors of foreign economic policy, private interests are directly involved in the process of policy-making; in most sectors governmental success is measured by its ability to promote and protect particular interests.

So far we have talked about foreign economic policy as a whole, rather than distinguishing between different strands of policy within this wide field. A minimal definition of 'policy' would be the avoidance of inter-governmental conflict over economic questions: a task which in itself requires a considerable amount of governmental activity, in managing or monitoring Britain's foreign economic relations. More positively, two wider tasks may be distinguished: the protection of British economic interests from damage by developments in the international economy, together with the promotion of those interests wherever possible; and the British contribution to intergovernmental discussions about the management and future development of the international economic order.[5] More widely still, policy may be defined as the reconciliation of economic objectives involved in these, often divergent, tasks with the pursuit of other, non-economic, foreign policy objectives.

Economists and others have criticized both the British government's choice of priorities among conflicting goals in economic policy and the balance struck between economic and non-economic objectives since World War II. Among economic priorities, three criticisms stand out. The first is that over the period 1945–67 financial considerations were too often preferred to industrial or commercial ones: that the demands of sterling and of currency management were given more weight than the needs of industrial exporters or the expansion of the domestic economy, that what would benefit the City of London was considered more important than what would benefit manufacturing industry. This imbalance was attributed partly to the dominance within the Treasury of the Overseas Finance division, and partly to 'the Treasury's submission', in turn, 'to the Bank's superior expertise'; 'the powerful alliance of the Bank of England and the Treasury', sharing the same orthodox attitude to international financial morality, biased the whole discussion of economic policy within Whitehall.[6] The second, closely linked to the first, is that the British government too often unquestioningly identified its interests with those of the international economic order – or, as harsher critics would have it, subordinated its national interests to those of the international economic order. It was not only that 'the Bank of England (as well as much of the City and the Conservative Party) seemed to think that there was a moral obligation to protect the reserves of the bank's overseas customers' but were less ready to admit the existence of a moral obligation to those who became unemployed through deflationary domestic policies and the avoidance of devaluation.[7] It was also that, in Whitehall discussions on policy, officials from the most powerful Departments 'often spoke as though they were more concerned for, say, the fate of EFTA, the Sterling Area or the Kennedy Round than for that of this country.'[8] The third criticism is that short-term objectives have too often been preferred to long-term ones, that the broader interests of the British economy and balance of payments have on successive occasions been sacrificed to immediate considerations of domestic politics or of international obligation. The curbs which the Labour government of

1964–70 placed on outward investment, for example, seemed both to academic and to industrial critics to sacrifice long-term advantages in order to save short-term costs.[9]

Two contradictory lines of criticism have been made about the balance struck between economic and non-economic objectives. The first, and the most widely circulated among economists, is that for too long Britain subordinated economic interests in foreign policy to what governments perceived to be the responsibilities of power: incurring heavy defence expenditure, thus directing resources from exporting industries, maintaining forces overseas, thus adding to the burdens on the balance of payments, maintaining the value of sterling, and thus abandoning one of the most potent economic instruments available for promoting growth.[10] Conversely, representatives of the radical tradition in British politics protest that increasingly from the early 60s, in foreign policy British governments have subordinated principle to economic advantage: failing to support the democratic government of Israel 'for fear of offending oil-rich, sterling-holding Arab sheikhs', demonstrating our goodwill to dictatorial governments in the hope of gaining further exports, or selling arms for primarily commercial reasons to regimes which suppress minorities and imprison their opponents.[11]

These criticisms are set out to demonstrate the unavoidable problems of reconciling conflicting goals within a large and complex field. The British government's ability to identify and to choose among divergent goals, as has already been suggested, has not always been high. Part of the explanation for this lay in the compartmentalized structure of Whitehall, part in the secrecy which, here as elsewhere, clouds the policy-making process; but part also lay in the limited perspectives of ministers as well as of civil servants. The willingness of successive Chancellors of the Exchequer to accept the financial orientation of their advisers, the willingness of Cabinets to accept a scale of priorities in which exports and economic growth were subordinated to sterling, the financial orthodoxy of successive Prime Ministers, reinforced and maintained the established Whitehall machine.[12] Most Foreign Secretaries displayed little interest in economic matters, and most Chancellors accepted a narrow definition of their role in debating foreign policy, thus maintaining the compartmentalization of issues into 'high foreign policy' and 'economic policy'. The relative lack of interest of Conservative Prime Ministers between 1951 and 1964 in international economic matters, as opposed to security, disarmament, and political summits, also inhibited the drawing together of the different strands of policy. The more active interest of both Mr Wilson and Mr Heath in economic policy, domestic and foreign, has in contrast contributed to the integration of Whitehall policy-making, with consequent effects on the machinery through which policy is evolved and managed.

If the strategic outlines of foreign economic policy are decided – or assumed – in general terms at high level, the management of foreign economic relations at middle and low level covers a very wide range of detailed transactions, and is handled on a day-to-day basis by relatively distinctive groups of officials and interests. The conduct of international monetary relations, for instance, includes an extensive administrative machinery for dealing with exchange control, managed on behalf of the Treasury by the Bank of England; it necessitates frequent decisions on flows of investment, and requires regular and discreet consultations between the Bank and companies whose operations involve large-scale transactions across the exchanges. Policy on inward and outward investment involves the British government in vetting foreign takeover bids for British firms, and in making representations to foreign governments when British-based companies come up against their anti-trust legislation or are expropriated without warning or adequate compensation. Foreign trade policy includes a great deal of detailed negotiation on tariff regulations and non-tariff barriers, comprehensible only to the really expert. International fisheries policy, except in periods of direct intergovernmental disputes, is a remarkably self-contained area, managed in conjunction with the fishing interests and the network of international bodies concerned by the Fisheries department of the Ministry of Agriculture (*not* by that Ministry's External Relations divisions), with one FCO department holding a watching brief. Successive intergovernmental negotiations for civil aviation agreements, peculiarly acrimonious because of the direct financial implication of the division of air traffic agreed to for government-sponsored airlines and for the balance of payments, are handled primarily by a division within the Department of Industry, in close cooperation with the airlines; again with a department of the FCO and the embassy concerned monitoring developments in case the dispute should emerge on to the political level. Every economic and industrial Department in Whitehall is involved in some aspect of international economic relations; and the volume of work is very considerable, both in Whitehall and in overseas posts, even if for the most part it can be handled by junior officials. The sections below follow the broad division between financial and commercial policy, accepted both in the pattern of intergovernmental organizations and in the institutional divisions of Whitehall, and illustrative examples are taken from the decision to devalue the pound in November 1967, and from the area of export promotion and export credit.

The Management of International Financial Policy

The Treasury is responsible for financial policy, and the Bank of England is its executive agent. That, at least, has been the formal position since the Bank was nationalized in 1946. The exclusiveness of the relationship between the Bank and the Treasury in financial matters, the special relationship between the Chancellor of the Exchequer and the Prime Minister, the Governor of the Bank's regular meetings with the Chancellor, his right of access to the Prime Minister, and his lack of contact with the rest of the Cabinet, including the Foreign Secretary, contributed a great deal to the isolation of international financial policy from wider considerations of foreign policy in the two decades after World War II.

The organization of the financial divisions of the Treasury has already been touched on in chapter 2. Successive reorganizations have reflected the institutional difficulties of reconciling the management of the increasing complexities and time-consuming discussions of international finance, with the need to relate British policy to domestic objectives. The criticism that in the 1950s 'the centre of gravity, in terms of capacity as well as achievement . . . lay in the large Overseas Finance Division' was partly met by the reorganization of Home Finance and Overseas Finance in 1962 into a single Finance Group with the aim of more closely relating international to domestic considerations.[13]

The Labour government in 1964 gave the newly-created DEA a coordinating role in some aspects of international economic policy; though policy-making on financial matters remained the responsibility of the Treasury, and the DEA's functions in this area were ultimately reabsorbed into the Treasury and the Cabinet Office. Early in 1973 Overseas Finance was again separated from Home Finance: recognizing the growing burden which multilateral consultations placed on the Overseas Finance divisions (now further increased by entry to the European Community) and drawing Home Finance closer to the National Economy Group, responsible for domestic economic management.

The most striking feature of the Finance Group in the early 70s was the smallness of its staff.[14] Its divisions were responsible for providing a financial perspective on every aspect of external relations under discussion within Whitehall, for briefing the Chancellor on the position he might take in foreign policy discussions, for giving instructions to the Bank of England on the management of the exchanges and of monetary policy as a whole, and for preparing for – and often attending – the regular multilateral meetings within the framework of the IMF, the OECD, and now also the EEC.[15] The impossibility of such a small group of officials giving more than the most cursory and superficial consideration to issues outside their immediate sphere of responsibility may account for the often criticized 'narrowness' of the Treasury perspective on questions of foreign policy, and the failure to take account of the economic and financial implications of foreign and defence policy decisions.

The exact nature of the relationship between the Treasury and the Bank of England is one of the cardinal mysteries of British government; only slightly illuminated by the Select Committee on Nationalized Industries' investigation in 1970.[16] Most commentators agree on the persistence of a 'basic imbalance between the Treasury's Finance Group and the Bank', attributed to the Bank's degree of independence from government, to the strength of its links with foreign central banks, to the political and economic influence of the City of London, and to the ambiguity of the Bank's position as both representing the government to the City and the City to the government.[17] Governors of the Bank, while appointed by the Chancellor, have far greater security in office. The retirement of Lord O'Brien in mid-1973, and his replacement by Mr Gordon Richardson, a merchant banker, marked only the fifth change in the office in fifty years, a period which had seen twenty-one Chancellors. The Governor dealt directly with the Chancellor, in the late 60s meeting him at least once a week, the nature of their relationship depending a great deal upon the personalities of the two men. As spokesman for the City and the financial community, the Governor would on occasion publicly criticize government policy. The overall imbalance between the Bank and the Treasury was further marked by the Bank's representation 'on nearly every economic committee' in the Treasury and in Whitehall and the absence of Treasury representation on policy-making committees within the Bank.[18] Until 1966 the internal operations of the Bank remained a mystery even to most officials in the Treasury, though from then on, slowly developing, a limited number of Treasury officials began to spend periods working in the Bank.

In considering international financial policy, two aspects of this imbalance between the Bank and the Treasury stand out: the Bank's more generous staffing, and the greater resources available to Bank officials to travel abroad on their own initiative to gather information and to consult with central bankers in other countries. In 1972 the Overseas Department of the Bank, which had just separated itself from the huge and largely executive Exchange Control Department, contained some 125 staff at administrative grade levels, with a narrower range of responsibilities than their opposite numbers in the Treasury. The Department was organized, not unlike a foreign ministry, into functional and regional divisions; the foreign languages its staff could command included Chinese and Russian, and it contained in addition a translation section. Geographical 'advisers' were expected to spend up to three months in every year travelling round their 'parishes', maintaining contact with foreign banks and reporting back on economic conditions in Latin America, Eastern Europe, the Middle East, Africa, or Asia. Their expenses were met from the Bank's own resources.

Not surprisingly, therefore, the Treasury depended heavily on the Bank for information and assessment of international economic developments; more particularly since, until the late 60s, economic reporting from embassies was accorded little respect within the Treasury. The Bank's access to detailed and up-to-date information about financial developments overseas and in the international markets was extended by its regular and informal contacts with British overseas banks in London, and with representatives of the many foreign banks operating in London, including several from Eastern Europe. 'The central banking family is very closely knit . . . almost every week of the year we have ten or twenty people in the Bank of England from other banks'[19] – some 500 or 600 visitors a year, who stayed from one or two days to three months at a time. Every two or three years, in addition, the Bank held a three month central banking course attended by nominees of other central banks: formally the 'Commonwealth' Central Banking Course until 1970, but by the early 70s opening its doors more widely. The greater inflow of members of foreign central banks than the movement of British bank officials outward reflected not only the pre-eminence of London as an international banking centre but also the Bank's continuing prestige and administrative reputation. In 1970 some thirty Bank of England staff were working on secondment in other central banks, mostly in senior positions in the central banks of the newer Commonwealth countries. The extent to which the Bank saw itself as part of a close international community separate from Whitehall is suggested by the contrast between the Governor's enthusiasm for inter-bank exchanges, and his 'reservations' about the desirability of encouraging exchanges with 'the government'. In early 1970 there were officials from the Board of Trade, the Treasury, and the Central Statistical Office in the Bank of England, but no Bank officials in Whitehall.[20]

During the 1930s the Treasury had developed its own limited net work of overseas representation, with permanent 'Treasury representatives' attached to British embassies in Berlin, Paris, Washington, and the Far East. The Washington and Far East posts (the latter resident in Kuala Lumpur) were maintained after 1945. The overwhelming importance of sterling-dollar relations throughout the 50s and 60s, together with the establishment of the headquarters of both the IMF and the World Bank in Washington, made the role of 'the UK Treasury and Supply Delegation' there crucial, and service on the delegation a prelude to promotion. In 1972 it amounted to five administrative-grade officials, the most senior an under-secretary, four from the Treasury and one (the Alternate Director of the World Bank) from the ODA.[21] The smaller office in Kuala Lumpur was concerned more specifically with sterling area matters; with the successful multilaterization of the sterling balances, and the effective ending of the sterling area by the regulations which accompanied the decision to float the pound in June 1972, its importance had diminished, and it was closed later that year.

In addition to their own direct contacts with other countries, both the Treasury and the Bank were actively involved in the regular round of multilateral consultations within the IMF, the OECD, the Bank for International Settlements (BIS) and (until it was wound up in 1972) the European Monetary Agreement. The regularity of these consultations had greatly increased at the beginning of the 1960s, in the wake of the return to full convertibility of European currencies in 1958 and the replacement of the dollar surplus by an emerging dollar deficit. OECD began operations in 1961, rapidly establishing a number of committees on financial, economic, and development issues. A succession of difficulties within the international monetary system in 1960 and 1961 led to the emergence of the Group of Ten within the IMF and the establishment of the multilateral 'Gold Pool' – in which Britain acted as agent for other governments in the London gold market – and of the General Arrangement to Borrow. Thereafter increasing instability and uncertainty progressively led to more frequent meetings. Working Party Three of the Economic Policy Committee of the OECD, one of the key meeting places for finance officials, had met every two months in the early 60s; at one point in 1970 it was meeting every three weeks. The period of more intensive consultation which began with the 'Nixon initiative' of August 1971 and extended through Britain's approach to and entry into the European Communities drew more and more national civil servants into still more regular intergovernmental discussions. One Treasury estimate suggested that in 1973 some 40 per cent of its administrative grade officials travelled abroad at least once on intergovernmental business, the more senior officials being the most frequent travellers. The second secretary in charge of the Finance Group reckoned under normal conditions to spend about a quarter of his working time abroad; under the exceptional conditions of the first three months of 1973 he had spent more than half his working time out of the country.

In many ways the formal meetings were less important than the opportunities these occasions provided for informal exchanges of views. It might not be too strong to talk about a degree of socialization among the officials who participate, certainly about a slowly shifting consensus on acceptable and unacceptable forms of international behaviour.

The purpose of Working Party Three is usually described as educational. The ultimate goal is a convergence of viewpoints through informational exchange among experts who hold high policy-making positions in their respective countries.[22]

Those attending are influential people in their own governments, and they are naturally sensitive to the opinions of their foreign counterparts.[23]

If discussions did not always produce agreement, 'the face-to-face meetings' at the BIS in Basle (as at Paris and Washington) over many years 'helped to promote a solidarity of viewpoint and a sense of mutual confidence which facilitated negotiations by telephone' during a crisis[24] Solidarity was reinforced by a common commitment to the maintenance of the international monetary system. It was generally agreed by British and foreign participants that central bankers represented a more close-knit, even a more closed, international club than did the parallel network of finance ministry officials: made even more close-knit by the Bank of England's connection in April 1972 to the direct conference telephone circuit linking the central banks of the EEC, which was used for discussions three times a day. Foreign Offices and diplomats, it may be noted, played no part in this network, concerned as it was with mainly technical matters – though some of these technical matters thinly concealed major political differences. Finance ministers were less closely involved than their civil servants, responsible as they were for a wider range of issues and distracted by their domestic political role; but the frequency of their meetings too was sharply increasing in the early 70s, within differing organizational contexts, and increased for Britain particularly with the approach to Community entry in 1972–3.

In these continuing discussions it was often difficult for British officials to distinguish between the interests of sterling and those of the international economic order as a whole. Many of the repeated monetary crises of the 1960s in effect revolved around sterling, and in several others sterling played a major role. The burden of Britain's international responsibilities was borne in upon Treasury officials not only by the Bank of England and by their own preconceptions, but also by the firm representations of foreign civil servants and central bankers, until the severe weakness of the British economy had impressed itself fully upon foreign opinion. As has been noted, the extension of massive international credits to support sterling, both before and after devaluation, carried with it an element of foreign intervention in British domestic politics – and not simply in domestic economic management. More than one member of the Labour government of 1964–70 recalled that the Chancellor insisted that the the Industrial Relations Bill of 1969, which caused so much acrimony within the PLP, was a necessary concession to international financial opinion, most of all to the IMF.[25] The IMF's attempts to impose conditions on the management of public expenditure and the expansion of domestic credit, in the 1968 and 1969 negotiations over the annual 'Letter of Intent', provoked press opposition and political resistance to what were seen as 'banana republic' terms.[26]

These negotiations, as well as the annual OECD country review, also offered officials the prospect of transnational coalitions – of gaining foreign support for views they wished to press on to ministers and within Whitehall. It was open to British participants in such discussions to suggest what recommendations the IMF or OECD might best press upon Whitehall. One consequence of multilateral surveillance of the British economy was thus to increase the influence of officials and to diminish that of ministers. However, ministers might on occasion revolt against the political interference which multilateral surveillance implied. Harold Lever, then Financial Secretary to the Treasury, flew unannounced to Washington in May 1969 to resist the terms the IMF was then seeking to impose. The Conservative government of 1970–4 was sufficiently annoyed by the tone of the 1970 OECD review of Britain's economic situation to exert pressure at the highest level to moderate the tone of its successor.[27]

Both the technical character and the technical requirements of international monetary management, as well as this distinctive transnational network, continued to separate this area from wider concerns of foreign policy in the more politicized atmosphere of the 1970s. 'To the outside world our discussions . . . must often seem theoretical and esoteric', Mr Barber, the Conservative Chancellor, remarked at the IMF annual meeting in September 1971; the technical complexities of Special Drawing Rights, floating currencies, crawling pegs, and stable but adjustable parities, kept discussions of direct political and economic significance to Britain off all but the financial pages of the quality press. The technical necessity of subjecting transactions with members of the sterling area to exchange control at the moment that Britain decided to float the pound, in June 1972, and the speed which the situation then prevailing forced upon the decision to float, meant in effect that a change of policy which had significant implications for future relations with, for instance, Australia was determined in isolation by the Bank and the Treasury.

The level of Foreign Office involvement in international financial policy had been traditionally low, and remained so until the late 60s, as did its expertise and information in this field: reflecting the rather lower priority given to economic matters than to security questions and high diplomacy, as well as the reluctance of diplomats to venture into an unfamiliar field. The Foreign Office had contained a small Economic Relations department since World War II, covering the whole field of foreign economic policy from exchange control to food supplies, from oil imports and arms exports to commerical policy; the Commonwealth Office contained a number of economic departments, organized in the early 60s according to international regions. With the merger of the two ministries in 1968 these were reorganized along functional lines, with a new Financial Policy and Aid department relating directly to the Treasury. The Plowden Committee's comment in 1964 that in overseas posts 'economic and commercial work are two sides of the same coin', and that 'an officer reporting on economic developments in a country overseas can easily become academic without the realities of day-to-day commercial and business affairs to guide him' reflected the then prevailing view that the first priority of embassy economic sections was to promote exports.[28] Not unnaturally therefore, information of use to economic policy-makers at home, as opposed to industrialists, was rather thin.

Successive sterling crises, devaluation, experience gained in the 1967 and 1969–70 discussions on EEC entry, appreciation among a number of Diplomatic Service officials that the FCO would increasingly lose out in Whitehall unless its members were able to contribute effectively to economic discussions – and perhaps also the stimulation of having, in the person of George Brown, a Foreign Secretary actively interested in economic issues – had combined to raise both the level of attention and the degree of expertise by the early 70s. Members of the Diplomatic Service began to be seconded to industry and to the City of London, and also to the Treasury. In 1969 for the first time a diplomat spent a period working in the Bank of England before going on to become head of the Financial Policy and Aid department, and in 1972–3 secondments of three months or so for training and 'acclimatization' before going out to overseas posts as financial secretaries or financial counsellors were beginning to become an accepted practice. Mid-career training in economics had spread. The Foreign Office had inherited a small number of specialized economists from the Commonwealth Office, organized from 1968 onwards into an Economists' department, though their prestige within the FCO several years later remained low; a service department rather than an influential contributor to policy formation. Not surprisingly, the quality of economic reporting from embassies and the respect the Treasury accorded to FCO advice had improved markedly. To some extent the bilateral relationship between the Treasury and the Bank had thus become a triangular relationship with the FCO; even if relations between the FCO and the Bank remained the weakest link in the triangle.

Improved cooperation between the Treasury and the FCO also reflected a welcome diminution of the established rivalry between the two Departments, which had amounted at times to antagonism. Relations between them had been at their worst in the 30s, when the Treasury had held to the view 'that economic affairs were its concern alone and that the Foreign Office should be confined to the more traditional spheres of diplomacy'.[29] Echoes of this antagonism were still evident in the comments of officials in both Departments at the end of the 60s, reflecting both the powerful influence of bureaucratic tradition and a certain continuing rivalry between the two most prestigious Departments in Whitehall.[30] Informal cooperation between Treasury divisions and FCO departments, however, was now becoming normal practice, encouraged by a rearrangement of Whitehall offices which by 1969 had led to the siting of most of the FCO's economic departments in the same range of buildings as the Treasury.

Relations between the two Departments nevertheless remained less close than those between the Foreign Office and the MoD. The explanation for this must lie partly in the prevailing perspectives of ministers, and the way in which the organization of the Cabinet and its committees. reflected these perspectives. There was little incentive for Foreign Office staff to put up papers on economic aspects of foreign policy when their political masters were not enormously interested in them; they did not therefore find themselves so regularly in contact with their opposite numbers in the Treasury. Nor was it easy for the FCO to gain a firm footing in interdepartmental economic discussions without the backing of its ministers in Cabinet and Cabinet committee. A number of FCO officials in the early 70s emphasized the need for at least one Foreign Office minister to have a degree of economic interest and expertise. Conversely, Treasury ministers were often too preoccupied with their immediate responsibilities to spare time and attention for wider aspects of foreign policy. The division of business between Cabinet committees, with economic matters coming normally under the Economic Policy Committee rather than the DOPC, as a rule with only a junior Foreign

Office minister attending, reinforced this separation. In consequence Foreign Office planning papers rarely received the attention in the Treasury that they received within the MoD, even when they touched on relations with countries where the economic dimension was far more important than the security dimension. In response to the 'Nixon initiative' of August 1971, a Cabinet committee to cover trade, monetary, and defence questions as they interrelated was set up; but its meetings became infrequent as soon as the immediate crisis was past.

Informed and interested opinion with regard to financial policy is concentrated primarily in the City of London, with a small body of academic economists and a smaller group of financial journalists widening the circle a little. A number of City associations – the Issuing Houses Association, the Corporation of Insurance Brokers, the Corporation of Foreign Bondholders – lobby the government and the press on matters relating to international economic policy; at least one, the Committee on Invisible Exports, was set up in reaction to the Labour government's domestic and foreign economic policy, to represent City interests more directly to the goverment. But few of these are concerned with the central issues of international financial policy or international monetary management; and the social characteristics of the City are such that formal lobbying is on most occasions far less important than informal influence. The Bank of England is the natural focus of City opinion, both formally through the representation of the main sectors of financial and industrial activity on its Court of Governors, and informally through the whole range of contacts between its staff and private bankers, brokers, and industrialists.[31] Particularly under a Conservative government, informal access to MPs and ministers helps to constrain the government's perception of possible choices of policy within the boundaries of what influential opinion in the City regards as practical or 'sound'.

The shifting consensus of academic opinion provides a not dissimilar constraint, reinforced by its transnational character. Leading monetary economists in Britain participate in a continuing debate with their fellows in the United States, the Netherlands, West Germany, and elsewhere. They are closely linked to each national government by their role as outside advisers and by the frequency of exchanges between goverment economic services and the academic world. In 1965 proposals for floating exchange rates were being put forward only by the more radical economists, frowned on by much established opinion and as such mistrusted by banking opinion; hence a British decision to float would have risked undermining financial confidence. The progressive acceptance of such ideas by respectable academic opinion in the following two or three years, culminating in the successful German float of 1969, had made it possible by 1972 for the British government to float sterling almost without arousing adverse comment. Had it attempted to do so in 1967, so far ahead of academic and financial opinion, reaction in the City and abroad would have been one of panic.

The secrecy which cloaks the British policy-making process remains at its deepest here, only slightly lessened by the Bank's greater openness to Whitehall. The complexity of the subject, the need for speed and complete secrecy in the management of the exchanges, the closeness and informality of contacts among those involved, partly explain this; reinforced by the lack of expertise in Parliament and the resistance of successive governments to a parliamentary committee on economic affairs. Until after the 1967 devaluation, powerful taboos suppressed debate on sterling; the Treasury's anxiety lest gloomy financial comment in the press should start a run on the pound led it to pay careful attention to strict management of news.[32] The extreme degree of secrecy in the discussion of policy alternatives however outlasted the $2.80 parity. Not only outside critics but many of those within the circle of privileged opinion found this unnecessary and inhibiting. One civil servant complained that the absence of an open debate on international financial policy made it more difficult to make ministers listen to 'scare stories', to re-examine their accepted assumptions, 'even to accept the realities of the situation'; as a result, decisions were postponed, alternatives avoided. Since ministers in turn were usually too busy to question their officials' assumptions, the only opportunities to challenge the accepted wisdom of the Treasury and the Bank arose, paradoxically, not in Whitehall or Westminister but in the multilateral environment of the OECD reviews and IMF missions.[33]

The process of policy-making which culminated in the devaluation of November 1967 was above all an example of decisions postponed and alternatives avoided. The question had come up for decision immediately the Labour government took office in October 1964.[34] A substantial minority of economists, including Professor Kaldor, who became one of the new government's leading economic advisers, had favoured devaluation for some months beforehand as part of the strategy needed for domestic economic expansion. Treasury papers prepared for incoming ministers included immediate devaluation amongst the alternatives offered. Yet within three days of taking office the three ministers most directly concerned, Mr Wilson, James Callaghan, the Chancellor, and George Brown, the new Secretary of State for Economic Affairs, decided that devaluation must be ruled out. The issue was therefore not considered by the Cabinet, and throughout the series of short-term exchange crises which hit the pound sterling in November 1964 the possibility of devaluation was rigorously excluded. The grounds on which this first decision was taken were political: that a Labour Party which was trying to prove itself as a responsible party of government could not allow itself to be labelled as the party of devaluation (as the Conservative opposition, referring to the Labour devaluations of 1931 and 1949, would certainly have called it), and that its narrow parliamentary majority would not survive such a controversial decision.[35]

On several occasions during 1965 economic advisers raised the possibility of devaluation with particular ministers or directly with the Prime Minister, but without either securing a hearing or at any point reaching the Cabinet or a Cabinet committee for discussion. But in the spring of 1966 official opinion within the Treasury began to argue the case for further deflation of domestic demand, and the DEA, with their minister's encouragement, prepared a set of detailed proposals based upon the premise of devaluation, intended for circulation to the Cabinet. The increased Labour majority in the general election of March 1966 had removed the most pressing domestic constraint. A seamen's strike from mid-May to early July, moreover, disrupted Britain's external trade and precipitated a run on sterling.

The question of devaluation therefore came to the Cabinet for the first time in July 1966. Reference to the Cabinet was made easier by Wilson's absence in Moscow, opening a trade fair and attempting to mediate between the Russians and the Americans on Vietnam; according to some accounts, this made it easier for George Brown to encourage the emergence of a 'pro-devaluation' faction within the Cabinet. The consensus of economic advice favoured devaluation. The sole economic alternative was to impose a more severe deflation of the domestic economy, which would mean increased unemployment and a cutback in social welfare expenditure. Discussion amongst ministers, however, was disjointed and inconclusive. The Chancellor supported the Prime Minister (on his return), a full consideration of the issue was avoided, and a package of deflationary measures was presented to Parliament. George Brown was dissuaded with difficulty from resigning from the government, and accepted instead a transfer to the Foreign Office.

The Cabinet did not discuss devaluation again until the decision had in effect been made, by the Prime Minister and the Chancellor, in consultation with the Governor of the Bank of England, on the weekend of 10–12 November 1967. It was presented with a fait accompli on 16 November, for confirmation and approval, in conditions of great secrecy and without the prior circulation of papers.[36] During the previous year official opinion in the Treasury had become more and more firmly convinced of the need for devaluation, though naturally the Bank of England had resisted it. In April 1967 a Treasury paper had argued that the proposed application to the European Community would have to be accompanied by devaluation; by the summer this had become the Treasury view. Once the decision was taken, Bank of England officials, those in the Treasury, and economic sections in embassies abroad worked to a carefully managed timetable for devaluation. Apart from a last minute failure, when an incautious reply by the Chancellor to a parliamentary question the day before devaluation was announced on 18 November sparked off a run on the exchanges, the operation was carried out in conditions of complete secrecy, with a degree of consultation with foreign central banks and with the IMF which many of those involved considered a landmark in successful international monetary cooperation.

The most striking aspect of this series of decisions was its successful containment within the Treasury, the Bank of England, and the Prime Minister's Office. The Foreign Office was not involved at any stage, until coded instructions were sent through the Diplomatic Wireless to overseas posts as part of the immediate preparations for devaluation. Even the DEA, established by the Prime Minister to counterbalance the Treasury, was unable to force the question open, except under the crisis conditions of July 1966. Prime ministerial determination, reinforced by the support of the Chancellor, successfully prevented the sterling parity from being discussed at Cabinet level as an issue of high policy, leaving the management of the exchanges and the raising of successive international loans to departmental ministers and senior officials.

The corrolary of this was the acceptance of an increasing degree of foreign intervention in British economic policy. In October and November 1964 a succession of senior officials and ministers travelled to Washington to discuss US conditions for supporting sterling.[37] In June and July 1965 Callaghan and a large number of Treasury officials visited Washington to hear American views on what steps were necessary to strengthen the British economy, and in August George Brown used the argument of American reservations about further monetary support to push the CBI and the trade unions towards accepting continued restraint on incomes policy. After the July 1966 crisis the opinion of European governments and the IMF became another direct constraint (which, as has been noted above, remained for some years after devaluation). More widely, dependence on American financial support acted as a constraint on British foreign policy, on Vietnam and on defence deployment in particular.[38]

Containment of the issue within the Departments concerned was facilitated by the suppression of debate outside Whitehall. The Conservative Party identified devaluation with political disaster; when it came, they denounced it as a 'defeat'. A substantial section of the Labour Party shared this attitude, including Mr Callaghan. The Liberal Party broke the taboo on discussing devaluation during the 1966 election campaign, when their economic spokesman, Christopher Layton, raised it in a television discussion. He was immediately and sharply attacked by the spokesmen of both other parties, and the subject was dropped. The argument that to mention devaluation was to weaken sterling and to risk a run on the exchanges was powerful, reluctantly accepted both by economists and by journalists. The Observer, the first newspaper to break ranks by discussing the possibility, in July 1966, was subjected to considerable governmental pressure to desist, which was maintained until the moment of devaluation.[39] This meant that Cabinet ministers in non-economic Departments had no readily available source of alternative advice to enable them to criticize existing policy. Parliament, even more, was uninformed and uninvolved.

The crucial gap between official advice and ministerial preconception was therefore not bridged. By and large, and under increasing protest, officials accepted as given the prime ministerial exclusion of devaluation as an economic alternative, and prepared papers and managed policy within the limits of that preemptive decision. But ministers had no other informal source of advice and criticism than their officials. By maintaining the (perhaps necessary) secrecy of the decision-making process, in order to protect foreign confidence in sterling, they also ensured that the costs of alternative policies, the wider choices involved, would not be clearly presented. As a result, choice was postponed until there was only one available alternative. The compartmentalization of policy also prevented a clear perception of the interrelationship between the East of Suez commitment, the role of sterling, and the evolution of policy towards the European Community. During the 1966 election campaign a committee of the most senior officials in Whitehall prepared a paper 'which re-examined the whole foundation of the government's economic and foreign policy', which was to be presented to the Prime Minister, the Chancellor, and the Foreign Secretary. Yet as soon as its first draft was completed, 'all copies (except one) were destroyed on the Prime Minister's personal instructions'.[40] It is unlikely that the Foreign Secretary or the Minister of Defence were aware of its existence. Earlier, in July 1965, the chief economic advisers in Whitehall had signed a memorandum arguing the case for devaluation, which was presented to the Prime Minister but which did not reach the Cabinet.

International financial policy between 1964 and 1967 was efficiently managed at the middle policy level. International support for the pound was ensured, lines of credit were extended; the management of devaluation itself was applauded by foreign governments. The failure was in the inability of official advisers and Cabinet critics to force the discussion of a major issue of policy at the highest level – because, at the highest level, the Prime Minister and the Chancellor were unwilling to consider it. This failure was compounded by the willingness of the international financial community to support existing policy, wishing, for their own purposes, to avoid the disruption which devaluation might bring, and pressing rather for harsher domestic policies which were less damaging to their own concerns. In consequence, Britain delayed devaluation until it was unavoidable; the final decision was not so much taken as accepted.

The Management of Commercial Policy

Many aspects of present-day commercial policy were already concerns of government a century or more ago. Organized industrial interests were active in the eighteenth century, as when in 1785 Josiah Wedgewood's short-lived General Chamber of Manufacturers 'helped to wreck Pitt's proposals for Anglo-Irish free trade'.[41] Though export promotion was not yet an organized activity, the Great Exhibition of 1851 included

among its objectives the furtherance of knowledge of British manufactures abroad. Cobden's Anglo-French Commercial Treaty of 1860
was followed by a succession of similar treaties with other European
countries, incorporating the 'most-favoured-nation' clause extending
bilateral tariff concessions to what became in effect a unified and, for a
while, a relatively free trade area. The rebuilding of protective tariffs
from the 1870s onwards brought sharper pressure from British industry
on the Foreign Office and the Board of Trade to intervene with other
governments on their behalf. Wartime economic mobilization between
1914 and 1918 necessitated a much closer relationship between government and industry and far more governmental intervention in import
and export trade, both intensified by World War II. The return to
protectionism between the wars added imperial preference, quotas, the
underwriting of export finance, and detailed bilateral bargaining. After
1945 the re-established international economic order imposed a multilateral framework on this pattern of bilateral negotiations, most importantly through the GATT.

Commercial policy 'involves the manipulation in Britain's favour of
the "rules of the game" of international trade'.[42] More broadly, it has
come since World War II to include a substantial government effort at
export promotion, which developed to enormous proportions during the
6os, as well as government programmes to reduce imports by assisting
domestic industry and expanding domestic agriculture. As the level of
tariffs was progressively reduced through multilateral tariff negotiations
during the 50s and early 60s, problems of non-tariff barriers – industrial
standards, health and safety regulations, discriminatory government
purchasing policies, and so on – became a major subject of negotiations.
Commercial relations also involve policy on inward and outward investment, affecting as it does both the balance of payments and the pattern
of British trade.

For more than twenty years after World War II British commercial
policy was conducted within established institutional and political parameters. The establishment of GATT, firmly supported by the United
States, the dominant economic power, 'permitted trade issues to be
discussed and resolved in their own realm, without intruding into other
areas of policy';[43] separated, perhaps artificially, from matters of 'high
foreign policy', except to some extent in relations with the state trading
countries of the Soviet bloc. Successive British governments were not
predisposed to question the wider political assumptions underlying this
compartmentalization. They were, after all, committed to the acceptance
of American leadership, to the principle of a liberal international
economic order enshrined in the Bretton Woods Agreement, and to the
conduct of Britain's economic as well as political foreign relations on a
global rather than a regional basis.[44] Thus at least until the late 60s the
conduct of commercial policy was mainly a departmental responsibility
managed by officials under the general supervision of their minister, in

close consultation with those industrial interests which officials were concerned to defend: in short, a classic case of middle-level policy. Major questions of principle seldom arose. Even during important multilateral negotiations, such as the Dillon and Kennedy Rounds, the detailed formulation of aims and the negotiation of agreements were handled by civil servants from the Board of Trade and the Foreign Office, within the guidelines agreed by ministers. The relative absence of urgency, and the more direct (and more necessary) involvement of private interests, made for more open policy-making than in international financial policy. If it was felt desirable to keep the government's intentions secret from its negotiating partners, it was a positive disadvantage in carrying British companies and industrial organizations along with government policy to keep them less than fully informed.

In Whitehall terms, the management of commercial policy has since the eighteenth century been the responsibility primarily of the Board of Trade and, less actively, of the Foreign Office. The 'question of the right relationship between the Foreign Office . . . and the Board of Trade' in commercial policy matters had attracted attention from both industrial interests and ministers since the last years of the nineteenth century, and was 'settled by the creation in 1917 of an independent department, the Department of Overseas Trade', whose ministerial head reported both to the Foreign Secretary and to the President of the Board of Trade.[45] But this in turn separated foreign trade policy from domestic trade and industrial policy, the other established responsibility of the Board of Trade, which was expanding with growing governmental involvement in economic management and under the pressure of the industrial problems of the interwar years. In 1946 the Department was abolished, its responsibilities and most of its personnel reabsorbed into the Board of Trade; its separate Commercial Diplomatic Service had already been merged into the Foreign Service under the 1943 reforms.

During the 60s and early 70s the Board of Trade went through a series of major reorganizations, reflecting changing ministerial views on the management and objectives of domestic industrial policy. In 1963 Edward Heath became Secretary of State for Industry, Trade and Regional Development, bringing additional domestic responsibilities to the Board of Trade. Under the Labour government of 1964–70 its functions were progressively reduced, partly to the DEA, increasingly to the Ministry of Technology; so that by 1969 it had become almost another Department of Overseas Trade concerned with little more than foreign commercial relations and export promotion. The returning Conservatives in 1970 merged this rump Board of Trade and the Ministry of Technology into the giant DTI; arguing amongst other advantages that by 'unifying this whole field of policy', it would avoid

an unreal dichotomy between the 'internal' and 'international' aspects of commerce and industry, i.e. between the department responsible for export promotion and overseas commercial policy and the department responsible for the bulk of the Government's relations with industry . . . it greatly simplifies industry's contacts with government.

It also argues that 'the unified structure will have advantages in the context of the possibility of our accession to the European Community'.[46] This unified Department lasted for three and half years. Its failure properly to bring together from its constituent divisions the domestic and international implications of energy policy, and the acuteness of the crisis precipitated by the Middle East war of June 1973 and the interruption of oil supplies which followed, led to the creation of a separate Department of Energy, in January 1974.[47] The minority Labour government which took office in March 1974 completed its dismemberment by dividing its remaining functions among three separate Departments for Trade, Industry, and Consumer Protection.

This succession of reorganizations illustrates the difficulty of drawing administrative dividing lines in policy areas which overlap domestic and international concerns – as did the similar internal redistributions of functions within the Treasury. But below the ministerial level there has been remarkable continuity in the divisions responsible for commercial policy and export promotion. Several of the senior officials in the Commercial Relations and Exports divisions (CRE) in 1970 had spent virtually their entire careers in this field, beginning in the tangled web of trade discrimination and bilateral negotiations between the wars.[48] One official then on the point of retirement had begun his career as private secretary to the leader of the British delegation to the Ottawa Conference which led to the establishment of imperial preference. Many of his opposite numbers in other countries had had similarly long careers, meeting each other for bilateral and multilateral conversations year after year, their mutual acquaintance and trust reinforcing the compartmental-ization of trade policy within a multilateral framework of established assumptions and institutions.

The five CRE divisions of the Board of Trade in 1969–70, reduced to four in a DTI reorganization at the end of 1972, contained between forty and fifty administrative-grade officials. CRE1 was responsible for overall commercial policy questions and for the management of British commercial policy within the context of GATT, of OECD, and of UNCTAD; its under-secretary bore the additional and traditional title of 'Adviser on Commercial Policy'. CRE2–5 were organized on a geo-graphical basis, managing bilateral negotiations and conversations and relations with regional organizations. Until the end of the 60s one of these divisions was effectively 'the Commonwealth division'. By 1970, when Commonwealth trade and the sterling area had declined in im-portance, and with the approach to Europe, responsibilities were re-distributed on more strictly geographical lines.[49] The volume of their work was increased by the proliferation of bilateral committees meeting regularly to discuss detailed questions of mutual interest. Three other divisions within the Board of Trade, continuing with little change under the DTI, dealt more directly with the promotion and control of exports: the issue of export licences, collection and dissemination of information on export opportunities, government sponsorship of and participation in trade fairs, liaison with the various government-assisted bodies encouraging businessmen to seek out exports, and cooperation with the Export Credits Guarantee Department (ECGD) – mostly low-level detailed executive work, rarely raising controversial points or questions of principle. ECGD was a separate Department responsible to the President of the Board of Trade: it had been set up in 1919 to deal with a number of 'temporary' problems in financing exports to the new states of Eastern Europe. It now performed a 'dual role as a Department responsible to central controls and as an insurer operating on basic commercial principles', an executive agency in the same relationship to the Board of Trade/DTI as Customs and Excise and Inland Revenue to the Treasury.[50] Its underwriting of exports followed primarily commercial criteria, but from 1962 onwards interest rates on export credits had been subsidized, and the assessment of applications took into account also considerations of domestic industrial policy and of political relations with the importing country.[51] Both the Board of Trade and the ECGD maintained a network of regional offices throughout Britain, to ease communications with industry and to ensure maximum use of their services to exporters.

Several functional departments of the FCO, most importantly Trade Policy and Export Promotion (merged into a single department, as Trade Relations, during 1973), and Commodities, were primarily concerned with commercial aspects of foreign policy.[52] Trade Policy related directly to CRE1 on multilateral commercial policy, tariffs and non-tariff barriers, and to CRE4 on general policy towards the sensitive area of East-West trade. FCO geographical departments were in regular and informal contact with the corresponding divisions of the Board of Trade/DTI, desk officer to desk officer, receiving copies of the same telegrams and consulting each other about the replies.

The two Departments were also closely linked by the commercial activities of overseas posts, in which effectively the Diplomatic Service operated on behalf of the CRE divisions. During the 60s, as emphasis on the overwhelming importance of exports grew, more and more stress was placed on commercial relations and the detailed pursuit of export opportunities by staff in overseas posts. By 1968 some 24 per cent of UK-based staff in overseas posts were engaged full time on commercial work, and a foreign tour in a commercial post no longer indicated that an official's career prospects were limited.[53] Consular posts, particularly in West European and North Atlantic countries, likewise devoted an increasing and often preponderant proportion of their attention to commercial work.[54] In 1970 in the United States, the biggest single export market, the direction of export promotion work was transferred from the Washington embassy to an enlarged British Trade Development Office in New York. By 1972 this office controlled 57 commercial officers in 16 subordinate posts, with substantial local staffs, costing over £2m. It reported back to the DTI and its regional offices and to the FCO's Export Promotion department, liaising with the Washington embassy and the FCO Trade Policy department on wider questions of commercial policy, but rarely if ever concerning itself with questions sufficiently relevant to political relations to warrant direct contact with the FCO North American department. These posts were also responsible for attracting American firms to invest in Britain.

The Treasury was naturally involved in commercial policy. Concern for the balance of payments gave it an immediate interest in import policy and export promotion. A possible surcharge or the imposition of temporary quotas on imports were among the various alternatives suggested by Treasury officials to the incoming Labour government in October 1964 to reduce the immediate balance-of-payments deficit (though opinions in the Treasury on the import surcharge were divided, from the moment of its acceptance by the government to its withdrawal under international pressure). The Treasury had a strong interest too in the growth of expenditure on export promotion to a total of £20–25m at the beginning of the 1970s, particularly in the proportion of the total which was spent abroad. Both the Treasury and the Bank of England had an interest in export finance, which they exerted in their relations with the ECGD on the side of creditworthiness rather than political or industrial desirability. The Ministry of Agriculture was also actively concerned: not only with the regulation of agricultural imports and with balancing the interests of domestic agriculture against those of foreign producers, but also as the sponsoring Department for the small agricultural industry and for exports of agricultural produce and machinery.

Industrial firms, singly or through the intermediary of industrial associations, were involved so closely in some aspects of commercial policy that it is difficult to draw a firm dividing line between official and private activities. The technicalities of tariff negotiations are such that official negotiations often require the advice of the industries on whose behalf they are bargaining. At the outset of the Kennedy Round in 1963 the Board of Trade suggested that the 'peak associations' interested – the FBI, the Association of British Chambers of Commerce, and so on – should form a joint committee as a convenient focus for continuing contact as the negotiations proceeded; in the later stages, when the discriminatory effect of the American Selling Price rule was under consideration, two representatives of the Chemical Industries Association moved to Geneva to be on hand for immediate advice. Representatives of industrial associations were frequently included on official trade delegations, most regularly on those to Eastern Europe, and a number of overseas British Chambers of Commerce received government subsidies. Exchanges of staff between Whitehall and industry, particularly between the Diplomatic Service and industry, and efforts to give personnel about to take up commercial posts abroad preliminary contacts with industry before they took up their posts, helped to cement relations between government and industry.

The closest interrelationship between government and industry until the 60s had been the establishment of the Import Duties Advisory Committee, a small non-ministerial government Department headed by a commission misleadingly named 'advisory', set up in 1932. It in effect operated until World War II as a Tariff Commission, dominated by the FBI and sympathetically attentive to the representations of trade associations.[55] In the 1960s, when government promotion of exports had become a consuming passion, dominating declared policy in a widening range of external relations, industry and government drew even closer together. The Dollar Exports Board, established in 1949 'under the aegis of the FBI, but . . . supported by a grant-in-aid from the Exchequer', was supplemented in 1960 by an Advisory Council on Middle East Trade and an Export Council for Europe.[56] In July 1964 these were reorganized under the BNEC, with twelve area committees dividing up the entire non-state-trading world. Originally BNEC was intended to be financed equally by government grant and industrial contributions, but as activities expanded industrialists pressed the government to provide all its regular budget. For 1968–9 this amounted to £906,700. Nevertheless BNEC itself remained 'an independent organization run by businessmen whose contribution in time and expertise is matched by the government which provides the funds for its day to day operations'.[57] Its area committees included senior officials from the Board of Trade and the Foreign Office; those covering developing countries included also representatives from the ODM. Two independent but associated Trade Councils, also supported by the government, assisted industry in the more sensitive questions of trade with Eastern Europe and China.

A certain disillusionment on both sides, besides the new Conservative government's declared opposition to subsidies to industry, was reflected in the abolition of BNEC in 1971 and its replacement by the British Overseas Trade Board, rather more closely under DTI control. After all the emphasis previously placed on promoting exports and giving maximum assistance to industry, Diplomatic Service as well as CRE officials had become somewhat sceptical. 'Businessmen,' one commented, 'want to be spoon-fed'; several others said that their hard work to discover export opportunities in foreign countries had failed to arouse industrial interest. Businessmen for their part still felt at arms length from Whitehall compared with their competitors in the Netherlands, West Germany, France, or, above all, Japan. They resented being allowed to sit on essentially executive committees but excluded from the vital Whitehall policy-making committees. 'The extraordinary cloak of secrecy' which governs consultations between government and industry, one oil company executive remarked, 'inhibits a full understanding between the two'. Certainly British constitutional traditions would resist that general blending of private industrialists and officials on policy-making committees in Whitehall for which some businessman seem to hope, though it has not been unknown for representatives of oil companies at least, to attend meetings of committees within Whitehall. On one exceptional occasion 'a high representative of the oil company involved in the Persian seizure of the Abadan refinery' was invited to attend a Cabinet meeting.[58]

Ministerial activity was often a matter of lending prestige and dignity to the conclusion of a commercial agreement or to British trade fairs and export drives. Major departures from established policy clearly required ministerial decision, and would be approved by the Cabinet; for negotiations in progress and less vital decisions ministerial approval at departmental level sufficed. But the successful compartmentalization of questions of trade policy within a relatively stable multilateral system meant that major departures were rare. Each approach to the European Communities, of course, raised questions of its commercial implications both for British and for Commonwealth trade, which attracted much attention in Cabinet and Cabinet committees. On the other hand British reluctance earlier on to concede that the EEC was more than an economic association is indicated by the assignment of British representation on the Spaak Committee in 1955 to a Board of Trade under-secretary. As towards the end of the 60s commercial policy again became more politically sensitive and more deliberately linked with other areas of intergovernmental relations, under the pressure of American discontent and the representations of the developing countries, so it became increasingly a matter for Cabinet discussion and for active ministerial concern. Questions from MPs on behalf of local industries, delegations from industrialists themselves, provided other channels for drawing particular problems to ministerial attention. But ministerial roles very often remained promotional rather than directly political.[59] East European countries especially pressed for ministerial presence during trade discussions. Ministers added prestige and publicity to major efforts at export promotion, such as the overseas tour of the British prototype of Concorde in 1973. A succession of ministerial visits in 1972 and 1973, including one by the Prime Minister, exerted pressure on Japan to increase imports from Britain and to lower its non-tariff barriers.

It is difficult to select any one representative example of the management of policy, because of the various and detailed issues under continuing discussion at different levels. In 1970, for instance, the annual meeting of the Anglo-Canadian Continuing Official Committee, chaired jointly by the Permanent Secretary to the Board of Trade and his Canadian equivalent, with representation from the Treasury, the Ministry of Agriculture, and the FCO, reviewed – among other outstanding issues – allegations of 'dumping' in heavy electrical transformer equipment, British restrictions on imports of Canadian apples, Canadian provincial taxes on imported whisky, the purchasing policy of Canadian government departments, the international trade in cereals, and the implementation of mutual concessions agreed in the Kennedy Round. One point at issue in the equivalent Anglo-Irish conversations was the non-tariff barrier presented by the Irish government's requirement that markings on pottery should be in Irish as well as English. The CRE under-secretary responsible for this question had travelled to Stoke-on-Trent for repeated discussions with industry, while the FCO had cautioned against unduly offending Irish susceptibilities. Discussions with the East German government, conducted (in the absence of British recognition) by officials of the CBI, involved some complicated and highly political manoeuvring over the establishment of a British 'Trade Office' in East Berlin, held out as a precondition for expanded trade. The issue of British participation in the project to construct an oil pipeline from the Gulf of Suez to the Mediterranean, to be examined more fully below, was more unusual than most. Against the normal containment of questions of export finance within the commercial and financial criteria agreed between the ECGD and the Treasury, it raised implications for bilateral political relations and for British policy in the Middle East which provoked considerable interdepartmental discussion, requiring reference to the Cabinet. Less unusually among issues in British foreign relations, it exercised officials, and occasionally ministers, for some three years in taking contingent decisions, without in the end coming to a successful conclusion.[60]

Proposals for an oil pipeline to relieve pressure on the Suez Canal and to accommodate the new super-tankers, too large to pass loaded through the canal, had been formulated before the Arab-Israeli war of June 1967. After the closure of the Canal a London based firm of engineering consultants, International Management and Engineering Group Ltd (IMEG), presented a detailed proposal to the Egyptian government, whose most pressing concern was to replace the lost revenue from Canal dues, estimated at around £95m a year. But the project was estimated to be economically viable even in competition with a reopened Canal, promising a major additional source of future revenue. Indeed, the SUMED project (as it came to be called) was later compared with the Aswan high dam and the industrial iron and steel complex (both financed by the Soviet Union, after American and West European hesitations and refusals) in its economic importance for Egypt. At first it was hoped that it might be financed by the World Bank, together with some oil companies and oil-producing countries. By mid-1968, however, it was clear that the World Bank would not participate, and both IMEG and the Egyptian government were talking about inviting a consortium of West European interests to undertake its construction, at an estimated cost of £60m. Kleinwort Benson, a British merchant bank which had contributed to financing a recent large-scale pipeline project in Iran, was already involved in detailed discussions. If British finance was provided, Egyptian sources suggested, there could be substantial benefits for British construction firms and engineering companies; if Western finance was not provided, they hinted, the Soviet Union might again be prepared to step in.

For the Egyptians the proposed construction of an Israeli pipeline from Eilat to Ashkelon presented a political as well as an economic challenge. European participation in a major project close to the truce line would give European governments a vested interest in preventing further fighting, and would represent a gesture of support for the Egyptian regime. The Egyptians therefore saw the issue of financial credits for SUMED as a test of European attitudes towards them, and by implication towards the Arab-Israeli dispute. The British government was concerned to improve relations with Egypt, and more generally with the Arab world, for political and economic reasons: to reduce Soviet influence in the Middle East, to protect oil company investments and oil supplies, to boost civil and military exports. Diplomatic relations between the United Kingdom and the UAR had been broken off in December 1965 and were not resumed until 1968, while Arab attitudes to Britain had not been improved by allegations of British military intervention during the June war.[61] As against this the domestic context for a reorientation of British Middle East policy was delicate. There was a large pro-Israeli lobby within all parties in the Commons, and the attitudes of many Conservative MPs were still coloured by Nasser's role in the Suez crisis. There was also an outstanding dispute over Egyptian confiscation of British-owned property in 1961, for which no compensation had yet been paid. Official awareness of the sensitivity of this issue was heightened by knowledge that one of the most valuable collections of private property confiscated was owned by a relative of an MP.

The multilateral character of the project, calling for a multinational construction consortium with proportionate financial credits underwritten by their governments, complicated the British reaction further. At various stages throughout the life of the project ECGD was involved in discussions with the credit agencies of the French, Dutch, West German, and other European governments. As the prospect of a successful application to the European Community opened, the desirability of presenting a common front on policy towards the Middle East – or, at least, of presenting a front acceptable to the French government – also became a factor of some significance to the Foreign Office.

After exploratory Egyptian conversations with British banks and construction firms in 1968 and early 1969, the attitude of the ECGD remained sceptical. Oil companies were reluctant to commit themselves to use the pipeline. They had already ordered supertankers to take oil round the Cape, and at prevailing charter rates experts doubted whether the pipeline would be economically competitive with these. Israeli bombardment of Egyptian installations, which in March 1969 knocked out the oil refinery at Suez, increased doubts about the pipeline's security. The British government therefore hung back, leaving it to a French-led consortium, with government support, to sign a construction agreement in July 1969. Together with Italian, Spanish, and Dutch companies, a number of British firms were involved in this consortium, under the leadership of Mitchell Construction: they included English Electric, Motherwell Bridge, Dunlop, and the (nationalized) British Steel Corporation. The French and Italian governments were each reported to have underwritten a quarter of the cost of the project, but the participation of these British companies depended on ECGD agreeing to underwrite their share, some £15m. In September 1969 the British government therefore came to its first conditional decision, taken primarily by ECGD within the limits of its established criteria, after consultation with the Treasury, the Foreign Office, and the British embassy in Cairo. Its 'guarded and less than enthusiastic' decision was to make a credit guarantee conditional, first on the conclusion of firm contracts with oil companies to use the pipeline, second on Egyptian settlement of outstanding debts and claims, third on the financial participation of oil-producing states (thus reducing Britain's total contribution), and fourth on the payment of dues by users not to the Egyptian government but to a consortium of European banks until the credit had been repaid.[62] These conditions were hardly such as to warm Egyptian hearts; the last condition was indeed the subject of later protests in the Egyptian parliament, as an infringement on national sovereignty. They were however appropriate for an official credit agency assessing an application from a government with one of the lowest international credit ratings, because of past defaults and outstanding debts.

During the next fifteen months ECGD continued to resist requests from interested British companies (and presumably also from the Foreign Office, at relatively low level) for a more positive response, while some of its conditions were gradually met.[63] The Kuwaiti government promised to contribute financial credits, though strained relations with Saudi Arabia prevented that country committing itself. After extended negotiations, four of the major international oil companies, including BP and Shell, contracted in December 1970 to use the pipeline, bringing the total commitment to some 80 per cent of capacity. This decision was heavily influenced by the sharp rise in international tanker rates, which had transformed the economics of the project. The absence of shelling across the Canal throughout 1970 had quieted doubts about security. As significant as all these developments, however, was the change of government in Britain, and the new Foreign Secretary's initiative to improve relations with the Arab world. Initial Egyptian reactions to the Conservative government had been hostile; Sir Alec Douglas-Home, in particular, was seen as 'a man of Suez'. But his visit to Cairo to attend President Nasser's funeral in October, and the major speech on Middle East policy which he made in Harrogate on his return, were noted by the Egyptians as evidence of a reorientation of British policy.

Accordingly in December 1970 the Egyptians launched a diplomatic offensive to persuade the British to provide a guarantee. They argued that British participation was the key to the whole project and that the Egyptian Foreign Minister's prospective visit to London in January (in response to an invitation from Sir Alec) would provide an appropriate occasion to sign an agreement. This forced the British government to take a more definite decision, with wider political overtones. It was evident that there was disagreement between Departments on the criteria which should govern the decision; the FCO made hopeful statements ahead of the ministerial visit, but the Treasury supported the ECGD's more critical attitude. The conflict between political and financial and commercial objectives was deep enough to necessitate a full discussion by the Cabinet. After preparatory work by officials, and consultations with other European governments, the Cabinet in early March 1971 gave its approval in principle to underwrite the participation of British firms in the project, 'conditional on certain arrangements relating to financial guarantees'.[64] In April the West German, Italian, Dutch, and Greek governments announced that they would join the French and British governments in extending credit. In July the construction contract was renegotiated, after adjustments for increased costs, and an agreement was reached on compensation for British property in Egypt. In September Sir Alec Douglas-Home's official visit to Cairo, set the seal on more cordial Anglo-Egyptian relations.[65]

The implementation of this high-level decision, once taken, depended not only on Whitehall officials and their opposite numbers in Paris, Rome, Cairo, and other capitals, but also upon the large numbers of companies and banks involved. The British construction member of the consortium first withdrew, was then replaced, and finally contracted for a smaller share of the work, throwing doubt on the consortium's ability to take up all of the British line of credit. The British Steel Corporation was unable to supply the steel pipe required, and was replaced by German and Japanese suppliers. There were further delays in the re-negotiation of contracts with oil company users and with the separate consortium of banks which was to provide the immediate finance, both affected by the rise in estimated costs during the previous two years. Not surprisingly, the most difficult point in the negotiations was over the question of the payment of dues into a blocked account outside the control of the Egyptian government. By the time this was settled, in May 1972, costs had risen even more, and the construction companies were claiming another adjustment in their contract. Proposed dates for the pipeline's opening were long past; the Israeli pipeline was already in operation; the oil companies had made alternative arrangements; tanker rates had again fallen. In September 1973 President Sadat confirmed that the scheme for a 'European' pipeline was dead. In December 1973 a new contract was signed with an American consortium, to be financed by Saudi Arabia and several Gulf states.

Activity within three Whitehall Departments over a period of years, repeated reference to ministers, and a Cabinet decision had therefore achieved no definite result. Yet indirectly the British had gained a number of political and economic advantages. Egyptian debts had been settled, if for a lesser sum than the British had claimed. British exports to Egypt rose; in 1972 the government extended a loan of £5m to cover exports of machinery and a further line of credit for £20m to cover industrial exports over the next four years. Exports of military equipment to Egypt amounted to £4m a year in 1971–2, although the British government was resisting Egyptian requests for less clearly defensive weapons. The political benefits were less tangible, but it might be argued that the more positive attitude of the British government and its European partners contributed to the Egyptian government's decision to expel 20,000 Soviet technicians in July 1972; it may even have eased the position of British-based oil companies in increasingly difficult operating conditions. Diplomatic officials would rarely expect or claim full success for their policies. They would more likely argue that without their efforts to maintain good relations with one of the leading Arab governments the position of British Middle East investment, of British exporters, and of Britain's supplies, would have been even more difficult. Hence in the Middle East too commercial policy issues had become more directly political than during the 60s. But the day-to-day management of policy and individual decisions was still necessarily handled within the limits of established institutional and political boundaries.

7: Aid, Information, and Cultural Policy

AID, INFORMATION, AND CULTURE are not vital to the central interests of British governments, as military security and economic welfare are. Except for the panoply of state visits and the occasional cultural extravaganza, there is little in the activities which they involve to attract ministerial attention or to win popular imagination. They have little in the way of a domestic constituency, and are thus vulnerable to political attack and budgetary reductions. In sharp contrast to defence or diplomacy, government action makes only a marginal contribution to the flow of international communications or to the transfer of knowledge and culture. With few exceptions, both aims and observable benefits are necessarily long-term rather than immediate. It is therefore more difficult to define objectives or to decide priorities. Policy represents an uncertain contribution to an ill-defined field, governed more by the accepted attitudes of the institutions responsible for its implementation and by established budgetary limits than by any clear conception of objectives or any generally accepted criteria for measuring performance.

Historically, British governments entered all these activities reluctantly and hesitantly, following the lead of other governments rather than taking the initiative itself. 'In the days of the old diplomacy it would have been regarded as an act of unthinkable vulgarity to appeal to the common people upon any issue of international policy'; until World War I came 'to degrade all international standards', and Her Majesty's government was forced by the vulgarity of Hitler and Mussolini to accept the need for international propaganda and for the promotion of British culture abroad.[1] As an imperial power Britain had as a matter of course assisted colonial development. As colonies reached independence British governments extended aid to help them through the transitional period. But the concept of aid as a long-term contribution to economic development did not become a conscious objective until the early 60s, in the wake of developmental policies emphasized within the UN and espoused by, for instance, the American government. A certain echo of this reluctant approach lingers in the institutional arrangements and the style of policy-making adopted, most of all in information and cultural activities.

In one sense these are all secondary aspects of foreign policy: pursued not for themselves but for the contribution they make to the achievement of other, primary, objectives. The objectives of aid policy, it is true, have been hotly debated between those who insist that the promotion of economic development is an end in itself and those who see it as an instrument of foreign policy. But few except the most dedicated development economists deny that Britain should be more generous in assisting its 'friends' and less generous to its 'enemies', should aim to give support to more democratic governments and to withhold support from dictatorial regimes. In information and cultural activity the instrumental character of policy is manifest. Their aim is to contribute to the creation and maintenance of a favourable image of Britain abroad, 'to give that impression of Britain and the British people which we should like foreigners to have' and, more immediately, 'to explain, support and gain acceptance for British policies'.[2] Their contribution to this image is of course rarely decisive. The total image of Britain in any foreign country is made up from remembered historical ties or conflicts embedded in the national literature and culture, the attitudes to Britain expressed by national leaders and the media, the characterization of British actions not only by British diplomats and news media but also by those of third countries, the behaviour of British residents, companies, and tourists in that country, the representational activities of the British embassy – a whole series of connected impressions on which the total activities of the British government can make only a marginal impact. The efforts of its information and cultural agencies are difficult to distinguish from those of, for instance, British personnel working on development projects, or from the local reputation of British firms as employers and suppliers of goods, in contributing to a favourable or unfavourable image of Britain abroad. But in many countries by the early 70s the aid relationship, cultural and informational activities, and the assistance provided by the British embassy for British companies, amounted to practically the entire official relationship between the two governments.

For those involved in these activities there is a natural tendency to see their work as an end in itself: to assume that impartial broadcasting, economic development, educational assistance or cultural exchange require no ulterior justification. To those concerned with the allocation of resources within a limited external budget, however, the cost of the BBC External Services, the British Council, British Information Services, and (less directly) of the aid programme must be justified in terms of their contribution to the achievement of foreign policy objectives, through their effect in creating a favourable atmosphere, in cultivating friendly relations with foreign governments and their domestic publics. The benefits to be hoped for from the cultivation of good relations include that haziest of concepts in business and politics, 'goodwill': the creation of favourable predispositions to British proposals and British interests in general, amongst politicians, officials, publicists, the economically powerful and the politically influential. From this the British government may hope to gain easier access to ministers and officials when needed, and also that its representatives will meet with a more ready response. It may hope too that good relations will benefit trade, as respect for Britain's image spills over into respect for British goods and friendly contacts with British officials extends to friendly contacts with British businessmen. 'Culture is the soft underbelly of business', as one official involved in the promotion of good relations remarked. Aid and technical assistance also have direct and indirect commercial pay-offs. The doctor trained in a British hospital is more likely to buy British medical equipment; the teacher trained under a British sponsored scheme is more likely to buy British books.

The problem for policy-makers is that these benefits are intangible: cumulative in their impact, long-term in their effect. The student at a British university may not become an influential member of his national government until some twenty years later; the habit of listening to the BBC is slow to catch on. Yet the priorities of British foreign policy necessarily change over much shorter time-spans. It is therefore peculiarly difficult to assess the utility of official expenditure or to determine priorities between different activities and different regions. Nor could there be any satisfactory yardstick for determining an appropriate level of official expenditure on information and culture. The field is vast, the market virtually inexhaustible. Goodwill is a non-quantifiable asset, though one much valued in international politics, as in business. Cultural expenditure, like prestige advertising and public relations, is justified less by the specific content of each presentation than by the faith that each action helps to create a favourable public image – or more specifically, for governments, to build up their country's credit abroad, in the uncertain currency of political influence.

Justification for governmental activity, and standards of measurement of its scale, are a little clearer in aid and development policy. To some extent expenditure on aid is a recognition of the uncertain and intangible influence of international opinion – the shifting consensus among governments and elites about what is and what is not acceptable and expected international behaviour. Nowadays any government of an industrially developed country which wants international respect must support an aid programme and make a contribution to economic development. Successive international conferences, innumerable UN resolutions, have insisted that this is a duty owed by the rich countries to the poor. British membership of various UN specialized agencies has imposed on it obligations to contribute its share. The developed countries have also evolved a broadly accepted yardstick of what level of expenditure is expected: the Pearson Committee's target of 1 per cent of GNP. In general outline, then, the size of the aid programme and its future growth have become an automatic obligation consequent on the government's status in the international community: maintained not so much in the hope of exerting influence as from a recognition that any significant reduction would damage Britain's image abroad.

Unlike information and culture, aid and development issues also have a small but active domestic constituency. By the end of the 50s voluntary organizations which had concerned themselves with famine relief and political groups which had worked to decolonize the British Empire began to share a common interest in longer-term economic development for poorer countries. Their growing awareness of the long-term problem was heightened by similar discussions in the United States and in other countries, converging in the UN commitment to make the 1960s 'the Development Decade'. The Labour government's creation of the ODM in 1964 owed much to the studies undertaken in opposition by party members committed to gaining a higher priority for economic development in government policy. In turn, the new ministry and the voluntary organizations interacted to create an active aid lobby, as economic retrenchment threatened cuts in the aid programme. From 1968-9 onwards the political skills of the aid lobby were demonstrated in the mobilization of support throughout the country to bring pressure to bear on Parliament, and in the mobilization of supporters in Parliament to bring pressure on the government to maintain and enlarge its expenditure on official aid.

The weakness of the aid lobby lay in the government's awareness that it reflected only a small minority of public opinion, however articulate that minority might be. The sympathy of the wider public might briefly be aroused by a major disaster, such as the Bengali floods and the subsequent civil war, or the Ethiopian famine; but there was far less sympathy, and still less understanding, for government expenditure on less immediate overseas projects among a public whose natural demands were for increased domestic social and economic expenditure or for lower taxes. Hence the efforts made by ODM and the aid lobby to inform and educate the wider public about the case for economic development – that is, to attempt to enlarge their domestic constituency. But if the domestic constituency for aid is weak, that for information and culture is almost non-existent. The British Council and the BBC External Services therefore devote some effort to informing domestic elites about the quality of their work and its contribution to Britain's standing abroad. When budgetary cuts threaten, they mobilize what domestic support they have to operate through whatever channels of influence are available; sparking off shoals of letters from foreign policy influentials in the quality press, making informal representations to ministers, and so on.[3]

Officials involved in all these activities seek also to generate domestic support and to protect themselves from reductions in expenditure by identifying their activities with the changing emphases of government policy. In 1966 and 1967 ODM economists were writing articles demonstrating that in balance-of-payments terms Britain gained more in increased exports from aid than the aid programme cost. In 1968 and 1969 the emphasis on export promotion as the declared first objective of overseas representation was reflected in the way the British Council stressed the contribution its efforts made to a favourable climate for British exports and in the additional domestic publicity the BBC gave to its external programmes on British products.[4]

Aid, information, and culture are handled predominantly at low level.

The political importance that the Labour government gave to economic development on its return to office in 1964 was initially reflected in the seat in the Cabinet accorded to its minister. But there was insufficient support in the party or outside to maintain this level of attention. Despite early protestations, aid was never defined as more than a secondary priority, and the size of its budget and the status of its ministry slipped steadily, retaining the occasional attention of senior ministers as much because of the efforts of the aid lobby and of its parliamentary supporters as because of its continuing existence as a separate Department. The Conservatives in 1970 brought the ODM within the orbit of the Foreign Secretary, as the ODA; on returning to power in March 1974, Labour restored its formal independence, as a gesture to the aid lobby.

Since World War II cultural and informational activities overseas have been managed by government agencies, without the prestige or support of a directly responsible minister. Here, more even than in aid policy, the influence of the Foreign Office remains far more decisive than in other aspects of external policy. Their strategic objectives, their geographical and functional guidelines, are laid down by Foreign Office departments.

The execution of policy by separate agencies – the BBC, the British Council, the COI, the ODA – increases its insulation from considerations of overall foreign policy. This is intensified by their employment of other autonomous agencies and nongovernmental bodies to carry out some of their responsibilities. Not surprisingly, this separation of functions among agencies concerned with overlapping aspects of overseas policy has led to a certain confusion of effort. 'In many aspects of the British Council's work', the Duncan Committee noted, 'there must be difficulty in determining how much of a particular activity is attributable to 'aid' or how much to 'overseas information''; yet 'for purposes of financial control, there is strict separation between the two budgets', funded respectively from the ODM and FCO votes, and coordination between the British Council and the ODM was not always very good. The importance attributed to the independence of British Council staff and offices abroad from the political control of the local British embassy also led, in the Committee's view, 'to duplication between separate organizations, and wastage of money and staff effort'.[5] 'The information services, the BBC and the British Council', another critic remarked, 'instead of being coordinated into a single arm of foreign policy, and judged by their respective contributions to British prestige abroad, are kept in separate compartments and in an often semi-competitive relationship.'[6] Part of the price paid for the autonomy accorded to the ODM/ODA, the BBC and the British Council – vigorously defended as it is by their members and by their domestic supporters – is that it makes coordination between them and with the total political direction of foreign policy so difficult. Yet this independence from immediate political direction was, of course, the objective in granting them autonomous status.

All three activities discussed here have been much less affected than defence and economic policy by the general trend towards multi-lateralism. British contributions to aid are made via the UN specialized agencies and a number of multilateral aid consortia in which it parti-cipates. From 1961 onwards the attitudes of the developed countries towards aid and development have been discussed in the OECD's Development Assistance Committee, and British entry into the EEC has added another multilateral framework for the discussion of policy on economic development. But throughout the 50s and 60s the proportion of British aid actually disbursed through multilateral channels remained small – a fairly constant 10–15 per cent of the total flow. Membership of the EEC and consequently of the European Development Fund sug-gested that this proportion would rise, but hitherto British aid policy had remained primarily a matter of bilateral government-to-government relations.[7]

In cultural and information activities multilateral cooperation was at best a fringe activity. The Council of Europe and NATO sponsored a number of educational and cultural activities, from discussions on school textbooks and student exchanges to the provision of scholarships and the presentation of prizes for academic work. The EEC Commission spon-sored a similar range of activities, in which the British government participated as a new member from 1973. But the vast bulk of informa-tion work and of cultural efforts remained either entirely under the con-trol of the government or subject to a series of bilateral agreements with the foreign governments concerned. Although all these were relatively new fields of foreign policy, the pattern of policy-making was in this respect traditional: bilateral, government to government, under the ultimate control of the Foreign Office.

Aid and Development
Government involvement in financial assistance for economic develop-ment overseas dates from the Colonial Development Act of 1929 and the more ambitious Colonial Development and Welfare Act of 1940.[8] After World War II Britain contributed to the budget of the World Bank and to the aid and development work of the various UN agencies (which in the immediate postwar period concentrated on 'relief and rehabilitation' in Europe and the Middle East); and expanded its own assistance to British overseas territories through the Colonial Development Corpora-tion (CDC, later the Commonwealth Development Corporation), estab-lished in 1948, through the research work and technical advice provided by a number of institutes in Britain, and through an extensive programme of technical assistance. Budgetary aid was also granted to such in-dependent and non-Commonwealth countries as Libya and Jordan, on political and military grounds.

The rationale for a long-term programme only began to emerge in

Britain and elsewhere in the late 50s. Britain had, after all, been itself a major recipient of economic and military aid from the United States until 1954–5. Acceptance of the principle of faster progress to political independence for the African territories carried with it acceptance of the need for some continuing economic assistance. A series of independence settlements provided for financial loans to replace grants formerly made to colonies, and for technical assistance to replace the work formerly undertaken by officials of the Colonial Service. These agreements incidentally made the newly independent countries responsible for the pensions of their former colonial civil servants, an issue which was to bedevil Britain's relations with its former colonies for years to come. Completion of the postwar recovery programmes in Western Europe, extension of the Cold War from Europe and the Middle East to Asia and Africa, and pressing demands for more rapid decolonization, combined to promote the concept of a continuing commitment to assist economic development in the poorer countries of the world. The motives behind this new commitment were mixed: a sense of post-imperial responsibility to the British Commonwealth, a desire to support the friendly and democratic governments which independence was intended to leave in most of Britain's colonies, concern for military security and for the future availability of military facilities, and acceptance of a certain moral obligation to reduce the gap between wealth and poverty in the world as well as in one's own country.

If motives were mixed and objectives uncertain, institutional arrangements were until 1964 dispersed, if not muddled. Technical assistance programmes had been brought together in 1961 into the new non-ministerial Department of Technical Cooperation. Financial aid was still in 1964 divided among five separate Parliamentary Votes, the responsibility of six Whitehall Departments: the Foreign Office, the Colonial Office, the CRO, the new and short-lived Central African Office, the Board of Trade, and the Treasury, which retained detailed control over all aid expenditure. The ECGD was responsible for long-term loans to independent countries to purchase British goods; the Bank of England was involved in the supervision of borrowing by colonial governments and newly independent states on the London market. The Ministry of Agriculture was responsible for British representation in the FAO and for the international commodity agreements which played so large a part in determining the export earnings of some Commonwealth territories; the Ministry of Education was responsible for the British contribution to UNESCO, which was increasingly devoting its main effort to economic and social development. There was no overall aid programme, as such, and no aid budget. The imposition of an aid 'ceiling' by the Treasury in 1964 was the first step towards a coherent assessment of priorities in terms of expenditure.

Since 1964 the institutional machinery has been shaped by the continuing debate about the proper objectives of policy and about how wide or narrowly its boundaries should be drawn. It has also been influenced by the growth and activity of the aid lobby, in Parliament and outside. There has been a close alliance between an unusually 'committed' Department and its domestic constituency, and the identification by that constituency of its promotional interests with the institutional independence and status in Whitehall of the Department it supported. For some time before 1964 the Overseas Development Institute (ODI, itself established in 1960 with financial support from the Ford Foundation and from British business), had been promoting the idea of a single Department responsible for policy on aid and development. 'The precise shape of the Ministry . . . was determined by a working group of Fabians set up early in 1964, with Thomas Balogh as Chairman.' Their ambitious proposals intended that the ODM should not be 'just an aid Ministry but (as its name implied) a department concerned with all aspects of policy affecting the Third World' – i.e. that development policy should embrace those aspects of policy on trade, food and agriculture, overseas investment and international monetary questions which concerned British relations with developing countries. The emphasis laid on a separate ministry outside the Foreign Office reflected the view of this group that development policies should not be subordinate to British political interests.[9] To ensure that Whitehall discussions should devote sufficient attention to development, the new ministry must be headed by a senior Cabinet Minister, with the authority to reconcile (and where necessary overrule) the conflicting views of the Treasury, the Bank, the Foreign Office, the Board of Trade, and the Ministry of Agriculture. The identification of the new ministry with the Labour Party's emphasis on economic development was strengthened by its inclusion as a commitment in the 1964 Labour Manifesto, as an earnest promise that Labour 'will give a dynamic lead in this vital field'. Many of the most active supporters of the charitable bodies which were now raising money for economic development were also members of the Labour Party; Harold Wilson himself was closely associated with the Freedom from Hunger Campaign, which had collected nearly £5m since its foundation in 1960, as well as with the older War on Want.

The first Minister of Overseas Development was Barbara Castle, an energetic and forceful personality with a firm base in the Labour Party, who had the confidence of the Prime Minister. Her Department was in effect an expanded Department of Technical Cooperation, from which its first Permanent Secretary came. Divisions formerly within the Colonial and Commonwealth Relations Offices, personnel from other Departments, and a small number of 'irregulars' from outside Whitehall were added to this nucleus. The post-colonial context of aid policy was reflected not only in the pattern of aid it inherited but also in the balance of its staff, more than a third of whom had worked originally in the Colonial Office (from which much of the staff of the DTC had been drawn). The new Department gained representation on the Whitehall network of interdepartmental committees responsible for the coordination of policy on trade, investment, and foreign relations, although it failed in its first attempt to dislodge the Treasury from the post of British executive director on the World Bank or to capture from the Board of Trade the leadership of the British delegation to the UN Conference on Trade and Development (UNCTAD). In August 1965 a coherent policy and programme for the Department and criteria for future policy were set out in a White Paper on *The Work of the New Ministry*.[10] This roundly declared that 'The basis of the aid programme . . . is a moral one', though it qualified its commitment by references to Britain's 'long-term economic advantage' and the assistance we must naturally give 'to our friends', reflecting the differences of view between the ODM and other Whitehall Departments which had participated in drafting the White Paper.

The publication of *The National Plan* in the following month, however, showed that the new ministry had been unable to resist economic pressures and the arguments of other Departments concerned to defend their spending programmes. 'The Government', it announced, 'have decided to restrain two major items of their overseas expenditure', defence commitments and overseas aid. Although it was 'fully aware of the importance of aid to the developing countries,' it found it necessary 'to scrutinise the aid programme with particular care so long as the United Kingdom balance of payments is under such great strain and we are faced with the need to repay the overseas indebtedness recently incurred'.[11] But it was not only concern about the deteriorating balance of payments which led the Cabinet to accept the need for restraint on aid expenditure, inspiring ODM economists to undertake detailed studies of the net burden of aid expenditure on the balance of payments in order to refute the charge that the aid budget contributed to the total deficit.[12] It was also that, when it came to a hard choice between spending priorities, overseas aid was grouped with support for the railways and scientific research among those 'other programmes' which would 'probably have to be slowed down to make room for the high-priority services'.[13] Not only was the projected aid programme cut, but between 1966 and 1967 total expenditure on aid fell. Throughout the period of office of the first Wilson government, in terms of UNCTAD targets for official and for total aid flows, the UK contribution to international economic development fell steadily, and the respectability of British aid statistics was preserved only by an increase in private investment in developing countries.

The status of the ODM declined with the diminished priority given to the aid programme. Mrs Castle moved to the Ministry of Transport in December 1965, in a minor government reshuffle. Her successor held the post for only nine months, and his successor in turn for only a year. In August 1967, when Reginald Prentice, a more junior minister, was made Minister of Overseas Development, the office was left out of the Cabinet. During the second half of 1968 there was considerable speculation that the ODM was about to be absorbed into the new FCO; this was

The Flow of British Aid, 1964–72 (£m)

	1964	1965	1966	1967	1968	1969	1970	1971	1972
Gross aid programme	191·2	194·8	207·2	200·8	203·0	210·8	213·8	268·9	303·6
Net official flows as % of GNP	0·53	0·48	0·48	0·45	0·42	0·39	0·37	0·41	0·40
Net private flows as % of GNP	0·45	0·54	0·39	0·29	0·30	0·64	0·64	0·63	0·56
Total flows in terms of UNCTAD 1% target	0·98	1·03	0·87	0·74	0·72	1·03	1·01	1·05	0·96

Note: Aid expenditure is given at current prices. The difference between the gross aid programme and net official aid amounted in 1968 to £30m, in 1972 to £62m, from the repayment of loans.

Source: British Aid Statistics.

firmly resisted by the aid lobby, helped by a friendly report on the ministry's work by the Estimates Committee.[14] Another campaign to protect the ODM from absorption was fought during the summer of 1970, in anticipation of the Conservative government's plans for the creation of a number of 'giant' Departments. Though this failed to prevent the subordination of the Department to the FCO, it did succeed in exacting a pledge from the new Minister of Overseas Development, Richard Wood, that 'the Ministry is not being destroyed', and that it would remain as a separate entity within the FCO.[15]

The 'failure' of the ODM, to its supporters, was partly a result of political and partly of institutional factors. Mrs Castle's 'main failure', a member of the ODI wrote in 1968, 'which was not so much hers as that of the Government as a whole, was that she found no way of giving her Ministry a secure vantage point in the structure of policy-making'. The 'root cause' of the decline in the ODM's standing after her departure 'was a deliberate removal of political support'.[16] This explanation is too simplistic. Initial expectations of the ODM's influence in Whitehall demanded that the objective of economic development should dominate the entire spectrum of British relations with the Third World, but there was never sufficient support for this within the Labour Party. It was not therefore simply the resistance of established Departments in Whitehall which defeated the ODM, nor 'the deliberate removal of political support' which brought it down. Rather, the development objective had never been sufficiently clear or appealing to override other, equally powerful, objectives; and the preoccupations of government sharpened ministerial awareness of their prior commitment to other objectives.

The Labour government's initial priorities were to increase the rate of domestic economic growth, to end the restraints placed on the economy by balance-of-payments deficits and to redirect government expenditure into expanded social programmes; internationally the aim was to maintain Britain's position as a global power and as a close ally of the United States. Few of these fitted easily with the promotion of overseas economic development. Economic aid was a reluctantly accepted drain on the balance of payments, reduced by tying a considerable proportion of it to the purchase of British goods and by holding back the proportion committed to multilateral aid, despite the ODM arguments on export gains from multilateral aid programmes. It was difficult to defend an expanding aid programme when cuts were being made in domestic projects equally included in the Labour Party Manifesto but which had more electoral appeal. To subordinate trade policy to development would mean sacrificing the interests of textile workers in Lancashire and shoe manufacturers in the Midlands to the interests of developing industries in other countries. The argument that the Labour government had not been elected to put British workers out of work had considerable force to members of the Cabinet, faced with an already existing unemployment problem. Whatever the declared policy of the Party in opposition, before 1964 and again between 1970 and 1974, it is difficult to rebut the reply of one left-wing MP to the development promises contained in the 1972 Labour *Programme for Britain*, that 'No future Labour Government could possibly consider endangering the livelihoods of our own people by putting them second to any others, whatever the reason.'[17]

The particular concern of the aid lobby in protecting the ODM from the Foreign Office was to prevent the subordination of development criteria in the formulation of aid policy to the political considerations which they feared the FCO would impose.[18] Economic development, it was argued by the aid lobby inside and outside Parliament, was necessarily a long-term exercise, easily damaged by the immediate twists and turns of political relations; the assessment of aid priorities should depend upon the needs of the recipients, not the wishes of the donor. There were, however, two problems with this demand. First, there was (and is) no agreed set of criteria for economic development; its prerequisites remain a subject of debate among economists, who lay changing emphases on the relative importance of infrastructure and industrialization, of urban or rural development, of technical education and population control. Political differences colour the emphases some advocates place upon state intervention and others upon private enterprise and foreign investment; on the right and on the left disillusioned critics have denied the value of development aid to the recipients as a whole. Secondly, supporters of the aid lobby themselves on occasion argued in favour of utilizing aid to reward friendly governments and punish detested ones – though their definitions of 'friendly' and 'unfriendly' differed somewhat from what they saw as the FCO perspective. It was strongly argued, for instance, that the post-Nkrumah regime in Ghana should be given more positive help with its burden of inherited debt than appeared to be possible within the confines of Treasury financial principles and the already-committed aid budget, in order to strengthen this re-established democracy.[19] Conversely, George Cunningham MP, an active supporter of development in the House of Commons, was among the many who wanted to break existing aid commitments to Uganda in 1973, finding it 'offensive and unnecessary' to continue to honour them 'if that country behaves in the manner in which Uganda has behaved towards this country and its own citizens.'[20] The choice among competing criteria for development is not self-evident or simple. The balance of geographical and functional priorities adopted necessarily depends upon wider considerations than economic development alone.

A further acute problem, not fully appreciated in 1964–5, was that of balancing long-term assistance to economic development with immediate assistance to areas suffering from large-scale natural disasters, within the limits imposed by the Treasury on the overall aid budget. If the political arguments for immediate assistance to Busia's Ghana failed to break through the boundaries of the aid budget, the political desirability of helping Malaysia and Singapore to offset the effects of the rundown of British forces in 1968, and the security need to meet Maltese demands for increased 'technical assistance' in 1972, did burst through. But these were recognized as special cases, and were charged to the parliamentary Votes of the FCO and the MoD. Contingency assistance to Zambia to compensate for the adverse effects of Rhodesian closure of the border, in early 1973, was also financed separately from the 'normal' aid programme. But the need to allow for unexpected contingencies and the difficulty of anticipating the rate of actual disbursements so as to reach but not exceed the aid ceiling led to repeated underspending on the aid programme between 1966 and 1970 – with the consequent loss of aid funds under the strict Treasury rule that expenditure could not be carried over from one year to another.[21]

To cope with this, some degree of flexibility in aid expenditure within the boundaries of the five-year projections for public expenditure was introduced in 1971–2. But this was not enough for the number and scale of immediate and unexpected claims upon the aid budget within the next two years. Although in 1971 the ODA was aware of the likelihood of severe famine in East Bengal in the wake of a disastrous cyclone and extensive flooding, the scale of that famine and the consequences of the partition of Pakistan strained the entire British aid programme. An additional £10m was provided towards relief in Bangladesh (as it became) in the financial year 1971–2, drawn partly from immediate economies in other sectors of the aid programme and partly from 'the switching of sums from later to earlier years in anticipation of special demands on the aid programme up to 1974–5'.[22] Other demands could not be met without a political decision at Cabinet level to divert additional resources to the aid programme. The settlement of the Sudanese civil war in early 1972 brought immediate requests from the Sudan government and the UN High Commission for Refugees for substantial economic assistance, yet Britain could only offer from an already overcommitted aid budget some £200,000. The Ethiopian famine and the southern Saharan drought brought other immediate demands. Sympathetic MPs, the charitable agencies of the aid lobby, and some sections of the press bitterly criticized the slowness and inadequacy of Whitehall's response and the reluctance of the authorities to agree to the diversion of sufficient RAF planes and army personnel to such civil disasters.[23] But to demand such a diversion of resources, without a clear indication of public support for it and without indicating from what other expenditure programmes the funds should be taken was to demand from the government a political reorientation for which the basic commitment was lacking. The only and unacceptable alternative, as these critics were forced to admit, was to divert funds from long-term development programmes.

The emergence of a politically conscious aid lobby was one of the unanticipated results of the high expectations and disappointed hopes of the period between 1964 and 1968. A number of charities had been active for many years before 1964 in raising money for famine relief, and more recently also for longer-term development. Save the Children Fund and Oxfam, the two oldest, had begun their work in the European context, during and after World War II, and had moved outwards from there to the developing countries. Several church-sponsored agencies were also raising money for poorer countries during the 50s. These were naturally caught up in the rising international concern with economic development at the end of the 50s. The UNA played more of a propagandistic than a fund-raising role in the early sixties, following the issues emphasized by UN agencies. In addition, like other voluntary organizations, it ran its own small programme of technical assistance, sponsoring volunteers to work overseas. The ODI, from its establishment in 1960, had played a rather more discreet role as a publicist for development.[24]

None of these bodies saw themselves as directly political bodies in 1964. UNA, perhaps the closest to a campaigning body, included the leaders of all three political parties among its honorary presidents; the others would have classified themselves, in differing degrees, as respectable rather than radical. In 1965, with considerable encouragement from senior officials from the ODM, five of the main charitable agencies, plus the ODI and the Catholic Institute for International Relations, established the VCOAD, with the three aims of coordinating project work overseas, of cooperating in their educational and publicity work in schools and colleges, and of representing the interests of the developing countries to the British government – this last a tentative step towards political lobbying.

Between 1966 and 1968 several events contributed to the evolution of an organized aid lobby. The publication by the British Council of Churches of a report on *World Poverty and British Responsibility* in 1966 was the first statement by an influential body of the need to take action to influence the government as well as to raise money for charity. Significantly, the study group which had drawn up this report had included three 'observers' from Whitehall – from the ODM, the Board of Trade, and the Ministry of Agriculture. The role of the churches, exercised both directly and through the agency of Christian Aid, was decisive in transforming these groups into a national movement over the following five years. The impact of the expenditure cuts of July 1966, chopping more than twice the amount raised by all voluntary aid agencies from the official budget, was to reinforce the arguments for a more political orientation: arguments now forcefully advanced by ministers and officials from within the ODM, who saw the agencies as much-needed allies. Further cuts in projected aid expenditure in the post-devaluation review of December 1967 were followed by the threat of yet further major reductions in the winter of 1968–9. The response of what now constituted a selfconscious lobby included a barrage of letters to the Chancellor of the Exchequer and to individual MPs, lobbies of the House of Commons, meetings in towns all over the country (organized often on the initiative of the local Council of Churches, a ready-made national network for action, together with branches of UNA and the charitable agencies), and 'Christmas Sign-Ins' for aid in various churches and cathedrals. The Minister for Overseas Development, Reginald Prentice, (who later resigned to work for a larger aid programme from outside the government rather than accept 'promotion' to another ministry) afterwards claimed that the aid budget eventually agreed 'would certainly have been lower if the aid lobby had not worked so hard', and might indeed have been reduced in absolute terms.[25]

From 1969 onwards the relationship between the ODM and the voluntary organizations stabilized into a close 'client'-to-'sponsor' relationship – though, in contrast to the relationship between interest groups and Whitehall Departments in most areas of domestic policy, the aid lobby was concerned not with its own interests but with promoting the cause of overseas countries, and with supporting the work of the ODM to that end. In 1968–9 the ODM contributed some £7,000 towards the VCOAD to assist with 'its educational and information activities as well as its coordinating role'.[26] By 1972–3 this had grown to £20,000, by 1973–4 to £25,000. In March 1971, in addition, the ODA and VCOAD between them set up the Standing Conference on the Second Development Decade, to which nearly seventy organizations affiliated, with the aim of widening the basis for public education about aid and development. In addition to their promotional and publicity work, voluntary organizations acted as agencies for the ODA, in for example administering the British Volunteer Programme, to which the ODA contributed 75 per cent of the cost. Their own extensive money-raising activities supplemented the official flow of aid, and provided firm evidence of the commitment of at least a section of the public to economic development. In 1968 the total aid flow from voluntary bodies was estimated at £17m; in 1972 at £19m. Their independent field operations overseas complemented the work of the ODA. In Biafra in 1969, in Bengal in 1971, they were able to operate where government officials could not go, and incidentally to provide valuable information on the economic situation to the ODA.

The relationship of the ODM/ODA to Parliament also reflected the effectiveness of the aid lobby, and its ability to mobilize its supporters. A small minority of MPs, some of whom had spent periods in former colonies or in development work overseas, was actively committed to a larger aid programme and to a broader definition of British policy on aid and development. The large majority accepted aid as a desirable objective, if not a high priority, which it was respectable to support. The report of the Estimates Committee in 1967–8 took the form more of a defence of the ODM and of the aid programme than of a critical examination of administration and priorities; the creation in April 1969 of a Select Committee on Overseas Aid institutionalized the parliamentary lobby.[27] This committee lapsed with the dissolution of Parliament in June 1970, to be reconstituted, after a great deal of lobbying, in the following December to complete its report. Its disbandment in 1971 set off a sustained campaign to establish a continuing committee, with broader terms of reference, to which the Conservative government yielded in December 1972. The existence of a Select Committee, like the independence of the ODA, had become a symbolic issue for the aid lobby.

The emphasis which from 1968 the voluntary organizations increasingly placed on publicity and education recognized the limitations inherent in representing a small (if vigorous) minority, and the force of the political argument that majority opinion was against it – though supporters of the aid lobby bitterly criticized political leaders for failing to give a positive lead to public opinion. Ministerial and opposition reaction to lobbying tended rather to increase the gap between declaratory policy and policy in practice: reaffirming their commitment to international development, but giving a lower priority to aid expenditure than to domestic programmes, and subordinating developmental considerations to the interests of British industry.

Hence the field was narrowly defined and the management of policy conducted at a relatively low level. What emerged, from 1968 onwards, was not the coherent development policy which enthusiasts had hoped for, but an efficiently managed aid programme, together with a developmental 'presence' on interdepartmental committees concerned with trade, long-term credits, international debt, and some other aspects of monetary relations. The ODM's defence of its position in Whitehall came to rest less on political muscle than on its expertise in developmental questions and the administration of aid. The aid planning process which emerged between 1967 and 1969 rested on the acceptance of the Treasury ceiling and the criteria for aid laid down in the 1965 White Paper. An annual aid framework was drawn up, for discussion with the FCO, the Board of Trade, and the Treasury, breaking down the aid programme into its regional and functional categories. From 1969 onwards this was supplemented by some 45 Country Policy Papers, which examined the economic situation and needs of the main recipient countries, the amounts contributed by other countries and by international agencies, the proposed amounts and priorities of British aid, and 'other relevant factors'.[28] These were discussed between the geographical divisions of the ODM and geographical desk officers in the FCO and Board of Trade, and sent for comment to the British embassy in the country concerned. From these, as revised and agreed, the shape of the aid programme for the next year and its projection beyond was put together, again within the ODM under consultation with other Departments.

It is hard for the outside observer to detect any significant changes in the pattern of policy-making with the transition from a separate ministry to an agency within the FCO in 1970. The ODA, and its minister, remained as a separate entity at the other end of Victoria Street from the Foreign Office; in 1972 there was still a Foreign Office department responsible for 'liaison with the Overseas Development Administration'.[29] The Treasury and the DTI played predictable roles, protecting and promoting their departmental interests, resisting the establishment of precedents on debt repayment which would provide a handle for less deserving debtors, looking for opportunities to 'do good to our exports through aid'.[30] Foreign Office geographical departments attempted to emphasize political factors against what they saw as the 'naivety' of the ODA. But the ODA itself remained responsible for the final shape of the aid programme, partly because this was its central interest, partly because its established expertise had won it the respect of the other Departments involved.

It is almost as hard to detect significant differences in the objectives of aid policy between different party administrations. Under the Conservatives, despite their more muted declared support for economic development, the volume of economic aid rose more rapidly – assisted by a less urgent concern for the balance of payments. Their commitment to private enterprise was reflected in the introduction of a new EGCD scheme to insure private investment in developing countries against non-commercial risks, and in a declared intention to use official aid to encourage private investment – though in this Britain was following almost every other OECD country.[31] The new government set in motion a review of aid priorities and objectives, conducted at under-secretary level under a general prime ministerial directive. But when this committee reported, after more than eighteen months' work, the emphasis only differed marginally from that laid down in Barbara Castle's White Paper. 'The make-up of the aid programme reflects a wide and complex range of developmental, political and economic considerations', institutionally represented in Whitehall by a stable relationship among different Departments, with only occasional ministerial intervention.[32]

Issues which overlap the boundaries of aid policy, so defined, could not be so conveniently handled. Debt questions, which loomed increasingly large in British relations with developing countries in the early 70s, were allocated to different Departments according to the importance it was felt should be attached to different considerations. On the Indonesian debt the Treasury took the lead, and provided the British representative on the 'Paris Club' set up to renegotiate it; over Ghana the problem was seen as so central to bilateral relations that the FCO played the leading role. The Indian debt problem was seen as so closely related to the whole question of India's economic development that the ODA handled it under this heading. If these ad hoc arrangements worked satisfactorily, the management of British policy towards UNCTAD was rather less happy. In 1963, when it was evident that the developing countries were pressing for a world conference on trade and development, 'the Board of Trade began to prepare briefs and especially to work out the implications with regard to GATT'.[33] Having thus seized the issue, the Board of Trade retained the leading role throughout the next ten years, despite the intervention of the Foreign Office and a later challenge from the ODM. Although the British government played a constructive role in the first UNCTAD Conference in 1964, its role in the second Conference in 1968 was largely passive. Its brief had been prepared through a series of interdepartmental discussions, at under-secretary level, over the previous twelve months, under the chairmanship of the Board of Trade. Reference to ministers had come only at a very late stage in the discussions, and the issue was never discussed in Cabinet or in Cabinet committee. At the third Conference, in 1972, there was some evidence of disagreement between the DTI and the FCO. It was reported that 'The Foreign Office has been privately expressing its distress at the speech by Mr Michael Noble, the Minister for Trade and head of the British delegation, at the opening session', and after Mr Noble's early departure Lady Tweedsmuir, an FCO minister of state, was sent to the closing stages of the conference.[34] The impression received is of a series of unsuccessful attempts to dislodge Board of Trade dominance between 1964 and 1972, from within both the ODM and the Foreign Office, which failed because the officials were unable to capture the attention of their ministers for long enough to raise the issue effectively to ministerial level and so to alter the established parameters of discussion.

The management of aid policy had thus become institutionally and conceptually compartmentalized. The changes from a Labour to a Conservative government and in the Department's formal status in 1970 affected the pattern of policy-making relatively little. It was hard to believe that the return of a Labour government in 1974, and the symbolic re-establishment of the Department's independence, would lead to any greater changes, without the commitment of the substantial and sustained political effort needed to raise this field of policy to a higher level. What pressures there were for change in 1974 came from elsewhere: from the erosive effect of inflation and the deteriorating exchange rate on the overseas operations of the ODM, from the wider constraints of EEC membership, and from the demands of the developing countries themselves for an overall reassessment of their economic relations with the developed world.

Managing Information and Promoting Culture

The structure of policy-making and administration for information and culture was shaped in the years preceding and immediately following World War II. John Reith began the BBC Empire Service, the predecessor of the (English) World Service, in 1932, on his own initiative, as a link to bind together the peoples of the British Empire; asking for financial assistance from the government only when it had established an audience overseas. The 'British Committee for Relations with other Countries' was set up in 1934, largely on the initiative of the Foreign Office; its activities grew rapidly as the need to counteract Italian and German efforts became more apparent. The BBC's Arabic Service was started in 1936 to combat the 'streams of anti-British propaganda' pouring out from the Bari Radio Station.[35] The Foreign Office had operated a 'British Official Wireless Service' since the dissolution of the wartime Ministry of Information in 1919, providing summaries of the British press to foreign newspapers through overseas missions; it had also maintained press attachés in the major embassies since the early 20s. As World War II approached, the information work of its overseas posts expanded, as did the support provided for them from Whitehall; until on the outbreak of war they were taken over by a re-established Ministry of Information.

The British propaganda effort during World War II was massive and highly professional, with some 6,000 officials (mostly temporarily recruited for wartime service) in the Ministry of Information in London and attached to embassies abroad. But as it was not considered appropriate to a democracy to retain what was in effect a ministry for propaganda after the end of the war, the future of the overseas information services was then considered by the various Departments and agencies concerned. The British Council had been granted a Royal Charter as an independent but grant-aided body in 1940, after a sharp controversy between Lord Lloyd, its chairman since 1937, and Sir John Reith. BBC External Services, vastly enlarged during the war to broadcast to occupied Europe, were returned to the control of the BBC – but were to be financed by a grant-in-aid from the Foreign Office. The Foreign Office and the Commonwealth Relations and Colonial Offices took over responsibility for informational services overseas. The COI was established to provide the technical services they needed, as well as to supply the information needs of home Departments. This compromise solution reflected not only the conflicting aims of the bodies involved, and the fierce attempt made by the Ministry of Information to retain its autonomy, but also a general reluctance to accept the propriety of ministerially-directed propaganda in time of peace.[36]

This administrative framework has persisted, with a few minor changes, since 1946. Ministerial responsibility has shifted with ministerial and governmental changes. From 1957 to 1962 the Chancellor of the Duchy of Lancaster, Dr Charles Hill, effectively acted as Minister of Information, with a seat in the Cabinet, coordinating both home and overseas information services. Between 1962 and 1964 the junior minister responsible for the Department of Technical Cooperation was made responsible for coordinating overseas activities. In 1964 the Minister of Overseas Development made a determined effort to take over responsibility for the British Council; but the downgrading of the ODM and the acceptance of the eventual merger of the Colonial and Commonwealth Relations Offices into the Foreign Office from 1965 on brought the determination of overall policy within the responsibility of the FCO, with the cost of these services falling on the FCO Vote.

The emphasis of wartime effort had been on occupied Europe, North America, and the Middle East. The period of drift which followed the war, with ministers uninterested and ministerial responsibility uncertain, with decisions effectively taken through a series of interdepartmental committees, with the information budget under constant pressure, gave little opportunity for a reorientation of priorities. The 'information ceiling' imposed by the Treasury on overseas activities had pressed down from £11·7m in 1948–9 to £9·8m in 1952–3, in a period of sharply rising prices. After some active lobbying from the British Council, the BBC, and officials responsible for information in Whitehall Departments, an Independent Committee of Enquiry was set up, under the chairmanship of Lord Drogheda.[37] Its report, in 1954, laid down the principles which were to guide British information policy for nearly twenty years afterwards. It accepted the extensive cutback in information effort in Western Europe since 1945, and recommended further reductions – against stiff resistance from the BBC, which regarded its wartime efforts as its proudest achievement. It accepted too, with some reservations, the similar cutback of effort in Latin America. What it recommended was a substantial build-up in the Cold War areas of the Middle East and South and South East Asia, expansion in the colonial territories as they moved towards autonomy and eventual independence, and the maintenance of whatever activities were possible in Eastern Europe (then limited solely to broadcasts by the BBC).[38] The Conservative government accepted these recommendations and the increased expenditure which they required. Between 1955 and 1962 the overseas information budget doubled. Its growth, and its regional priorities, were reinforced by the Conservative reaction to Suez, which blamed the inadequacies of British propaganda for contributing to the failure. Consequently there were increasing activities of all kinds in the Middle East.[39]

Under the pressure of rising costs and successive reviews of public expenditure, a long period of retrenchment began in the mid-60s. The post-devaluation cuts of 1967–8 forced the British Council to withdraw completely from eight countries and the BBC to close some of its smaller overseas operations, including the Albanian and Hebrew Services. Both bodies had to some extent taken on the protective colouring of prevailing fashionable priorities by first emphasizing their contribution to aid and development, and then, after 1966–7, to exports; though for British Information Services, which were 'selling' government policy and concentrating their efforts more in developed countries, only the second of these rationales was available. It was not until March 1972, when Britain had successfully negotiated entry into the EEC, that any major change in priorities was announced. On prime ministerial initiative, an additional £6m over four years was now to be provided to expand cultural exchanges with Western Europe and assist the BBC to develop its European links.

Within the FCO, from 1968 on, the determination of information policy rested with the five information and cultural policy departments, reporting to the same assistant and deputy under-secretaries. The largest, the Guidance and Information Policy department, provided 'guidances' to overseas posts on government policy or ministerial statements, and background briefings for the use of information officers and of embassy staff as a whole. It was also generally responsible for the operations of official information services overseas, for the overseas information activities of the COI, and for 'liaison with BBC External Services'. The Cultural Relations department was responsible for 'matters requiring consultation between the Foreign and Commonwealth Office and the British Council' and for a number of other bilateral and multilateral educational and cultural questions.[40] Cultural agreements with Eastern Europe, the Soviet Union, and China were handled by a separate Cultural Exchange department, in recognition of the peculiar difficulties and the political sensitivity of government activities in this area. The Information Administration department was responsible for the budgetary control and financial priorities of the overseas information services, the overseas operations of the COI and the BBC, and the British Council, as well as for the allocation to overseas posts of sponsored visits to Britain. The Information Research department performed a more ancillary role, producing reports on international developments, primarily within the socialist countries, for restricted circulation in Britain and abroad. In addition, the News department, which reported directly to the Permanent Under-Secretary, briefed the British and the foreign press in London, issued statements, and dealt with varying degrees of informality with some 150 journalists a day.

Apart from the direct involvement of the News department, those activities most clearly subject to Foreign Office control were the information services overseas. Separately established (as the British Information Services) in the larger and more important countries, they were the responsibility of full-time or part-time information officers in smaller missions. These were staffed by the Diplomatic Service itself, which had decided against maintaining a separate class of information officials at the time of the merger with the Commonwealth Service. DS officials who demonstrated a flair for information work might expect to spend two or three periods during their career in information activities in Whitehall or abroad; beyond that, it was argued that a familiarity with the overall priorities of British foreign policy was an essential part of information work, which only the generalist could provide. Locally-recruited staff in the larger missions provided continuity at executive level. For background material – pamphlets, films, articles for the local press, speakers, and exhibitions – the information services relied on the COI, which also handled the sponsored visits to Britain of foreign 'influentials' nominated by overseas posts. Nearly three-quarters of the COI's staff time and over 40 per cent of its budget were spent on over-seas information activities. FCO officials at home and abroad expressed satisfaction with the wide range of services it provided. An investigation conducted by Sir Gordon Newton in 1970–1 on the possibility of hiving off the COI's presentational services to private agencies, in accordance with the Conservative's commitment to reduce the role of government, apparently found that no private agency could match the COI in terms of costs or speed of delivery, and in consequence was never published.[41]

The BBC External Services are financed through the FCO Vote, but are otherwise an integral part of the BBC, cherishing their independence of government direction. The FCO is responsible for the size and the overall allocation of the External Services budget, and hence for major decisions about the distribution of broadcast services. The BBC is responsible for the content of programmes. It is affected, of course, by changing attitudes on government priorities, and is made aware of ambassadorial strictures on some programmes, but it remains entitled to decide the emphasis of its programmes independently. Its output during the Suez crisis, when it broadcast reports of domestic criticism of the government's action instead of the firm support which the government expected, is still cited as an argument against accepting the guidance of the Foreign Office on policy matters. No other example so sharply emphasized to its overseas audience the impartiality and independence of its programmes, on which its international reputation so largely depends.[42]

By 1972 the BBC had sunk from its wartime position as the world's largest external broadcaster to fifth place in the international league table, surpassed not only by the United States and the Soviet Union but also by China and West Germany. For many years capital expenditure had been insufficient, so that reception from old and inadequate trans-mitters was poor. An additional £5m had been granted in 1971 for capital improvements after a Whitehall review on behalf of the Con-servative government, supplementing its annual expenditure of some £10m. The BBC had additionally performed something of the same role in developing broadcasting services in the new Commonwealth countries as had the Bank of England for their central banks: seconding staff, assisting with training, providing advice and broadcasting material, and maintaining continuing links through the Commonwealth Broadcasting Conference. In this it overlapped with the ODA, as in providing broadcasting and television material to foreign networks it overlapped with the COI – though the BBC's more straightforward concern was with 'good broadcasting', as against the COI's interest in providing documentaries on British manufactures and the like.[43]

The British Council also stands a little apart from the FCO, despite their close working relationship overseas. Like the BBC, it is a public corporation, dependent upon the government for overall direction and for its funds but with 'a considerable degree of real independence from Government control' to safeguard 'the non-political character' of its work.[44] The impression of distance from the FCO partly reflects the lingering myth that it is not a fully governmental body – a reality in the 1930s, when a substantial proportion of its funds were provided by private industry, but increasingly unreal since World War II. A small part of its income comes from such self-financing activities as charges for English-language teaching; the rest is provided by the FCO, which retains a dominant voice in the geographical distribution of its efforts. It also, by convention, approves the appointment of British Council representatives to foreign countries – where they are likely to have regular contacts with the resident British mission, and in many places are formally included within it as cultural attachés, under a bilateral cultural convention. Moreover the FCO takes the lead in negotiating and renegotiating the network of cultural conventions and agreements under which the British Council operates, as matters of intergovernmental relations. The Council itself is governed by an Executive Committee of notables, academics, industrialists, civil servants and MPs (not unlike the Arts Council), assisted by a number of advisory committees. Its professional staff are not members of the civil service; convinced of the intrinsic value of their work, they resent what they perceive to be the FCO's patronizing attitude to it and its inferior status.[45]

In regard to information and culture, the FCO geographical departments play a less direct role than overseas missions, merely offering occasional advice or making representations. The CRE divisions of the DTI were involved in the commercial aspects of informational work; in addition the DTI granted £18,000 to the British Council in 1971–2 and 1972–3 to support its more directly commercial activities. The ODA was much more directly drawn into discussions of the work of the British Council, which acted as an agency for it in educational aid and many aspects of technical assistance; just over a third of the British Council's budget of £15·5m in 1971–2 (and £17·6m in 1972–3) was provided under a grant-in-aid from the ODA, separately accounted for from the FCO grant. The other major Department involved was the Treasury, naturally cast in an apparently antagonistic stance in respect of expenditure in which ministers had little or no interest, which showed no immediate return but which adversely affected the balance of payments.

Thus the FCO acted as a buffer between the agencies and the Treasury, resisting Treasury 'attacks' with shifting defences of information work, and enforcing unavoidable cuts on the agencies.[46] The British Council was particularly bitter about the imposition of an immediate £500,000 cut on its budget in 1967–8, subordinating the long-term character of its work to the immediate needs of the economic situation; though, as the FCO not unreasonably replied, 'when overall reduction in public expenditure has to be achieved, it would be difficult to select the Council for exemption'.[47]

The absence of ministerial preoccupation with information policy for extended periods left the determination of policy in the hands of officials: proceeding therefore within the incremental limits of interdepartmental bargaining, the stable positions of the Treasury, the Foreign Office, and the agencies making for an overall stability of policy. Ministerial disquiet with the reaction abroad to the Suez invasion had prompted Dr Hill's appointment, temporarily elevating the oversight of information services to Cabinet level. Hardly surprisingly, his period of office coincided with a sustained expansion of the overseas information services. His removal to the Ministry of Housing in 1961 left the agencies, as they saw it, to the 'death of a thousand cuts' at the hands of the Treasury. Information and culture were never prime concerns for any Foreign Secretary; it was not therefore until after prime ministerial intervention in 1972 that there was any decisive change of direction. Parliamentary interest was low; the Expenditure Committee's report on the British Council in 1971 was the first parliamentary investigation since 1948, and was not debated until a year after its publication.[48] MPs' scepticism about the value of British Information Services was increased by the amount of unsolicited literature they received from foreign embassies in London, which they immediately consigned to the wastepaper basket. The press campaign which the Beaverbrook newspapers and others had run against the 'extravagance' of the British Council and the ineffectiveness of British Information Services in foreign countries in the late 40s and early 50s had long since died away; but it had not been replaced by any more positive appreciation of their work.[49]

Hence policy evolved gradually, mainly at low level within Whitehall, its insulation from foreign policy as a whole increased by the institutional independence of the agencies. Disputes between the agencies and the Departments which controlled them were themselves largely limited to Whitehall; only when major cuts were threatened did the BBC and the British Council actively appeal for support to a wider audience. There was of course little room for differences between British Information Services and the FCO, since their role and that of the information officers of overseas missions were clearly defined as the communication of government policy. The British Information Services staff belonged to the Diplomatic Service; the COI's accepted role was as a provider of material and of technical services.

With the BBC and the British Council, however, both separate organizations with their own staff and organizational rationale, at least two consistent differences between their perspective and that of the FCO are apparent. The first is the difference of emphasis between the FCO's insistence that activities should be aimed at the 'influential few', and the tendency of the British Council, and still more of the BBC, to want to attract mass audiences as well. The Foreign Office argument derives from the need to maximize influence by concentrating limited resources where they will be most effective: the agencies' resistance to this rests upon their concern with the longer term, when existing elites may well have been overthrown and new unknowns emerged to take their place. The difference of emphasis between the FCO and the BBC over the relative priorities to be attached to the English-language World Service and to the vernacular services, for instance, revolves around this issue, with the Foreign Office arguing that 'the BBC's external services will have the greatest effect upon the educated and professional classes, for whom English will often be the main lingua franca', and the BBC replying that it is not always the educated and professional classes alone who exert political influence.[50]

The second underlying difference is between the FCO's view of information and cultural activities as instruments of foreign policy, and the natural tendency of independent agencies to view their work as an end in itself. To a broadcaster, professional satisfaction is derived from good broadcasting and a large and attentive audience, not from presenting the policies of the British government or from following the changing priorities of successive Foreign Secretaries. To a cultural attaché or a British Council representative, the transmission and enjoyment of culture is to some extent its own justification, contributing it is hoped to a shared sense of civilization and a greater affection for Britain, but not to be costed in terms of direct political gains. The Duncan Committee (p. 99) noted a not dissimilar 'tendency for information sections in overseas missions to . . . acquire as it were a life of their own; the machine is there and is a good machine and it is not difficult to find useful work for it to do'.[51] This tendency, indeed, extends to overseas missions as a whole. Cultural work is enjoyable; a successful orchestral concert or ballet performance may give a sense of achievement and satisfaction to an ambassador and his staff out of all proportion to its potential political influence. Reaction in the British embassy in Moscow to the expulsion of 105 Soviet diplomats in the summer of 1971, for instance, was overlaid with remorse that it had ruined a carefully prepared Musical Week, which had brought a splendid programme of concerts to entertain the musical elite of Moscow.

Different perspectives on time-scale lie at the back of both these disputes. Necessarily, FCO officials are concerned with immediate policy and with short-term results. The agencies with reason reply that it takes long years to establish the British Council's position in the cultural life of a foreign country, and years more before the benefits may be reaped, so that to twist and turn with every shift of British foreign policy is to risk destroying the value of work already done. Likewise the BBC argues that only a regular service over a period of years can provide the basis for influence in a crisis. 'Only if the BBC is there in the autumn and winter can it be there in the spring', as the director of External Services argued after the Czech invasion of 1968.[52]

Assessment of priorities between different activities is as difficult as determining priorities within each particular area. The marginal contribution of official efforts, within a universe of cultural and communication exchanges, is almost impossible to measure; the British Council hardly attempts to measure it, though British Information Services in New York and elsewhere compile statistics on the use made of their material and the professions of those who subscribe to their publications, while the BBC conducts a limited number of audience surveys in countries where this is allowed.[53] The Duncan Committee (p. 17) adopted the rough and ready yardstick of comparison with the scale of French and German efforts, discovering that Britain spent considerably more on information work in overseas missions and considerably less on cultural activities. But it would be difficult to argue that the allocation of French or German expenditure was in any sense more rational than the British, given their different cultural and informational priorities and the marked divergence between the German emphasis on broadcasting and the French on language teaching and literature. We are dealing here with imponderables, hardly amenable to measurement or cost-benefit analysis; habit, guesswork, and a natural preference for concentrating on what one believes one can do best necessarily shape the pattern of activity.

The size of the effort which should be mounted is equally difficult to assess. The total budget for overseas information and culture amounted to some £38m in 1972–3, half the amount allocated to overseas representation, a seventh the size of the aid budget, less than 2 per cent of the defence budget. Arguably, as the Duncan Committee suggested, some information work is superfluous, attempting to meet the inexhaustible demands of the uninfluential; but equally persuasive arguments can be made that the effort is too small. One African diplomat, asked in 1969 to prepare a brief for his minister on how his country should cast its vote in the UN Assembly on Gibraltar, discovered a handsomely bound exposition of the Spanish case in the archives, presented by their embassy, but was unable to obtain any statement from the British embassy. In the summer of 1972, as the Anglo-Icelandic fisheries dispute worsened, the only published account of the issues at stake was that provided by the Icelandic government. If English is already a lingua franca, then arguably the British Council's language-teaching efforts abroad are redundant. But it may also be argued that the different perspective which is gained by learning English within a

British rather than an American context is valuable enough to maintain a distinctive effort. The choice to an extent is arbitrary; it goes beyond the authority of officials, yet usually remains below the attention of ministers.

The advantages and disadvantages of the degree of autonomy of the BBC and British Council are not much easier to balance. Both agencies fiercely defend their autonomy as essential to their reputation abroad. Yet there is force in the argument that this is just a 'smokescreen', that when 'it is hard enough to get foreigners to admit the non-governmental character of *The Times*', the sacrifice of local prestige and of political co-ordination involved in, for instance, the separation of the British Council from embassies abroad is scarcely worth the marginal gain in credibility.[54] There have, it is true, been occasions when the activities of the British Council have been left undisturbed after a rupture in diplomatic relations. But equally, there have been occasions when the British Library has been the target for crowds protesting against the policy of the British government, or when the BBC has been the focus of attacks by governments with which official relations are still maintained. The independence of the BBC's reporting on developments in foreign countries embarrassed the British government in attempting to improve relations with Egypt in 1971–2, and in its relations with India in 1972–3. Here again, the choice is to an extent arbitrary, depending upon the pre-conceptions of those involved and upon inherited inhibitions about the British government directly engaging in propaganda. Perhaps 'it is not possible for the Information Services of a democracy to do a satisfactory job in peacetime'.[55]

Yet within the limits set by its institutional structure, by the absence of ministerial and parliamentary interest, and by the conflicting pressures of the Treasury and the Foreign Office, the management of British information and cultural policy operates well. In retrospect, officials considered the failure to reorient efforts towards Western Europe at the time of the first application to the EEC in 1961 to have been a major mistake. But such a reorientation was beyond the authority of those directly involved in the field of culture and information, and would have required an expansion in their budgets. It would also have required a readjustment of the then dominant rationale of the British Council – its commitment to educational and cultural development. When a decision was eventually taken, at a higher level, to step up activities in Western Europe, the Foreign Office and the agencies revived and put into action plans which they had put up unsuccessfully in previous years. Whitehall and Westminster investigations of the administration of cultural and information activities has found them on the whole to be efficient and effective; though uncertainty as to the purpose or the proper extent of direct information work has led to more qualified approval of the efforts of British Information Services. For evident political reasons, in Eastern Europe and the Soviet Union the cultural and information effort fits more directly into the framework of overall British policy, as an instrument of foreign policy operating within the guidelines laid down.[56] Information and cultural policy is low-level policy par excellence, and the institutional machinery of British government handles low-level policy, within each separate compartment, well.

Part III: Patterns of Relations

8: The Atlantic Area

IT WILL BE CLEAR from the preceding chapters that the character and range of British relations with the industrialized countries of Western Europe and North America are now qualitatively different from those between Britain and the mostly non-industrialized countries of the rest of the world. The Duncan Committee's distinction, in discussing the pattern of British representation overseas, between what it termed 'the Area of Concentration' and 'the Outer Area' provoked a good deal of disapproving comment, both within the Diplomatic Service and outside; but if its terminology was tactless, the distinction was incontestably right. It had resulted from two different developments in British foreign relations since World War II: the establishment of relations with a large number of new countries, mostly newly-independent ex-colonial territories, and the increasing closeness of governmental and non-governmental links between Britain and its main military, economic, commercial, and cultural partners.

'When I joined (the Foreign Service) in 1930', a member of the Duncan Committee recalled, 'there were only about 40 or 50 countries you could go to. They were all pretty stable and they were all much the same, although you led a slightly more sophisticated existence in Paris'.[1] In 1972 British missions were accredited, residentially or non-residentially, to some 137 countries. The 67 accredited foreign missions in London in 1950, when postwar intergovernmental relations had returned to a semblance of 'normality', had grown to 80 in 1960, to 122 in 1970, and 131 in 1972, roughly doubling the number of embassies and high commissions in London in twenty years.[2] In addition, the British government maintained limited relations with three further governments to which it did not then extend full recognition – North Vietnam, Taiwan, and the German Democratic Republic – and had informal contacts with another three governments with which formal relations were temporarily suspended – Rhodesia, Syria, and Congo (Brazzaville).

Whatever superficial similarities the diplomat of the 1930s may have seen between the overseas postings he might expect, his successor of the 1970s had few illusions about the sharp differences he would find between the various posts he might take abroad – in their contacts with Whitehall, with Westminster, and with non-governmental groups at home, and in the balance and diversity of the work.

Such differences in relations between Britain and other states – differences of intensity, priority, and formal status – have always existed. In the nineteenth century they were distinguished by gradations of representational rank (until competitive pressure for prestige devalued the ambassadorial title), as well as by the admission of some states to conferences of 'the powers' and the exclusion of others. Yet there is a radical difference in the conduct and context of British relations with the industrialized countries of the North Atlantic area today – a difference not just compared with relations among 'the powers' before World War II but also compared with relations with the rest of the world. In the first place, Britain's perceived high policy interests are now concentrated in this area: economically and commercially at stake in relations among the industrialized democracies, militarily at stake in their common concern with European security. This convergence of economic, industrial, security, and political interests is perhaps less novel than the interpenetration of governments, of financial, industrial, and commercial operations and of societies which has accompanied it. British relations with the United States, the Netherlands, France, or Denmark have therefore passed far beyond the limits of Foreign Offices, embassies, commercial and consular relations, and occasional ministerial visits.

What is significant about a country of this type is that our relationships with it involve us in contacts over a much wider range of government and society than has been usual in traditional diplomacy, and that these contacts are concerned with many topics which have in the past been conventionally regarded as belonging to the domestic affairs of sovereign states.[3]

Relations within this 'area of concentration' are distinctive along a number of clearly identifiable planes. They are multidimensional: they cover virtually the whole range of politically significant intergovernmental relations. They are multilateral: they are conducted as much through international organizations as through bilateral channels, and there are few issues of concern to no more than two countries. They arouse a relatively high degree of domestic interest in Britain, reflected in the organizations which constitute their domestic 'constituency' and in the continuing attention of substantial sections of informed opinion. Their affairs are regularly reported in the British press, particularly when they concern British interests. Business interests, and often also political and promotional groups, maintain regular contacts with their opposite numbers and lobby their own and each other's governments; MPs follow intergovernmental developments, meet each other formally and informally and use the information so gained in questioning their own governments. There are regular ministerial visits and interministerial contacts, involving the Prime Minister, the Chancellor of the Exchequer, the Minister of Defence, and a large number of senior and junior ministers, besides the Foreign Secretary and his departmental ministers. To underpin these, officials from almost every Department in Whitehall are to some extent involved in the management of intergovernmental relations.

The oldest of these networks of close and continuing intergovernmental communications, from the highest levels downwards, was the 'special relationship' established between Britain and the United States during World War II and maintained in a less intensive fashion for twenty or twenty-five years after the war had ended. Built upon an existing network of economic, social, and cultural ties and upon the wartime identity of interests between the two governments, an impressive degree of intergovernmental cooperation was achieved, both through the wartime joint boards and through less formal links between national officials; guided and directed by the meetings between the Prime Minister and the President and between members of the British and American Cabinets.[4] After the war there were sufficient common economic and security interests and objectives to provide the basis for continuing exchanges of information, consultations, and cooperative activities; these were strengthened by the mutual confidence between the two governments and by the extensive personal ties between officials within each administration built up during the war. Meetings between Prime Minister and President continued once, twice, three or even more times a year, supplemented by a considerable transatlantic traffic in ministers and ministerial advisers. At lower levels similarly close relationships, between members of the armed services, between the two country's intelligence services, between 'the Anglo-Saxons' in international commercial and monetary negotiations, and between members of embassies in third countries extended the area of mutual understanding and common purpose. The shared assumptions of informed opinion in the two countries made for an intellectual similarity in the context within which policy-makers on both sides of the Atlantic formulated policy, as was perhaps most sharply evident in the parallel official and unofficial debates on strategy in Britain and in the United States throughout the 50s.

The gradual cooling of this bilateral Anglo-American relationship during the 60s went hand in hand with the growth of a more diffuse and multilateral pattern of relations, linking Britain less exclusively to a predominantly West European group of countries. British resistance to multilateralism, evident in its attitude to successive European organizations from the Council of Europe to EFTA, as well as in its reluctance to support the delegation of any substantial degree of authority to OEEC/OECD or NATO, was breached by the Conservative government's first application to join the EEC and by British initiatives in establishing

ELDO and ESRO. Outside the English-speaking world the network of elite contacts and social and cultural intercommunication was still flimsy, though contacts among like-minded politicians in the party internationals, successive generations of student exchanges, the growth of 'town-twinning' and above all the growing links between British and continental industrialists and businessmen provided some foundations for mutual understanding. Links between governments and their administrations had to be deliberately forged, through a succession of ministerial visits and meetings, through the establishment of bilateral links between officials, and through the efforts of embassies on both sides. The cumulative experience of collaboration – with European and American partners within the extending consultative structure of NATO and with the various organizations constituting 'the international money circus', with European partners in joint technological projects and within the Euro-group – had, by the time that the renewed negotiations to join the European Communities reached a successful conclusion, accustomed the British government to conducting important aspects of its foreign relations through multilateral channels, and to using bilateral relations as a necessary means of preparing for and of supplementing institutionalized multilateral negotiations.[5]

Governmental management of such intricate relations necessarily reflects their complexity. The importance of the issues at stake for British foreign policy as well as vital sectors of domestic policy necessarily brings into play the Cabinet Office, No. 10, and the whole Whitehall structure of interdepartmental committees and consultations. Preparations for multilateral meetings of heads of government involve most Departments in Whitehall in months of drawing up briefs and agreeing positions, a massive weight of paper to be condensed into summary form; senior officials from the Cabinet Office and from the major Departments will accompany the Prime Minister to the meeting. Preparations for bilateral heads of government meetings, while less complex, similarly require a cooperative effort throughout Whitehall, orchestrated by the Cabinet Office. The intensity of relations between the major home Departments and corresponding ministries in the most important West European and North American countries, reflected less in contacts between ministers than in those between officials at senior and junior levels, both reduces their need for the FCO as an intermediary and makes it more difficult for the FCO to keep track of the shifting pattern.

The active and regular involvement of Prime Ministers and Cabinet ministers in this 'new' diplomacy has in many ways added to the difficulties of managing relations between governments. Personal relations between the British Prime Minister and the American President, between the Foreign Secretary and the Secretary of State, had significantly influenced the course of the Anglo-American relationship during the postwar period, most crucially in the antagonism between Eden and Dulles in the three years before the Suez crisis. Where good personal relations were established, it was easy for leaders to place too great a reliance on friendship and mutual confidence, and give too little attention to the constraints of domestic politics or the difficulties of implementing their general agreements in detail. At moments of crisis politicians on either side too often 'took their own word for what constrained the other side, played their own hunches, drew their own conclusions'; confident of their own expertise, they tended to disregard the advice of their specialist advisers and the interpretative reports their embassy sent back.[6] Nor did acquaintance always mean clear communication or exact mutual understanding: 'imprecision is commonplace when such as these engage in casual conversation'.[7]

Increasing ministerial and prime ministerial involvement in relations with Britain's major European partners during the 60s enlarged the difficulties. The language barrier added to the dangers of imprecision or mutual misunderstanding, either on the telephone or in personal meetings, as at Rambouillet in 1962. Multilateral 'summits' increased the gap between surface bonhomie and detailed exchange of views: the larger the number of foreign leaders the less easy it is for ministers to appreciate their respective domestic circumstances and constraints. Moreover the range of issues discussed at such meetings – strategic, technological, economic, and industrial as well as the traditional concerns of high foreign policy – made it more difficult adequately to brief already over-burdened ministers on complex questions. Mr Wilson once found himself 'abducted' by the French Prime Minister and his advisers for a discussion on the role of gold in the international monetary system, separated from all his own expert advisers. On other occasions as Prime Minister his discussions with the French ranged over comparisons between the two countries' computer industries, cooperation in the production of military aircraft, nuclear energy, French and British policy in the Middle East since the Suez crisis, the Vietnam war, and, of course, relations between Europe and the United States.[8] The style of Anglo-French relations throughout the 60s and early 70s reflected another effect of personal diplomacy on foreign policy-making: that the distribution of power within the government with which Britain is dealing affects the way in which Whitehall itself formulates and conducts policy. Given the presidential nature of French foreign policy-making and the demands of protocol, it was of limited use for the Foreign Secretary to lead intergovernmental discussions. It had to be the Prime Minister who spoke to the President; and this necessarily increased the influence of the Prime Minister's private secretary and personal advisers and decreased that of the Foreign Office. The declining involvement of the State Department in the conduct of American foreign policy under President Nixon had a not dissimilar effect. The succession of presidential advisers who passed through London expected to talk to their 'opposite numbers' in the Cabinet Office rather than to be shunted off to the Departments, marginally increasing the importance, influence, and workload of the Cabinet Office at the expense of the FCO, the Treasury, the DTI, and the MoD.

Below the highest level, the continuing relationship between government Departments and their equivalents in other national capitals (described in previous chapters) has gone far to undermine the solidarity of the British government's position vis-à-vis its major partners. Coalitions of common interest across national boundaries – of armed services, central bankers, or ministries of finance or agriculture – have only marginally weakened Whitehall's ability to coordinate policy at the centre; but the context within which policy is made has been considerably affected. This is partly because officials and ministers are aware of differences of opinion within other national administrations and are naturally drawn in to support those whose opinions are closest to their own. Partly, too, the advice which officials render to ministers already reflects the official assessment of what would or would not be acceptable to their foreign colleagues, so that ministerial choice is limited by existing intergovernmental understandings. More than this, established patterns of mutually satisfactory relations between officials concerned with 'technical' subjects create a certain bureaucratic resistance to ministerial interference. One official, for example, remarked that in the DTI his colleagues resisted suggestions that ministerial discussions within the Anglo-German Economic Committee should go into questions of detail because 'they don't want their contacts raised to this level'.

The role of the FCO has been sharply affected by these developments. At least within their own fields of responsibility, the Treasury, the MoD, the DTI, and the Ministry of Agriculture have become sufficiently closely concerned with, for example, the American, German, or Dutch governments, and sufficiently familiar with their domestic political and administrative constraints to consider themselves as well informed as their opposite numbers in the Foreign Office, and more expert. Since with these governments the whole range of British external relations is involved, all departments within the FCO have at least a tangential involvement in the bilateral and multilateral relationships; whether through 'political' conversations about extra-European developments or through the watching brief functional departments hold over the management of technical relations. At the departmental level the growing importance of multilateral relations has been reflected in the leading role played by functional departments and the ancillary position of geographical departments. The part played by the Western European department in managing relations between Britain and, say, France or Italy is far more modest than that of the Latin American department in relations with Argentina or the West African department with Sierra Leone; it does not go much beyond providing briefs and speeches and managing arrangements for incoming and outgoing ministerial visits. It was an indication of the diminishing intimacy between Britain and the United States that it was felt necessary in 1971 to create a separate North

America department, to focus attention within the FCO on the bilateral relationship and to provide briefs.[9] The perceived importance of relations with these 'Western' industrially developed countries for British interests, and the active involvement of other Whitehall Departments, has meant that within the FCO proposals have regularly risen above departmental level for consideration and decision, to involve under-secretaries, junior ministers, or even the Secretary of State. More than in the FCO, the overall pattern of bilateral relations has been pulled together in the embassy abroad: itself more fully integrated into the flow of Whitehall policy-making by improved communications and increasingly also by contacts with visiting British officials, and representing through its contingent of seconded home civil servants the interests of other Departments than the Foreign Office alone.

Such close relationships are of course reciprocal. West European and North American embassies in London report back to their home governments on differences within Whitehall, and encourage their ministers and officials to intervene to influence the debate through the appropriate channels. Officials of foreign governments give evidence to parliamentary and official committees, thus helping to shape opinion in Britain. The Plowden Committee on the Aircraft Industry in 1965, for instance, heard oral evidence from representatives of four US, three French, and two German government agencies.[10] The US government's interest in the evolution of opinion in Britain (and in other allied countries) from the early 1950s onwards went so far as to sponsor regular opinion polls on attitudes to the USA, to NATO, and so on.[11]

Cross-national links between non-official opinion are naturally thickest between Britain and the open societies of the industrialized countries of Western Europe and North America. The concentration of British trade and investment has drawn businessmen and trade unionists into closer contact with their opposite numbers in this area. Parliamentary Assemblies, party internationals, even tennis matches and skiing competitions bring MPs together. Contacts at international conferences and institutes, through studies at foreign universities, even through intermarriage, spread the net wider; while the mass public have come to mingle in the same Mediterranean resorts, and to share at least the superficial common culture of films and TV programmes. Links formed for non-political or only partly political reasons are nevertheless available for use for political ends – for the exchange of information, for coordinated lobbying of national governments. The interpenetration of government administrations is paralleled by a gradual interpenetration not only of economies but also of societies, longest-established within the English speaking world but now spreading among the countries of Western Europe. It can no longer be accurate to describe political relations between such countries in foreign policy terms alone.

The importance of multilateral channels in the conduct of intergovernmental relations within the non-communist industrially developed world which constitutes Britain's 'area of concentration' makes it easier to define its membership organizationally than geographically. Britain's main allies, its major partners in international economic management and in social and technological cooperation, formed by the early 70s a series of overlapping groups of some fifteen to twenty countries, with the United States and the members of the European Communities at its core. A definition in terms of British overseas trade or inward and outward investment, which have become increasingly concentrated within

Britain's Leading Partners in International Organizations

	EEC	NATO	OECD	IMF Group of 10	BIS Board	Council of Europe	Commonwealth
W. Germany	X	X*†	X	X	X	X	
France	X	x †	X	X	X	X	
Netherlands	X	X*†	X	X	X	X	
Italy	X	X*†	X	X	X	X	
Belgium	X	X*†	X	X	X	X	
Luxembourg	X	X*†	X			X	
Denmark	X	X*	X			X	
Ireland	X		X			X	
United States		X	X	X			
Canada		X	X	X			X
Norway	x	X*	X			X	
Sweden	x		X	X	X	X	
Switzerland	x		X	X²	X	X	
Austria	x		X			X	
Iceland	x	X	X			X	
Greece	x	X*	X			X	
Turkey	x	X*	X			X	
Portugal	1	X	X				
Japan			X	X			
Australia			X				X
New Zealand			X				X

Notes:

[1] In early 1975 the new Portuguese government was negotiating an association agreement with the European Community. Finland, not shown here, has also concluded an association agreement with the EEC.

[2] Switzerland is an anomaly here, as a non-member of the parent International Monetary Fund. The Group of 10 thus has in practice eleven members.

* denotes a member of the Eurogroup.

† denotes a member of Western European Union (WEU).

x denotes an association agreement with the EEC and the looser French association with NATO.

the industrialized societies of the non-communist world, provided a not dissimilar picture, though with some anomalies. Fifteen countries accounted for almost two-thirds of British exports in 1970. Only three of these were geographically outside the North Atlantic area, and only South Africa was for most purposes outside the multilateral intergovernmental network which linked the countries of the industrialized world. A definition in terms of communication flows, of newspaper and journal circulation, educational exchange, mail, telephone and travel would show a similar concentration of British overseas links – though again

Principal British Markets and Sources of Supply, 1973 (£m)

Imports from (cif)		Exports to (fob)	
United States[a]	1,622	United States	1,522
W. Germany	1,351	W. Germany	785
France	980	France	678
Netherlands	912	Irish Republic	626
Sweden	740	Belgium-Luxembourg	621
Canada	736	Netherlands	604
Irish Republic	527	Switzerland	521
Italy	504	Sweden	514
Denmark	478	Canada	414
Japan	443	Australia	404
Belgium-Luxembourg	442	Italy	386
Republic of South Africa	400	Republic of South Africa	374
Australia	341	Denmark	329
Finland	332	Japan	273
Western Europe	7,920	Western Europe	6,283
EEC	5,197	EEC	4,030
EFTA	2,371	EFTA	1,746
Sterling Area outside Europe	2,822	Sterling Area outside Europe	2,195
Developed countries	1,016	Developed countries	947
Developing countries	1,806	Developing countries	1,248
North America	2,358	North America	1,936
Latin America	482	Latin America	355
Soviet Union and Eastern		Soviet Union and Eastern	
Europe	550	Europe	323
Rest of the world	1,699	Rest of the world	1,318

[a]Including dependencies.

Source: COI, *Britain's external trade and payments* (1974).

with some anomalies – a bias towards the English-speaking world in terms of communication and educational exchanges and towards the Mediterranean in terms of travel.

Within this group of countries the United States, France, and the Federal Republic of Germany were clearly the most important to Britain in terms of political significance, economic interaction, and ministerial and official interchange. Next in importance came the second rank member states of the EEC – Italy, the Netherlands, and Belgium – and Canada. The intensity of intergovernmental contacts among these, the predominance of multilateral relations, the formal structure of joint commissions and committees and the informal links which supplement them, have left to British embassies, to the FCO, and to the central Whitehall machinery a number of problems for bilateral consideration and consultation. The most important of these (most often rising to the ministerial level) is the establishment of priorities: choosing which objectives to press most urgently upon the leaders of other governments and which to leave at the official level. In its relations with the United States between 1964 and 1967 the Labour government clearly gave first priority to financial and economic questions, and muted its criticisms of other aspects of American policy accordingly. The Conservative government in early 1973 resisted pressure from Australia and New Zealand to make public representations to the French government over its nuclear testing programme because it was reluctant to irritate Paris when 'more important' British interests were at stake in Anglo-French relations. An ancillary task for the FCO and for the central machinery is to single out from the mass of technical issues under discussion bilaterally and multilaterally those likely to be politically sensitive and alert ministers to pitfalls ahead. Given the continuing importance of bilateral perceptions among national governments even as closely linked as these, of each other as 'friendly' and 'responsive', or uncooperative and unresponsive, a considerable amount of work at all levels is needed to oil the wheels of diplomacy and to smooth over personal relations between political leaders: avoiding misunderstandings, handling the traffic in visitors, maintaining a friendly atmosphere. Preparation for multilateral negotiations themselves involve a great deal of bilateral consultation, assessing each other's initial positions and likely sticking points, lobbying within each other's administration for preferred policies, building coalitions and attempting to trade advantages. As a case study, British relations with Germany – after the United States arguably the most important of Britain's partners in the early 70s is more fully explored in the next section.

It is more difficult to define the limits of the Atlantic area than to describe its core. The Scandinavian countries are less central to British interests than those of continental Europe; yet in terms of intergovernmental organizations, security, industrial and commercial interests, their combined importance to Britain is far from negligible. Australia and New Zealand have close continuing social and cultural as well as economic ties with Britain, though they are less involved in the multilateral relations of the North Atlantic area. Switzerland, South Africa, and Japan are all for very different reasons special cases. The gradual integration of Japan into the economic and organizational network of the industrial world has been limited by cultural and linguistic barriers and by distance. The integration of Switzerland is limited by its self-imposed neutrality.[12] Portugal, Spain, Greece, and Turkey, on the fringe of this area in terms of organizational membership and political acceptability, and economically and commercially more dependent upon it, loom larger among the concerns of British foreign policy-makers than their economic and security significance to Britain alone would suggest. Their importance to American security policy and to French and Italian Mediterranean policy, as well as the constant pressure of domestic groups and MPs on the government to make representations about their treatment of detainees or their internal policies, necessitate a more active British involvement. Perhaps the best evidence that these Mediterranean countries are seen by British informed opinion as culturally and socially part of the Atlantic area is the degree of attention given to their shortcomings in civil liberties and constitutional standards, reflecting not only the existence of personal links with their elites and opposition groups but also the many historical associations which lead British critics to apply stricter standards to the behaviour of their governments than to that of governments in other areas of the world.[13] Relations with one of the smallest of these second-rank countries, Iceland, are discussed in more detail later in this chapter.

The increasing importance of intergovernmental organizations to the conduct of foreign policy has created particular management problems for Whitehall. Those organizations which have fairly strictly defined fields of responsibility, which in turn fit fairly easily within the responsibilities of a single Whitehall Department – such as the BIS, the Group of Ten, or the European Conference of Ministers of Transport – give rise to fewer problems than those which overlap the interests of several Departments. (Some of these, such as ELDO, ESRO, and the succeeding European Space Conference, have been discussed in earlier chapters.) Since the postwar period Britain has maintained permanent missions to the most continuously active or important of these – the Council of Europe, OECD, NATO, and the European Communities – which report back to interdepartmental committees in Whitehall at different levels.[14] The impact of European Community membership on British foreign policy-making will be discussed in the last chapter; the example of NATO will be examined in more detail below.

Bilateral Relations: West Germany

British relations with Germany are heavily overlaid with historical memories and associations. World War II and the adverse image of Germans and Germany which it re-established and sharpened in British public opinion still retained a certain force twenty-five years later. However, the postwar occupation, with its substantial 're-education' programme, involved a large number of Britons in administering German territory and created a network of close personal and official ties. British troops, stationed in Germany continuously since 1945, have made both for a bond and an irritant between the two countries, most often an irritant through the repeated haggles over agreements on offsetting the foreign exchange costs since the ending of their occupation status in 1955. Differences of opinion, often deeply felt, on policy towards Eastern Europe, on the relative importance of Britain's intra- and extra-European commitments, and on the adequacy of West German efforts to support Britain's application to the European Communities, made for an uneasy relationship through much of the 60s. It was only in 1968–9 that underlying suspicions on both sides were dispelled, with the British decision to withdraw from East of Suez and to concentrate its defence policy on

Europe, with the evolution of the 'Ostpolitik', and with the satisfaction expressed on both sides with their experience in technological collaboration and economic and monetary cooperation.[15]

Anglo-German relations span the entire range of politically significant external affairs; and in almost every dimension of that relationship West Germany ranks as one of Britain's two or three most important partners. The military and security relationship for long remained predominant, at least until the successful completion of the Ostpolitik with the negotiation of a basic treaty between the East and West German governments in November 1972. The British government, together with the American and the French, was closely involved in these negotiations by virtue of its continuing occupation status in Berlin; regular consultation between the three 'occupying powers' and the West German government was therefore necessary throughout the protracted negotiations. The evolution of NATO policy towards détente and the approach to the CSCE also required close cooperation between the UK and German governments. Fortunately, there was no repetition of the misunderstandings of the late 50s, when Germans of all parties suspected that Britain was prepared to bargain away their security and their commitment to Berlin in return for an uncertain easing of tension, and British politicians of all parties saw the Germans as unnecessarily rigid and uncompromising.

Political consultations on other foreign policy matters grew closer as Britain approached membership of the EEC and as West Germany approached membership of the UN. Mutual interests in the Middle East provided a basis for the bilateral exchange of views and information. The external relations of the European Community, as well as a shared interest in expanding trade and in ensuring supplies of raw materials, supported similar exchanges on African and Asian questions. So too did British responsibility for Rhodesia: breaches of sanctions by West German companies were brought to the attention of their government, and at the time of the 1972 Olympic Games the two governments were in constant touch about the sensitive issue of Rhodesian participation, from the arrival of the Rhodesian team in Munich to its eventual withdrawal.

The military relationship extended by the end of the 60s through exchange of officers and joint training schemes to strategic discussions and joint procurement. Britain and Germany were the leading members of NATO's Eurogroup, the closeness of the relations between their defence ministries and their armed forces matched only by the Anglo-Dutch relationship. Almost a quarter of the British army and a substantial air force were stationed in West Germany, with the strategic reserve in Britain primarily committed to its reinforcement. German forces trained in Britain, under long-standing arrangements which had now outlived initially adverse public reactions. British and German chiefs of staff regularly held bilateral and multilateral discussions. 'The most important single project' in Britain's military development programme in 1972, 'both on military grounds and from a financial and industrial point of view', was the Anglo-German-Italian Multi-Role Combat Aircraft,[16] Britain and Germany were partners with the Netherlands in developing the nuclear fuel centrifuge, involving both governments and private companies. Cooperation in civilian technology, in the context of ELDO, ESRO, CERN, and so on, had become extensive, if not always successful. Here, as in so many other dimensions of Anglo-German relations, bilateral cooperation took place within a multilateral framework.

Economic links were as close. West Germany was Britain's second largest overseas market in 1972, taking 6·1 per cent of British exports, and the second largest source of British imports, providing 7·5 per cent. British investment in Germany was considerable and growing; German investment in Britain, while as yet on a much smaller scale, was being actively encouraged by the British government.[17] With a bilateral trade balance which was tilting more definitely in Germany's favour, the British government was also engaged in major efforts at promoting exports to Germany. In monetary matters, cooperation between the Bank of England and the West German Bundesbank kept officials in daily contact with each other.

The closeness of Anglo-German cultural links reflected both the legacy of the occupation period and the German government's continuing enthusiasm for the widest possible range of cultural exchanges with its West European partners. In 1972 the British Council spent twice as much on activities in Germany as in France. The Federal Republic's cultural efforts towards Britain were rather larger, though dwarfed in scale by the exchange programmes with France established under the Franco-German Treaty of 1963. There were numerous town-twinning schemes and sponsored exchanges of schoolchildren and students. Even so, governmentally-sponsored contacts were only a small part of the volume of cultural and social interchange between the two countries. Elite contacts, encouraged in the postwar years by both governments through such institutions as the Wilton Park Centre, were by now self-sustaining. The three political parties in both countries shared membership of party internationals and of party groups in European assemblies. Bilaterally, the annual Königswinter Conferences, organized by the Deutsch-Englische Gesellschaft since 1949, had achieved the status of a continuing dialogue between political establishments, bringing together MPs, journalists, academics, ministers, and officials to discuss major problems of mutual interest. Tourism, student travel, intermarriage (encouraged by the stationing of British troops in Germany and the training programmes for German troops in Britain), helped to build links between the wider publics and to break down old stereotypes. Business and financial activities, British and German subsidiaries of German and British firms, created closer ties. German orchestras toured Britain, British pop groups toured Germany, without any need for official encouragement or sponsorship; radio and TV programmes were shared or exchanged.

Relations between the two governments therefore took place within the context of two interlinked societies, reading each other's newspapers, supporting or opposing each other's political campaigns.[18] The closeness and extensiveness of intergovernmental relations had in its turn led to interpenetration between the two administrations. Formal links existed in almost all fields – the Permanent Mixed Commission which supervised the Anglo-German Cultural Convention, the Anglo-German Economic Committee, for instance – but the characteristic nature of Anglo-German exchanges was their informality: they had grown up, in sharp contrast to the formally established structure of Franco-German consultation, little by little since the mid-6os, until by 1972 German officials in several ministries considered their consultations with their British opposite numbers to be fully as frequent and as extensive as those with the French, and closer in terms of mutual confidence.

The most intimate relationship was that between the two defence ministries. When Helmut Schmidt moved from defence to the German Finance Ministry,

what appalled him most . . . [he says] were the poor contacts at ministerial level within the Atlantic alliance. At defence he had known daily what was in the mind of Denis Healey . . . or Peter Carrington or the American Defence Secretary, and they knew his ideas.[19]

The personal relations established between the British and German Defence Ministers, particularly since 1968, were paralleled by the close personal contacts between officials and serving officers at all levels within their ministries, who were in regular direct touch by telephone as well as through written channels and through bilateral and multilateral meetings. The overwhelming importance of NATO and the Eurogroup to the bilateral relationship will be immediately apparent. But to a considerable extent the success of the Eurogroup was built upon the closeness of bilateral Anglo-German understanding, and within NATO the Anglo-German link provided the core of the European response to American pressure. On NATO questions the two Foreign Offices played a part in the relationship; on Eurogroup matters neither Foreign Offices nor embassies were much involved. The comment by a German official that the members of the Eurogroup aim through their mutual cooperation 'to strengthen each defence minister's hand in his own Cabinet' indicates the extent to which national solidarity had been transformed.

The link between finance ministries remained until after Britain's entry into the EEC weaker, and subject still to occasional misunderstandings. In early 1973, for example, the British government's resistance to the establishment of the European Monetary Cooperation Fund in Luxembourg, on the political grounds that it was undesirable to disperse Community institutions from Brussels, was interpreted by the German Finance

Ministry as an attempt by the Treasury and the Bank of England to concentrate the financial institutions in London – a failure in communication which would have been almost unthinkable in the field of defence. Shared membership of committees and working groups of international economic organizations, including from mid-1972 those of the European Community, had developed contacts between those officials most directly concerned with international financial questions, but had not yet affected the outlook of either ministry as a whole.

The DTI related to its German equivalents through most of its divisions. For those concerned with the sponsorship of joint technological projects, this had become by 1972 a close working relationship, involving industrial companies and the administrations of both countries. Senior officials, ministers, the Treasury, and the FCO were involved when a new project or major changes in an existing programme were under discussion, but day-to-day work was conducted by middle-ranking civil servants. With British entry into the European Communities, Anglo-German commercial relations become almost entirely multilateral. Desk officers responsible for bilateral economic and commercial relations continued to exist, but in both ministries some scepticism was expressed as to their necessity. The Ministries of Agriculture had a number of long-established contacts through their External Relations divisions and through common membership of international commodity agreements and fisheries organizations. The enormous increase in the interaction between the two ministries involved in British participation in the Common Agricultural Policy, however, required positive efforts during 1972-3 to improve the level of mutual acquaintance and mutual understanding.

These increasingly close contacts between domestic Departments and the high level of political communication between the two governments deeply affected the role of their foreign ministries, whose respective geographical departments played at best an ancillary role: servicing ministerial visits, providing background briefs, drawing the attention of functional departments to bilateral aspects of their work. The North Europe and North American department of the Auswärtiges Amt had in 1972 three desk officers dealing with eleven countries. The FCO West European department, in contrast, had three desk officers (almost half its staff) working on German matters alone; but this was mainly due to the amount of detail involved in the negotiations on Berlin and in aligning the two governments' relations with East Germany, which diminished a little with the ratification of the basic treaty.[20] Almost all Foreign Office departments were concerned in Anglo-German relations: holding a watching brief on the political implications of functional cooperation between home Departments, involved in multilateral and bilateral political consultations, and so on. In few of these consultations were foreign ministries alone involved. The dispute over the Iceland fisheries in 1971-3, for instance, which affected the German deep sea fishing fleet as well as the British, required close and confidential discussion between the two Foreign Offices; but necessarily also involved the two fisheries departments and defence officials in the pattern of consultation and in the evolution of agreed policy.

Within the FCO, policy on relations with West Germany was made not by departments but by under-secretaries, in close consultation with ministers. The major interests of other Whitehall Departments in different aspects of the relationship made regular coordination of policies and priorities indispensable, through the Cabinet Office and the interdepartmental committee structure, at under-secretary and at ministerial level. The occasional failure to coordinate policy has pointed up its necessity and also the high level at which priorities must be agreed. In November 1968 the Foreign Office was pressing the German government to support the British application to join the European Community more positively in its discussions with the French; at the same time the MoD was engaged in yet another series of negotiations on offset payments. A speech by the Chancellor of the Exchequer while on a visit to Bonn, reprimanding his his German colleagues for not 'pulling their weight' in international financial negotiations, provoked an adverse reaction in the German press and temporarily set back progress in the other discussions. The FCO sees its role in Whitehall as pulling together the different threads of even the closest bilateral relationship; but the direct engagement of other major Departments implies that it can only act, at best, as *primus inter pares*.

Increasing ministerial and prime ministerial contacts have made personal relations at the top a significant factor. By the early 70s discussions between the British and German Prime Ministers had become at least an annual event. European 'summits' provided opportunities for bilateral conversations outside the formal multilateral framework, and the two Prime Ministers were occasionally in direct touch by telephone. The warmth or lack of warmth of this personal relationship, the degree of mutual understanding achieved, affected the whole tenor of relations between the two governments. Contacts between ministers (and not only between those responsible for defence and foreign policy) had become an accepted part of their regular activities, through visits and multilateral meetings, and on the telephone. In the first three months of 1973 one or more British ministers arrived in Bonn every week, and the traffic in the other direction was almost as heavy. In almost every case these discussions were ancillary to multilateral negotiations, preparing the ground, explaining national positions, lobbying for support.

To a considerable extent the traditional functions of embassies had thus been bypassed. Yet the workload and staffs of the British embassy in Bonn and the German embassy in London were expanding rather than contracting in this period. The Bonn embassy was the second largest British mission, with 178 UK-based staff in Bonn and in subordinate posts. Its size and activities partly reflected the continuing peculiarity of the British position in Germany. During the active period of the Ostpolitik, between 1969 and 1972, a number of embassy staff were fully occupied, in liaison with the French and American embassies and the German government, in the 'Bonn Group,' which coordinated the allies' approach to East Germany and to the Berlin question. The ambassador was also British high commissioner in Berlin, where the British Military Government contained a substantial diplomatic element, headed by a minister. The presence of British forces in Germany naturally added to embassy work, from a more active role in intelligence and assessment (in cooperation with military headquarters) to the minutiae of obligations under status-of-forces agreements: negotiations over military accommodation, compensation to landowners for damage to crops, and the like.

The slackening off of political work with the completion of the active stage of the Ostpolitik coincided with the approach to Community membership, which affected the work of both embassies. The establishment of direct contacts between ministries which had not previously been much concerned with each other's work reduced the traditional role of the embassy as intermediary still more. But it increased the demand for documentation and reports, on aspects of domestic policy such as industrial retraining or social security which had not previously been of direct interest to the other government, and it brought new requests, for embassy staff to keep abreast of thinking in domestic ministries between visits, to make representations on axle weights or on the harmonization of animal foodstuff regulations. The British embassy in Bonn had added an agricultural attaché in early 1973 to handle the detailed traffic of day-to-day queries and contacts in the European Community's most developed area of policy. To keep in touch with multilateral developments, the Bonn embassy received copies of all telegrams between London, Brussels, and other Community embassies; it was harder to keep the embassy informed about telephone contacts and direct discussions between officials from domestic ministries, though briefings were regularly provided, for instance, on developments in financial and monetary relations. Staff in both embassies agreed that 'the great days of bilateral relations are over', and that their future shape was likely to be less diplomatic, more that of a 'task force' of civil servants from foreign ministries and from home Departments maintaining a permanent presence in each other's capitals, to supplement the established network of direct contacts.

The ease of travel and communication between London and Bonn, the range and importance of topics under continuing discussion between the two governments, had by 1972 transformed Anglo-German relations beyond anything a diplomat of Harold Nicolson's generation would have dreamed of. This was a government-to-government relationship, within the context of closely linked societies and economies, and within the framework of common membership of influential multilateral organizations.

Bilateral Relations: Iceland

If British relations with West Germany represent the innermost core of the Atlantic area, those with Iceland reflect its outer limits. No British minister regards it as vital to be on personal terms with his Icelandic opposite number, or to ensure that his officials are in regular contact; no senior official under normal circumstances would regard relations with Iceland as one of his top priorities. There are three main dimensions of politically significant relations between Iceland and Britain: security, trade, and fisheries. Of these, only the last was by the early 70s primarily a bilateral relationship, although even here Britain's links with other governments could not be disregarded.

Anglo-Icelandic relations have a long and chequered history. English boats were trading with Iceland and fishing in Icelandic waters as early as the fifteenth century. In times of friendship, Icelanders remember that English traders kept Iceland prosperous by breaking the Danish trade monopoly; in times of tension, they remember their unruly and piratical behaviour.[21] English and Scottish trawlers developed the modern Icelandic distant water fisheries in the twenty or thirty years before the First World War, considerably assisted by a treaty of 1901 in which Denmark accepted the British definition of territorial waters for its Icelandic subjects. A central theme in Icelandic nationalism has been to reverse this 'betrayal' of Icelandic interests and to extend their fishing limits from three miles outwards towards their broad medieval claims. In 1948, only four years after independence had been achieved, the Althing passed a law proclaiming its right to control fishing within the limits of the Icelandic continental shelf; in 1952 the government unilaterally extended the limits to four miles, drawn between headlands. Britain, as the principal nation fishing in Icelandic waters, was the natural focus for antagonism and the natural leader of foreign resistance to Icelandic claims. From 1953 to 1956 British trawlermen enforced a landing embargo on Icelandic fish in British ports; from 1958 to 1961, after a further extension of the limit to twelve miles, the British government gave naval protection to its trawlers fishing in Iceland waters.[22]

On the other hand, the British market had been the basis of Icelandic economic expansion since direct landings of fresh and frozen fish from Icelandic boats began between the wars, and remained its largest export market until the late 60s. The British military occupation of Iceland in 1940 had not been unwelcome and had left behind many personal ties. Britain, with Norway and Greenland, was Iceland's nearest neighbour. Glasgow, London, and Copenhagen are first ports of call for Icelanders travelling abroad, visited each summer by Icelanders in large numbers coming to shop and see the sights. For the Icelandic government the relationship with Britain, the fisheries question apart, remains one of the most important aspects of Icelandic foreign policy. In 1971 Britain was its second largest market, taking 13·2 per cent of Iceland's exports, and with West Germany its largest source of imports, each country providing

14·7 per cent.[23] Britain was a leading member of NATO, and of EFTA – which later Iceland had joined, after much hesitation in 1970. The British government maintained the third largest of the ten foreign missions in Reykjavik (after the United States and the Soviet Union) with five UK-based staff.

The imbalance of the relationship is evident. Iceland ranked 31st among British export markets in 1970, and only in the fish trade provided a significant percentage of British imports. The 500 or so Icelandic citizens in Britain, studying at colleges and universities or engaged in business, represented one of its smaller foreign communities, though they were one of the largest Icelandic communities abroad. Relations with Iceland did not arouse much public interest. Only two groups were directly interested: the economically involved, concentrated in the distant water fishing ports of Hull, Grimsby, and Fleetwood and organized into the British Trawlers' Federation (for the owners), the Trawler Officers' Guild (for the skippers and mates), and the Transport and General Workers' Union (for the deckhands and dockers); and the 'friends of Iceland', a very small number of people scattered across the country whose links with Iceland as visitors or businessmen gave them a continuing interest, unorganized until the 1971–3 dispute led to the establishment of a formal Friends of Iceland group. An Anglo-Icelandic Parliamentary Group had existed since an IPU visit to Iceland in 1965, meeting roughly twice a year – its members mainly MPs with fishing interests in their constituencies, and only occasionally in touch with the two diplomatic members of the Icelandic embassy.[24]

Icelandic relations matter to Britain partly because fishing in Icelandic waters has been a small but useful source of employment and of 'home-produced' food, and has in turn been represented by a well organized and geographically concentrated constituency. In 1970 almost a quarter of British landings of demersal fish (bottom-feeding fish such as cod, haddock, and plaice) were caught in Icelandic waters, amounting to 60 per cent of landings at Fleetwood, 50 per cent at Grimsby, and 40 per cent at Hull. In all three towns fishing was a major industry; in Fleetwood the dominant one. Here was a clear domestic interest, pressed on the Government by local MPs as well as by the interests involved. But British fisheries policy was not concerned with Iceland alone. British trawlers fished also off the coasts of Greenland, the Faroes, Norway, and the Soviet Union; the British government, with Iceland, was a member of the North-East Atlantic Fisheries Commission, concerned with the regulation and conservation of international fisheries.[25] West Germany had a substantial stake in the Icelandic fisheries and a parallel agreement with Iceland to that which Britain had signed in 1961, and Belgian trawlers were also involved. Preparations for the UN Conference on the Law of the Sea threatened British shipping with a general extension of territorial limits; to yield to the Icelandic case, it was argued in 1971–2, might therefore set an unwelcome precedent.

The military importance of Iceland to Britain and to all NATO countries bordering the Atlantic (most of all the Americans) was its strategic position across Soviet shipping and submarine lanes to the southern Atlantic. Iceland's only contribution to NATO, as a member state without armed forces, was its acceptance of the Keflavik base: manned by American troops, but used also by British reconnaissance aircraft. Any dispute between NATO member-states which involved the threat of force must involve the alliance as a whole. Icelandic membership of EFTA and the British approach to the EEC involved the two countries in a further multilateral relationship. Together with the other non-applicant EFTA members, Iceland negotiated a trade agreement with the European Community during 1971–2; with which the British government was naturally concerned.

The management of British relations with Iceland under the 'normal' conditions of 1961–71 reflected the dominance of functional and multilateral questions over bilateral, and the relatively low level of perceived interests. Security relations were handled, as part of Britain's involvement in NATO, through the FCO Western Organizations department and the Defence Secretariat. The fisheries relationship was handled primarily by the Fisheries department of the Ministry of Agriculture, with the FCO Marine and Transport department holding a watching brief. From 1970 onwards the Ministry of Agriculture's External Relations division was marginally involved in EEC-related questions of fisheries policy, as negotiations got under way. The negotiation of a new airline agreement in 1971–2, arising out of BEA's claim to a share of the now-thriving traffic between London, Glasgow, and Reykjavik, was handled by a delegation from the DTI, with some support from the FCO Aviation and Telecommunications department. In the Western European department the desk officer for Iceland was responsible also for bilateral relations with Norway, Denmark, Finland, and Sweden, with an assistant who covered in addition Austria, Switzerland, and Italy. With such a wide coverage, his work was inevitably concerned mainly with briefings and arrangements for ministerial visits; the desk was itself unoccupied for two months in early 1972, when relations with Iceland were again becoming sensitive.

The small British embassy in Reykjavik received one diplomatic bag a month – in contrast, for example, to the daily bag to Brussels – to supplement telegrams; its members felt, not without some reason, that their own despatches aroused little interest in the Foreign Office and sometimes went unread.[26] The British Council's small programme in Iceland had been cut in 1966 as an economy measure, leaving a COI allocation of four sponsored visits to Britain a year as the sole governmental information effort. In London, decisions on policy towards Iceland rarely rose above departmental level, relying upon informal consultation among desk officers, supervised by heads of department. The involvement of ministers was almost entirely formal. In fisheries, close and continuing links between officials and interests in Britain, and between these, fisheries scientists, and their colleagues abroad, added up to a very self-contained transnational network. The Director-General of the British Trawlers' Federation was in touch with the Fisheries department at least once a week; the handful of MPs for deep-water fishing constituencies were also in direct contact. The responsible officials in London and Reykjavik had worked on international fisheries questions for ten years or more; they knew each other personally and were familiar with the domestic constraints within which the other worked.

The defeat of the Icelandic government in a general election in the summer of 1971 and its replacement by a coalition pledged to unilateral abrogation of the 1961 treaty and extension of the fisheries limit to fifty miles opened a more active period in Anglo-Icelandic relations: shifting the level at which policy was managed to a higher level, involving first junior and then senior ministers, provoking extensive press coverage and limited parliamentary interest – though never arousing much public interest or disagreement between political parties. In July 1971 the new Icelandic government served notice to terminate the 1961 agreement and to bring a fifty-mile limit into effect on 1 September 1972. Consideration of the British response drew in a larger number of officials. The section of the Defence Secretariat concerned with the navy was involved because the question of naval protection for British trawlers would have to be considered. (The decision to station frigates in the area of Iceland was itself, of course, a ministerial matter, which would clearly have to be approved by the Cabinet.) The FCO Legal Advisers were actively involved, the more so because of the provision under the 1961 agreement for reference to the International Court of Justice of any dispute over extension of the limits. When the case reached the International Court, the Attorney-General led the British team. The FCO's United Nations department also sent a desk officer to interdepartmental meetings, in preparation for a possible Icelandic appeal to the General Assembly.

The interest of this dispute to the observer derives partly from the entirely legitimate reasons which the three Whitehall Departments most directly concerned found for coming to sharply differing interpretations of the British national interest, giving rise to a succession of lengthy meetings, and frequent reference to ministerial level. These were conducted within the DOPC framework, which included ministerial and official sub-committees for maritime and seabed matters. The Minister of State in the Foreign Office with responsibilities for functional and United Nations matters, Lady Tweedsmuir, represented the FCO and led the early ministerial discussions in Reykjavik and London, in consultation with junior ministers from the Ministries of Agriculture and Defence. The official committee which shadowed ministerial meetings met formally at under-secretary level, with more junior representation from departments less centrally involved. The position of the Fisheries department, as the sponsoring department for the trawler industry, was that the government must defend Britain's established interests by all legitimate means. As the main point of contact between Whitehall and the trawler industry, its officials found themselves playing an intermediary role, explaining the wider governmental constraints to the fishing interests and the needs of the trawlermen to their Whitehall colleagues. The MoD's main concern was with the importance of Keflavik to NATO, and the importance of not jeopardizing the future availability of the base. It was also concerned about the diversion of four or five frigates from other duties, if required to give naval protection, because of a shortage of frigates for other commitments.[27] The FCO perception of the dispute primarily in terms of multilateral maritime interests was reflected in the lead role taken by the Marine and Transport department, with its supervising assistant under-secretary leading British official delegations to Reykjavik. Its main concern was to avoid prejudicing the British position at the Law of the Sea Conference by making bilateral concessions on more than an interim basis, and it was particularly anxious that Britain should act entirely within the framework of international law.

Left to themselves, the foreign ministries of both governments could satisfactorily have settled the dispute in the fifteen months between the announcement of the extension of the limits and its coming into effect in September 1972. Each understood the other's position and recognized the need for a compromise. Domestic constraints were however too strong for this. The Icelandic government was a coalition, in which the most left-wing party (to which the Fisheries Minister belonged) was interested in using the dispute to improve its political standing, and if possible also to carry Iceland out of NATO. In Britain the government's reluctance to sacrifice the interests of the distant-water fisheries without at least a show of resistance was strengthened by the growing campaign from inshore fishermen against what they saw as the sacrifice of their interests involved in accepting the European Community's common fisheries policy; no government could afford to be seen to be neglecting fishing interests across the board at a delicate stage in the negotiations for entry.

Preliminary ministerial and official conversations therefore failed to reach agreement. In April 1972 the British government instituted proceedings with the International Court, while attempting to reach an interim arrangement with Iceland through a further set of talks in Reykjavik and London; in August 1972 the Court granted an interim injunction against Icelandic enforcement of the new limit, which the Icelandic government immediately rejected. From September onwards the Icelanders relied on the severity of winter conditions and the denial of Icelandic havens to trawlers identified as fishing within the new limits, and also on harassment by their coastguard vessels, to disrupt the British trawler fleet and force a withdrawal. The British government found itself resisting stronger and stronger pressure from all sides of the trawler industry – the owners, skippers, and deckhands having combined for the purpose into a Fisheries Joint Action Committee – and from their MPs to provide naval protection: responding by chartering first one and then up to four unarmed ocean-going tugs to shield the trawlers from interference, which took up position from January 1973 onwards. In May 1973, when the trawlers had survived the winter with catches almost unimpaired, the Icelandic patrol boats began to fire live rounds at British vessels. The trawlermen then withdrew from Icelandic waters, protesting vigorously to the British government, and the frigates which had been hovering in the area were sent in. The summer of 1973 brought matters close to a breach of diplomatic relations, and Iceland also served notice on the US government to review the Keflavik agreement. Considerable diplomatic activity within NATO, involving the Foreign Secretary and attempts by the NATO Secretary-General to act as mediator, brought pressure to bear on both sides. At last, after the management of the dispute had risen to prime ministerial level, two days of discussions at No. 10 in October 1973 succeeded in reaching a compromise interim agreement.[28]

A number of aspects of the management of this dispute should be noted. First, the embassy in Reykjavik was only marginally involved in the evolution and management of British policy. Negotiations were handled throughout by a mixed delegation from Whitehall, under FCO leadership. The embassy itself acted as a post-box and as a source of day-to-day reporting; its staff was not reinforced until after the commitment of the navy in May 1973, when a spokesman from the News department was sent out for a month to handle the press, and was expelled by the Icelandic government after his first news conference. Secondly, governmental contact with the interests involved was close and continuous, reflecting both the established relationship of confidence between the Fisheries department and the British Trawlers' Federation and the belief by officials that the trawlermen would more easily understand the government's inability to meet all their demands if they were aware of the negotiating situation. BTF members were included in several delegations to Reykjavik; while in London the Marine and Transport department was in direct contact with MPs – an indication of the non-partisan nature of political divisions on the issue. Thirdly, Whitehall Departments were not monolithic in their approach to the dispute. Within the Foreign Office there were inevitably differences of perspective between the three departments most actively concerned, reflected partly in the transference of the temporary 'Icelandic Unit' desk from Marine and Transport to Western European department as the dispute became more directly political. Fourthly, the degree and the level of ministerial involvement rose as the domestic and international implications of the dispute widened; culminating in the Prime Minister's meeting with the Fisheries Joint Action Committee in No. 10 just before the final and successful negotiations. Lastly, the multilateral dimension was far more important than the bilateral one. Iceland raised the question at the NATO Ministerial Meeting in June 1972, and active diplomacy among NATO members continued from then until the end of the dispute. The Icelandic trade agreement with the EEC, completed in July 1972, was suspended at the insistence of Belgium and Germany until a settlement satisfactory to all parties had been reached. Consultation with the German government throughout was extremely close; the two governments pursued parallel cases before the International Court and parallel negotiations with the Icelandic government, although the Icelanders resisted all attempts at a trilateral meeting.

With the conclusion of the dispute, Anglo-Icelandic relations fell back to their normally low level, of bilateral contacts within a multilateral framework, characteristic of British relations with countries on the fringe of the Atlantic area. Another, more conservative, government took office in Iceland in 1974, pledged to a further extension of fishering limits to 200 miles. But they were prepared to negotiate the introduction of this with the British, and the evolution of discussions within the UN Law of the Sea Conference had made it clear that a 200-mile limit would soon become the international norm. It seemed unlikely in the extreme that such a bilateral dispute would recur.

Multilateral Relations: NATO

The British government played a leading role in the negotiations which led up to the signature of the North Atlantic Treaty in 1949 and in the subsequent establishment of NATO. Yet throughout the 50s Britain's attitude to the integrated machinery for military command and political consultation was ambivalent. While strongly committed to the alliance as such, the government gave a higher priority to its defence and political relationship with the United States. The commitment of conventional forces to NATO was seen as bringing Britain few political benefits, and from 1955 on as a wearisome burden on the balance of payments. Consistently, therefore, the NATO commitment was rated lower than the independent nuclear deterrent or the extra-European role. But the gradual reorientation of British foreign and defence policy towards Europe during the 1960s, the decline of the 'special relationship', and the efforts of successive governments 'to prove ourselves good Europeans' brought about a natural reorientation towards NATO as an integrated organization, and after the decision to withdraw from East of Suez the British government emerged as one of the strongest proponents of closer cooperation within NATO. Denis Healey, as Minister of Defence, had already taken a leading part in remodelling NATO strategy and reshaping its nuclear planning and military structure during 1966 and 1967.[29] During 1968 he took the initiative in sounding out European defence ministers on ways to concert their contribution to the alliance and to respond to growing American pressure for the

European members to play a larger role. It was this that led to the creation of the Eurogroup at the beginning of 1969.

Changes in the organization of NATO during the 60s had also involved the British government in a widening network of intergovernmental committees and political, technical, and military consultations. French withdrawal from the alliance organization in 1966, and the consequent move of NATO headquarters from Paris to Brussels, was followed by changes in the machinery of alliance planning. An integrated International Military Staff was established, reporting to the Military Committee, and the Tripartite Standing Group was replaced by a more integrated structure for strategic planning. The 'Harmel' Report of 1967 on 'Future Tasks of the Alliance' committed the member governments to 'use the Alliance constructively in the interest of détente' through closer political consultation and cooperation, primarily in East-West relations, but also in relations with countries outside the NATO area.[30] The creation of the Eurogroup added a further tier of committees and working groups. By the early 70s, therefore, the British position in NATO was one of active and positive commitment which involved ministers and officials in a wide range of multilateral consultations on alliance-related topics.

The central importance of NATO to British defence policy, already discussed in chapter 5, is illustrated by the commitment of the overwhelming preponderance of British forces to the alliance. The British Government also contributed £1¼m to the cost of the NATO international secretariat, 19·5 per cent of its total cost, and £8½m under the Ministry of Defence Vote towards common headquarters expenses.[31] In effect, British defence policy focused on the NATO commitment.

The commitment of forces and finance was, however, only one dimension of British involvement in NATO. Political consultation within the alliance had developed an extensive network of regular contacts at all levels. The North Atlantic Council met regularly at ministerial level twice a year, with foreign ministers representing national governments, and weekly at the level of permanent representatives. Daily contacts between members of permanent delegations, and regular meetings of foreign ministry officials concerned with particular policy areas in Brussels, underpinned the North Atlantic Council with a continuing exchange of information and views. During 1972 these political discussions focused above all on preparations for the European Security Conference, on the associated proposals for East-West negotiations on mutual reductions of forces, and on keeping alliance members informed about the progress of the Soviet-American SALT talks and on the four-power discussions on Berlin: all matters of prime importance to British security policy. The Anglo-Maltese dispute over payments for military facilities involved active NATO consultations in Brussels, and Italy and other alliance members contributed to the payments eventually agreed.[32] Political consultation was supplemented by the exchange of political, economic, and military intelligence, through a similar pattern of daily contacts among delegations and regular meetings of experts from national capitals; the annual 'intelligence conference' lasted up to a month. These fed into the formal committee structure, and were serviced by the civil and military international staff.

French withdrawal from the military organizations had led to a rather more formal separation between political cooperation among the fifteen, working up to the North Atlantic Council, and defence cooperation among the fourteen, working up to the Defence Planning Committee. This met at the level of defence ministers twice a year, and at the level of permanent representatives fortnightly or more often; it in turn co-ordinated the work of a large number of associated committees and working groups. Support, supply, and procurement generated a great deal of activity, with direct financial implications for national govern-ments. In 1972 there were 143 working groups in the Defence Support sector alone – dealing with equipment specifications, research and development, and possibilities for joint procurement – attended by the responsible officials from national capitals and operating under the umbrella of the Conference of National Armaments Directors. On the Budget Committee and the Infrastructure Committee (and their sub-sidiary working groups) national governments supported their own firms in bidding for contracts for pipelines, radio and radar equipment, and the like. Many of these all-alliance groups were by 1971–2 paralleled by similar working parties among the ten Eurogroup members, aiming at closer cooperation in procurement, training, military communications, and logistics, within the framework of the European Defence Improve-ment Programme. To oversee these, Eurogroup defence ministers met three times a year. National military representatives worked within a separate framework, serviced by the international military staff and reporting to the NATO Military Committee, which met three times a year at the level of national chiefs of staff and 'in permanent session' in Brussels at the level of military representatives.

All international organizations are subject to pressures to expand their range of activities; this often makes for some duplication between different organizations. In the case of NATO external pressure was in-creased by occasional proposals from member governments to improve the 'image' of the alliance at home by demonstrating that it was not only concerned with military matters. Thus after extensive consultation on economic questions during the rearmament efforts of the early 50s had led to a considerable overlap with OEEC, it was agreed to transfer those activities away from NATO. Other NATO activities included a small cultural programme of fellowships and scholarships. President Nixon's proposal in 1970 for a Committee on the Challenges of Modern Society, despite a rather reluctant response from some European governments, considerably enlarged the traditional concerns of the organization. In 1972 British officials and 'national experts' were participating in working discussions and pilot studies of urban transportation, sewage treatment, health services, road safety, environmental planning, disaster assistance, and coastal and inland water pollution. The CCMS too had its own fellowship programme, administered by a high-level selection panel with British representation.

To handle the daily traffic of exchanges of information and committee work the British government maintained a large permanent delegation of 43 UK-based staff, and a small group of five Military Representatives, all based within the Brussels headquarters complex. The delegation itself was fairly evenly balanced between the Diplomatic Service and the MoD in terms of personnel; the Permanent Representative and his deputy were both drawn from the Diplomatic Service. Its civilian character and the easy cooperation among its sections are notable, reflecting the understanding achieved between the MoD and the FCO during the previous decade and the degree of trust between the civilian and military hierarchies within the MoD. Its internal organization was tailored to the structure of NATO committees, with the FCO element primarily concerned with political consultation, information, and intelligence, and the MoD element handling defence planning, crisis management, and procurement. The defence planning section had also provided the secretariat for the Eurogroup from its establishment in 1969 until the beginning of 1972. Thereafter this work was shared with other delegations, as first the Germans and then other Eurogroup members succeeded to the chairmanship. The Military Representatives – five senior officers from the three services headed in 1972 by a full General – were formally separate from the UK delegation proper, housed until the end of 1971 in a separate wing of NATO headquarters.[33]

The delegation's immediate points of contact in Whitehall were the parallel departments within the FCO and the MoD, Western Organizations department and a division of the Defence Secretariat (DS II) reporting to the Assistant Under-Secretary of State (Defence Staff). The ambassador and his deputy related directly to their supervising undersecretaries. From these, policy questions were formally referred to other affected parts of Whitehall and where necessary fed into the interdepartmental machinery reporting to the DOPC. The Treasury was the most directly involved third Department: its Defence (Policy and Materiel) division received copies of most telegrams from the delegation, and was necessarily drawn in to all policy discussions which involved potential expenditure. Delegation members concerned with collaboration in procurement related directly to other sections of the Defence Secretariat, and to the Procurement Executive (from which two of them had come). Formally, again, the Military Representative and his staff reported to the Chiefs of Staff Secretariat, and through the Chiefs of Staff where necessary to the DOPC.

In practice pressure of business and intensive communication between Whitehall and Brussels and among the Departments in Whitehall concerned made for a much more fluid relationship. In the course of a year the delegation was likely to be in direct contact with almost every department in the FCO, and to receive members of most departments in Brussels. Disarmament Department, for instance, was directly concerned with alliance discussions on force reductions; geographical departments took part in political consultations. The situation within the MoD was not dissimilar. Several thousand journeys were made each year by some hundreds of London-based officials to NATO headquarters, from the FCO, the MoD, the Procurement Executive, the DTI, the Department of the Environment (primarily for meetings within the framework of the CCMS and the Science Committee), and the Cabinet Office; some MoD members of the delegation travelled to London monthly throughout the year. Direct phone links between London and Brussels, both open and secure, supplemented communication by telegram and telex. Officials at both ends expected to be in touch by telephone daily; one delegation member frequently spoke to his opposite number in Whitehall four or five times a day. Perhaps as important, personnel postings knit the different sections together.[34] The delegation worked, effectively, as an extension of Whitehall, playing an active part in drawing up the instructions to which its members worked. Familiarity with Whitehall thinking and confidence in each other made possible flexible interpretation of instructions, in the light of changing negotiating positions. Sometimes members were prepared to go against their instructions, and explain why. The high morale of officials in the delegation and in those sections of Whitehall most involved reflected their feeling that they were engaged not simply in political representation but in collaborative intergovernmental policy-making, negotiating decisions which bound the British government on high-level issues, which linked them directly to the central core of Whitehall policy-making, the Cabinet and the Cabinet Office.[35]

Since ministers were actively involved in NATO affairs, and questions were frequently referred to ministerial level (to DOPC or to the full Cabinet) because of their policy implications or on expenditure grounds, the attitudes and standing within the Cabinet of ministers had great influence on contacts at lower levels. Identity of outlook and interest between successive Ministers of Defence and Foreign Secretaries, once the decision to withdraw from East of Suez had been taken, naturally tended to place them and their supporting officials in an informal coalition against the Chancellor of the Exchequer and the Treasury. The European Defence Improvement Programme, for instance, was 'a joint assault on the Treasury', carried through the Cabinet and its subordinate committees.

Bilateral contacts had grown closer as NATO committee work had expanded. Officials within the Defence Secretariat frequently telephoned their opposite numbers in other capitals, most often in Bonn and in the Hague. Political discussions between Foreign Offices, through embassies or direct, attempted to build coalitions or mitigate opposition before multilateral negotiations. In 1972 British military staffs were also holding separate staff talks with the Germans and the Dutch. Awareness of differences within each other's administrations made it possible to choose points of contact in order to influence internal policy discussions, thus making it more difficult to maintain a monolithic national position. Officials in Whitehall suggested that it was not unknown to use direct contacts with other national capitals deliberately to by-pass both their permanent delegations, infected with the camaraderie of NATO head-quarters.

A limited number of non-governmental organizations are supported by NATO and by the British government, to maintain and enlarge the circle of informed opinion sympathetic to the alliance. NATO supports the Atlantic Treaty Association and its junior affiliate, the Atlantic Association for Young Political Leaders, which has sponsored several international conferences. In 1972 the FCO gave £19,000 to the British Atlantic Committee, the British affiliate of the Atlantic Treaty Associa-tion, 'to assist the organization in the promotion of knowledge and under-standing of the North Atlantic Treaty Organization', and £300 to the international Atlantic Information Centre for Teachers to assist in its educational work.[36] The North Atlantic Assembly, a semi-official body of parliamentarians who met to discuss alliance questions, received an FCO grant of £21,560. On more strategic questions, informed opinion was already organized within such bodies as the IISS and the RUSI, in which Ministry of Defence and FCO officials regularly participated.

In the early 1970s relations within NATO could be taken as exemplary of a general trend within the Atlantic area. Government officials had become so close to their opposite numbers in other national administra-tions that the solidarity of government positions had been effectively undermined. The regular and rapid exchange of views at all levels, from Cabinet minister to principal, made personalities and personal relations often as important as formal positions; understanding or mistrust between two Cabinet ministers or between, say, the British and Dutch Ministers of Defence could significantly affect the evolution of policy. A proliferation of bodies and committees and considerable duplication of work resulted from the fact that high-level discussions escaped the compartments imposed by organizational boundaries, overlapping responsibilities, and different memberships. Already in 1972 many of the Foreign Office officials holding political discussions within NATO were also engaged in consultations within the Davignon framework; in 1973 the deputy permanent representative led the British delegation to the first round of negotiations on mutual force reductions. Barring a major upheaval in relations among the developed industrial countries, the prospect for other organizations with similar memberships and shared concerns seemed likely to follow the experience of NATO: witnessing a closer involvement of national governments in cooperative policy-making, covering a widening area of issues.

9: The Non-Atlantic Countries

The distinction which the Duncan Committee made between the pattern of British relations with what it called the 'inner' and the 'outer' areas related to more than the contrasting styles of diplomacy which, it suggested, were required. It was not only that it did not see the actions of any governments outside the advanced industrial world as 'likely to impinge on the day-to-day conduct of British Government business in quite the way that we expect the countries of the first group to do (p. 13)', or as giving rise to any comparably wide-ranging or intensive network of relations with Britain. It was also that political relations between governments were no longer seen as the prime concern of British diplomacy. The virtual completion of the long-drawn-out process of decolonization and the withdrawal from military involvement outside the North Atlantic area (completed by the East of Suez decision) had in its view ended the potential for the exertion of British political influence, and with it ended Britain's direct political interest in the attitudes and policies of outer area governments. 'Political relations between governments are significant', the Committee remarked, only 'when one or other party is in a position to exert political influence' (p. 46). Without political responsibilities to require active diplomacy or the military potential to underwrite it, British interests in the extra-European world, with some few exceptions, had become primarily economic and commercial, the cultivation of good relations at a low level through the promotion of trade, the encouragement of cultural exchanges, the provision of aid and technical assistance, the promotion and protection of British investment, and (one of the oldest and most basic diplomatic concerns) the protection of British citizens abroad.

The largest exception to this neat division, as the Committee noted, was the Soviet bloc, on the edge of the inner area geographically, economically, politically and culturally (p. 13).[1] British interests in Eastern Europe remained in the early 70s emphatically more political than commercial, both because of the concentration of British security interests in Europe and because of the peculiar obstacles in the way of expanding trade with state-trading countries. Britain's interest in Eastern political developments, as a member of NATO, was sharpened by the approach to the CSCE, bringing East-West relations to the edge of a genuine multilateral framework in a way that the UN Economic Commission for Europe, the only regional multilateral organization which had bridged the European divide, had never managed. Political

relations between governments were made more sensitive by the attention both sides paid to the threat of subversion and espionage, and to the
coverage of their domestic affairs and foreign policy in each other's press
and broadcasting media. The expulsion in September 1971 of 105 Soviet
diplomats whom the British government suspected of political, military
or industrial espionage led to a sharp deterioration in Anglo-Soviet
relations which took nearly two years to repair. Negotiations with the
East German government in early 1973 on the establishment of diplomatic
relations paid particular attention to the number of diplomats each
country was willing to accept.[2] The formality of inter-governmental
relations is emphasized by the importance East European governments
attached to treaties, protocols, and formal agreements, reinforced where
possible by joint commissions or bilateral committees, covering not only
consular relations and cultural exchanges but also trade, scientific
research, and technological collaboration, often in considerable detail.[3]

The traditional quality of bilateral relations with Eastern Europe is
suggested by the symbolic importance attached to ministerial visits, as
formal indications of good relations, and by the active interest the Soviet
Union displayed in late 1972 and in 1973 in visits to the USSR by the
British royal family.[4] The gradual expansion of tourism throughout
Eastern Europe and the ambivalent attitude of those governments to the
activities of foreign visitors had increased the burden and the delicacy of
consular work, aiding British citizens arrested for smuggling Bibles or
drugs or for such 'innocent' activities as aircraft-spotting. Commercially,
as we have seen, a great deal of diplomatic effort was needed to achieve
relatively little. Apart from the USSR itself, Poland, and Yugoslavia,
British trade with Eastern European countries was miniscule; in 1970
Bulgaria imported barely half as many British goods as Iceland.

Relations with South Africa and Israel are also exceptional cases:
distinctive because of the domestic political sensitivity of British policy
towards them, and in the case of South Africa also because of the substantial British economic involvement and the link, through the unre-
solved Rhodesian dispute and through residual defence commitments,
with the attitude of other African states to Britain. The active interest of
a substantial body of MPs in relations with Israel and South Africa, the
voting strength, effective organization, and economic and social influence
of the Jewish population of Britain, and the existence of active lobbies on
all sides necessitated regular ministerial attention to their affairs, and not
infrequently brought decisions about British policy towards them before
the Cabinet.

In 1969 it seemed appropriate to the Duncan Committee to group
together the other 90–100 countries with which Britain maintained
relations in a single category, 'the outer area': as developing countries,
suppliers of raw materials and importers of British goods, but as of far
less political significance than the Atlantic countries. Five years later it
had become clear that the supply of raw materials, above all oil, was

among the most politically-charged aspects of Britain's foreign relations. Well before the Middle East crisis of October 1973 and the emergence of 'the oil weapon', a rising awareness of the sensitivity of oil and mineral supplies was apparent in the conduct of British foreign policy. The Conservative government's initial coolness towards the military government of Nigeria, on coming into office in 1970, gave way to a growing solicitude for Nigerian attitudes, marked by the welcome given to Nigerian officials visiting London and by successive ministerial visits to Lagos, culminating in General Gowon's state visit to London in June 1973 – the first Commonwealth African head of state to be thus formally honoured.[5] In December 1973 President Mobutu of Zaïre followed him, to be received 'by the Queen, members of the Royal Family, the Prime Minister and other dignitaries with all the pomp and circumstance befitting the leader of a country which contains some of the world's richest mineral deposits'.[6] The increasing ability of the oil-producing states to act in unison (through OPEC) and to use their economic strength for political ends made the need for political information and for the exercise of such influence as could be exerted through diplomatic means more starkly urgent than had been apparent a few years earlier – as did the explicit linking of oil and economic relations with the Arab-Israeli conflict, and through that with the attitude and involvement of the superpowers in the Middle East.

British relations with the countries of Asia, Africa, and Latin America are not of the same order of political significance. They are less often multilateral in character, more easily conducted through Foreign Offices and embassies. They arouse a relatively low degree of domestic interest in Britain; where organized groups concerned with their relations with Britain exist, they are generally small, and well known to the FCO department concerned. Their affairs receive relatively little attention in the British press, except during revolutions or natural disasters, or when British interests are threatened or British citizens involved. There is little direct contact between their elites and informed opinion in Britain, except for those Britons who specialize academically or commercially in particular regions. Ministerial contacts and visits are less frequent and more formal: the two-hour discussion at No. 10, followed by a similar session in the FCO on 'questions of mutual interest' for representatives of the larger countries, talks with junior ministers in the FCO and DTI for the rest.

Relations with these countries range over a number of matters of secondary importance to Britain, rarely sufficient so to warrant more than a very occasional reference to ministerial level, though cumulatively of considerable weight. Since withdrawal from East of Suez economic relations have become predominant. Over a quarter of Britain's exports went to the developing countries of Asia, Africa and Latin America, a declining proportion but still by no means a negligible one. Imports from them include many highly important raw materials – as we have seen – as well as many foodstuffs. British investment in many developing countries has been substantial and is still continuing; the provision of services, from sea and air transport to insurance, substantially adds to Britain's invisible earnings. Expatriate populations of British citizens, non-European holders of British passports, British businessmen and teachers working abroad, British tourists, and in some countries British 'drop-outs' have extended consular work and threatened occasional political embarrassment. The aid programme and the work of the British Council provided a more positive bilateral link; with some countries indeed, aid administration and technical assistance now constitute almost the entire intergovernmental relationship.

As we have seen in chapter 5, residual military commitments and interests remained into the early 70s; though, with the exceptions of the Anglo-Malaysian Defence Agreement and a small commitment of British officers and pilots in Oman, this had now shrunk to training agreements and the use of the military in support of prestige, goodwill, or commercial aims. Royal Engineers built roads and bridges in Thailand, Afghanistan, Ethiopia, Kenya, and Zaïre, amongst many other countries; RAF transport planes assisted with relief supplies in East Bengal and West Africa. British ships and aircraft made goodwill visits, and helped to promote sales of British defence equipment; officers of foreign armed services were trained at British military academies and visited Britain for staff courses.[7]

Active diplomacy reflected this limited range of concerns. A great deal of time-consuming work at low level was often involved in such matters as the negotiation of agreements on airline routes and overflying rights. Protection of British investment and the promotion of British trade necessitated contacts between the FCO and embassies and British businessmen, and discreet advice, as well as representations to governments. Complicated and long-drawn-out negotiations over expropriated British property and trade debts dogged British relations with a growing number of countries, often with the successor regimes to those responsible for incurring them. Frequently these ended only in an agreement to fund them on a longer-term basis through a multilateral creditors' 'club' – a far cry from the era when the British government occupied Egypt to foreclose on a loan, or took over the Chinese Imperial Customs. In 1972 the FCO Latin American department was still trying to secure Brazilian compensation for the nationalization of British-owned utility companies, and less actively pursuing compensation for expropriated Argentinian tramways; the East African department was making representations to Tanzania about the expropriated property of British Asians. Political representations were most often concerned with government attitudes to questions coming up for discussion in the UN and its agencies or in international conferences, and in Africa also with explaining British policy on Rhodesia and South Africa. Officials, usually supported by their ministers, hesitated to express too enthusiastic support or too strong disapproval of any particular regime. The consensus throughout the Diplomatic Service was that trade counted for more than moral disapproval, that a country in regular balance of payments deficit could not afford the luxury of delicate scruples. The rapid turnover of regimes and instability of governments also discouraged more than a correct and slightly distant relationship, combined with the most discreet contacts with such opposition or exile groups as seemed to threaten the regime in power.

Until the mid-6os a firm dividing line could have been drawn through the developing countries according to their membership or non-membership of what was still called on occasion the 'British' Commonwealth. The very real ties which had bound Commonwealth countries to Britain in a privileged relationship not shared by other countries were gradually eroded during the 6os: preferential access to British government Departments, Commonwealth consultative machinery in defence, economic, scientific, and educational matters, privileged access to British political reporting and intelligence on third countries through the CRO and through cooperation among Commonwealth embassies, unrestricted access for Commonwealth citizens to Britain (first restricted in 1962), above all British willingness to grant special treatment to Commonwealth interests and complaints.[8] The biggest breaking-point came over Rhodesia, on which both the Labour government and, more strongly, the Conservative opposition felt that criticism from Commonwealth African countries was unsympathetic to the real dilemma Britain faced, and unconstructive. Difficulties over immigration added to the disillusionment; the legacies of empire somehow seemed less glorious when they appeared in such strength in Wolverhampton or Bradford. The growing Soviet involvement in India in the late 6os and the Indian government's declining attachment to Britain marked the end of a special relationship which had symbolized the multiracial Commonwealth for a generation of Englishmen.[9] The successive collapse of the democratic governments which in the passage to independence British administrators had worked so hard to establish destroyed the illusion that British traditions and standards of behaviour could be transplanted into other cultures, and could serve as a continuing link between like-minded nations.

What remained in the early 70s was a continuing network of trading and financial links, cultural and social ties, which reflected the strength of historical relationships. Almost all of the 253 Commonwealth organizations which a handbook in 1965 had listed remained active, linking universities, armed services, youth groups, professional bodies, and religious organizations – and a number of new bodies had been added.[10] British aid, as we have seen, was still overwhelmingly concentrated on Commonwealth countries; common language, shared traditions of administration and education, made for continuing closeness in governmental and private training programmes and technical assistance. British investment and companies remained on the whole more deeply involved in Commonwealth than in non-Commonwealth countries, though the nationalization (or 'Africanization') policies of some Commonwealth governments had considerably reduced this, and the scale of new British investment in such countries as Zaïre was beginning to alter the pattern. In spite of increasingly tight restrictions on migration, travel, student interchange, short-term and long-term migration were all far higher between Britain and Commonwealth countries than with non-Commonwealth countries. Significant communities of Jamaicans, Trinidadians, Bengalis, Pakistanis, and Indians in British cities had given those countries' high commissions a special role in British society, advising 'their' communities on their social and political behaviour and keeping them in touch with developments 'at home'.

Yet it would be difficult to isolate from these continuing bilateral ties a peculiarly 'Commonwealth' element; while the multilateral dimension, never as great as the mystique of the Commonwealth has suggested, had declined to infrequent 'Commonwealth Meetings' of heads of government and to a range of low-level cultural and aid links – handled, since 1965, no longer by the CRO but by the intergovernmental Commonwealth Secretariat. The table on p. 250 suggests that, according to one crude but simple indicator, those non-industrial states which remained most important to Britain after the withdrawal from East of Suez were without exception Commonwealth members. The preponderance of business in relations with India and Pakistan, however, mainly reflected the pressure of applicants for entry to Britain and the substantial British aid effort in the Indian subcontinent: nearly a quarter of the staff in both countries listed in the 1972 *Diplomatic Service List* were specifically concerned with immigration matters. The importance of Nigeria as a source of raw materials, above all oil, as an export market, and as one of the most influential African governments was becoming sharply evident to Whitehall. The Singapore and Australian missions had absorbed some of the former staff of the Political Office of the Far Eastern Command, with regional responsibilities.

Some legacies of Britain's overseas empire remained, as sources of inescapable embarrassment to the British government: small and scattered territories, many scarcely viable as independent states, some coveted or claimed by their neighbours, difficult to disengage from without offending neighbouring governments or the more nostalgic elements of British opinion. In the Caribbean, the 'revolt' in Anguilla which had considerable embarrassed the Labour government in 1969 was followed by less severe troubles in Bermuda and a threatened secession in the Bahamas. The Guatemalan claim to British Honduras necessitated the maintenance of separate British embassies in a number of small Central American countries where British interests alone would not have justified residential missions. Rhodesia, above all, exercised the machinery of foreign policy-making and management: each new development, each response to initiatives from the Rhodesian government or from other

Major British Overseas Missions, 1968, 1973: No. of UK-Based Staff

1968		1973	
1. Germany	212	1. United States	217
2. United States	206	2. Germany	178
3. Pakistan	122	3. France	101
4. India	116	4. India	94
5. France	101	5. Australia	86
6. Nigeria	84	6. Pakistan	83
7. Far Eastern Command,		7. Nigeria	70
Political Office	83	8. European Communities	68
8. USSR	64	9. USSR	62
9. Italy	62	10. South Africa	60
10. South Africa	62	11. Italy	59
11. Japan	56	12. Japan	54
12. Malaysia	55	13. Canada	47
13. Persian Gulf	51	14. NATO	43
14. Kenya	51	15. Spain	40
15. Australia	50	16. Turkey	40
16. Turkey	49	17. Singapore	39
17. NATO	48	18. Belgium	39
18. Canada	45	19. Poland	39
19. UN, New York	44	20. UN, New York	37
20. Iran	43		

Source: Civil Estimates, HC 126-II, 1968–9; Supply Estimates, HC 114-II, 1973–74.

Note: These totals comprise UK-based staff at missions and subordinate posts in the countries listed, and do not include locally-engaged staff. Total Diplomatic Service staff in the USA in 1973, including locally-recruited staff performing mainly routine commercial, consular and secretarial work, was 764; in India, reflecting the burden of consular and immigration work, it was 508, compared with 512 in Germany and 325 in France. In 1968 the total number of staff in the United States had been higher than in Germany, 761 against 554.

African states, requiring not only explanations from British missions throughout independent Africa but also the most careful ministerial presentation to British domestic opinion.[11] The decision in 1971 to yield a small group of islands in the Persian Gulf, the Greater and Lesser Tumbs, to Iran rather than to its Arab claimants required a careful assessment of the balance of disadvantages to Britain, referred to ministerial level for clearance. The Iranian government's satisfaction had to be offset by the half-anticipated Libyan response, which seized the excuse to expropriate BP's extensive investments.

Government management of relations with the developing countries in the earlier 70s was still contained primarily within the FCO. The geographical departments of the ODA and the three CRE divisions of the DTI whose responsiblities covered these countries, were closely involved in many policy discussions. Other DTI divisions, responsible for oil and for other raw materials, for outward investment and for civil aviation, were drawn in on matters relating to their competences; the Sugar and Tropical Foodstuffs division of MAFF, together with its 'rest of the world' External Relations division, were similarly involved. Sections of the Defence Secretariat were concerned with military visits and training; the MoD also had a direct interest in arms sales. But the numbers of those needed to be actively involved was rarely so large as to require more than informal consultation, orchestrated by the FCO departments concerned. In contrast to relations with Atlantic countries, the geographical departments of the Foreign Office most often played the leading role. Indeed, the level at which relations were most commonly handled provided desk officers in these departments with a satisfyingly wide scope for taking initiatives and decisions. A first or second secretary in his late 20s might find himself drafting, say, a convention on sealing in Antarctica, and coordinating the British government's position in negotiations with Argentina over the establishment of a regular air service with the Falkland Islands, a question not without potential domestic political embarrassment if the government was held to be insensitive to the interests and independence of the 2,000 islanders. In contrast, service in a small overseas mission, most of all a 'marginal embassy' with three or four home-based staff in, say, a Central or South American country, must have become one of the least satisfying of diplomatic posts.[12] These embassies could not hope to play a significant part in discussions on policy at home, on the infrequent occasions when questions of policy relating to their country arose. They combined the promotion of British exports and the protection of British citizens and interests with the uncomfortable role of providing targets for local dissidents and revolutionaries. The light weight of specifically Commonwealth business within the FCO was suggested by its management within one small department, reporting to the same under-secretary as the Caribbean and Dependent Territories departments – a massive reduction from the separate Department of State of ten years before, with its own Cabinet minister and two junior ministers. Ministerial involvement in bilateral relations with most developing countries was largely formal, receiving visitors and 'showing the flag' on visits abroad. They were drawn in more actively only at times of acute crisis.

The multilateralization of intergovernmental relations has also affected the management of British policy towards the non-Atlantic countries, if far less directly than towards the countries of the inner area. Britain's political and economic interest in the affairs of such regional intergovernmental organizations as the OAU and OPEC is reflected in a continuing need for information and political reporting and the occasional exercise of active diplomacy. As a permanent member of the UN Security Council and a leading member of many other global organizations and agencies now numerically dominated by the developing countries, the

British government needs to maintain a not inconsiderable official presence on a mass of committees, at conferences and at their headquarters. A brief discussion of the management of British policy within the UN framework therefore follows two case studies in bilateral relations with one Commonwealth and one non-Commonwealth country – Ghana and Ethiopia.

BILATERAL RELATIONS: GHANA
by CHRISTOPHER CLAPHAM

Relations with Ghana exemplify the intricacies of the post-colonial situation. At the base of the relationship is the fact that Britain created the Gold Coast, and ruled it for some seventy-five years, until independence in 1957. From the British viewpoint, the legacy of this period is a fairly simple one: colonialism created interests and linkages with Ghana which, while not of the first importance, are none the less well worth maintaining. The Ghanaian position is much more ambivalent: Britain has been much more important to Ghana than ever Ghana has been to Britain; the links between the two have been to an appreciable extent imposed by Britain or created in a framework of British dominance; and their maintenance, especially when they are difficult for Ghana to dispose of, tends therefore to carry colonialist overtones.

It is accordingly not surprising that, while the general context of the relationship has been mainly shaped by Britain, its condition in the short term has depended mostly on the nature of the Ghanaian response. This has varied according to the regime in power in Accra and the immediate problems which it has faced. The post-independence government of Kwame Nkrumah and the Convention People's Party (1957–66) combined policies of assertive Pan-Africanism, anti-colonialism, and non-alignment with the maintenance of a surprising amount of the relationship with Britain, expressed both in economic and in symbolic terms. Only at the very end of his regime was Nkrumah forced to make any decisive break with Britain, when he complied with the OAU's resolution to break off diplomatic relations over Rhodesia in 1965 in order to maintain his position as a radical in continental politics. The National Liberation Council (1966–9) which took over after the 1966 coup, and its successor, Dr Busia's Progress Party government (1969–72), were both led by men with extensive British training and sympathetic attitudes towards the United Kingdom; Busia had spent his exile during the Nkrumah period in Britain, and returned there after his fall in 1972. When diplomatic relations were re-established soon after the coup formal relations between the two countries became much more friendly. But by now events had moved too far for it to be possible to re-establish really close relations, and economic pressures, in particular the debts issue and demands for greater Ghanaian control of the economy, raised problems which had largely been avoided under the politically much more radical government of Nkrumah. When, in January 1972, the National Reformation Council of Colonel Acheampong ousted Busia, many of the personal factors which had affected the relationship with Britain were removed, and a clearer view of what remained – from the British as well as from the Ghanaian standpoint – became possible.

From the British point of view Ghana stands in the middle rank of the developing countries. In West Africa it is overshadowed by Nigeria, with eight times its population and a far larger share of British trade and investment – aside from the major foreign policy issue raised by British involvement in the civil war. Ghana lacks the capacity to impinge on British interests demonstrated by Kenya and Uganda over the Asians' issue, by Rhodesia and South Africa over the White South, and by Egypt over the Suez Canal. Yet as a member of the Commonwealth, a still substantial trading partner, and a country with a wide range of economic, cultural, and official contacts with Britain, it looms far larger in Britain's foreign relations than does, for instance, the neighbouring Ivory Coast, whose corresponding (and much closer) post-colonial links are with Paris. Only a small proportion of these links could be described as directly 'political'; the major diplomatic preoccupations of each state scarcely affect the other (though with some exceptions from the Ghanaian side). Political issues mostly arose in the early period, when Nkrumah championed the nationalist movements in the then British colonies and took an assertive role in world diplomacy which, in the long term, Ghana had not the resources to support. It is indicative of this that first Nigeria and then Tanzania and Zambia have taken over from Ghana the role of guardian of African interests in dealings with Britain over Rhodesia.

The more durable continuing links may be grouped into first, economic exchanges, and second, the contacts between Britain and members of various Ghanaian elites. Economically, Britain has been by far Ghana's most important trading partner. It has consistently been the largest supplier of Ghana's imports, though its share of the market declined fairly steadily from 43 per cent in 1958 to 27 per cent in 1969. In all but four years between 1958 and 1969 it was also the largest receiver of Ghana's exports, with a share which dropped from 29 per cent in 1958 to 13 per cent in 1965, and then picked up to 25 per cent by 1969. By contrast, Ghana in 1969 was the 40th largest receiver of Britain's exports with 0·5 per cent, and the 35th largest provider of its imports, again with 0·5 per cent, an imbalance which indicates the skewed nature of the relationship and its far greater importance to Ghana than to Britain.[13]

The trade figures have been affected by such Ghanaian government actions as exchange controls and trade with the communist bloc, but have not given rise to any major intergovernmental issues between the two countries. These have arisen much more from capital movements – both public and private, the role of British firms in Ghana, and the Ghanaian reliance on a single crop, cocoa, which is subject to enormous fluctuations in price. The single most important issue throughout the period since 1966 has been the Ghanaian government's indebtedness to British companies and, through ECGD underwriting of their export contracts, to the British government. Many of these debts arose from contractor-financed deals for capital projects arranged between British firms and the Nkrumah government between 1961 and 1966. Since 1966, when it was realized that Ghana had incurred obligations which it could not possibly meet, they have been the subject of numerous re-scheduling arrangements between Ghana, Britain, and other creditor countries. In February 1972 many of them were repudiated by the new Acheampong government, but negotiations continued intermittently. A British government offer made in November 1972, which would effectively have written off some 40 per cent of the debt, received no reply until May 1973. Meanwhile the total of short and medium-term debts had risen, as a result of the brief exchange-control liberalization of the Busia regime, to about £100m. Because of the debt repudiation British capital aid to Ghana was suspended, though technical assistance of some £1m p.a. was maintained.

Nkrumah's regime was surprisingly little involved in the affairs of British companies in Ghana. However, since 1968 every Ghanaian government has restricted the role of foreign business, whether by reserving certain areas of economic activity to Ghanaians (as in the Ghanaian Business Promotion Act of 1970), or by taking 55 per cent shares in foreign extractive industries and 40 per cent shares in foreign banks (as has happened since 1972). This affects especially Ashanti Goldfields, now part of Lonrho, and the British banks. Here the British government was unwilling to get involved, so long as some form of compensation acceptable to the companies was forthcoming – though where this was to come from, given Ghana's current indebtedness, was another matter. On another economic issue, both Britain and Ghana took active parts in formulating the International Cocoa Agreement which came into effect in 1973.

The cultural dimensions of the relationship are more pervasive, though less easily detailed. All members of the Ghanaian elite speak English and a high proportion of them have been educated in the UK. The institutions which they control – the law, the civil service, the universities, the army – have been constructed on British models and conducted initially by expatriates, mostly British, who have now generally handed over to Ghanaians, mostly trained in Britain. As has been suggested, the legacy of this has been ambivalent, especially in institutions like the army and universities, which are caught between colonial standards and a nationalist orientation; the post-1972 military regime, for example, is much less deferential to the UK than was its 1966–9 predecessor. Even so, there are multiple contacts which continue to be maintained through professional associations, the high number of Ghanaian students still present in the UK, Anglo-Ghanaian marriages, Britons serving in Ghana, and so on. The imbalance of the relationship is as clear here as in the economic sphere: there are many ways in which the British connection is important to Ghana but virtually none in which the Ghanaian connection is important to Britain. The flow of language, culture, and education has been entirely one-way; the former expatriates do not occupy the same roles in the British social and political structure as the 'been-tos' do in the Ghanaian; and the Ghanaian community in Britain – some thousand – is slight compared with the West Indians or the Pakistanis.

The focal point for official relations, from the British viewpoint, is the Ghana desk in the FCO West African department. The 'desk' itself is a more elaborate organization than, say, the Ethiopia desk, employing a desk officer and some four assistants rather than a single individual, and Ghanaian affairs are more often the concern of the head and assistant head of the department, since Ghana is the second most important country with which they have to deal. Occasional issues go to the supervising deputy under-secretary, but it is unusual for anything to go beyond this since there are few aspects of Anglo-Ghanaian relations which are of general political concern. During the Busia regime, when Dr Busia paid several visits to Britain and was received by the Prime Minister and the Foreign Secretary, the need for top-level briefings was greater. Since then contacts at this level have been almost non-existent; nor have visits to West Africa by Foreign Office ministers included any to Ghana.

The Ghana desk, like any other, acts as a clearing house for aspects of Anglo-Ghanaian relations arising anywhere in the official machine, but overwhelmingly its concerns are economic. It views itself principally as the custodian of British economic interests. Among these in the early 70s the debts issue was salient, not so much because of its importance in the total range of Anglo-Ghanaian economic transactions as because it required action through official channels in a way that most such transactions do not. The desk officer acted as convenor of an ad hoc committee on the debts, to which other interested parties were invited according to the subject matter. These might include representatives of functional departments inside the FCO, of other Departments of State such as the Treasury, the DTI, and the ECGD, and of other creditor countries whose common approaches to Ghana were coordinated by Britain (as the major creditor involved). More specialist activities may be handled by outside Departments and reported to the desk; the main British role in formulating the International Cocoa Agreement was carried by the MAFF, though the FCO was involved in contacts between the UK and Ghana as co-vice-chairmen, and in trying to persuade other consumers, notably Germany and the USA, to sign the draft agreement.

The British high commission in Accra appears at first sight to be fairly large, with a UK-based staff of thirty-four, though at £172,000 p.a. in 1973–4 it was in fact no more than the fiftieth most expensive British mission abroad, a position which accorded closely with Ghana's ranking in the trade figures.[14] It carried out the usual functions of political reporting, export promotion, and the administration of technical assistance. The British Council, with libraries in Accra and Kumasi and expenditure for 1973–4 of £128,000, had its sixteenth largest mission in Ghana, though it ranked lower than Ethopia with £173,000 and well behind Nigeria with £550,000.[15]

The Ghanaian high commission in London had an accredited staff of thirty-four, two-thirds of the German total of fifty.[16] This was probably a a measure more of historic attachments and West African bureaucratic inflation than of its diplomatic importance. Its functions included looking after the Ghanaian community in Britain, especially the students, and acting as a contact point for would-be visitors and investors. It also aimed to create a favourable climate of opinion about Ghana, through, for example, talks by the high commissioner in receptive settings like the Royal Commonwealth Society, or contacts with the magazine *West Africa*; as against this, it attracted some publicity as one of the leading foreign missions incurring unpaid car parking fines.

Though Britain and Ghana are both members of the Commonwealth, the opportunities which this provided for diplomatic contact were fairly limited. It is a useful forum when the parties have anything which they want to discuss, through the Commonwealth Prime Ministers' Meeting for example, but does not provide for automatic multilateral contacts over routine matters in the same way as, say, the EEC. Nkrumah used it, and during 1970–2 Dr Busia was one of the very few African Commonwealth leaders with whom Mr Heath found himself in accord, but its overall role in official Anglo-Ghanaian relations appears to be fairly slight.

Because there are so many personal connections between Britain and Ghana and because the official relationship has often been strained (initially because of Nkrumah and latterly because of the debts issue), unofficial connections have played a significant part in the total relationship. Elite contacts take place largely through informal channels. There was in 1972, for example, no Anglo-Ghanaian society, by contrast say with the Anglo-Sierra Leone Society or the Britain-Nigeria Association. This was mainly because Britons interested in Ghana have tended to be partisan, favouring either Nkrumah or, more often, Busia and the group who were in opposition for nine years after independence, whereas both Sierra Leone and Nigeria had a much less controversial post-colonial period, in which such links could more easily be formed. Nor was there any parliamentary group with a special interest in Ghana – again in contrast to Nigeria. Perhaps the most important single point of contact was a magazine, *West Africa*, which was produced in London and provided a weekly commentary on the Ghanaian and Nigerian scene.

Commercial relations are more closely organized. The London cocoa market is the major international point of exchange for Ghana's most important commodity. London is also the headquarters of the West Africa Committee, which groups the main British and foreign firms operating in West Africa. It maintains a small secretariat and a 'political adviser' – Sir Evelyn Hone, former Governor of Northern Rhodesia – though it seldom deals directly with the FCO. Other links are maintained by bodies like the West Africa section of the London Chamber of Commerce and by individual companies such as Lonrho which have large Ghanaian interests.

Anglo-Ghanaian relations take place principally within the context of the London-centred network which links the United Kingdom radially to each of her former colonies. In the years since independence its importance has weakened to some extent with the development by each country of closer connections with its neighbours, but no multilateral pattern has taken their place. Though there are various other elements in the relationship, the main British concern at the official level since the abandonment of the British African empire has been the maintenance of economic links, which from the Ghanaian viewpoint imply dependence on the former colonial power. This is where the main strains in the relationship arise, indicated in particular by the debts issue and the takeovers of British companies. These issues have had considerable symbolic and some practical significance to Ghanaians, but they have aroused little attention in Britain and have been dealt with at the lower and middle levels of the official machine.

BILATERAL RELATIONS: ETHIOPIA
by CHRISTOPHER CLAPHAM

Britain's relations with Ethiopia originated in the great expansion of British overseas commitments in the second half of the nineteenth century. Ethiopia then came to impinge on British interests both through its proximity to the Red Sea route to India and the East and its frontiers with British-controlled territory in Kenya, Somaliland, and the Sudan. A permanent British legation was established in Addis Ababa in 1897. From then until the Italian invasion of 1935–6, Britain occupied perhaps the third most important place in Ethiopia's foreign relations, after Italy and France, though the importance of this relationship to Britain was no more than peripheral. It was concerned principally with boundary-maintenance between Ethiopia and the British territories, with the activities of British subjects – mostly Indian traders – in Ethiopia, and with a certain amount of covert and never very decisive involvement in internal Ethiopian politics. This period ended with Mussolini's invasion in 1935 – almost the only occasion when Ethiopia has been in the forefront of Britain's diplomatic consciousness – when Ethiopia was in effect sacrificed to the appeasement-oriented requirements of European diplomacy. The Emperor Haile Selassie found refuge in Bath.

The liberation of Ethiopia in 1941, largely by British forces, gave Britain a temporarily dominant position there. It then controlled all of

Ethiopia's neighbours except the tiny French Somali coast, directly administered the Somali-inhabited Ethiopian territories of the Haud and Ogaden, and provided Ethiopia with government advisers and a military training mission. English became the second official language of the empire (after Amharic), and the British Council and British-run schools were established in Addis Ababa. But the British presence was steadily run down during the later 1940s and most of the 1950s. The British Military Mission and the British Council were withdrawn in 1951, though the latter returned in 1958. Britain ceased to administer the ex-Italian colonies of Somalia and Eritrea in 1951 and 1952 respectively, and the Haud and Ogaden in 1954–5. The Sudan became independent in 1956, British Somaliland in 1960, and Kenya in 1963, and with the withdrawal from Aden in 1967 the last British possession in the region disappeared.

British withdrawal from East Africa and the southern Red Sea has removed the basis for the old Anglo-Ethiopian relationship, and there is at present no area in which the present relationship is vital for either side. The cost of the Addis Ababa embassy, at £140,000 in 1973–4, placed it fifty-ninth among British missions abroad, rather lower than Libya and higher than the Sudan, and considerably lower than African states with major British interests such as Egypt or Kenya. But even though Britain had no real direct stake in the country, Ethiopia impinged on British interests at several points. First, at least until the 1974 coup, Addis Ababa was the main African diplomatic centre, as the headquarters of the OAU and the UN Economic Commission for Africa, and hence a useful listening post in any crisis which involves British interests in Africa, of which by far the most important have been the Rhodesian issue and the Nigerian civil war. Pan-African rather than purely Ethiopian affairs took up much of the embassy's time, and led for example to Harold Wilson's visit in 1968 to confer with Haile Selassie over Nigeria. Secondly, Britain retained a residual interest in the Middle Eastern and Red Sea arenas which are central to Ethiopian foreign policy, and sympathized with Ethiopia's goal of maintaining a dominant position in the Horn of Africa.[17] Hence the sale of Canberra bombers to Ethiopia was readily agreed to when the Ethiopians requested it in 1967 (though the British approached the sale primarily from a financial rather than a strategic viewpoint). Here the position of Ethiopia may affect British concerns in Kenya, in the use of the Red Sea as an international water-way, and more indirectly in the Gulf.

In economic terms, Britain ranked fifth as a supplier of Ethiopia's imports (some 10 per cent of the total, after Italy, West Germany, Japan, and the USA), and seventh as a receiver of its exports, with a mere 3.2 per cent of the total.[18] As a proportion of Britain's total trade, that with Ethiopia is insignificant. Technical assistance of £0·4m in 1969 was high in proportion to British exports of £6·5m and imports of £1·6m in the same year, and in addition a £2m interest-free British loan was negotiated. On the defence side, Ethiopian officers have been trained at Sandhurst and other British institutions, though the proportion is small compared with those who have gone to the USA, and there have been several well-publicized British army expeditions to Ethiopia.

These links are not specially important from an economic or military viewpoint, and are best seen as offshoots of an assortment of Anglo-Ethiopian contacts which can broadly be classified as 'cultural'. The British presence in the early 70s was consistently higher than can be accounted for by 'hard' diplomatic or economic objectives. The British Council, with a 1973–4 budget of £173,129, maintained in Ethiopia its tenth largest overseas operation and subsidized the leading secondary school in Addis Ababa. The British community, with 2,651 residents in 1969–70, was the fourth (after Yemen, Italy, and the USA); most of its members were engaged in education, medicine, and related activities.[19] The 2,491 British tourists in 1969–70 constituted the third largest national contingent after the USA and France, and British interest in Ethiopia had been boosted by the Queen's state visit there in 1965 and more recent visits by other members of the royal family, as well as by a very popular series of TV programmes. On the Ethiopian side, contacts at the elite level had been created chiefly by education. Several members of the imperial family went to English public schools, and in 1969 there were 113 Ethiopians (6·2 per cent of Ethiopian students abroad) in British institutions of higher learning. Medical treatment has also brought Ethiopian notables to Britain. Contacts of this kind, involving a small number of people in elite positions, were extremely vulnerable to the changes in Ethiopian domestic politics resulting from the military take-over in 1974.

Relations between Britain and Ethiopia are for the most part carried out at a low level and through a small number of official channels. Within the FCO, they are supervised by a desk officer within the East Africa department, and most routine matters are dealt with at the desk level. Most of the decisions required are of a kind that can be taken by the department, or at most by the supervising assistant under-secretary; it is rare for any decision to need to go higher than this. No general policy issues have arisen for many years, and contacts with higher levels are restricted to such things as briefings for visiting dignitaries. The functional departments of the FCO (apart from the ODA) and other Departments of State in Whitehall are involved only occasionally and on an ad hoc basis. A decision like that to agree to the Ethiopian request for Canberras, originating with the ambassador in Addis Ababa, would require clearance by the MoD and DTI, as well as checking with the embassy in Somalia.

The British embassy in Addis Ababa had in 1973 a UK-based staff of 19, of whom the ambassador, counsellor, and a first or second secretary managed the Chancery, while the rest had specialized responsibilities for trade, technical assistance, consular work, and so forth. Most official contacts between Britain and Ethiopia were carried out through the embassy, partly because it was larger and more competent than the Ethiopian embassy in London, but equally because the personal conduct of Ethiopian foreign policy by the Emperor and his advisers before the 1974 military takeover meant that effective contacts could often only be made in Addis Ababa. Official contacts were generally between the ambassador and the Minister of Foreign Affairs, or at lower level, rather than with the Emperor direct. The embassy also acted as a listening post for the OAU. The British Council administered much of the British technical assistance programme as the agent of the ODA, a position recognized by a special agreement with the Ethiopian government in 1969; it also ran a library and other cultural activities in Addis Ababa, and supervised British volunteers. The Ethiopian embassy in London had an accredited staff of five. Very little of Anglo-Ethiopian relations has been carried out through international agencies, except in the 1966–8 period when Ethiopia was a member of the UN Security Council.

Channels for unofficial relations were likewise few. At the semi-official and elite level, there was an active Anglo-Ethiopian Parliamentary Group, chaired by Sir Bernard Braine, which provided hospitality for visiting Ethiopians, and an Anglo-Ethiopian Society which held dinners at the House of Lords and (in conjunction with the Ethiopian embassy) issued a news magazine on Ethiopian affairs. Like the Queen's State Visit in 1965, these typify the combination of high-level social contact and negligible political contact which characterized so much of Anglo-Ethiopian relations in the years before the deposition of the Emperor. Economic interest activity, for example, did not extend beyond the occasional efforts of particular firms or individuals. The most important non-official relations, rather, have sprung from attempts by groups and individuals in Britain to influence developments in Ethiopia through personal contacts and human appeals. The Ethiopian famine of 1973 was brought to the world's attention by a BBC programme, which thus helped to precipitate the events which led to Haile Selassie's downfall. His deposition, and the execution (in November 1974) of several Ethiopians with strong British connections, abruptly changed the position. Leaders of the Anglo-Ethiopian Society became involved in raising funds for Ethiopian exiles in Britain, and so attracted hostile comment from the new military regime. Thus, the cultural relationship became the prisoner of the groups in each country which had fostered it.

Anglo-Ethiopian relations in the early 70s were peripheral to the interests of both countries, and the channels through which they were conducted were simple and few. In both political and economic fields, they were no more than is necessary to maintain a steady level of uncontroversial contacts, and to iron out the occasional problems which such contacts give rise to. The salience of the cultural contacts was all the more noticeable for the absence of more tangible links, and these contacts, with the British technical assistance programme which to an appreciable extent springs from them, were what Anglo-Ethiopian relations are chiefly about. There remained an imbalance in the relationship, in that Britain was still consistently more important to Ethiopia than Ethiopia to Britain, but only in the immediate post-liberation period has this been marked enough to strain relations. Indeed, the absence of economic pressures or post-colonial strains has helped to induce the relaxed and gentlemanly atmosphere which, at least until 1974, characterized the Anglo-Ethiopian relationship.

MULTILATERAL RELATIONS: THE UNITED NATIONS

The British government played an active part in the negotiations which led to the establishment of the UN and its associated agencies before the end of World War II. A British diplomat acted as temporary secretary-general to the San Francisco Conference, and a large number of Britons went into the UN Secretariat. Britain became one of the five permanent members of the Security Council and, as befitted a great power, was automatically given a seat on the Economic and Social Council and on the governing bodies of other specialized agencies. During the UN's most prestigious period, in the late 50s, each General Assembly saw a substantial party come out from London to reinforce the delegation, led by the Foreign Secretary. In 1960 the Prime Minister himself led the delegation for a short period, and in 1965 Mr Wilson as Prime Minister addressed the General Assembly.

Yet successive British governments and their officials displayed an ambivalent attitude towards the UN, compounded of criticism of the inefficiencies, ineffectiveness, and empty and time-wasting rhetoric which they saw as characterizing global international organizations, and critical support for the objects of those organizations, combined with proposals for reform. Britain's ability positively to influence the UN was limited from the UN's early years on by its defensive position as an imperial nation in a decolonizing world. The Labour government's enthusiasm in 1964 to demonstrate its internationalist commitment was swamped by the reaction of the ex-colonial countries to the Rhodesian crisis; Lord Caradon's proposals for a UN peacekeeping force could not command a hearing in such an atmosphere. The British posture within the UN (and within many specialized agencies) has therefore been largely defensive: resisting hostile resolutions and proposals to increase activity and expenditure, protecting its interests, and attempting initiatives only when it saw some chance of success.

The UN and its agencies touch upon almost all aspects of British external relations, but only rarely concern high policy issues in any decisive way. Even when resolutions on major international issues come before the Security Council, the diplomatic activity behind them is likely to have taken place largely outside the UN context, in direct conversations between like-minded governments. Diplomacy within the UN is more often tactical than strategic, agreeing forms of words rather than deciding overall policy. The United Nations is no longer a major forum for the exchange of information among national delegations; Whitehall officials in 1972 could not remember any telegrams from Britain's UN delegation which were not specifically concerned with UN matters. The Foreign Secretary still found it convenient to attend the autumn General Assembly for a week or so, to take the opportunity for private and informal conversations with the foreign ministers of other governments, though he spent little or no time on the floor of the Assembly or of any of its committees.[20] The public character of the Security Council and the General Assembly placed a special burden on the Permanent Representative, whose speeches might appear on TV throughout the United States and in many other countries during a major crisis. Much British activity within the UN represented pure political diplomacy: explaining the British government's position across the whole spectrum of foreign policy, defending its policies and interests, caucusing with and lobbying the representatives of other governments on proposed resolutions, trading support and votes, agreeing on nominations for elected representatives on important and unimportant UN bodies.

In addition to political diplomacy a mass of economic, social, humanitarian, scientific, and legal questions was discussed, often in considerable technical detail, within the UN's own structure of subordinate committees and within its associated agencies. In 1972, for example, British delegations attended (among many others) the annual assemblies of the WHO, the ILO, and the IAEA, and the biennial conference of the UNESCO, while British representatives took part in the often lengthy meetings of such committees as the UN Special Committee on the Question of Defining Aggression, the Outer Space Legal Sub-Committee, the International Lead and Zinc Committee, the inter-agency Committee on Natural Resources, the Working Group on the UN Development Programme (UNDP), the Sub-Committee on Minorities of the UN Human Rights Commission, the UN Pensions Fund, the UN Commission on International Trade Law, and the Committee on the Rationalization of Procedure. By virtue of its status as a permanent member of the Security Council and its position as a major financial contributor, the British government was a member of the executive boards of all UN agencies, which met regularly in between assemblies. Major UN conferences required British representation throughout the long series of preparatory meetings and a substantial delegation to the conference itself.

It was difficult for the British government to avoid taking part in these myriad conferences and committees. Both ministers and officials saw Britain as a 'responsible' member of the international community, a self-image which did not fit with boycotts and 'empty chairs'. British interests might be threatened, 'intemperate' criticisms of British policy made, in almost any forum – requiring at least a watching brief from a single representative. Scarcely any committee, however technical, was free of potential political content and embarrassment. Other governments did not respect the convenient boundaries of diplomatic discourse as well as the British: the question of South African representation, for instance, arose in even the most technical assemblies. In some, major British interests were clearly at stake, as for example in the 1972–3 Law of the Sea Conference preparatory discussions on the extension of territorial waters and fishery limits. In others hardly any item on the agenda was of direct interest to the British government. The unavoidable burden of business at the middle and lower levels therefore necessarily involved a large number of officials and others in a great deal of time-consuming activity. The desirability of ensuring that representatives in different gatherings do not vote for contradictory resolutions, of maintaining a coherent policy on international organizations, kept the machinery in Whitehall busy in following the progress of different bodies, providing briefs on policy and sending out instructions.

A further significant aspect of Britain's relationship with the United Nations is financial. The bulk of the £40m allocated within the external budget to subscriptions and contributions to international organizations in 1972–3 went to the UN and its agencies. Britain was assessed for the fourth largest contribution to the UN budget – 5·9 per cent – after the United States, the Soviet Union, and France. In 1972–3 this amounted to £4,150,000. It was assessed at 7·39 per cent of the FAO budget, amounting to £1,128,000, at 5·5 per cent of UNESCO's budget, amounting to £873,000 – and so on, from the World Meteorological Organization to the Universal Postal Union. Like British representation on committees, this was a largely automatic obligation; there was little freedom of manoeuvre. Established organizations expanded their activities, new agencies were created, and Britain as a responsible member of the international community contributed its share. Treasury resistance to additional expenditure across the balance of payments, and well-grounded suspicions of the wastefulness of many agencies and of duplication of effort by overlapping organizations here again placed British representatives on the defensive, resisting proposals from the majority of developing countries for expansion of activities and larger budgets. British policy towards UNESCO, for instance, had for some years 'largely aimed at keeping down the overall UNESCO budget'.[21] At its 1972 Conference Britain and eighteen other West and East European countries voted against the budget proposed for 1973–4. When it was nevertheless carried by a majority of 75 votes, Britain's contribution automatically rose to £1,136,000.[22]

The requirements of British representation in these various organizations were met partly by maintaining permanent missions and partly by extensive travel. The UK Mission to the United Nations in New York contained in 1972 37 UK-based staff, all (except one seconded Treasury adviser) from the Diplomatic Service, with a senior ambassador as Permanent Representative. The Mission to the International Organizations at Geneva, which handled relations with EFTA as well as with a number of global international organizations, contained 28 UK-based staff, including a small number seconded from the DTI. The six-man UK Delegation to the Conference of the Committee on Disarmament shared the same building in Geneva. A counsellor and first secretary in the Vienna embassy acted respectively as UK Alternate Governor on the IAEA and representative to the UN Industrial Development Organization; a counsellor in the Rome embassy, on secondment from the ODA, was designated as FAO representative, assisted where necessary in committee work by a first secretary and heavily reinforced by a delegation from the ODA and the Ministry of Agriculture during conferences. A principal in the ODA acted as UK Deputy Permanent Delegate to UNESCO in Paris, travelling over as needed.[23]

The New York mission worked within an annual cycle of activity, rising to its peak during General Assemblies, and servicing committees in New York and elsewhere during the rest of the year. Although the reduced importance of the General Assembly meant that regional specialists no longer came out from the FCO to boost the delegation, the workload of Assembly sessions and committees still required some reinforcement. Two MPs from the government party came out each year to sit on the Third and Fourth Assembly Committees, dealing with human rights and colonial questions; a second Legal Adviser from the Foreign Office joined the delegation for the Assembly period. The entire delegation to the Disarmament Conference regularly moved to New York for the General Assembly. Delegations to more intermittently active bodies were drawn from New York, Geneva, the Foreign Office and other parts of Whitehall, depending on geographical convenience and topic; one member of the New York delegation, for instance, had spent more than a fortnight each at meetings in Santiago, Nairobi, and Stockholm during a twelve-month period in 1971–2, in addition to his regular commitments in New York. Representation to more technical committees was led by diplomats only when the novelty of the topic or the depth of potential political pitfalls were seen to require it. On some sub-committees and working groups the British representatives were drawn from outside the civil service, and larger delegations might include non-official members; the secretary-general of the British Trawlers' Federation, for instance, attended the preparatory meetings from the Law of the Sea Conference. The mixed British delegation at a lengthy meeting of the legal committee of the International Civil Aviation Organization (ICAO), in Washington in September 1972, to discuss legal proposals to curb hijacking, was led by a senior solicitor from the DTI. A meeting of the Scientific and Technical Sub-Committee of the UN First Committee, earlier in 1972, was attended by a DTI official, a member of the Science Research Council, and the deputy director of the

Radio Astronomy Department at Slough, with some assistance and advice from the New York mission. Major conferences require larger and more complex delegations. Given the novelty of the subject, the number of Whitehall Departments with interests potentially affected, and the uncertain division of responsibilities within Whitehall, it was only after much effort that the British delegation to the 1972 Stockholm Conference on the Environment was reduced to 45.

The main point of contact in London for the New York and Geneva delegations was the United Nations department of the FCO: divided into separate departments for political questions and economic and social questions for some years before, but combined during 1972 in the hope of reducing duplication of effort and saving staff. These large departments had reported to the same supervising under-secretaries, who also supervised the geographical departments responsible for Middle Eastern and African questions. UN agencies were the prime responsibility of the Whitehall Departments most directly concerned, with the British subscription met from their Parliamentary Vote. The Department of Employment thus led on the ILO, that of Health and Social Security on WHO, the ODA on FAO and UNESCO. A number of other FCO departments, those concerned with marine and transport questions, aviation, disarmament, science and technology, were also regularly drawn in on matters relating to functional agencies, and might on occasion play a leading role. The relatively low level of British interests involved in most international organization questions enabled coordination to be managed on a fairly informal basis. It was extremely rare for international organization matters to be taken up within the DOPC structure; when they rose to ministerial level for approval, they were most often referred to junior ministers. The formal structure of the Steering Committee on International Organization, established in 1946, existed only in the shape of working groups and sub-committees, convened as needed.[24] The role of the FCO UN department on questions for which it did not provide the Whitehall lead was to ensure a degree of coherence between different technical discussions and to alert other officials to politically sensitive issues.

Liaison between London and delegations 'in the field' was effected on two levels. The UN department, or other departments and divisions for functional agencies, was responsible for preparing briefs on the general line of policy to be pursued, agreed amongst the affected sections of Whitehall, and modified from time to time as occasion demanded. Delegations worked within these general instructions, and referred back to Whitehall for specific clearance or approval as negotiations proceeded. During Security Council meetings a telephone line would often be kept open to London, continuously manned at both ends; for less urgent situations an evening telegram, taking advantage of the time differential between New York and London, could usually bring a reply in time for the next morning's session. General satisfaction was expressed by officials involved at the efficiency and flexibility of these arrangements, and at the opportunities provided for delegation members to take part in writing their own instructions; 'policy evolves', one official suggested, 'by a process of osmosis'. For some major negotiations, the same senior official led the delegation and was responsible for coordinating the preparatory work in Whitehall. Here again, continuity and coherence were assisted by cross-postings between Whitehall and the permanent missions. In 1972 one of the two supervising under-secretaries and one of the two assistants in the FCO UN department shared recent experience of the New York delegation; the head of Chancery in Geneva had previously been an assistant in the UN department. Ministerial involvement was relatively limited, both in Whitehall and abroad. One of the ministers of state in the FCO had general responsibility for international organization questions; status and prestige required her and colleagues from other Departments to play a part in international conferences, in addition to keeping an eye on the evolution of policy in Whitehall.

As has already been suggested in chapter 4, a small and fairly self-contained public of interested and informed opinion exists on the UN and related international organizations. The FCO's UN department keeps in close touch with the UNA and encourages it in various ways; it also maintains contact with the two parliamentary groups most directly concerned. The UN Advisory Group to the FCO is chaired at its occasional meetings by the responsible minister of state, though the departmental officials play a more active role. The national committees for other UN agencies all, to one degree or another, relate very closely to the Whitehall Department responsible. One peculiarity characterizing multilateral relations is that the UN itself maintains an Information Office in London, in regular contact with informed opinion. In New York the British delegation in 1972 included two information officers, one of whose responsibilities was to handle the considerable traffic in interested British visitors to the UN. Consultative status for international non-governmental organizations with the UN or with its agencies brings British groups which play a prominent part in international associations, for example the Anti-Slavery Society, into direct touch with the permanent missions.

The pattern of British relations with the UN and its agencies, therefore, represents a good example of British foreign policy on the middle and lower levels. The more directly political aspects of UN affairs are managed between London and New York, mainly within the Foreign Office network and with only occasional ministerial involvement. The experiment of making the Permanent Representative a minister of state, in the person of Lord Caradon, from 1964–70, did not significantly alter the established pattern. Ministers are drawn into the formulation of policy at a fairly late stage, unless their subordinate officials are unclear about their general attitude on a line of policy; they come in to add prestige and legitimation, to make the opening speech at a conference or to sign a carefully-prepared agreement. In the more technical agencies and committees, the compartmentalization of policy-making is high.[25] The officials responsible, the small number of outside experts and representatives of interested groups, may meet the same crowd of foreign delegates at the same international conference year after year. At this level, policy evolves slowly over a period of years within a shifting multi-lateral context, only indirectly affected by political inputs from the top, and only distantly related to the perceived high policy issues of British foreign policy.

10: Conclusion: The Wider Debate

IN ONE SENSE, British accession to the European Community, in January 1973, should have transformed the whole context of foreign policy-making. In principle, Britain was abandoning the pursuit of an independent foreign policy, to adhere to a Community 'determined ... to construct an ever closer union among the peoples of Europe on the foundations already laid': bringing together agricultural and industrial policy, foreign as well as domestic commercial and financial policy, coordinating the 'political' dimension of the foreign relations of member states, and perhaps eventually extending this coordination to national defence policies.[1] Opponents of British membership assumed that the alternatives presented themselves in these terms. The issue, to them, was independence versus European federation, parliamentary sovereignty versus subordination to Brussels. The government's response was more to emphasize the long and uncertain road that lay between Community entry and the achievement of political union than to deny the importance of the change.

Yet, in another sense, entry into the European Community was only a further step in an evolutionary process, which had begun with the establishment of a number of multilateral intergovernmental organizations in the postwar period and continued throughout the 1950s and 1960s. As we have seen in previous chapters, successive governments of different parties have accepted (if sometimes reluctantly) the necessity and desirability of an increasing multilateralization of Britain's foreign relations, and the extension of multilateral relations to areas of policy previously regarded as matters of domestic politics. If British governments had resisted the political aims and implications of the European Coal and Steel Community and later of the EEC and Euratom, they had played a leading role in the establishment and operation of NATO, the OEEC, WEU, EFTA, ELDO and ESRO, and the Eurogroup. Even while the Labour government was considering its position on renegotiating the terms of Community entry and protecting the sovereignty of Parliament, in 1974, it accepted almost without debate British membership of the International Energy Agency – the powers of which appeared to infringe parliamentary sovereignty (and to foreclose freedom of action in domestic policy) far more within its field than the Community itself. To present the issue of Community membership in the absolute terms of sovereignty versus integration was therefore fundamentally to misunderstand the nature of Britain's international predicament. Interdependence had already eroded the old barriers between foreign and domestic policy; what remained was more the shadow of sovereignty than the substance.[2]

British membership of the European Community was a novel departure in four senses. First, it made explicit what had previously been implicit: that Britain's freedom of manoeuvre in both foreign and domestic policy was becoming tightly constrained by the actions and attitudes of foreign governments. Second, it brought together within a single framework a number of issues which had formerly been discussed separately within different intergovernmental organizations. Third, the wide competences of the Treaty of Rome extended the subject matter of intergovernmental discussion and collaboration still further; and fourth, it seemed to open the long-term prospect of uniting a wide range of intergovernmental contacts within an institutional structure which could exert a degree of democratic control. British withdrawal from the Community would not remove the need for continuing intergovernmental cooperation – as members of the Labour government rapidly appreciated in the months after their return to office in March 1974. It would merely alter the context of collaboration and the relationships between the various governments involved. Only a British rejection of the constraints which bound it to its partners in Western Europe and the North Atlantic area – involving withdrawal from NATO and the other intergovernmental organizations and an attempt at economic autarky – or the collapse of the existing international economic system and of the collaborative pattern of European defence and security, could free its government from the consequences of interdependence.

The impact of these developments on the formulation and management of foreign policy in Britain has been examined in some detail in previous chapters. It remains here to summarize the argument made. Dependence on the cooperation of other states means that decisions on British policy can no longer be so clearly taken: rather, Whitehall can only formulate negotiating positions, making preliminary 'decisions about desired decisions' to guide its negotiators in the process of multilateral bargaining. There has been, then, a considerable loss of autonomy in policy-making, not only in questions of foreign policy but also in many areas traditionally considered primarily domestic. Moreover, British membership of international organizations carries with it the acceptance of a number of largely automatic future obligations – not only in the European Community, but to one degree or another in most of the ninety or more organizations to which Britain subscribes.[3] When a UN agency expands its activities, the British contribution to its budget rises. When a new aid consortium is established or a new Special Drawing Right subscription is agreed, Britain is expected to pay its share; when an Atlantic plan for sharing energy resources or recycling petrodollars is proposed, Britain is expected to play its part in it. It is sometimes possible to stand out against one's partners or against the majority within a large international organization; but until now British policy-makers have been reluctant to stand out against their partners too defiantly. A not insubstantial part of Britain's external budget, as well as significant (perhaps even central) areas of its external relations, are determined within organizations in which Britain's representatives have only one voice among many.

Another consequence of these developments is that the solidarity of national governments in their relations with their closest partners has to a considerable extent been undermined. Foreign governments intervene in Whitehall discussions, supporting some ministers or Departments, combating the arguments of others. Coalitions of interest occasionally cut across the formal barriers of national sovereignty and evade the apparatus of central coordination; the common interest of finance or of defence ministers and their subordinate officials has often proved strong enough to support intervention in each other's domestic discussions.[4] The aim of the central machinery in some instances has indeed become to maintain the unity of the British position on a particular issue while taking advantage of differences within other governments to influence their decision in Britain's favour.

A further consequence is that the balance of authority between ministers and officials in policy-making has been tilted a little further in favour of the latter. They necessarily carry the main burden of representation in international consultations; ministers have domestic responsibilities which limit their freedom to travel abroad. The agenda for ministerial meetings, the preliminary papers on which ministerial discussions are based, emerge from a series of official committees. The major lines of national policy may be laid down under ministerial supervision, and the heads of agreement returned for ministerial approval. But the parameters within which ministers thrash out their final agreement will to a very considerable extent have been determined by the initiative, personal qualities, and assumptions of their civil servants, often without the possibility of more than a cursory reference back to ministerial level. Ministers may still make policy, in the overall sense; but in the context of international organizations it is perhaps more accurate to say that policy is evolved rather than made, and it is continually evolving below them. If this is true of ministerial control, it is even more so for parliamentary accountability. Entering a negotiation, with their civil servants searching out the boundaries of possible advantage and the scope for compromise, ministers not unnaturally refuse to commit themselves to a definite statement of intent. When after much effort a multilateral package has at last been tied up, they are naturally reluctant to reopen it in response to parliamentary pressures.

A still wider consequence is that foreign policy has ceased to be a discrete field, separated from domestic politics both in the nature of the issues and the management of policy. It would be more appropriate to talk about a foreign policy dimension across the whole range of domestic politics, demanding particular attention from particular ministers, civil servants, and commentators, but inseparable from the major issues of domestic debate. But the belief that foreign policy remains a separate matter dies hard – protected by the institutional divisions of Whitehall and of other national administrations, by the existence of separate Diplomatic Services, by the weakness of Parliament and the traditional perspective of politicians, and by the similar institutional divisions between critics outside – between diplomatic and political correspondents and between the academic disciplines of international relations, economics, and politics. Even when participants and commentators have accepted that foreign policy-making in their own country is rooted in domestic concerns and pressures they still perceive the foreign policies of other countries as emerging out of a separate process, largely internal to the government. In the autumn of 1973, for instance, British press comment on German 'intransigence' on the composition of the proposed European Community Regional Fund concentrated on suggestions of a split in the German Cabinet; there were only passing references to parliamentary and public attitudes. A French academic patiently explained to a conference in London in the same year that the British must understand that, although their own government exercised effective freedom in conducting its foreign policy, the French government had to pay more attention to public opinion.

The consequences of all these developments for Whitehall are likely to be far-reaching in the long run. The linking of different issues, of trade concessions and the maintenance of troops in Europe by the US government, of axle weights and road haulage licences by the French, of cultural exchanges and technological cooperation by the Soviet Union, make it more difficult to keep policy areas in separate compartments. Increasingly, and unavoidably, issues in intergovernmental negotiations overlap the responsibilities of different Whitehall Departments, however the boundaries between them are drawn. The management of policy in Whitehall has therefore been pushed towards the centre, placing a heavier burden on the network of interdepartmental committees and the senior officials who most frequently attend them, and also on the Cabinet Office and its constituent units. Whether or not Britain remains a member of the European Community, this trend towards a reinforcement of the centre at the expense of departmental autonomy seems likely to continue. Indeed, it might well be argued that the intricacies of coordinating the international dimension of British policy outside the European Community, handled as it would be through a larger number of separate but overlapping multilateral discussions, would require a good deal more effort from a larger Cabinet Office than would coordination within the Community context. Yet there must be a limit to how far policy can be pushed towards the centre, before the determination of priorities collapses under the weight of detail. Much of the day-to-day management of British relations with other countries, interleaving as they do with the management of domestic policy, must continue to be handled by different Departments. What seems most necessary, therefore, is that the HCS should be made more aware of the inter-governmental implications of their responsibilities and should be alerted to look for issues which may exacerbate relations on a higher level.

Because of these trends towards greater coordination at the centre and greater direct involvement of home Departments and home civil servants in foreign relations, the role of the Foreign Office has become far less clear than it was fifteen or twenty years ago. In the 1950s very few home civil servants travelled abroad. They communicated with their opposite numbers in other governments (except within the Commonwealth, and in some areas except in the US government) only through the Foreign Office or with its permission. External relations divisions held low status in most Departments, as handling questions of only marginal importance to their central responsibilities. Unquestionably at that time 'the central core or central column of the policy-making machinery' in foreign policy was 'the Prime Minister-to-Diplomatic Service hierarchy', which functioned 'as the gatekeeper' between domestic politics and the international environment.[5] By the early 1970s the position was far less simple. The involvement of home Departments and their ministers in significant areas of foreign policy was now considerable. Senior officials in many Departments had gained experience of international negotiations, and regularly took part in multilateral discussions; direct communication with the corresponding officials of other governments, by telephone and telex, was an accepted and regular occurrence.

In 1969 the Duncan Committee reiterated that the special role and 'particular expertise of the Foreign and Commonwealth Office and the Diplomatic Service lies in dealing with other countries and this will be a central requirement into the foreseeable future. . . . The Foreign and Commonwealth Office is in this respect a co-ordinating Department'. 'It might however be argued', the Committee admitted, 'that with the increasing importance of economic matters in Britain's relations with other countries the Foreign and Commonwealth Office will eventually have little useful function to perform' (p. 66). Certainly, as home Departments have become more active in intergovernmental relations, the particular expertise of the FCO has become less vital, more a useful supplement to continuing departmental contacts than an indispensable requirement for departmental policy-making. As Britain has relinquished world power status and the traditional issues of foreign policy have declined, so the authority of the Foreign Office in Whitehall has diminished. The FCO's reaction has been to create a succession of functional departments, to cover each new aspect of intergovernmental relations as it grows; but these divert the FCO from its 'particular expertise', without being able to compete in expertise with the home Departments whose responsibilities they cover.

There is always likely to be a useful role in Whitehall for an organization providing information on developments in foreign countries and advice on their likely reaction to British policies in one field or another, and acting as a point of first contact in Whitehall for overseas missions. But it is not self-evident that this same organization should claim a strategic role in ordering the priorities of policy as they affect other countries. Considerations of administrative politics and career expectations have led some Diplomatic Service officials to hope that the FCO will establish such a position – but similar considerations must lead the home Departments to resist such an attempt. The increasing interdependence of domestic and foreign concerns implies that such a strategic role can only be exercised within a structure which oversees the whole spectrum of domestic and foreign policy. That can only be the Cabinet, the Cabinet Office, and their dependent committees. The establishment of the Assessments Staff and the European Unit within the Cabinet Office rather than within the FCO suggests the line of future development.

Such a development must call into question the separate existence of the Diplomatic Service. Career patterns and expectations necessarily influence perspectives. The persistence of a widespread assumption within the HCS in the early 1970s that foreign policy was 'a separate area, outside the normal policy process' owed much to its institutional separation, not only as the responsibility of the Foreign Office within Whitehall but as the careful guarded expertise of a separate élite.[6] Awareness throughout Whitehall of the implications of domestic policy for intergovernmental relations, and the relevance of intergovernmental relations to domestic policy, is therefore inhibited. Conversely, diplomats whose work abroad in the industrialized countries of the North Atlantic area is increasingly concerned with technical detail and domestic considerations lack both the expertise in technical fields of policy and the direct experience of the domestic constraints on policy needed to master their new roles. Against the reluctance of most home civil servants to travel and the resistance of the Diplomatic Service to any further erosion of its administrative territory, it will be necessary to work at least towards a closer integration of overseas missions in industrialized countries with Whitehall and to widen exchanges between the Diplomatic and Home Civil Services, if not yet towards an eventual merger of the two.

Much of the discussion so far is relevant only to the management of British relations with the countries of the Atlantic area, forming only a small proportion of the states of the international system but the central focus of defence and technological cooperation, the main market for British exports and the main source of manufactured imports (though not of raw materials). Outside this area there will remain for the foreseeable future a need for a corps of specialists, expert in languages and foreign cultures, prepared to spend a considerable proportion of their careers abroad, in conditions of frequent discomfort and occasional danger, attempting to exercise many of the traditional skills of diplomacy.

It is likely that the management of British relations with these countries will continue to resemble the traditional pattern of foreign policy-making, and to require the continued existence of a specialized Department in Whitehall to alert domestic Departments to matters affecting their interests. The trend towards multilateralism, it is true, is also evident here: in the attempted Euro-Arab dialogue, in the apparent strength of OPEC, in the Lomé Convention between the forty-six African, Caribbean, and Pacific states and the European Community, potentially even in relations between East and West Europe. But the different character of their governments and the far narrower range of shared concerns still sharply distinguishes the management of British relations with these hundred or more countries from the management of interdependence within the industrialized Atlantic area.

The Wider Debate

It has been a recurring theme in this study that the secrecy of the policy-making process delays the re-examination of existing assumptions, reinforces the institutional separation of policy management into separate compartments, and inhibits awareness within and outside Whitehall of the interconnection between foreign and domestic issues. At the lower level, of the administration of day-to-day policy on matters of little perceived significance, the Whitehall machinery operates well. At the middle level, of the management of issues of continuing importance to sections of Parliament and the public, within the limits imposed by established foreign policy assumptions and by the prevailing pattern of relations with other governments, the process of policy-making satisfies most demands. Affected interests are consulted – if not as fully as they would always wish; decisions are taken as rapidly as the situation requires, and are as rapidly communicated to those responsible for implementing them. Accountability to Parliament for decisions taken, and ministerial control over the evolution of policy, are not as firm as democratically inclined critics would like; but this is a weakness throughout Whitehall, not one peculiar to matters of foreign policy.

The crucial failure is at the higher level. Time and again, since World War II, questioning of the assumptions underlying foreign policy has successfully been suppressed. Alternatives have been denied, choices avoided; decisions once taken presented as inevitable, scarcely ever re-examined. The most remarkable aspect of the long story of Britain's relationship with the European Community is that at no point has there been a clear public presentation of the alternatives, no wider debate in which the government attempted to educate public opinion and the opposition to emphasize the political consequences, not only of entry, but also of staying out. The Labour government's attitude to the referendum campaign, at the beginning of 1975, seemed only to compound this failure: looking on it as something to be got out of the way as quickly as possible, in a month's campaign, rather than as a long-delayed opportunity to enlighten the public. Over the East of Suez commitment, over devaluation, the issues at stake were as firmly evaded, the choices as determinedly obscured. Over the whole range of British foreign policy, established assumptions continued to determine the direction of policy long after the international environment to which they related had been transformed, long after outside critics had questioned their relevance. The special relationship with the United States, the idea of the Commonwealth as a 'family' which looked to Britain for leadership, the role of sterling, the importance of the independent deterrent: all these and other guiding assumptions clothed British policy when they were long since threadbare. If government is the exercise of choice over strategic decisions, then the record of British foreign policy-making since the war must be adjudged a poor one. At times, the process of government has seemed to be dedicated to the avoidance of choice.

This criticism is not novel.[7] Nor does it differ greatly from similar criticisms of domestic policy-making in, for instance, the management of the British economy. Opinions, however, differ as to whether the central cause lies in the machinery and practice of Whitehall, the pragmatic approach of ministers and civil servants, or the restricted character of the British political debate. In the early 60s reformers hoped to achieve much by institutional change within Whitehall in foreign and domestic policy. The compartmentalization of policy within departmental divisions was to be overcome by strengthening the central apparatus. The consensual style of interdepartmental decision-making was to be counterbalanced by the creation of larger planning staffs, to question established interdepartmental compromises and provide a source of initiative within Whitehall. The introduction of new techniques of policy analysis and review would make for a more rational determination of policy priorities. To some extent these institutional reforms achieved their aims – though the intractability of questions of foreign policy, above all of costing and forecasting accurately enough for rational decision, limited their effectiveness. They represented the 'belief that institutional reform on a broad front can of itself act as a catalyst in bringing about far-reaching changes'. But 'in practice this has meant that institutional reform has often been advocated as an alternative to the much more difficult task of modifying attitudes and behaviours in society' as a whole, above all in political society.[8]

Certainly, the style of Whitehall policy-making, the established assumptions of civil servants, 'the pragmatic approach to events' and the commitment to consensus and compromise have contributed to the slow pace of Britain's adjustment to a changing international environment and to its declining economic and military capabilities.[9] But the civil service cannot bear the whole weight of criticism. There have been at least two attempts at a fundamental reconsideration of the priorities of foreign policy within Whitehall – the work of the Future Policy Committee between 1958 and 1960, and the high-level official review of foreign policy objectives during the 1966 general election.[10] The first stemmed from a prime ministerial initiative; the second apparently took place on the initiative of the officials themselves. Both failed because they were unable to attract the attention or interest of the Cabinet, in the first case because ministers were more concerned with immediate matters, in the second because the resulting papers were deliberately prevented from reaching the Cabinet. If the Foreign Office was slow to appreciate the significance of the European Communities in 1957–8, the firmness of its conversion in the early 60s was such as to arouse the criticism of the doubters. It was not the fault of officials within the Treasury that the Cabinet did not consider devaluation between 1964 and 1967.

Civil servants, moreover, might justifiably reply to outside criticism that it is not their job to question the fundamental assumptions of government policy. That belongs to the *political* domain: to the Prime Minister, the Cabinet, to individual ministers, to Parliament and the political parties. Politicians do not expect to be contradicted on major policies by their civil servants; with some justification, they tend to treat the long-term views of planning staffs as less important than the views of fellow-ministers, fellow-MPs, and their party as a whole. It is not only expecting too much of the civil service to ask it to generate its own wide-ranging criticisms of its working assumptions; it is also profoundly undemocratic, unless such criticisms are linked to a wider debate.

An ideal model of British government would picture the Cabinet as an informed group of political generalists, surveying the balance of policy across the whole range of domestic and foreign issues. In practice, Cabinet ministers are far too preoccupied with departmental policy to keep abreast of developments in other areas, far too concerned with immediate problems to have leisure for more long-term considerations. Ministers have time only to deal with issues and opinions which are forced upon their attention. The problem is that

by and large there is nothing in the British political system, unlike that of the United States, for example, which imposes upon a British Government the need to take into serious account views and information which have not emerged from within the formal machinery established for the administration of foreign affairs and subject, ultimately, to its control.[11]

Politicians share with their civil servants the same intellectual tolerance of ambiguity, the same preference for compromise over open confrontation, which leads to the concealment of objectives and the avoidance of choice – a cast of mind which sharply distinguishes debate upon domestic and foreign political objectives in Britain from the parallel debate in, say, France. How then is it possible to create the conditions which would force upon governments the need to consider information and answer views originating outside Whitehall?

The mechanisms developed within Whitehall to promote the re-examination of objectives over the last decade have contributed something to narrowing the gap between internal consideration of policy and outside criticism. Departmental planning staffs have acted as a bridge between Whitehall and informed opinion, explaining developments in government policy and carrying alternative views back to Whitehall. The Labour government of 1964–70 reportedly looked to junior ministers as a source of new ideas and criticism, as less weighted down by administrative and political responsibilities and as more in touch with party thinking and informed opinion. But junior ministers have not always had the standing to hold the attention of their superiors. Most of them, particularly within the overseas Departments, were themselves heavily burdened with business; the Conservatives, from 1970, decreased their number. The establishment of the Central Policy Review Staff, as a semi-political body with the ear of the Cabinet, and the appointment of a small number of political advisers to ministers in Whitehall, have narrowed the gap a little further. Political advisers have proved of particular value in alerting ministers to party criticism and partisan debate.

Yet the gap between the internal debate within Whitehall and the debate outside – in Parliament, among informed opinion, in the press and in the parties – remains wide. If civil servants have become more open in their contacts with academics in the last ten years, they have become less open with the press – for the most persuasive of reasons, that under both the Labour government of 1964–70 and the Conservative government of 1970–4, ministerial insistence on secrecy about government intentions had led to a series of investigations, from Cabinet to principal level, in pursuit of 'leaks' on foreign and domestic issues.[12] There has been little or no outside investigation of the Whitehall machinery for the management of foreign policy, and little or no commissioning of outside research on problems of foreign policy except for the fields of defence and economic development. The one major investigation, by the Duncan Committee, was limited in its terms of reference and in the time made available, and on its own admission was 'not able to conduct research in depth' (p. 16). In retrospect, its members expressed dissatisfaction both with the shortage of time and with the inadequacy of research.[13] Sometimes major debates could take place within Whitehall without even the most expert opinion outside being aware of their existence.[14] The introduction of 'Green Papers', as a means of encouraging discussion before the line of future policy had been determined, had not extended into any fields of foreign policy. The conclusions of internal re-examinations of policy were not always published. The Newton Report on the COI and information services, in 1971, and the Conservative government's redefinition of priorities in aid, were filed away unseen and undiscussed outside Whitehall.

If, in the perspective of the last ten years, there have been some marginal improvements, in the degree of contact between officials and expert opinion, in the availability of information to parliamentary committees, the long-term view still suggests how much more restricted the debate on foreign policy has become. The nineteenth-century practice of publishing despatches and blue books on diplomatic negotations disappeared with World War II. The series of committees and commissions which investigated major setbacks in foreign and defence policy, the Roebuck Committee on the Crimean War, the Select Committee on the Jameson Raid, the Royal Commission on the Dardanelles, had no parallel after Suez. Characteristically, an official account of the diplomacy and management of the Suez operation, undertaken on the initiative of senior civil servants, is reported to have been declared secret for 100 years, in contrast to the normal thirty year rule foɪ official documents.[15] The Labour government of 1974 came into office, as had its predecessors, committed to a more open flow of information in domestic and foreign matters. But beyond the gesture of Mr Jenkins's visit to Washington, in January 1975, to investigate the working of the Freedom of Information Act, nothing had happened within their first twelve months of office to suggest any major change of policy, or even to foreshadow a relaxation of the Official Secrets Acts.

The consequences of this continuing barrier between Whitehall and the debate outside are several. First, it maintains the boundaries established between different compartments of policy, discouraging the reexamination of assumptions which underpin different fields – that the East of Suez commitment protected British investment and British trade, that sterling was a diplomatic asset – and the reordering of priorities between different fields. In spite of advances in the application of cost-benefit techniques and programme analysis and review, no effort has been made to consider the comparative benefits achieved from expenditure on different instruments of foreign policy: at least, no effort which has reached the attention of Parliament or the press. The defence budget, the aid budget, the information budget, are determined separately within separate expenditure ceilings. Clearly, no exercise in cost-benefit analysis could hope to overcome the many imponderables which cloud the discussion of foreign policy; but an attempt to set out the assumptions behind the existing pattern of external expenditure, in outline, would help to clarify governmental and parliamentary debate.[16]

Secondly, this barrier reinforces the conservatism of Whitehall and limits ministerial access to new ideas. It is difficult for ministers to follow, even on occasion to discover, the debate about alternatives which goes on below them; the hierarchical procedures of Whitehall will have filtered what reaches ministerial desks into an acceptable compromise. Officials in their turn find it difficult to capture ministerial attention for unorthodox proposals, and hesitate to put up ideas which they are doubtful that the minister would approve. Reportedly one of the early discoveries of the CPRS was that ministers had ideas which their officials were completely unaware of, on topics which their officials hesitated to broach for fear of ministerial disapproval. Officials look to ministers for initiatives on redefining policy, while ministers look to officials. If the formulation of policy were less confined within Whitehall, a number of civil servants have argued, it would be far easier for new ideas to take root, at ministerial and at official level.

Thirdly, debate outside is both limited and discouraged. Informed opinion, it is true, has little difficulty in following the evolution of policy, at least in outline. What *is* difficult is to discover the government's intentions on future policy, and so to contribute to the internal debate. But the effort required to uncover information and to piece it together is sufficient to limit the circle of those so informed to the professionally concerned and the economically interested, and to small numbers even of those. The growth of an intelligent interest in foreign policy matters within a wide circle is not encouraged.

Fourthly, the opposition is not informed or educated. The exclusion of Parliament from the internal debate, the unsatisfactory qualities of foreign affairs debates, and the continuing weakness of parliamentary committees in foreign policy matters, keep from the alternative government an awareness of the constraints imposed on government policy by cost and by the international environment.[17] As a result, parliamentary confrontations take place too often on unreal issues; and incoming governments have to undergo a long and painful learning process before they can come to balance their objectives with the capabilities available and with the possibilities offered by the international environment. Between 1964 and 1967 the underlying weakness of the Commonwealth, the declining importance of the American connection, and the increasing importance of relations with continental Europe were all slowly borne in upon the Labour government. In 1970 they were replaced by a Conservative opposition which had re-committed itself to East of Suez, and had given undue credence to reports of Soviet naval intentions in the southern Atlantic and the Indian Ocean. In its turn the Labour opposition between 1970 and 1974 paid more attention in evolving its alternatives in foreign policy to party perceptions than to developments outside, to go through a similarly painful learning process on its return to office. One reason for this, it may be suggested, is the weakness of the floor of the House of Commons as a forum for informed debate. The real debates in Parliament take place upstairs, within the parties themselves: in private, if not in secret.

Fifthly, the wider public is thus not educated or led. If Parliament and the press are only partially aware of the constraints which govern the development of policy, of the growing interdependence between domestic and foreign objectives, then the uninterested public is likely to be in almost total ignorance. This would matter less if politicians were less anxious, on the European Community issue as on other earlier issues, to avoid too sharply disturbing public opinion or going against the limits of what they perceive to be publicly acceptable. Mr Macmillan's 'attempt to sidle into Europe' may perhaps have been the clearest example of 'the non-leadership qualities of British governance';[18] but the second and and third applications to join the European Communities were not distinguished by a markedly firmer lead to public opinion, or a markedly more open debate. Some Labour ministers privately justified their delayed decisions on East of Suez withdrawal and on devaluation, amongst other reasons, by arguing that public opinion would have been unprepared for earlier withdrawals from entrenched positions. But they had done little to prepare public opinion.

Lastly, the government itself is denied the benefit of a sharper clash between articulated alternatives. 'In order to choose, the decision-maker must be reasonably clear about the nature of the alternatives'.[19] Improvements in the Whitehall machinery over the last ten years have helped to clarify the choices available to ministers and to the Cabinet as a whole. But the political context in which they operate, the parliamentary and party environment, does not provide a similar impetus. 'Ministers, ineffectively challenged, lack the stimulus to face, first in their own minds, then among their counsellors, and finally in their policies, the full force of problems.'[20]

'Is it utopian to suppose that one day we can set ourselves long-term objectives at home and abroad, and then work steadily and successfully towards them?'[21] Necessarily, such an ideal must remain utopian: the international environment is too uncertain, the conflicting pressures of domestic politics too intractable. But it is possible to move some way towards a clearer definition of alternatives and priorities. Some further progress, indeed, can still be made within the existing limits of constricted debate. A Cabinet Office unit for strategic planning and for the examination of the overlapping assumptions of departmental policies could be established, either as an extension of the Assessments Staff or of the CPRS or as a separate unit. The number of political advisers in Whitehall could be expanded into a system of ministerial cabinets, keeping ministers informed on the departmental discussion at lower levels and on the debate outside and providing *political* briefs on proposals from other Departments. The provision of expert advice and criticism from outside sources could be improved, and the sources themselves better provided for. There is as yet no equivalent to the relationship between the National Institute for Economic and Social Research and the Treasury in the field of foreign policy. A Foreign Service Institute, or a reoriented and better financed Chatham House, would seem desirable.

Beyond this, however, as Edward Heath said when Leader of the Opposition:

Some of us would like to see further developments in what is published. We would like, for example, to see a deeper analysis of foreign policy, defence policy and home policy in addition to the daily comments and reports. This is a sphere in which the Government can set an example. There should be much greater freedom of discussion about the issues that arise and the alternative courses open to the Government to follow in dealing with them.[22]

For any government which wished to 'set an example' there are a number of fairly straightforward lines of reform. An annual statement of policy, perhaps accompanied by an analysis of the external budget and its various programmes, would help to concentrate minister's minds, to focus debate in Parliament and to inform the interested public. The publication of Green Papers 'from time to time on particular issues so that they can be debated and discussed before conclusions are arrived at' would encourage a more informed political debate.[23] A parliamentary committee on foreign affairs would help to educate the opposition. The publication of a regular bulletin on foreign policy problems, along the lines of the *Department of State Bulletin*, would make it easier for the interested observer to keep abreast of developments.[24] The Labour government's Foreign Secretary, James Callaghan, himself put forward several of these proposals soon after he came to office in March 1974.

Foreign policy is not an idol to be hidden in the temple, untouched by profane hands. The world is getting smaller and as it does so, it gets more dangerous to live in unless we regulate our relationship with other countries and even other continents. [What is needed is] . . . to consider how we can secure full and open debate about these issues which affect such problems as peace and war, riches and poverty, liberty and oppression.[25]

In the past, the realization in opposition of the desirability of such a full and open debate, carried over into the first intentions of new governments, has led to only minor improvements once the habit of government has again taken hold. 'In Britain governing is *meant* to be a mystery': perhaps that is at the root of the problem.[26] The ever increasing interdependence between the issues of foreign and domestic policy make it a matter of urgency that foreign policy-making in Britain should become a less mysterious process.

Sources

THE FOLLOWING LIST includes only the principal published books; all others are set out in the notes to the separate chapters. In order to shorten the references to them, there follows a full list of UK Command papers and House of Commons papers, which are referred to merely by number and date in the notes.

PRINCIPAL PUBLISHED BOOKS

Beloff, Max. *The future of British foreign policy*. London, 1969.
Boardman, Robert & A. J. R. Groom. *The management of Britain's external relations*. London, 1973.
Brown, George. *In my way*. London, 1971.
Butler, Lord. *The art of the possible*. London, 1971.
Darby, Phillip. *British defence policy east of Suez 1947–68*. London, 1973.
Gordon Walker, Patrick. *The Cabinet*. Rev. ed. London, 1972.
Gladwyn, Lord. *The memoirs*. London, 1972.
Kirkpatrick, Sir Ivone. *The inner circle*. London, 1959.
Mackintosh, John P. *The British Cabinet*. 2nd ed. London, 1968.
Strang, Lord. *The Foreign Office*. London. 1955.
Vital, David. *The making of British foreign policy*. London, 1968.
Waltz, Kenneth N. *Foreign policy and democratic politics: the American and British experiences*. Boston, 1967.
Wilson, Harold. *The Labour government 1964–70*. London, 1971.

UK COMMAND PAPERS

Cmd 9138, Apr 1954. Overseas Information Services; summary of the report of the Independent Committee of Enquiry (Drogheda Report).
Cmnd 2097, July 1963. Central organization for defence.
Cmnd 2276, Feb 1964. Committee on Representational Services Overseas 1962–3, Report (Plowden Report).
Cmnd 2592, Mar 1965. Statement on the Defence Estimates 1965.
Cmnd 2736, Aug 1965. Overseas Development: the work of the new ministry.
Cmnd 2764, Sept 1965. The National Plan.
Cmnd 2853, Dec 1965. Committee of Enquiry into the Aircraft Industry, Report. (Plowden Report).
Cmnd 2901, Feb 1966. Statement on the Defence Estimates 1966.
Cmnd 2902, Feb 1966. 1966 Defence Review.
Cmnd 3357, July 1967. Supplementary statement on defence policy.
Cmnd 3638, June 1968. The civil service, vol. 1: Report of the Committee 1966–8 (Fulton Report)
Cmnd 4107, July 1969. Review Committee on Overseas Representation 1968–9, Report (Duncan Report).
Cmnd 4290, Feb 1970. 1970 Defence White Paper.

Cmnd 4506, Oct 1970. The reorganisation of central government.

Cmnd 4656, Apr 1971. British private investment in developing countries.

Cmnd 4814, Nov 1971. A framework for government research and development (Rothschild Report).

Cmnd 4836, Dec 1971. Review Body on Top Salaries, 1st report (Ministers of the Crown and Members of Parliament).

Cmnd 4891. Statement on the Defence Estimates 1972.

Cmnd 5178, Dec 1972. Public expenditure to 1976–7.

Cmnd 5231, Feb 1973. Statement on the Defence Estimates 1973.

Cmnd 5248. Supply Estimates 1973–4 (Memo. by Chief Secretary to the Treasury).

Cmnd 5341. Fisheries dispute between the United Kingdom and Iceland, July 14, 1971 to May 19, 1973.

Cmnd 5445, Oct 1973. An account of the British aid programme; UK memo. to the Development Assistance Committee of the OECD.

HOUSE OF COMMONS PAPERS

HC 222 & 254, 1957–8. Estimates Committee, 6th Report.

HC 252, 1958–9. Estimates Committee, 3rd Report (Commonwealth Relations Office).

HC 282, 1962–3. Estimates Committee, 10th Report (Military expenditure overseas).

HC 42, 1963–4. Estimates Committee, 2nd Report (Transport aircraft).

HC 302, 1963–4. Estimates Committee, 9th Report (Military expenditure overseas).

HC 162, 1964–5. Estimates Committee, 6th Special Report (Sittings of subcommittees overseas).

HC 148, 1965–6. Estimates Committee, 2nd Report.

HC 349, 1966–7. Select Committee on Agriculture, 1st Special Report.

HC 54, 1967–8. Parliamentary Commissioner for Administration, 3rd Report.

HC 365, 1967–8. Estimates Committee, 6th Report (Promotion of exports).

HC 442, 1967–8. Estimates Committee, 7th Report (Overseas aid).

HC 213, 1968–9. Select Committee on Science and Technology, 2nd Report (Defence research).

HC 362, 1968–9. Public Accounts Committee, 3rd Report.

HC 57, 1969–70. Select Committee on Members' Interests (Declaration), Report.

HC 258, 1969–70. Select Committee on Nationalized Industries, 1st Report (The Bank of England).

HC 299, 1970–1. Select Committee on Overseas Aid, Report (with appendix and Proceedings of the Committee).

HC 304, 1970–1. Expenditure Committee, 1st Report (The British Council).

HC 629, 1970–1. Select Committee on Science and Technology, 5th Report (UK space activities).

HC 19, 1971–2. Expenditure Committee, 3rd Special Report (The British Council).

HC 344, 1971–2. Expenditure Committee, 5th Report (Diplomatic staff and overseas accommodation).

HC 393, 1971–2. Select Committee on Parliamentary Questions, Report.

HC 450, 1971–2. Expenditure Committee, 7th Report (Public expenditure and economic management).

HC 516–1, 1971–2. Expenditure Committee, 9th Report, vol. 1.

HC 159–11, 1972–3. Supply Estimates 1972–3, class II (Commonwealth and Foreign).

HC 269, 1972–3. Expenditure Committee, 9th Report (Visit by Defence and External Affairs Sub-Committee to Ottawa and Washington).

HC 399, 1972–3. Expenditure Committee, 12th Report (Nuclear weapon programme).

HC 114–1, 1973–4. Supply Estimates, Class I (Government and finance).

HC 114–11, 1973–4. Supply Estimates, Class II (Commonwealth and foreign).

HC 114–111, 1973–4. Supply Estimates, Class III (Home and Justice).

Notes

Chapter 1. Introduction

1 John Locke, *The second treatise of government* (Oxford, 1948), pp. 72–3.
2 David Vital, *The making of British foreign policy* (1968), p. 49.
3 F. S. Northedge, reviewing Vital (n. 2) in *International Affairs*, July 1969, p. 524.
4 Joseph Frankel, *The making of foreign policy: an analysis of decision-making* (1963), p. 1.
5 Harold Nicolson, *Diplomacy*, rev. ed. (Oxford, 1963), p. 67.
6 Ibid., p. 28.
7 Ibid., ch. 7.
8 Cmnd 4107, July 1969, Review Committee on Overseas Representation 1968–9, *Report*, p. 22 (hereafter Duncan Report).
9 Graham Allison, *Essence of decision: explaining the Cuban crisis* (Boston, 1971), p. 4.
10 There is room for a comparative study of the relationship between the status of a country's Foreign Service and the formulation and management of its foreign policy; contrasting, perhaps, the United States and West Germany with Britain and France.
11 Charles E. Lindblom, 'The science of muddling through', *Public Administration Review*, 1959, p. 86.
12 To deny the existence of any discoverable 'national interest', one Whitehall official commented, is like telling a doctor that there is no such thing as a cure. Even if a doctor (or a diplomat) will admit intellectually that the concept is impossible to define, his professional self-respect depends on its adoption as a working assumption.
13 This aphorism is attributed to Don K. Price, of Harvard University.
14 James N. Rosenau, ed., *Domestic sources of foreign policy* (New York, 1967), pp. 34–41.
15 C. Wright Mills, *The power elite* (New York, 1956), p. 245.
16 What follows is an adaptation to the British political system of a framework developed by Theodore Lowi for the analysis of American foreign policy, set out in 'Making democracy safe for the world', in Rosenau, pp. 295–331. C. J. Friedrich, in R. B. Farrell, ed., *Approaches to the study of international and comparative politics* (Evanston, 1966), 97–119, suggests a similar division.
17 Helen Wallace, in *National governments and the European Communities* (London, 1973), pp. 39–43, notes the tendency for foreign ministries to seek to impose a 'political' framework on sectoral issues claimed by other ministries.
18 Duncan Report, p. 18. The Queen's Award for Exports and the use of the honours list to reward leading exporters can be seen as attempts to raise the symbolic importance attached to this unglamorous activity.
19 Walter Bagehot, *The English Constitution*, with introd. by R. H. S. Crossman (London, 1964).
20 Andrew Shonfield, in *Observer*, 31 Dec 1972.
21 George Brown, *In my way* (1971), ch. 9.

22 Harold Wilson, *The Labour government* (1970), pp. 768–70.
23 Henry Kissinger, *American foreign policy* (New York, 1969), p. 20.

Chapter 2. The Whitehall Machinery
1 Cmnd 2276, Feb 1964 (hereafter Plowden Report), paras 87 & 410.
2 Lord Strang, *The Foreign Office* (1955), p. 147.
3 Ernest Davies, MP, 'The Foreign and Commonwealth Services', in W. A. Robson, ed., *The civil service in Britain and France* (London, 1956), p. 72; Hugh Thomas, ed., *The Establishment* (London, 1959); Anthony Sampson, *Anatomy of Britain* (London, 1962); Vital, ch. 5.
4 Cmnd 3638, June 1968.
5 FCO, *The merger of the Foreign Office and the Commonwealth Office*, Oct 1968, p. 8.
6 This list is taken from R. G. S. Brown, *The administrative process in Britain* (London, 1970), pp. 31–4.
7 These, with the Finance department, Protocol and Conference department, and Office Services, accounted for some 700 personnel of all grades (HC 159–II, 1972–3).
8 HC 54, 1967–8; R. G. S. Brown, *The administrative process in Britain*, p. 103.
9 The Duncan Report, p. 56, noted that in 1969 there was a total of 309 administrative-grade personnel in the geographical and functional departments of the FCO, not including a further 28 in information and 39 in administration. This is over twice as many as the 126 administrative personnel in the Treasury, which similarly holds to informal working methods.
10 HC 159–II, 1972–3.
11 It might alternatively be argued that it was the reduction in the FCO's ministerial strength which made a further reduction in the number of senior officials impossible.
12 Although no assigned responsibilities were ever publicly announced, this system did receive occasional notice in the press. Thus in the *Guardian* of 24 Feb 1970, for instance, Maurice Foley was described as 'the Minister responsible for relations with African Governments south of the Sahara'.
13 Strang, *Foreign Office*, p. 116.
14 627 HC Deb., 1996, 28 July 1960.
15 The flow of policy within the FCO is discussed further in ch. 4. For a more extended discussion of the FCO see Christina Larner, 'The Foreign and Commonwealth Office', in Robert Boardman & A. J. R. Groom, eds, *The management of Britain's external relations* (1973), pp. 31–73.
16 In 1972 there were overseas posts in 18 Spanish-speaking countries, with a total of 183 home-based staff, compared to posts in 17 Arabic-speaking countries, with 217 home-based staff (HC 159–II, 1972–3).
17 *Georgia Journal of Int. & Compar. Law*, Autumn 1971, contains two useful articles on the work and status of the FCO Legal Advisers.
18 See, for instance, A. N. Oppenheim & Ian Smart, 'The British diplomat', in Boardman & Groom, pp. 75–116.
19 Cmnd 4506, Oct 1970, p. 11.
20 The Plowden Report, para. 27, had similarly outlined the 'main tasks' of the three overseas services as: advice, negotiation, the cultivation of friendly relations, trade promotion, information work, protection of British persons and interests, and technical assistance.
21 *The Times* leader, 17 July 1969; Duncan Report, p. 52.
22 Duncan Report, p. 60.
23 Plowden Report, para. 171.

24 Strang, *Foreign Office*, p. 18.
25 The distinction implied here between the character of British interests in different categories of countries was not fully accepted by the Diplomatic Service.
26 Douglas Hurd, 'Splendours and miseries at the FO', *Sunday Times*, 8 June 1969.
27 David Spanier, *Europe, our Europe* (London, 1972), p. 91.
28 Parallels are occasionally drawn with the situation in American and German overseas posts, where conflicting loyalties and separate channels of communication with the national capital have sometimes resulted in incoherence and inconsistency. For the Duncan Committee's discussion of this point see ch. X, esp. pp. 126–7, and Annex Q, p. 202, which recommend the abolition of the distinctions between different terms of service abroad, and the acceptance of direct secondment to the Diplomatic Service.
29 Sampson, *The new anatomy of Britain* (London, 1971), p. 302; Sam Brittan, *Steering the economy* (Harmondsworth, 1970), p. 26.
30 Plowden Report, paras. 16, 61; Duncan Report, pp. 29–30, 128.
31 Vital, p. 49.
32 Sir Frank Figgures, 'The Treasury and external relations', in Boardman & Groom, p. 161.
33 Lord Bridges, *The Treasury*, 2nd ed. (London, 1966), provides a fuller account of the division of responsibilities within the Treasury in the mid-60s.
34 Richard A. Chapman, 'The Bank of England: not a nationalised industry or a public corporation, but a nationalised institution', *Parliamentary Affairs*, Summer 1971, p. 209.
35 *Civil Service List*, 1972, cols 287–381. The Directorate of Economics (C), for instance, included among its varied responsibilities 'Advice on unremunerative railway services, Channel Tunnel and rural buses'.
36 John P. Mackintosh, *The British Cabinet* (1968), p. 454; Patrick Gordon Walker, *The Cabinet* (1972), p. 115.
37 Gordon Walker, p. 88.
38 Mackintosh, *The British Cabinet*, p. 458.
39 Lord Butler, *The art of the possible* (1971), p. 181. It was suggested by members of the Labour government that Arthur Bottomley's removal from the CRO in the July 1966 reshuffle was due to the Prime Minister's belief that he would oppose a settlement with Rhodesia, at a time when an agreement appeared possible.
40 Gordon Walker, pp. 87–9.
41 Mackintosh, *The government and politics of Britain* (London, 1970), p. 62. The minister in question was Douglas Jay, who had prepared a paper countering the arguments for applying to join the European Community.
42 Colin Seymour-Ure, 'The disintegration of the Cabinet and the neglected question of Cabinet reform', *Parliamentary Affairs*, Summer 1971, pp. 196, 200.
43 Mackintosh, *The British Cabinet*, p. 278.
44 Cmnd 2097, 1963.
45 Such visits, not unnaturally, are something of an attraction to departmental ministers. Pressure for foreign visits, particularly to European countries, built up to such an extent in the late 60s that the FCO attempted to impose an informal system of priorities.
46 *Civil Service List*, 1973; Cmnd 5248, Mar 1973, p. 52. These figures do not include the Historical Section or the Central Statistical Office.
47 George Brown's allegations in his memoirs, p. 147, that 'we had No. 10 Downing Street trying to maintain a private Foreign Office in exactly the same way' as the White House, during his period as Foreign Secretary,

referred to this single official; and are perhaps best understood in terms of the atmosphere of mutual suspicion which pervaded the Labour government in 1966 and 1967.

48 These sentiments from officials were expressed in similar terms to the author from members of most home Departments in Whitehall. The attitude is not of course unique to civil servants in Britain. Compare, for instance, Harold Malmgren's comment in 'Managing foreign economic policy', *Foreign Policy*, Spring 1972, p. 61: 'At present, the State Department is perceived by other departments and by Congress to be the spokesman for foreign nations. Even some Foreign Service officers see themselves in this role.'

49 Sir Edward Playfair, 'Who are the policy-makers?', *Public Administration*, 1965, p. 267.

50 Lord Strang, *Home and abroad* (London, 1956), p. 303.

51 Sir Cecil Parrott, quoted in *Sunday Times*, 14 Apr 1968.

52 Lord Chalfont, 'The praying mantis of Whitehall', *New Statesman*, 6 Nov 1970. But see also the reply from Michael Stewart, MP, ibid., 30 Nov 1970.

53 Ronald Butt, 'A too rigid diplomacy', *The Times*, 13 Mar 1969; David Wood, 'Schizophrenia at the Foreign Office', ibid., 26 Oct 1970.

54 Vital, p. 98.

55 It may also be noted that in the early 60s this political suspicion of the civil service extended, for the Labour Party at least, to the whole of Whitehall. See the Labour Party's evidence to the Fulton Committee in *The Civil service*, vol. 5, June 1968, p. 655.

56 The Labour government in March 1974 continued this innovation, bringing in the party's international secretary from Transport House; though his salary was met from public funds.

57 Sir Frederick Hoyer-Millar, PUS Foreign Office, in evidence to HC 232, 1957–8, qu. 1507. He went on: 'In a properly managed Department, as we understand it, if there is any sort of dispute between departments or Under-Secretaries or Deputy Under-Secretaries, I have to settle it first. We try to avoid ever going to the Minister and saying that half the Foreign Office thinks this and the other half thinks that: will he decide it?'

58 Lord Gladwyn, *The memoirs* (1972), p. 176.

59 George Brown (pp. 129, 162) writes as if his practice was an innovation; but reportedly several of his predecessors had held similar, if rather less stormy, meetings.

60 Mr Heath, in 1970, chose as his Press Secretary an FCO official with whom he had worked during the first British application to the EEC. Mr Wilson in 1964 had similarly chosen as his first private secretary a man who had served in his private office in the Board of Trade thirteen years before.

61 Figures for resignations, but not the reasons given for resigning, were provided in a written answer to a parliamentary question (570, HC Deb 86, 22 May 1957). One of the few who did resign on this issue, Evan Luard, later returned to the Foreign Office as a Labour minister.

62 *The Times*, 21 Feb 1970.

63 Cmnd 5178, Dec 1972, pp. 26–8.

64 HC 344, 1971–2, pp. 10, 25.

65 HC 254, 1957–8, qu. 293 & p. 402.

66 Ibid., Sir Frederick Hoyer-Millar in his evidence, qu. 1452, for instance, asked specifically for a margin of £2m per year.

67 HC 344, p. 11.

68 Ibid., pp. 15–18.

69 Duncan Report, Annex D, p. 170.

Chapter 3. The Flow of Policy

1 Thus Harold Nicolson, in his novel *Public faces*, has one of the FO private secretaries complaining to a colleague that 'This telephone business is becoming a curse. Instead of sending telegrams or even messages to the Communications Department in the ordinary way, these lousy Embassies have developed a habit of telephoning to you or me. It gives them a sense of personal contact with the Secretary of State' (Portway ed., 1969, first publ. 1932), p. 215.

2 Twenty years before Lord Strang had similarly noted the difficulty of checking the expansion of communications traffic, given the improving capacity of the channels available and the expanding range of subjects covered. 'In the devising of policy at the centre one can never know enough about the facts on which it must be based; and the more facilities there are for obtaining information from the outposts, the more untiringly it must be sought' (*Foreign Office*, p. 41).

3 Dudley Seers, 'The structure of power', in H. Thomas, ed., *Crisis in the civil service* (London, 1968), p. 100.

4 Robert Carr, the Home Secretary, in defending the secrecy of government documents concerned with foreign affairs in the debate on the Franks Committee report on the Official Secrets Act, observed that 'A great deal of information of a confidential character is exchanged between Britain and her allies on the understanding that it will not be divulged . . .' (858 HC Deb., 1899, 29 June 1973).

5 A not inaccurate picture of the scale, classification, and potential value of an embassy's archives is contained in John Le Carré's novel, *A small town in Germany*.

6 Simon Winchester in *Guardian*, 17 June 1971. In the House of Commons on 14 May 1971 the Minister for Overseas Development, Richard Wood, had stated that he was 'awaiting reports from charitable associations and from the United Nations High Commission before deciding on the Government's response'.

7 *Sunday Times*, 11 Feb 1973; Geoffrey McDermott, *The Eden legacy* (London, 1969), pp. 133–9.

8 Thus, for instance, the heads of mission to the six European Community countries, to the Communities in Brussels and to EFTA met with the British negotiator, George Thomson, and officials for two-day discussions in June 1969 and March 1970, and the seven ambassadors to East European countries met with ministers and officials for a four-day conference in London in April 1972 (*The Times*, 10 Mar 1970; *Guardian*, 15 Apr 1972).

9 Britain's resources, in terms both of prestigious schools and good hospitals, as well as the residual ties of affection for this country retained by statesmen who were trained or educated here, and also the convenience of London airport as a stopover point during intercontinental journeys, all boost the flow of important foreign visitors, adding to the opportunities available for direct consultations and to the burdens on ministerial time.

10 Civil Service Commission leaflet inviting applications for Assistant Research Officers in the Diplomatic Service, Feb 1973.

11 Eli Kedourie, *The Chatham House version* (London, 1970), pp. 352–3; Chatham House Annual Reports.

12 Its function as an institutional memory for the Foreign Office has been assisted by the provision from within its ranks, over a period of years, of the official interpreters for the Foreign Secretary and the Prime Minister in Russian, Chinese, and Arabic.

13 An interesting case-study of this system, already in operation in the mid-1930s, is to be found in 'A clearing with Spain', pp. 201–78 in F. M. G.

Willson, *Administrators in action* (London, 1961), vol. 1. During the Anglo-Spanish negotiations of 1934–5 the Commercial Secretary in Madrid was writing direct to the Department of Overseas Trade, the Treasury representative direct to the head of Spanish Exchange Control; both he and the Bank of England representative also made 'almost daily' telephone calls to their home offices while negotiating in Madrid. Records of these were, however, taken and circulated together with other material among the interested parties in Whitehall, and thus a coherent British position was maintained throughout.

14 Lord Butler (p. 229), notes that for the Victoria Falls Conference of June–July 1963, which led to the agreed dissolution of the Central African Federation, the four Whitehall Departments most concerned 'produced the most massive briefing', which was later 'used by my advisers to provide the framework of my speeches'. During the Labour government's approach to the European Community in 1967 Mr Wilson circulated '140 pages of fairly closely printed foolscap' to his Cabinet colleagues. These were supplemented by 'a further series of authoritative papers, some of them very lengthy and on almost every issue raised' (*The Labour government*, pp. 373, 386). Few ministers can have read more of these than the opening summaries and the annotations added by their official advisers.

15 The origins and development of the JIC are discussed in Gladwyn, p. 95, and in F. A. Johnson, *Defence by committee* (London, 1960), ch. 10. Public reference to the Assessments Staff, however, hardly extends beyond the pages of *Who's Who*.

16 Roger Hilsman, *To make a nation; the politics of foreign policy in the administration of John F. Kennedy* (New York, 1967), p. 565.

17 *Her Majesty's Diplomatic Service* (Civil Service Commission & COI, 1970 ed.).

18 'Decision-taking in the Foreign and Commonwealth Office', memo. from Sir Paul Gore-Booth, PUS, 21 Oct 1968; reprinted (as an indication of the preferred pattern of Whitehall decision-taking) as Annex 3 to Sir Richard Clarke, *New trends in government* (London, 1971).

19 *Graduate Careers in the Diplomatic Service* (Civil Service Commission & COI, 1967, p. 21).

20 See also, for comparison with Gore-Booth's memorandum, a similar circular prepared by one of his predecessors in 1949, which lays particular emphasis on qualities of judgment: 'Conduct of Office Business', reprinted in pp. 207–13 of Sir Ivone Kirkpatrick, *The inner circle* (1959).

21 'Decision-making in the Foreign and Commonwealth Office', para. 6.

22 Adapted from Strang, *Foreign Office*, p. 155.

23 Ibid., p. 156.

24 The quotation is, again, from Strang, p. 155. The extent to which official descriptions of current procedures matched Lord Strang's description of procedures twenty years before in itself provides an example of the influence of institutional structures and practices on policy-making.

25 Cited by Larner, in Boardman & Groom, p. 59.

26 Gordon Walker, p. 44.

27 Ibid., p. 118.

28 Harold Wilson (pp. 609–11), presents the Soames affair as a Foreign Office coup, successful against his more cautious reaction because his imminent departure for Bonn prevented him from bringing prime ministerial and Cabinet counter-pressures to bear. In the case of the invasion of Czechoslovakia, intelligence reports had allowed a certain amount of official preparation.

29 In normal circumstances the Foreign Office is manned at night by a rota of duty officers, who have the use of an apartment in the Foreign Office building, and who can take immediate action when urgent reports come in.

30 *Diplomatic Service List*, 1972, p. 11.
31 J. G. March & others, *Organizations* (New York, 1958), p. 185.
32 T. Balogh, 'The apotheosis of the dilettante', in Thomas, *The Establishment*, p. 34; A. H. Birch, *The British system of government*, 2nd ed. (London, 1967), p. 200.
33 In Robson, *The civil service in Britain and France*, p. 78.
34 Vital, pp. 109, 110.
35 See e.g. Michael Banks, 'Professionalism in the conduct of foreign policy', *International Affairs*, Oct 1968, pp. 720–34; or Geoffrey Goodwin in Michael Leifer, ed., *Constraints and adjustments in British foreign policy* (London, 1972), pp. 40, 50.
36 Larner, in Boardman & Groom, p. 69.
37 Philip Darby, *British defence policy east of Suez*, 1947–68 (1973), p. 144.
38 Cmnd 4506, para. 44.
39 Nevil Johnson, 'Editorial: the reorganisation of central government', *Public Administration*, Spring 1971, p. 9.
40 The Plowden Committee noted that pay scales were lower than in the rest of the Diplomatic Service, fewer of the staff established and career prospects poor; but observed that 'We do not think that the Research cadre could necessarily expect promotion prospects of the same order as those of regular career officers' (paras. 332, 330).
41 Gladwyn, p. 108.
42 Darby, pp. 17, 141.
43 Plowden Report, para. 225.
44 Duncan Report, Annex D, pp. 170–2.
45 For an illustration of this difficulty, see the attempted 'Measurement of success in the export promotion work of the Diplomatic Service', in HC 344, 1971–2, pp. 13–18. But the foreign policy field is not alone in facing difficulties in relating costs to objectives and in assessing the marginal benefits of extra expenditure on the degree of success or failure achieved. 'Although studies are in process, there is currently no way of estimating the marginal contribution of an additional policeman to the campaign against crime' (R. G. S. Brown, *The administrative process*, p. 80).
46 Duncan Report, pp. 44–5. Significantly, it commented that 'Without new machinery and procedures, strategic thinking on organisational questions seems unlikely to get the high-level attention it deserves'.
47 Cmnd 4506, para. 44.
48 This 'inevitablist' approach to foreign policy-making was perhaps most sharply illustrated by the Labour minister who argued that any government, of whatever party, would have made the decision to withdraw from East of Suez no sooner than July 1967 and no later than January 1968, and any opposition would have opposed it; rubbing his point home by outlining the arguments with which a Labour opposition would have opposed it.
49 Kenneth Waltz, in *Foreign policy and democratic politics* (1967), comes to this general conclusion, though he attributes it to the dominant style of British politicians and to the patterns of political debate. 'The processes of politics in Britain do not readily result in a sequence of confrontation and resolution; rather, they tend toward evasion, confusion of issues, uncertainty, inactivity, and stalemate' (p. 264).
50 John Day, 'A failure of foreign policy: the case of Rhodesia', in Leifer, *Constraints and adjustments in British foreign policy*, p. 151.
51 Ibid., p. 162.
52 Quoted by Seers, in Thomas, *Crisis in the civil service*, p. 98.
53 Seymour-Ure, *Press, politics, and the public*, p. 40.

Chapter 4. The Domestic Context

1 For a full discussion of the opportunities for parliamentary discussion of foreign policy, and an examination of their use, see Peter G. Richards, *Parliament and foreign affairs* (London, 1967), esp. ch. 5.

2 One newly-elected MP's unsolicited postbag included in September 1970, a month when Parliament was not sitting, material from eight foreign embassies and from four British and two American pressure groups. Anthony Barker & Michael Rush, *The Member of Parliament and his information* (London, 1970), pp. 108–17, discuss the regular flow of diplomatic 'glossies' in some detail.

3 The IPU sends some 14 or 15 Members to its annual conference and a smaller number to the annual spring meeting held in a different country each year. In the late 60s it also sponsored some half-dozen visits abroad every year, each of around five MPs. The CPA, within a rather more closely knit international community, sponsored some ten foreign visits a year, involving 40 to 50 MPs.

4 Leading opposition Members, as well as backbenchers of all parties, travel abroad in this way. From 1951–6, for instance, Harold Wilson acted as economic adviser to Montague L. Meyer, a firm of timber importers. 'He went overseas for the Meyer organisation; he met other businessmen in the country; he helped to promote East-West trading relations' Marcia Williams, *Inside Number 10* (London, 1972, p. 104).

5 Foreign observers at trials in Athens in January 1973, for example, included Paul Rose, MP, representing 'the Campaign for the Release of All Political Prisoners in Greece', and Dr Maurice Miller, MP (*Guardian*, 18 Jan & 1 Feb 1973).

6 Including a partial delegation to the European Parliament and substitute delegates to the Council of Europe Assembly, these involved 58 MPs and 18 peers.

7 Dame Joan Vickers, MP, was, for instance, UK delegate to the UN Status of Women Commission in 1962–3.

8 Forty-five of these, from the Anglo-Afghan to the British Yugoslav Parliamentary Groups, were affiliated to the IPU and 13 to the CPA.

9 In 1969–70, for example, the Indo-British Group was holding monthly 'curry lunches' at the Indian High Commission, which up to 30 of its 100 members attended at any one time.

10 *Who Does What in Parliament*, no. 5, 1973, pp. 56–69.

11 Eight Conservative MPs in the 1970–4 Parliament were former members of the Diplomatic Service. A further five Conservatives and one Labour Member had served in the Colonial Service, while another Labour MP had earlier worked to organize African trade unions in Kenya. Wartime and immediate postwar service linked individual MPs with countries as diverse as Germany, Yugoslavia, and Indonesia.

12 Hugh Noyes, in *The Times*, 15 Dec 1972, considered Mr Callaghan's contribution to the first of these, as Shadow Foreign Secretary, to be 'one of the finest displays of political dexterity we have seen for some time, . . . tossing satisfying sops to his comrades in the Tribune group of left-wing MPs while at the same time delicately refraining from committing himself or the Shadow Cabinet to anything'.

13 Peter G. Richards, 'Parliament and the parties', in Boardman & Groom, p. 252. Two of these twelve debates concerned Northern Ireland, two relations with South Africa, two relations with Nigeria during and after the civil war.

14 HC 393, 1971–2, app. 9, Memo. from the Table office, House of Commons.

15 One or two MPs claimed to have had questions suggested to them by friends in the Foreign Office concerned to make sure that a matter for which they are responsible is brought to the attention of the Foreign Secretary. No civil servant would admit to such a tactic, involving as it does a deliberate attempt to bypass the official hierarchy; but it is quite possible, given the number of informal contacts between officials and those MPs with overseas experience, that this does happen from time to time.

16 Kirkpatrick, p. 209.

17 Richards, *Parliament and foreign affairs*, p. 110. An analysis of Parliamentary Questions during the 1962–3 session, for instance, showed that fourteen MPs were responsible for just over half the oral questions on foreign affairs. Of these, ten were identifiably 'left wing' on foreign policy within the Labour Party; the single Conservative had opposed his government's withdrawal from Suez, and was later to become a member of the Monday Club's Rhodesia Committee.

18 580 HC Deb., 710, 19 Dec 1957.

19 670 HC Deb., 1015, 30 Jan 1963.

20 HC 349, 1966–7, p. 3.

21 For the opposing views, see J. P. Mackintosh, 'Failure of a reform', *New Society*, 28 Nov 1968, p. 791, and the contributions of Alfred Morris & James Johnson to Alfred Morris, ed., *The growth of parliamentary scrutiny by committee* (Oxford, 1970). William Rodgers, MP, a Labour junior minister in the Foreign Office, claimed in *Socialist Commentary*, Apr 1971, p. 13, that George Brown as Foreign Secretary had at first been attracted by the idea of a parliamentary foreign affairs committee, but had abruptly changed his mind when he realized that it would investigate questions of policy.

22 HC 282, 1962–3 & HC 302, 1963–4.

23 Nevil Johnson, *Parliament and administration* (London, 1966), p. 63.

24 Colin Turpin, *Government contracts* (Harmondsworth, 1972), p. 41.

25 HC 57, 1969–70, app. 7, qu. 623.

26 Cmnd 4836, Dec. 1971, para. 42b.

27 HC 162, 1964–5, 'Sittings of Sub-Committees Overseas', contains an early discussion of this question, which was becoming more acute as more and more dependent territories were given their independence.

28 HC 629, 1970–1. One committee member had also visited French Guiana with an international group of MPs from European countries, as guests of ELDO, which maintained a rocket base there.

29 HC 339, 1972–3, para. 3. See also HC 516–1, 1971–2, para. 3.

30 Adam Raphael, in *Guardian*, 9 July 1973, estimated that British companies operating in South Africa had raised wages paid by a total of £5m since the committee announced its investigation.

31 Mark Abrams, 'British elite attitudes and the common market', *Public Opinion Quarterly*, Summer 1965, pp. 236–46. Mr Abrams's sample broke down in terms of occupations as follows: 26 per cent professors and administrators, 18 per cent civil servants, 15 per cent business, 10 per cent professions, 9 per cent communicators and 'artists', 7 per cent clergy, 6 per cent politicians, and 9 per cent others.

32 D. C. Watt, 'The nature of the foreign policy-making elite in Britain', *Personalities and powers: studies in the formulation of British foreign policy in the twentieth century* (London, 1963), pp. 1–15.

33 William Wallace, 'The role of interest groups', in Boardman & Groom, p. 272. This group, which produced an influential report on aid policy, also contained a distinguished foreign political exile, Dr K. A. Busia.

34 The information in this paragraph is drawn from *Who's Who*, 1970.

35 *The Times* of 3 May 1972, for instance, recorded on its court page a luncheon

at the Belgian Embassy at which the Belgian Prime Minister entertained four Cabinet ministers, several leading Labour MPs, and a number of officials from several Whitehall Departments. The Prime Minister's dinner in his guest's honour included a larger number of MPs, officials, businessmen, and trade union leaders. On the same day the CBI entertained the ambassadors of the Scandinavian countries, and the Minister of Overseas Development entertained British and American parliamentarians and others attending an international conference.

36 *Guardian, The Times*, 18 Apr 1973.

37 Preamble to RIIA Charter.

38 HC 114–II, 1973–4, pp. 25 & 72.

39 Vital, p. 87. On the origins of ISS see also Geoffrey Williams & Bruce Reed, *Denis Healey and the policies of power* (London, 1971), p. 139, and Laurence W. Martin, 'The market for strategic ideas in Britain: the Sandys era', *American Political Science Review*, Mar 1962, p. 34.

40 Alastair Buchan's successor as director of the International Institute for Strategic Studies, as it later became, was another former defence journalist, François Duchene, of *The Economist*. Hugh Hanning, previously defence correspondent of the *Guardian*, was editor of the *RUSI Journal* from 1968 to 1970.

41 By 1972, for example, *The Times* had only one diplomatic correspondent, without the one or more assistants of earlier years. The disappearance of a corps of separate Commonwealth correspondents had also reduced numbers and widened coverage.

42 Seymour-Ure, *The Press, politics and the public*, p. 258.

43 Philip Elliott & Peter Golding, 'The news media and foreign affairs', in Boardman & Groom, p. 315, give a geographical breakdown of national dailies and the broadcasting companies in May 1971.

44 Brittan, *Steering the economy*, p. 90.

45 *Diplomatic Service List*, 1972, p. 7; the wording of this part of the Planning Staff rubric had remained unchanged since 1967.

46 For the origins of these two panels, see William Wallace, in Boardman & Groom, p. 273.

47 Michael Howard, reviewing Roger Morgan, ed., *The study of international affairs: essays in honour of Kenneth Younger* (London, 1972) in *Sunday Times*, 13 Aug 1972. Professor Howard was himself at this time a member of Chatham House's Research Committee.

48 Since no regulations controlling the activities of voluntary organizations in the foreign policy field exist in Britain, no assessment of the numbers of different organizations is possible. The author attempted to compile a list of such groups from references to their activities in the quality press during the academic year 1969–70. This source alone yielded over 300 organizations, though some were only temporary 'campaigns'.

49 In 1970 five of the thirty-one CBI committees were concerned with international questions: the Europe Steering Committee, chaired by Derek Ezra of the National Coal Board, the Overseas Committee, chaired by the CBI President, Sir Arthur Norman; the Overseas Investment Committee, chaired by Sir Duncan Oppenheim of British-American Tobacco who had for some years been Chairman of the Council of Chatham House; the International Labour Committee and the Overseas Scholarship Board (CBI, Annual Report, 1969 & 1970). In 1973 the CBI divided its Economic Committee into three to cope with 'the increased diversity of its economic activities'; one of these, the Financial Policy Committee, was to be responsible for overseeing 'aspects of domestic and international monetary policy which are of interest to industry' (*The Times*, 4 May 1973).

50 794 HC Deb., 1711, 29 Jan 1970.
51 In the exceptional case of the ILO, employer and trade union representatives are formally required to be part of the British delegation. The Ministry of Agriculture has customarily included representatives of the NFU and the National Union of Agricultural Workers on the UK delegation to the FAO, meeting all the expenses involved, while its Fisheries Department has found it useful to take representatives of the British Trawlers' Federation to bilateral and multilateral meetings.
52 The Society for Anglo-Chinese Understanding and the Anglo-Rhodesian Society are clearly more politically engaged than the Anglo-Belgian Union and the Anglo-Norse Society. For a fuller discussion of interested and promotional groups in the foreign policy field, see William Wallace, in Boardman & Groom, pp. 265–83.
53 Support for voluntary organizations is not confined to specific country societies. The Victoria League for Commonwealth Friendship reported in 1969 that various goods contributed by High Commissions to the Commonwealth stall at its 'Christmas market' had contributed generously to the £4,000 which the event added to its funds. Other Commonwealth High Commissions provided goods for a stall run by the Movement for Colonial Freedom that year, similarly combining promotion of their countries' products with support for a sympathetic pressure group.
54 Ian Waller, 'Pressure politics: MP and PRO', Encounter, Aug 1962, noted the strenuous efforts of the Central African Federation to influence British opinion through this means.
55 HC 252, 1958–9, p. 56, cited by Kenneth Robinson in W. B. Hamilton & others, eds, A decade of the Commonwealth, 1955–64 (Durham, North Carolina, 1966), p. 100.
56 Darby, p. 325.
57 According to Patrick Keatley, in the Guardian, 29 June 1973, their Foreign Minister had been waiting in Geneva for the result of the election. The embarrassment which his arrival caused was reflected in the four day interval before he was able to meet Conservative ministers.
58 B. C. Koh, 'Cultivating Kim', Problems of Communism, Jan–Apr 1971, p. 82.
59 The Times, 30 Oct 1970.
60 HC 57, 1969–70, App 18 & 20.
61 Christopher Driver, The disarmers: a study in protest (London, 1964), p. 93 & passim.
62 Apart from one concert, a lieder recital, and a small art exhibition, the major event the Fanfare for Europe programme listed for Manchester was a series of 'Films from EEC Countries'.
63 Ian Waller, 'The press and politicians', in Richard Rose, ed., Studies in British politics (London, 1966), p. 178.
64 The D-notice system and the operations of the Defence, Press and Broadcasting Committee are described in the report of a 1967 Privy Council committee of inquiry, Cmnd 3309, and in a long letter from the spokesman of the Committee's Press and Broadcasting Section published in The Times, 10 Aug 1973.
65 For the 1967 episode, see Wilson, pp. 373–6.
66 A partisan view of this case by the journalist himself is given in Jonathan Aitken, Officially secret (London, 1971).
67 Robert Carr, Home Secretary, 858 HC Deb., 1899, 29 June 1973.
68 D. C. Watt, 'Foreign affairs, the public interest, and the right to know', Political Quarterly, Apr–June 1963, p. 123.
69 British academics have been heard to complain that these are made more

freely available to American academics by the British embassy in Washington than by the FCO to their fellows over here.

70 Sir Maurice Dean, in a Discussion Report published by RUSI in 1971, *Does the present central organisation of defence meet the requirements of the seventies?*, p. 3.

71 HC 450, 1971–2, and evidence of Patrick Jenkin, MP, Chief Secretary to the Treasury, to this Committee.

Chapter 5. Defence and Technology

1 The concept of a distinctive 'role' East of Suez did not develop fully until the late 50s; until then the continued necessity of maintaining British bases and forces in the Indian Ocean area was taken for granted.

2 In 1968–9 the defence budget was second only to social security in size among government spending programmes. In 1972–3, four years after the decision to end the East of Suez role, it remained the third largest spending programme (at £3,003m), after social security and the education budget (at £5,050m and £3,569m, respectively), accounting for just under 11% of total public expenditure (Cmnd 5178, Dec 1972, table 2A).

3 The management of Britain's relations with NATO are more extensively discussed in ch. 8.

4 Alastair Buchan, *The implications of a European system for defence technology* (London, 1967), p. 3.

5 *Sunday Times*, 2 July 1972, 29 Apr 1973.

6 Cmnd 5231, Feb 1973, pp. 18–19.

7 *Sunday Times*, 30 Jan 1972; *The Times*, 31 May 1972.

8 Anthony Eden, *Full circle* (London, 1960), p. 367.

9 Mackintosh, *The British Cabinet*, pp. 278–86. Colonel Maurice Hankey, the head of the CID Secretariat at the outbreak of war in 1914, became head of the Cabinet Secretariat as well on its establishment by Lloyd George in 1916.

10 Michael Howard, in *The central organisation of defence*, pp. 5–13, provides a brief history of the evolution of the structure of defence policy-making between 1945 and 1963. Chs 7 & 8 of William P. Snyder, *The politics of British defence policy*, 1945–62, examine the separate service ministries and the incoherent incrementalism which characterized so much of defence policy-making in that period.

11 Howard, p. 23.

12 Peter Nailor, 'Defence policy and foreign policy', in Boardman & Groom, p. 225.

13 Mr Healey's intention, set out in the 1970 Defence White Paper, had been to end 'the long tradition under which there has been a Minister associated specifically with each Service', and to retain only one or more Parliamentary Secretaries with functional responsibilities, under the Minister and his deputy Minister of State (Cmnd 4290, Feb 1970, p. 12). This process progressively reduced the ministerial strength of the MoD, from 7 in 1964 to 6 in 1967, and to 5 in 1970.

14 Cmnd 2097, July 1963, p. 2.

15 Cmnd 2592, Mar 1965, p. 13.

16 The terms are those of Michael Howard, p. 53.

17 Cmnd 5248, p. 58.

18 In the FCO of 1972, one of the two under-secretaries supervising Western Organizations department, the head of Defence Department, and one of his supervising under-secretaries, were among the graduates of the Imperial Defence College (at it had been titled until 1971). The head of the Planning

Staff had just published a book on the political applications of limited force, *Gunboat diplomacy*, written while on a year's secondment to the ISS.

19 Howard, p. 12. It may be noted that the majority of civil servants spent their entire career within one Department, becoming, so to speak, 'Navy men' or 'Army men' in the eyes of serving officers.

20 On the post-1957 manoeuvrings, see Snyder, pp. 166–9 and Andrew Pierre, *Nuclear politics: the British experience with an independent strategic force, 1939–70* (London, 1972), pp. 193–5.

21 *Guardian*, 10 June 1972.

22 Darby (p. 159n.) suggests that 'the Treasury made various attempts to review defence spending' in terms of its overall level and effectiveness at the end of the 1950s, 'but its efforts met with very little success'.

23 The quotation is from Field-Marshall Sir Richard Hull, who was Chief of Defence Staff 1965–7, in a published discussion held at the RUSI in January 1971, on the subject *Does the present central organisation of defence meet the requirements of the 1970s?*

24 Cmnd 2902, Feb 1966, p. 20.

25 For a discussion of the position in the late 50s, see Laurence W. Martin, *American Political Science Review*, Mar 1962, pp. 23–41.

26 Rear-Admiral Morgan-Giles, in *Does the central organisation of defence meet the requirements of the 1970s?*, p. 13.

27 HC 399, 1972–3, p. xvii.

28 HC 269, 1972–3, p. ix.

29 Several reports from the Public Accounts Committee refer to this 'affair': in the 1966–7 session, HC 571, and in the 1967–8 session, HC 154, HC 169, and HC 192.

30 Where not otherwise footnoted, the account here follows that of Darby, chs 7–9. For a parallel study of the major defence review of 1957 and of the constraints upon the Conservative government at that time, see William Wallace, 'World status without tears', in Vernon Bogdanor & Robert Skidelsky, eds., *The age of affluence, 1951–64* (London, 1970).

31 Peter Thorneycroft, then Minister of Defence, speaking in the House of Commons, 31 July 1963 (682 HC Deb., 478).

32 690 HC Deb., 469–70, 26 Feb 1964.

33 Christopher Mayhew, in *Britain's role tomorrow* (London, 1967) p. 134, notes the danger in fixing such a ceiling, in that once it 'is agreed, it ceases to be in the departmental interest of any minister except one – the Minister of Defence – to ensure that commitments are reduced to match'.

34 According to Williams & Reed, *Denis Healey*, p. 172, the American administration linked its willingness to provide monetary support for sterling to a 'reconsideration' of the TSR-2 project.

35 See, for instance, the series of articles in *International Affairs*, Apr 1966.

36 Wilson, p. 297.

37 Gordon Walker, p. 128.

38 Cmnd 3357, July 1967, p. 12.

39 Williams & Reed, pp. 222, 227.

40 Gordon Walker, p. 133.

41 So far as the author could discover, neither the Labour government nor the Conservative opposition consulted the CBI on its views about the contribution a military presence made to political and economic stability during this period. A CBI mission visited Singapore on its own initiative in 1968, to investigate how far the base areas could be converted to industrial use; and was astonished to be provided by the services with individual umbrella-bearers to protect its members from the rain. It returned with its scepticism about the value of the base strengthened.

42 Cmnd 2853, Dec 1965, p. 28. It wisely added that 'to fulfil this role, the industry must be successful'; if it produced only a string of failures 'it will, by virtue of its symbolic role, simply exacerbate the nation's discontent and self-distrust'.

43 Wilson, p. 334.

44 *Old world, new horizons* (The Godkin Lectures, delivered at Harvard in March 1967), (London, 1970), p. 45.

45 Cmnd 2853, p. 27. The Committee however regarded this as a 'supplementary foreign policy argument' to 'the main defence argument for having a domestic industry capable of supplying major weapons systems . . . that it provides a measure of independence in British foreign policy, especially in circumstances where we might have to consider using force' (p. 25).

46 Wilson, pp. 63, 332.

47 The Minister of Supply, Aubrey Jones, declared in the 1958 defence debate that 'we would welcome the development of the ballistic missile as a joint project with any other European country' (583 HC Deb., 500, 26 Feb 1958) – though he cannot have spoken for the government as a whole. According to Andrew Pierre (p. 222), Peter Thorneycroft and Julian Amery (the Minister of Aviation, successor to the Minister of Supply) held exploratory talks with the French government during 1962 on the possibility of an 'entente nucléaire', covering both nuclear weapons and delivery systems.

48 Norman J. Vig, *Science and technology in British politics* (Oxford, 1968), p. 36–43, and ch. 5, *passim*.

49 Wilson, p. 562.

50 The FCO, for instance, argued strongly within Whitehall against reconsideration of the Channel Tunnel: a tangible, if costly, symbol of Britain's European commitment dear to the heart and economic interest of the French government.

51 HC 42, 1963–4, para. 88.

52 HC 629, 1970–1, para. 15. Not unnaturally, civil servants in other Departments complained of the 'narrowness' of the Treasury's approach. Six different Departments held responsibilities for various international activities in the space field, relating to different intergovernmental organizations.

53 HC 148, 1966–7, p. 97. The responsible FO under-secretary dissociated his Department from the whole convention as completely as he could, though he admitted that legal advice had been provided. 'I think it is fair to say that the initiative for the formation of ELDO was not something which the Foreign Office took' (p. 95).

54 HC 629, 1970–1, pp. 245, 247.

55 L. C. J. Orchard, in *Weapons procurement, defence management and international collaboration* (London, Oct 1972), outlines the functions of the Procurement Executive. This also includes a description of the Executive's machinery for international collaboration.

56 Michael Heseltine, quoted in Roger Williams, *European technology: the politics of collaboration* (London, 1973), p. 149.

57 *Productivity of the national aircraft effort*, Report of a Committee appointed by the Minister of Technology (London, 1969). One of its conclusions (in sect 6) was that the Ministry 'should review critically their experience of collaboration projects and seek ways of implementing the policy which are more compatible with efficiency and speedy execution of the work'.

58 HC 362, 1968–9. para. 42.

59 Cmnd 4814, Nov 1971, p. 19. It added, 'if this organization is to exercise any form of oversight of trans-departmental and trans-national science, this distribution of disciplines needs revision'.

60 HC 222, 1957–8, p. 297. He went on to explain: 'I did not mean to say that nothing is being done, but as far as I am aware there is no universal pattern; each country is dealt with *ad hoc*. . . .'

61 The American organization, and the French sales organization established in the same year, are described in John Stanley & Maurice Pearton, *The international trade in arms* (London, 1972), ch. 5, which also includes a description of the development of the British organization.

62 'Promotion of Exports of Defence Equipment', Memo from the Ministry of Technology and the MoD, in HC 365, 1967–8, pp. 347–50.

63 Annual Statements on Defence, 1969–73.

64 Stanley & Pearton, pp. 106–10.

65 Differing accounts of this decision are given in George Brown, pp. 170-4, and Harold Wilson, pp. 470–6.

66 According to Andrew Wilson in *Observer*, 31 Dec 1967, Mr Healey was also swayed by the cancellation of the proposed development of an island base on Aldabra, immediately after devaluation. Without Aldabra, overflying and staging rights in South Africa became necessary to maintain the East of Suez role.

67 The account here is taken primarily from cuttings in the Chatham House press library.

68 The Minister for Overseas Development, for instance, who was reported as among those attending the DOPC meeting on 1 July, could be expected to adopt a cautionary position (*The Times*, 2 July 1970).

69 According to Hugh Stephenson (ibid., 9 Oct 1970), there had 'never, in the experience of many senior civil servants, been an occasion where Whitehall has been so unanimously convinced that a proposed piece of government policy was wrong'. It would be interesting to know how many Cabinet Ministers' minds were changed by the detailed briefs put up by their Departments and by their assumption, in office, of their departmental role.

70 HC 213, 1968–9, para. 130; Cmnd 2901, Feb 1966.

Chapter 6. Economic and Commercial Policy

1 Keith Middlemass, *The diplomacy of illusion* (London, 1972), pp. 259–60.

2 In 1972 a professor in one of Britain's leading university departments of economics replied to an invitation to take part in a conference on the politics of the international economy: 'The teaching of international economics in this university does not concern itself with politics in any way.'

3 Robert Gardner, in Robert W. Cox, ed., *International organisations: world politics* (London, 1969), p. 282.

4 Fred Hirsch, *Money international* (Harmondsworth, 1969), p. 36. The argument here is developed in more detail in William Wallace, 'The management of foreign economic policy in Britain', *International Affairs*, Apr 1974, pp. 251–67.

5 These roughly approximate, in the economic field, to Arnold Wolfers's distinction between 'possession' goals and 'milieu' goals: *Discord and collaboration: essays on international politics* (Baltimore, 1962), pp. 73–80.

6 Henry Roseveare, *The Treasury: the evolution of a British institution* (London, 1969), pp. 317, 321, 322. Mr Roseveare is referring here primarily to the situation in the 1950s.

7 Wilfred Beckerman, *The Labour government's economic record, 1964–70* (London, 1972), p. 14.

8 Roger Opie, 'The making of economic policy', in Thomas, *Crisis in the civil service*, p. 63.

9 See, for instance, W. B. Reddaway & others, *Effects of United Kingdom direct investment overseas* (Cambridge, 1968).

10 See, for instance, Seers, in Thomas, *Crisis in the civil service*, p. 102.

11 The quotation is from Peter Calvocoressi, in Tyrrell Burgess, ed., *Matters of principle: Labour's last chance* (Harmondsworth, 1968), p. 49.

12 Though the inhibiting pressure of their official advisers is suggested by Sir Edward Playfair's self-image of the civil servant 'as the guardian of some form of public interest . . .' in effect, against ministers. 'When I was concerned with overseas finance I found that Ministers of all parties were always terribly ready and willing to break the letter or the spirit of international agreements; it was our job to say: "You cannot do that – the country's good name counts" ' (*Public Administration*, 1965, p. 267).

13 Roseveare, p. 317.

14 The outlines of Treasury internal organization are set out in the annual *British imperial calendar and civil service list*. A fuller account of the division of responsibilities within the Treasury in the mid-6os is given by Lord Bridges, ch. 8.

15 One Treasury official remarked on his sense of shock at first seeing a brief to the Chancellor before a Cabinet discussion on foreign policy, during the Nigerian civil war, which began, 'This is, of course, partly a moral issue . . .' but then went on to discuss the question entirely in terms of its potential impact on the balance of payments. In the committee structure of Whitehall, however, this is the Treasury's proper role.

16 HC 258, 1969–70.

17 Brittan, *Steering the economy* (rev. ed., Harmondsworth, 1971), p. 82; Michael Artis, *Foundations of British monetary policy* (Oxford, 1965), p. 44. Artis further identified a persistent attitude of 'preoccupation with the independence of the Bank from the Government machine' among Bank officials.

18 The quotation is from Sir Douglas Allen (then Permanent Secretary to the Treasury), in evidence to HC 258, 1969–70, qu. 25.

19 Sir Leslie O'Brien, Governor of the Bank of England, ibid. qu. 933.

20 Sir Leslie O'Brien, ibid., qu. 2141, 2144.

21 Although the Delegation was sited in the British embassy, its distinctiveness was suggested by its separate appearance in the annual Civil Service Lists under the heading, 'Treasury Representatives Abroad.' Other Whitehall Departments second their officials to the Diplomatic Service when abroad.

22 Robert W. Russell, 'A preliminary assessment of small-group behaviour in the international money circus', unpubl. paper, Harvard Center for International Affairs, 1972, p. 23.

23 John Williamson, 'Constraints on economic sovereignty', in Leifer, *Constraints and adjustments in British foreign policy*, p. 173.

24 Russell, p. 24.

25 The alternative would have been to have continued with severe restraint on prices and incomes, a no less difficult task in terms of domestic politics.

26 Brittan, p. 396.

27 On the question of international monetary surveillance in general, see Robert W. Russell, 'Multilateral surveillance, consultation, and the adjustment process', in Hans W. J. Bosman & Frans Alting von Geusau, eds, *The future of the international monetary system* (Tilburg, 1969).

28 Cmnd 2276, Feb 1964, para. 234.

29 Max Beloff, *New dimensions in foreign policy* (London, 1961), p. 24. 'It was held by a number of [diplomats] that some of the now admitted weaknesses of British foreign policy in the interwar years had been due to the encroachment by the Treasury upon the rights and privileges of the Foreign Office' (p. 23).

30 The degree of Foreign Office irritation was suggested by Sir Ivone Kirk-patrick's response to an MP's question as to whether 'it would be a good idea to have an officer from the Treasury in the Foreign Office?' 'No, I do not, nor do I think it a good idea to have an officer from the Treasury in any other Department' (HC 254, 1957–8, qu. 2522).

31 In 1970 the 11 non-executive members of the Court included 4 directors of merchant banks, 5 directors of industrial or construction companies, 1 trade unionist, and 1 director of a trading company. The last of these, William Keswick, was a brother of J. H. Keswick, referred to in ch. 4, and a fellow-director of Matheson & Co. Another member of the Court, Sir Val Duncan, the chairman of Rio Tinto-Zinc, had chaired the Duncan Committee the previous year. Another, Sir John Stevens, was Chairman of the East European Trade Council; his merchant bank, Morgan Grenfell, played a leading role in financing this politically sensitive trade. Much of his earlier career had been in the Bank of England, and he had served as head of the Washington delegation before moving to the private sector.

32 John Barr, in 'The city editors', *New Society*, 28 Apr 1966, quotes a financial journalist as saying, in justification of his hesitancy in print: 'During the crisis last autumn, just one bad story could have devalued the pound'.

33 According to one official, furthermore, the shape of the forthcoming British Budget was 'intensively discussed' within Working Party Three in early 1968: a privilege not accorded to the Cabinet, let alone to any committee of Parliament.

34 Where not otherwise footnoted, what follows is based upon the accounts in Brittan, pp. 282–366, and in two newspaper articles, 'The count-down to devaluation', *Sunday Times*, 26 Nov 1967, and 'Devaluation – who was to blame?', by Peter Jay, *The Times*, 23 Nov 1967, supplemented by interviews.

35 The government could have strengthened its parliamentary position by coming to an arrangement with the nine Liberal MPs, whose party, before the election, had criticized the emphasis placed upon sterling; but this was also excluded on political grounds.

36 Wilson, pp. 445–6. 'The Cabinet met at 10.30 a.m. I said that the agenda as circulated was in abeyance . . . I then told them of our decision, and called on the Chancellor.'

37 Anglo-American consultations are extensively discussed in Henry Brandon, *In the red: the struggle for sterling, 1964–6* (London, 1966).

38 The extent of attempted American intervention is suggested by President Johnson's personal request, 'at the worst moment' of the July 1966 crisis, for a token British military commitment to Vietnam (Wilson, p. 264). The amount of attention Mr Wilson devoted to the Vietnam issue between 1965 and 1968 is partly explained by his need to balance the opposing pressures of the US government and of his parliamentary left wing.

39 'In 1967, there were "requests" from Downing Street not to keep "rocking the boat" by suggesting devaluation and, on one occasion, a nasty little interview, at the Bank of England when a high official demanded to know why, since I clearly liked Britain so little, I did not emigrate' (Anthony Bambridge, *Observer*, 3 Oct 1971).

40 Peter Jay, *The Times*, 23 Nov 1967.

41 A. R. Ilersic, *Parliament of commerce* (London, for Ass. of British Chambers of Commerce, 1960), p. 2.

42 Peter Byrd, 'Trade and commerce in external relations', in Boardman & Groom, p. 174.

43 Richard N. Cooper, 'Trade policy is foreign policy', *Foreign Policy*, Winter 1972–3, p. 19.

44 Britain's commitment to Commonwealth preference did not entirely fit in

with these assumptions and involved governments in disputes with the Americans; though it, too, was seen as a natural consequence of an accepted political commitment which gave Britain a global perspective.

45 Beloff, *New Dimensions in foreign policy*, p. 23.

46 Cmnd 4506, Oct 1970, para 20.

47 The FCO also suffered some administrative uncertainties in handling oil matters. Its Oil department, separated from its parent Commodities department in 1969, was merged at the beginning of 1973 into a larger Energy, Industry and Science department; and again separated the following autumn into an independent Energy department. These changes in both ministries reflected and reinforced uncertainties about the objectives of policy in this area. Representatives of the oil industry claimed that the changes were disruptive of established relations between government and industry at the middle level.

48 An excellent case-study of the management of commercial negotiations in the 1930s is 'A clearing with Spain', pp. 201–78 in Willson, *Administrators in action* (vol. 1). This disentangles the roles of the BoT, the Department of Overseas Trade, the Treasury, the FO, the ECGD, the Bank of England, the Department of Mines, the Colonial, Dominions, and India Offices, the Ministry of Agriculture, the Customs and Excise, and the Madrid embassy in a complicated bilateral negotiation.

49 The work of the CRE divisions is described in a BoT memo. printed in HC 365, 1967–8, pp. 23–6.

50 ECGD, *Review of Exports Credits Guarantee Department* (London, Mar 1972), p. 6.

51 For information on the ECGD I am indebted to research being undertaken by Malcolm Brown for a Ph.D. at Manchester University.

52 The range of responsibilities of these departments is set out in the annual *Diplomatic Service List*. Among the listed responsibilities of Commodities department in the 1972 *Diplomatic Service List*, p. 7, for instance, copper, coffee, sugar, and textiles were subjects of important international negotiations. Citrus fruit imports, another of its concerns, raised particular problems in terms of relations with Mediterranean countries and entry to the EEC.

53 Byrd, in Boardman & Groom, p. 178. This chapter provides a much fuller account of the organization of commercial policy than can be provided here.

54 The Duncan Report, p. 73, provides a regional breakdown of commercial staff abroad in 1958 and 1968.

55 J. W. Grove, *Government and industry in Britain* (London, 1962), p. 333.

56 Grove, pp. 344–5. The FBI merged with two other associations in 1965 to become the CBI.

57 BNEC, *BNEC area councils and committees* (London, 1970), p. 4. For an official description of BNEC, see pp. 14–16 of HC365, 1967–8, and the evidence of BNEC representatives to this Committee.

58 Gordon Walker, p. 110.

59 One officially characterized the purpose of some ministerial travel with the comment: 'For public relations purposes we can always produce a Minister'.

60 A further reason for choosing this example was that the departmental differences it provoked were well covered in the press: the Egyptian government's interest in pushing the British government into participating, the potential involvement of merchant banks and construction companies, and the parallel discussions within other West European governments, all helped to reduce the degree of secrecy. What follows relies primarily upon the resources of the Chatham House Press Library, supplemented by interviews with officials.

61 There was no foundation in these allegations of British aircraft involved in bombing attacks, broadcast from Cairo; British ships and aircraft had kept

well away from the combat area. But the Cabinet had discussed the possibility of military intervention to reopen the Straits of Tiran during the early
stages of the crisis, an action which would effectively have committed British
forces to the Israeli side.

62. *Financial Times*, 26 Sept 1969.

63 Other European governments appear to have made not dissimilar conditions,
if in the French case much less publicly; which suggests a degree of consultation between credit agencies. Egyptian efforts throughout the long
series of negotiations to press different governments into firm commitments
by presenting other governments' promises as more definite than they were
led to a succession of over-optimistic newspaper reports, originating from
Cairo and Beirut; and doubtless encouraged the European participants to
keep each other fully informed of their real intentions.

64 *Egyptian Gazette*, 19 Mar 1971.

65 The symbolic importance of this visit for Britain's image in the Middle East
was underlined by the widely published photograph of Sir Alec Douglas-
Home sitting astride a camel in front of a pyramid.

Chapter 7. Aid, Information, and Cultural Policy

1 Nicolson, *Diplomacy*, p. 92.

2 Plowden Report, para. 27.

3 Fears that the new Labour government was about to impose substantial cuts
on the BBC's External Services, in March and April 1974, led to a scarcely
veiled appeal for public support for their efforts and the publication in *The
Times* of over a dozen supporting letters, from amongst others from Lord
Trevelyan, from the Director of the Anglo-German Association, and from
the Chairman of the International Council of Jews from Czechoslovakia.
According to *The Times* (19 Apr 1974), the BBC's protective efforts also included requests to the export directors of a large number of companies for
their views on the value of their broadcasts in assisting sales abroad.

4 A good example of this is a memo. prepared by the British Council in early
1970 for the Expenditure Committee, on 'The Sales of British TV and Radio
Equipment in Ethiopia and the Extent to which these have been helped by
British assistance to the Mass Media Centre' (HC 304, 1970–1, pp. 410–11).
Not uncharacteristically, this memo. noted that in spite of the opportunities
provided by British assistance, and 'although the attention of British manufacturers has been drawn to the growth of this market, no interest was
shown'; increased sales were made instead by French, Dutch and Japanese
companies.

5 Duncan Report, pp. 108, 111. It added that 'it is hard to see why there should
be sinister interpretations of the fact that the Council's cars or accounting
services may be provided by the Mission' (p. 110).

6 Beloff, *The future of British foreign policy* (1969), p. 38.

7 Cmnd 5445, Oct 1973, p. 4.

8 ODI, *British aid – 1: Survey and comment* (1963), p. 7.

9 Dudley Seers & Paul Streeten, in Beckerman, p. 122.

10 Cmnd 2736, Aug 1965.

11 Cmnd 2764, Sept 1965, p. 71.

12 See, for instance, Andrzej Krassowski, 'British aid and the British balance of
payments', *Moorgate & Wall Street Review*, Spring 1965 (by a staff member
of the ODI), and Bryan Hopkin and others, 'Aid and the balance of payments', *Economic Journal*, Mar 1970, pp. 1–23 (a revised version of an
ODM paper circulated earlier within Whitehall).

13 Cmnd 2764, p. 179.
14 HC 442, 1967–8.
15 805 HC Deb., 1023, 3 Nov 1970.
16 John White, 'Rich countries and poor', in Burgess, *Matters of principle*, p. 63.
17 Mrs Renee Short, MP, in a letter published in *The Times*, 5 Sept 1972.
18 See, for instance, the letter from the Chairman and Secretary of the UNA in *The Times*, 29 Sept 1970, for a statement of this view.
19 The close association of Dr Busia with members of the aid lobby, while in exile in London, increased the sense of identification with his regime; he had, for instance, been a member of the British Council of Churches committee which produced the report on *World poverty and British responsibility* in 1966. The overthrow of Busia's government by the military was, in the opinion of several observers, partly attributable to its failure to renegotiate the burden of debt.
20 853 HC Deb., 619–26, 22 Mar 1973.
21 See the comments of the Select Committee on Aid, in HC 299, 1970–1, pp. 14–15.
22 Cmnd 5445, p. 4.
23 On the Sudan see, for instance, the article by John Barry in *Sunday Times*, 7 Jan 1973, 'How Britain robs the poor to help the poor'. On the Southern Sahara, see Hugh Hanning, 'Short measure', in *Guardian*, 4 Aug 1973.
24 In what follows I am relying heavily on an unpublished M.A. thesis by Judith Young, *The evolution of an aid lobby in Britain*, 1962–70 (Manchester Univ., 1970).
25 Speaking to a UNA meeting at the House of Commons, 16 Dec 1969. He claimed, for instance, that the Chancellor of the Exchequer had received 'over 1000 letters in one week on the subject'. See also the appreciative comments on 'the campaigns organized in 1969 by pro-aid voluntary societies', in ODA, *An account of the British aid programme* (1970), para. 29.
26 ODA, *An account of the British aid programme* (1969), para. 114.
27 The ten members of this committee in 1970 included a former member of the Colonial Service, two Conservative MPs with extensive business interests in the Third World, and several active members of UNA and British Council of Churches committees.
28 R. B. M. King, *The planning of the British aid programme* (London, 1971).
29 This was one section of the Financial Policy and Aid department. Some of its members had attempted to secure their own disbandment in 1971, on the ground that they ought now to be superfluous, but without result.
30 Treasury witness to HC 442, 1967–8, qu. 1410.
31 Cmnd 4656, Apr 1971.
32 Cmnd 5178, Dec 1972, p. 23.
33 Rosalyn Higgins, *The administration of UK foreign policy through the UN* (New York, 1966), p. 26.
34 *Observer*, 5 & 21 May 1972.
35 Lord Birkenhead, *Halifax, The life of Lord Halifax* (London, 1965), p. 375. Halifax was also much concerned about the 'Nazi beaver-like propaganda in Central Europe'. 'The Italian press was hostile, anti-British intrigue was in progress in Egypt, Palestine and Arabia . . .'
36 Kirkpatrick, pp. 199–204, and Sir Robert Marett, in *Through the back door: an inside view of Britain's overseas information services* (Oxford, 1968), ch. 11, describe the debate and the evolution of a compromise on the postwar arrangements.
37 Marett, p. 147.
38 A summary of the Drogheda Report was published, as Cmd 9138, Apr 1954.
39 Lord Hill, *Both sides of the hill* (London, 1964).

40 *Diplomatic Service List*, 1972, pp. 11, 8.

41 For the COI, see Rl. Inst. of Public Admin., *The government explains* (London, 1965), and Sir Fife Clark, *The Central Office of Information* (London, 1970).

42 Foreign Office members have commented, in reply, that this is a mistaken emphasis. At the time of the Suez invasion the Foreign Office was of the same opinion as the BBC, in opposition to the Cabinet. The Suez incident is discussed by Kenneth Lamb in 'Disclosure, discretion and dissemblement', in *Secrecy and foreign policy*, by Thomas M. Franck & Edward Weisband (New York, 1974).

43 For the BBC External Services, see annual *BBC Handbooks*. Also J. F. Wilkinson, 'The BBC and Africa', *African Affairs*, Apr 1972, pp. 176–85, and Maurice Latey, *Broadcasting to the USSR and Eastern Europe* (BBC Publications, 1974).

44 British Council *What is the British Council?* (1967), p. 2.

45 For the British Council, see Annual Reports, which contain each year in addition to a review of activities an article on some aspect of the Council's work.

46 The language in which FCO officials in the information field described their relations with the Treasury was consistently combative. 'We are always altering our arguments to meet changing Treasury tactics', one official remarked, 'and they are always changing their method of attack.'

47 HC 19, 1971–2, p. 3.

48 HC 304, 1970–1; 830 HC Deb., 1351–1432, 9 Feb 1972.

49 Paul Cave & Keith Waterhouse, *Britain's voice abroad: a Daily Mirror spotlight on propaganda* (London, 1956), attacked in particular the indolence of the director of the Governor's Information Office in Cyprus, Mr Lawrence Durrell, who appeared to spend half his day writing novels.

50 Duncan Report, p. 103, which sets out the FCO argument succinctly.

51 The Committee reiterated the FCO view that 'unlike commercial or political work, which if necessary at all are necessary in their own right, information work is essentially ancillary in character . . .'

52 Quoted in *The Times*, 21 May 1970.

53 The *BBC Handbook*, 1972, p. 108, for instance, reported a survey in urban Kuwait which suggested that four-fifths of the adult population listened regularly to the BBC Arabic Service. This was one of the highest percentages ever recorded for a foreign audience.

54 Treasury evidence, HC 222, 1957–8, qu. 816; Max Beloff, 'The projection of Britain abroad', *International Affairs*, July 1965, p. 485.

55 Kirkpatrick, p. 199.

56 For a study of this area, see Richard Speaight, *Cultural interchange with East Europe* (Centre for Contemporary European Studies, Univ. of Sussex, Research Papers, No. 2, 1971).

Chapter 8. The Atlantic Area

1 Sir Frank Roberts, 'Great men, evil men, ambassadors', *Listener*, 11 Jan 1973, p. 43.

2 Figures from 1972 *Diplomatic List*, from December 1972 *London Diplomatic List*, and from Melvin Small & J. David Singer, 'The diplomatic importance of states, 1816–1970', *World Politics*, July 1973, pp. 592–7. According to Small & Singer, in 1970 more governments were accredited to the Court of St James than to any other nation states.

3 Duncan Report, p. 14.

4 Bruce Russett, in *Community and contention: Britain and America in the 20th century* (Cambridge, Mass., 1963), p. 179, noted that a similar network of inter-allied bodies was set up in 1917–18, but that it was far less effective than during World War II.

5 For a fuller discussion of these developments, see William Wallace, 'British external relations and the European Community: the changing context of foreign policy-making', *Journal of Common Market Studies*, Sept 1973.

6 Richard E. Neustadt, *Alliance politics* (New York, 1970), p. 73.

7 Ibid., p. 101.

8 Wilson, pp. 90–3, 403–12.

9 Before this the United States, together with the Arctic and Antarctic regions and the whole of Latin America, had been the responsibility of the American department. Relations with Canada had, of course, been the responsibility of the CRO until the merger in 1968.

10 Cmnd 2853, Dec 1965.

11 These polls, sponsored and paid for by the US Information Agency, are on file in the Roper Public Opinion Research Center, Williamstown, Massachusetts.

12 In terms of FCO departmental organization Japan was in 1972 linked with China, Taiwan, Korea, and Mongolia in the Far Eastern department, and South Africa with its neighbours in the Central and Southern African department; though relations with Japan, in particular, were also the active concern of most of the functional departments of the FCO, and its importance to Britain was reflected in the succession of Cabinet and non-Cabinet ministers who travelled to Tokyo.

13 These four countries, together with Malta and Cyprus, were in 1972 the responsibility of the FCO Southern European Department.

14 From 1960 onwards the Geneva UK Mission to the UN and to GATT also serviced EFTA. Beloff (*New dimensions in foreign policy*) discusses the adjustment of Whitehall to the demands created by these organizations between 1947 and 1959.

15 The evolution of British policies and attitudes in the twenty years from the war's end to the Queen's long-expected state visit is discussed by D. C. Watt in *Britain looks to Germany* (London, 1965).

16 Cmnd 4891, 1972, p. 41.

17 Exact figures on the value of total investment are difficult to assemble; one British official suggested that the book value of British investments in West Germany amounted to £400–£500m, but that the market value of the largest British company's assets in Germany, those of British Petroleum, was itself above £400m. Some idea of the scale of investment flows may be gained from figures provided by the German Economics Ministry: German investment in Britain, 1952–72, DM 733m; British investment in Germany 1961–72, DM 3,038m.

18 One Conservative MP, faced in 1972 with the task of persuading his constituency association to support his government's policy on Community entry, invited a Christian Democrat colleague to come and address them. Their close acquaintance had sprung not only from successive Königswinter Conferences but also from service together in European assemblies.

19 *The Economist*, 5 Jan 1974.

20 'Inner-German' relations were the responsibility in Bonn not of the foreign ministry but of the Chancellor's Office.

21 Icelandic memories are long. Haldor Laxness, the novelist, cited the murder of the Governor of Iceland by English fishermen in 1468 as one of his countries' grievances against the English, in discussing the 1972–3 fisheries dispute (*Observer* 27 May 1973).

22 On this dispute, see Morris Davis, *Iceland extends its fisheries limits* (Oslo, 1963).

23 Basic Statistics of Iceland, 1972, Ministry of Foreign Affairs, Reykjavik.

24 Fisheries Dept, Ministry of Agriculture, 1971.

25 This was established in 1959, supplementing the older International Council for the Exploration of the Sea, which had coordinated research into fish stocks. Its other members were Belgium, Denmark, West Germany, France, Ireland, the Netherlands, Norway, Poland, Portugal, Spain, Sweden, and the Soviet Union.

26 In April 1972 a British official arrived in Reykjavik for exploratory talks which the Icelandic government and the British embassy had emphasized were to be entirely secret, to discover that the FCO News department had announced his visit, and the BBC had broadcast it to Reykjavik. The reader may note that the management of bilateral relations with the rest of Scandinavia does not greatly differ from that of relations with Iceland.

27 No more than three frigates were ever on station in Icelandic waters during 1973; but a larger number of ships was necessary to provide regular relief for the ships on station.

28 An account of the dispute from July 1971 to May 1973, from the British side, is given in Cmnd 5341, June 1973.

29 According to Williams & Reed, in *Denis Healey*, p. 256, 'the formation of the Nuclear Defence Affairs Committee and its subsidiary Nuclear Planning Group, although attributed to McNamara, in fact owed much more to Healey, who pushed them into existence and made them work'.

30 Text of the Harmel Report, NATO Information Services, Brussels, Dec 1967.

31 HC 159–II, 1972–3, 2; Class VIII, 7.

32 The biannual meetings of foreign ministers also provided a convenient opportunity to discuss problems of bilateral relations outside the formal framework. At the December meeting in 1972, for instance, Sir Alec Douglas-Home raised with the Turkish Foreign Minister the matter of Timothy Davey, a British boy jailed in Turkey on drug charges, which had provoked a campaign in the British press (*The Times*, 9 Dec 1972).

33 Their move to the same corridor as the civilian delegation, to ease communication, reportedly shocked the military representatives of some other member governments, who believed that civilians should be excluded from military matters whenever possible. Although the delegation ranked with those to the UN and the European Communities as one of Britain's largest multilateral missions, it was much smaller than those of some other alliance members. The German delegation was twice as large, the American over three times as large.

34 The deputy Permanent Representative in 1972 had previously spent three years as chief of the Assessments Staff. One of the under-secretaries in the Cabinet Office responsible for defence policy had just returned from several years' secondment to the NATO International Secretariat, as had the Assistant Under-Secretary (Defence Staff) in the MoD. Not infrequently the Treasury officials responsible for vetting proposals for collaborative expenditure were seconded from the MoD.

35 The observer might detect in the attitudes of FCO personnel a confidence that they were 'on the inner circle' of policy-making, to the exclusion not only of diplomats in outer area embassies but also those serving in West European embassies and in the geographical departments of the FCO. 'This is the place where things happen'; 'bilateral diplomacy is dying'.

36 HC 114–11, 1973–4.

Chapter 9. The Non-Atlantic Countries

1 The Duncan Committee also placed Australia and Japan marginally outside its categorization of 'the Area of Concentration'; perhaps by 1972 the active involvement of Japan, at least, in commercial and monetary negotiations affecting the entire advanced industrial world, and the increased traffic in Anglo-Japanese discussions at all levels, would have led them to a different opinion.

2 *Guardian*, 24 Jan 1973.

3 At the annual meeting of the Anglo-Soviet Joint Commission for Trade, Technical, Scientific and Economic Relations in April 1973, for instance, Mr Peter Walker, as leader of the British team, signed a detailed protocol which agreed upon 'mutual interest' in research on solid state physics and biology and the establishment of an intergovernmental committee on environmental engineering, amongst other items (*The Times*, 19 Apr 1973).

4 The Duke of Edinburgh accompanied Princess Anne to Kiev for the European Horse Trials in September 1973. Neither, however, visited Moscow.

5 The invitation for an official visit was issued by Sir Alec Douglas-Home during his visit in February 1973, and accepted remarkably rapidly.

6 *The Times*, 12 Dec 1973.

7 The 1972 Statement on the Defence Estimates (Cmnd 4891, Feb 1972), p. 35, noted that 'In 1971 more than 4,000 officers and men from over 60 different countries attended a wide variety of courses within the United Kingdom.'

8 Hamilton & others, *A decade of the Commonwealth 1955–64*, give an overview of these links and the contradictory pressures for closer and looser intra-Commonwealth ties.

9 In 1962 the Chinese invasion of India had brought an immediate response from the British government in military assistance, on a scale equivalent to that of the US, giving continued substance to 'the long-assumed moral obligation to the defence of India' (Darby, p. 231).

10 *Handbook of Commonwealth organisations* (London), for the Federation of Commonwealth Chambers of Commerce, 1965.

11 At the time of the report of the Pearce Commission in 1972 ministers were also involved in presenting policy to foreign opinion. The Minister for Overseas Development, Richard Wood, visited Lagos to show the Nigerian government a copy of the report before publication; Lord Carrington, Minister of Defence, followed him to explain the evolution of British policy after publication.

12 The Duncan Report, p. 50, described 'the minimum scale of representational capacity' as consisting of two diplomatic staff and a UK-based clerical-grade archivist-cum-secretary. In 1973 three missions were at this minimum level: those to Mongolia, Togo, and Tonga. A further ten, to seven Latin American countries, Brunei, the Malagasy Republic, and the Holy See, contained only four UK-based staff.

13 UN, *Yearbook of international trade statistics*, 1968–9.

14 HC 114–II, 1973–4, pp. 10–11.

15 British Council Annual Report, 1973–4.

16 *London Diplomatic List*, Dec 1972.

17 See IISS, *Conflicts in Africa*, Adelphi Paper No. 93 (1972).

18 Ethiopia, *Statistical abstract*, 1970.

19 Ibid.

20 One official remarked that the General Assembly had taken the place of royal marriages and funerals as a convenient opportunity for private diplomacy. Its value for the British government was greatest in affording an opportunity to meet a number of ministers from outer area countries.

21 Higgins, *Administration of UK foreign policy through the UN*, p. 32.

22 *The Times*, 25 Oct 1972. The 19 countries which opposed the budget contributed between them some 75 per cent of the total.

23 *Civil Service List*, 1972, col 587.

24 Higgins, pp. 4–5, describes the structure of this Steering Committee, and
notes that in the mid-60s 'what was once the central coordinating machinery
for UN questions is now one thread in a web of interwoven committees'.

25 Higgins noted (p. 29) that policy-making towards the Intergovernmental
Maritime Consultative Organization, the only UN agency with headquarters
in London, was 'very self-contained' within the Shipping Policy Division,
the Marine Safety Division, and the Maritime Division of the BoT (now the
DTI). 'Very few decisions need to be taken at higher than the under-
secretary level. Day to day coordination with other departments is done at
the level of principals . . . This is, in short, a very self-sufficient branch of
United Kingdom policymaking.'

Chapter 10. Conclusion: The Wider Debate

1 The quotation is from the preamble to the Treaty of Accession, Cmnd 4862,
Jan 1962, p. 1. 'Political' consultations of course took place outside the Community framework, strictly defined.

2 This development is discussed more fully by William Wallace in *Journal of
Common Market Studies*, Sept 1973, pp. 28–52.

3 Table VIII in Cmnd 5248, Mar 1973, lists British subscriptions to 87 public
international organizations amounting to £48m in all. These do not include
subscriptions to the World Bank or to other international development
agencies for aid purposes.

4 But Richard Neustadt, in *Alliance politics*, explores the problems of 'muddled
perceptions . . ., disappointed expectations and paranoid reactions' to
which the mutual penetration of the British and US governments led over
the Suez and Skybolt affairs (p. 56).

5 Vital, p. 90.

6 The quotation is from a home civil servant seconded to the Cabinet Office,
reflecting on his own perceptions of foreign policy.

7 See, for instance, Waltz (*Foreign policy and democratic politics*), who powerfully argues this case; Vital, ch. 5; Beloff, *The future of British foreign
policy*.

8 Nevil Johnson, *Public Administration*, Spring 1971, p. 1. For an optimistic
view on the amenability of foreign policy questions in the future to more
rational techniques of forecasting and planning, see Nigel Forward, *The field
of nations* (London, 1971). Mr Forward wrote this study while on leave from
the MoD.

9 The quotation is from Vital, p. 98.

10 See above, chs. 5 & 6; for the Future Policy Committee see also Darby, pp.
143–5. Public reference to the 1966 review has so far been limited to press
reports.

11 Vital, p. 78.

12 Gordon Walker, p. 32, notes that under the Labour government 'the question
of particular leaks was somewhat angrily discussed' in Cabinet, and sometimes the Prime Minister charged the Lord Chancellor to inquire into the
source of a leak', questioning ministers as well as civil servants. The energy
with which the police pursued the source of the 'leak' on the future rail network in 1972, referred to in ch. 4, was noted by officials within the FCO, as
elsewhere in Whitehall. Several useful essays on the British case are to be
found in T. M. Franck & E. Weisband, eds, *Secrecy and foreign policy*

(London, 1974). Mr Gordon Walker, in one of these contributions, remarks that 'the national tendency to secrecy in Britain is very strong and is part and parcel of the Cabinet system' (p. 49).

13 Sir Frank Roberts, *Listener*, 11 Jan 1973; Andrew Shonfield, 'In the course of investigation', *New Society*, 24 July 1969, pp. 123–5.

14 The author particularly remembers an exchange at a discussion meeting in London in early 1972 at which an oil consultant remarked on the absence of any debate on the implications for British foreign and domestic policy of energy problems over the next ten to twenty years, comparable to the lively debates then under way in the United States and West Germany. One of the several civil servants present replied: 'You say that we don't have an energy debate? You should come and join us in Whitehall.'

15 *The Times*, 10 Jan 1972. Mr Macmillan as Prime Minister was reported to have insisted on this extension of the embargo.

16 Mr F. T. Blackaby, the Deputy Director of the National Institute for Economic and Social Research, proposed such an examination of external expenditure in terms of assumed objectives and the contributions of particular budgetary programmes to their achievement, in a paper to the British Association for the Advancement of Science in September 1972. Andrew Wilson had argued for a similar exercise, in criticizing the incrementalism of the post-devaluation defence cuts, in *Observer*, 31 Dec 1967.

17 Thus Richard Crossman reflected in his diary on 3 Jan 1965: 'Looking back to October, I am impressed by our extraordinary innocence when we took over. We proceeded to do a number of things by almost instantaneous decision, all of which seem to me now to have been ill-judged.' He specifically cites the import surcharge as an example of this innocent misjudgement (*Sunday Times*, 2 Feb 1975).

18 Waltz, pp. 263–5.

19 Frankel, *The making of foreign policy*, p. 198.

20 Waltz, p. 265.

21 Mayhew, *Britain's role tomorrow*, p. 11.

22 740 HC Deb., 1685, 8 Feb 1967.

23 James Callaghan, MP, as Foreign Secretary, speaking to the Diplomatic and Commonwealth Writers' Ass., 10 Apr 1974 (FCO News dept text).

24 The novelty of such a development is lessened by the existing publication by the FCO, for restricted circulation, of its unattributable monthly reviews.

25 James Callaghan, MP (as in n. 23). Mr Callaghan also suggested an annual White Paper on Foreign Policy in this speech.

26 Richard Neustadt, 'White House and Whitehall', in Richard Rose, ed., *Policy-making in Britain* (London, 1969), p. 292.

Index